Paris
FOR
DUMMIES®
2ND EDITION

by Cheryl A. Pientka

WILEY

Wiley Publishing, Inc.

Paris For Dummies®, 2nd Edition

Published by
Wiley Publishing, Inc.
909 Third Avenue
New York, NY 10022
www.wiley.com

Copyright © 2003 by Wiley Publishing, Inc., Indianapolis, Indiana

Published simultaneously in Canada

No part of this publication may be reproduced, stored in a retrieval system, or transmitted in any form or by any means, electronic, mechanical, photocopying, recording, scanning, or otherwise, except as permitted under Sections 107 or 108 of the 1976 United States Copyright Act, without either the prior written permission of the Publisher, or authorization through payment of the appropriate per-copy fee to the Copyright Clearance Center, 222 Rosewood Drive, Danvers, MA 01923, 978-750-8400, fax 978-646-8700. Requests to the Publisher for permission should be addressed to the Legal Department, Wiley Publishing, Inc., 10475 Crosspoint Blvd., Indianapolis, IN 46256, 317-572-3447, fax 317-572-4447, or e-mail permcoordinator@wiley.com

Trademarks: Wiley, the Wiley Publishing logo, For Dummies, the Dummies Man logo, A Reference for the Rest of Us!, The Dummies Way, Dummies Daily, The Fun and Easy Way, Dummies.com and related trade dress are trademarks or registered trademarks of Wiley Publishing, Inc., in the United States and other countries, and may not be used without written permission. Frommer's is a trademark or registered trademark of Arthur Frommer. Used under license. All other trademarks are the property of their respective owners. Wiley Publishing, Inc., is not associated with any product or vendor mentioned in this book.

For general information on our other products and services or to obtain technical support, please contact our Customer Care Department within the U.S. at 800-762-2974, outside the U.S. at 317-572-3993, or fax 317-572-4002.

Wiley also publishes its books in a variety of electronic formats. Some content that appears in print may not be available in electronic books.

Library of Congress Cataloging-in-Publication Data:

Library of Congress Control Number: 2003101833

ISBN: 0-7645-5494-8

ISSN: 1531-765X

Manufactured in the United States of America

10 9 8 7 6 5 4 3 2 1

WILEY is a trademark of Wiley Publishing, Inc.

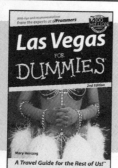
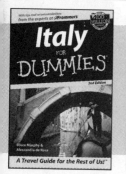

About the Author

Cheryl A. Pientka is a freelance journalist and a literary scout. She's the co-author of both *Frommer's Paris From $80 a Day* and *France For Dummies,* and a contributor to *Frommer's Europe on $70 a Day.* A graduate of Columbia University Graduate School of Journalism and the University of Delaware, she lives in New York when she can't be in Paris.

Dedication

To Sean Stevens, navigator extraordinaire, and to the memory of my father, Philip E. Pientka.

Author's Acknowledgments

A big *merci* to the following: Barbara Tolley, who so graciously let me begin work late; Myka Carroll and Kelly Regan; my moms Mary Anne Pientka and Alicia Patterson Giesa; and in France, Margie Rynn, Olivier and Julien Bardon, and Karen Fawcett. Thanks also to John, Claire, Eric, Tyler, Andy, Gramps & Grandmother, Justine Fontinell, Jayne Pliner, Michael Schneider, Nellie Stevens, and the staff and volunteers at Animal Haven shelter in Flushing, Queens, for their terrific work and patience.

Publisher's Acknowledgments

We're proud of this book; please send us your comments through our Dummies online registration form located at www.dummies.com/register/.

Some of the people who helped bring this book to market include the following:

Editorial

Editors: Myka Carroll, Associate Editor; Mike Baker, Kathleen Dobie, Project Editors

Copy Editor: E. Neil Johnson

Cartographer: Roberta Stockwell

Editorial Manager: Christine Meloy Beck

Editorial Assistant: Melissa Bennett

Senior Photo Editor: Richard Fox

Front Cover Photo: © John Lawrence/ Getty Images

Back Cover Photo: © Robert Frerck/Odyssey/Chicago

Cartoons: Rich Tennant, www.the5thwave.com

Production

Project Coordinator: Erin Smith

Layout and Graphics: Amanda Carter, Seth Conley, Carrie Foster, Stephanie D. Jumper, Michael Kruzil

Proofreaders: Dave Faust, Susan Moritz, Carl Pierce, **TECHBOOKS Production Services**

Indexer: TECHBOOKS Production Services

Publishing and Editorial for Consumer Dummies

Diane Graves Steele, Vice President and Publisher, Consumer Dummies

Joyce Pepple, Acquisitions Director, Consumer Dummies

Kristin A. Cocks, Product Development Director, Consumer Dummies

Michael Spring, Vice President and Publisher, Travel

Brice Gosnell, Publishing Director, Travel

Suzanne Jannetta, Editorial Director, Travel

Publishing for Technology Dummies

Andy Cummings, Vice President and Publisher, Dummies Technology/General User

Composition Services

Gerry Fahey, Vice President of Production Services

Debbie Stailey, Director of Composition Services

Contents at a Glance

Maps at a Glance

Table of Contents

Introduction

*I*f you've never been to Paris, you may be amazed to find so much to like! Many of the city's monuments and historical buildings positively gleam following recent renovations. The quays along the Seine have been widened for more foot traffic, providing space for such month-long events as Paris à la Plage, which recently turned the city's riverbanks into umbrella-strewn beaches with palm trees and lounge chairs. Opportunities for culture abound in Paris's dynamic theater and music scene and eclectic museum and gallery exhibits. In the spring and fall, celebrities and media fight for front-row space for the shows of top French clothing designers; even a quick glance in Paris's store windows attests to the city's love affair with fashion and objets d'art. Paris is a gathering place — adults meet in cafés to discuss their day, while young people congregate around place d'Italie and the Bastille to inline skate, skateboard, or ride their *trotinettes* (scooters).

If you haven't been to Paris in a dog's age, you're in for some changes. First of all, forget that stereotype about rude Parisians; the city's much friendlier. Many more people are willing to try out their English to help visitors, and service at stores and in restaurants can be downright warm when visitors take the time to acknowledge storekeepers and waiters with a pleasant *bonjour.* Monuments have been restored: The gold leaf on the Opéra Garnier's exterior is positively sparkling, and its interior (with a Marc Chagall mural) glows from its recent million-dollar scrubbing. This city noted for past glories has also entered the 21st century at full speed. Everywhere people talk on tiny cellphones. You won't see a conductor in the Métro's Meteor line because the train drives itself. Architecture has a decidedly futuristic flair: The buildings of the Cité des Sciences et de l'Industrie, a park and museum complex, include a huge sphere on which movies are shown, and the giant Bibliothèque Nationale de François Mitterand is shaped to resemble an open book. It all demonstrates France's eagerness to embrace the future.

But in some things Paris remains timeless. The city's beauty takes your breath away with graceful rounded beaux arts buildings, willowy arching bridges, green parks and squares, the spires and domes of famous churches and cathedrals, and the pink light of the setting sun reflecting off the river that is its heart.

About This Book

Consider this a textbook of sorts that you won't have to read from front to back, and certainly one you won't be tested on! Basically *Paris For Dummies* presents you with to-the-point information on Paris that's fun and easy to access. I explain very basic information about the city for readers who have never visited, but I also include points of interest for the seasoned traveler.

Conventions Used in This Book

Again, *Paris For Dummies* is a reference book, meaning you may read the chapters in any order you want. I use some standard listings for hotels, restaurants, and sights. These listings enable you to open the book to any chapters and access the information you need quickly and easily.

Other conventions used in this book include the following:

- ✔ The abbreviations for credit cards are AE (American Express), DC (Diners Club), MC (MasterCard), and V (Visa).

- ✔ Hotels, restaurants, and attractions are listed in alphabetical order so that moving among the maps, worksheets, and descriptions is easier.

- ✔ I include the Paris *arrondissements,* or administrative districts, in each address to give you a better idea of where each place is located. Paris is divided into 20 arrondissements, which spiral out like a snail shell from the first arrondissement in the very center of Paris (abbreviated *1er* in French), to the 20th on the outer edges of the city (abbreviated *20e*). The arrondissement number appears after the street address in each citation in this book. For example, "123 bd. St-Germain, 6e," indicates the building numbered 123 on the Boulevard St-Germain is in the 6th arrondissement. To get an idea of where each arrondissement is located, consult the "Paris at a Glance" map in Chapter 1. Street abbreviations used throughout the book include not only *bd.* (boulevard), but also *rue* (street), *av.* (avenue), *place* (square), *Bis* (an odd phrase generally meaning an address between two buildings), *Ter* (terrace), or *quai* (quay or riverbank).

- ✔ To help you orient yourself, I also give the nearest Métro (subway) stop for all destinations (for example: Métro: Pont Marie).

- ✔ Although exchange rates can and do fluctuate daily, the price conversions in this book were calculated at the rate of one euro (the local currency) to one U.S. dollar. Because the dollar and the euro were virtually equal in value at press time, prices are provided only in euros. For more information about the euro, see Chapter 12.

✔ All hotels and restaurants in this book are rated with a system of dollar signs to indicate the range of costs for one night in a double-occupancy hotel room or a meal at a restaurant, from "$" (budget) to "$$$$$" (splurge). Check out the following table to decipher the dollar signs. For more specific guidelines, consult Chapter 8 for hotels and Chapter 14 for restaurants.

Cost	Hotel	Restaurant
$	Under 100€	Less than 20€
$$	100€–150€	20€–30€
$$$	150€–215€	30€–50€
$$$$	215€–300€	50€–75€
$$$$$	More than 300€	More than 75€

Foolish Assumptions

As I wrote this book, I made some assumptions about you and what your needs may be as a traveler. Maybe this is your first trip to Paris. Or maybe you visited long enough ago that you went to the Jeu de Paume to see Impressionist masterpieces and wouldn't know that you can see them today at the Musée d'Orsay. Maybe you're traveling to Paris on business and have only a day or two to spend in the city. Or maybe you're visiting a second or third time and want to see what you missed on previous visits.

Whatever your circumstances, this book is for you. You want a book you can look at on the go, a book that won't have you wading through pages of information to get to the news you can use. Yet you still want descriptions of the best accommodations and ideas of where to eat in the city's more than 2,000 restaurants. You want opinions, you want the straight scoop, and you want some fun. *Paris For Dummies* is for you.

How This Book Is Organized

Paris For Dummies is divided into eight parts (the last of which contains two appendixes). If you read the parts in sequential order, they can guide you through all the advance planning aspects of your trip and then get you off and running after you're in the City of Light.

Part I: Getting Started

These four chapters introduce Paris and touch on everything you need to consider before planning a trip. The pros and cons of each season are given, as well as hints to develop a realistic budget, and a host of options are available to travelers with special needs or interests.

Part II: Ironing Out the Details

These chapters give you the nitty-gritty of trip planning, with the answers to questions such as: Should you use a travel agent or go it alone? Is travel insurance a good idea? What kind of accommodations should you use in Paris? Why don't you have to pay full price at hotel chains? Some of the city's best moderately priced hotels (with a few super-budget and some deluxe resorts thrown in for good measure), are listed here, as well as advice on how to tie up those frustrating last-minute details that can unnerve the most seasoned of travelers.

Part III: Settling into Paris

Get oriented in Paris in no time. These three chapters give you tips on everything from navigating your way through customs to getting to your hotel from the airport to discovering Paris neighborhood by neighborhood.

You find out how to use the city's terrific transportation system, why you shouldn't rent a car here, and what to know when you hail a cab. You make sense of the euro, and find out where to turn if your wallet gets stolen.

Part IV: Dining in Paris

Paris is known for its fine food, and the chapters in this part help you choose some of the best restaurants for your taste and budget. I list everything from moderately priced to haute cuisine restaurants, so you can discover that a fine meal is truly an art in itself. I also reserve a chapter to provide you with street food and light fare options for those occasions when you don't have the time, or the desire, for a full-course meal.

Part V: Exploring Paris

This part has everything you need to know about Paris's top sights — how to get to them, how much they cost, and how much time to devote to them, as well as handy indexes by sight, type, and neighborhood to make them easier to find. There are kid- and teen-specific sights, as well as information on orientation and other tours, a shopper's guide to Paris, three recommended itineraries, and five great day-trips if you're in the mood to get out of town.

Part VI: Living It Up After the Sun Goes Down: Paris Nightlife

Nothing is more beautiful than Paris at night when the city's monuments are lit up like a stage set where anything can happen. This part gives you everything you need to know about seeing plays, opera, ballet, and live music as well as which nightclubs and bars are fun. It's honest about whether those spectacles for which Paris has come to be known — the cabarets — are truly worth it. You uncover how to find out what's going on and where you can get reduced-rate tickets. You even get the lowdown on how Parisians dress for a visit to a classy bar.

Part VII: The Part of Tens

What *For Dummies* book would be complete without a Part of Tens? Included is a quick collection of fun tidbits: a digest of reading suggestions, and recommendations for the best place to relax with a picnic — a very Parisian pastime!

Part VIII: Appendixes

Not to be upstaged by the Part of Tens, the appendixes provide you with quick glimpses of Paris and the French way of life. Appendix A is called a *Quick Concierge,* because it answers those nagging "Where do I go?" and "How do I do this?" questions that inevitably come up on a trip. And, so you won't have any trouble communicating, I provide you with a glossary of English-to-French translations of basic vocabulary and health, travel, and (of course) shopping terms in Appendix B.

Icons Used in This Book

The little pictures in the margins are meant to draw your attention to especially useful text. Explanations of what each icon means follow.

This icon is a catchall for any special hint, tip, or bit of insider's advice that can help make your trip run more smoothly. Really, the point of a travel guide is to serve as one gigantic tip, but this icon singles out those nuggets of knowledge you may not have run across before or of which you can make immediate use.

This icon pegs the best bargains and juiciest money-saving tips. You may find a particularly value-conscious choice of hotel or restaurant, a discount museum or transportation pass, or simply a way to avoid spending more than you have to.

 You'll see this icon whenever something needs your particular attention. When you need to be aware of a rip-off, an overrated sight, a dubious deal, or any other trap set for unsuspecting travelers, this icon alerts you to that fact. These hints also offer the lowdown on the quirks, etiquette, and unwritten rules of the area so you can avoid looking like a tourist and, instead, be treated more like a local.

 This icon, in addition to flagging tips and resources of special interest to families, points out the most child-friendly hotels, restaurants, and attractions. If you need a baby sitter at your hotel, a welcoming relaxed atmosphere at a restaurant, or a dazzling site that delights your child, look for this icon. Information is included regarding larger, family-sized rooms at hotels and restaurants that serve meals that go easy on your little ones' tummies.

 Sometimes a great hotel, restaurant, or attraction may be a bit out of the center or require a bit of effort to get to. This icon alerts you to these secret little finds, and you can rest assured, no spots are included that aren't truly worth the energy. This icon also signifies any resource that's particularly useful and worth the time to seek out.

Where to Go from Here

To Paris! The City of Light is for everyone, and *Paris For Dummies* shows you just how accessible it can be. Included is a selective list of some of the best hotel, dining, and touring options along with insider info to help you make informed decisions. Follow the advice laid out here, and you'll want to return to Paris again and again. Because, as author Honoré de Balzac once said, in Paris there will always remain an undiscovered place, an unknown retreat, and something unheard of.

Part I
Getting Started

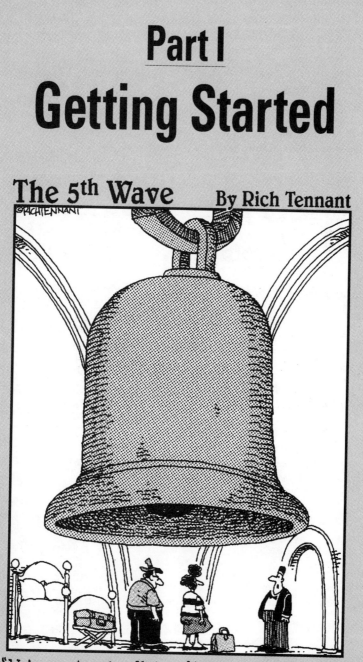

The 5th Wave   By Rich Tennant

"Welcome to the Hotel d'Notre Dame. If there's anything else I can do for you, please don't hesitate to ring."

In this part . . .

*A*re you a stranger to Paris? Or has it been a loooong time since you last visited? Then (re)introduce yourself to the city and whet your appetite to find out more about it. In Chapter 1, you get an overview of Paris and why it's such a great place to visit. Chapter 2 makes it easier to decide when to go — and why some times may be better than others to go. In Chapter 3, you discover how to plan a reasonable budget based on prices in Paris and get some cost-cutting tips. In Chapter 4, you find specially targeted advice for families, seniors, travelers with disabilities, and gay and lesbian travelers.

Chapter 1

Discovering the Best of Paris

In This Chapter

▶ Explaining why Paris is a wonderful place to visit

▶ Condensing Paris history into a nutshell

*Y*ou're planning a visit to Paris, and you may feel a bit overwhelmed. With so many museums to visit and monuments to see
you're probably asking which ones should you see first, and frankly,
which ones are a waste of time? If this is your first visit to Paris, friends
most likely are telling you about the incredible food and multi-starred
chefs. But, again, facing the choice of so many different types of French
cuisine is enough to make you want to stick to tried-and-true McDo
(French for McDonald's) and just have a cup of wine with your fries.

Take it easy. Know up front that, much as you'd like, you simply won't
be able to do and see it all. And, by rushing to visit so many places,
you may miss what perhaps is Paris's greatest attraction of all: a way of
life in which relaxing in a café and watching the world go by are natural
parts of the day. After you realize that you don't have to tour to
exhaustion, you can appreciate Paris the way it was intended to be
enjoyed — on bridges and streets meant for strolling and exploring.

You'll discover that the **Louvre** Museum is as incredible as its reputation and that the views from the **Eiffel Tower** are stunning — but did
you know that the views from department store **Samaritaine** also are
pretty spectacular? You'll find that crossing the **Seine** on footbridge at
sunset is indeed one of the world's most romantic strolls, but rowing a
boat in the **Bois de Boulogne's Grand Lac** ranks up there, too.
Whatever you do, you'll quickly discover that Paris is more of an experience than merely a city, and each visitor experiences it in an entirely
individual way.

This chapter is designed to put your mind at ease about your visit and
gives a face to the place that's the heart of all of France. The "Paris at a
Glance" map should help, too.

Paris at a Glance

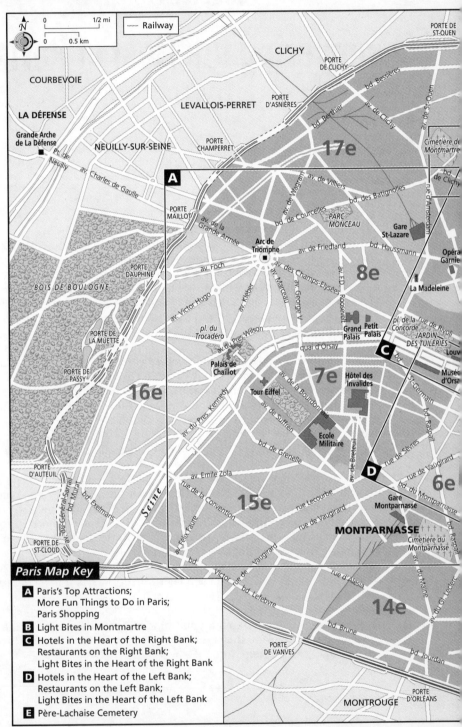

0 | 1/2 mi
0 | 0.5 km

--- Railway

PORTE DE
ST-OUEN

CLICHY

PORTE
DE CLICHY

COURBEVOIE

bd. Bessières

LEVALLOIS-PERRET

PORTE
D'ASNIÈRES

bd. Berthier

av. de Clichy

LA DÉFENSE

Grande Arche
de La Défense

NEUILLY-SUR-SEINE

PORTE
CHAMPERRET

PORTE
MAILLOT

Pl. de
Neuilly

av. Charles de Gaulle

17e

Cimetière de
Montmartre

bd.
de Clichy

rue d'Amsterdam

rue de Clichy

av. de Wagram

av. de Villiers

bd. des Batignolles

av. de Courcelles

PARC
MONCEAU

Gare
St-Lazare

av. de la
Grande Armée

bd. de Courcelles

Arc de
Triomphe

av. de Friedland

bd. Haussmann

Opéra
Garnier

av. Foch

av. des Champs-Elysées

8e

La Madeleine

BOIS DE BOULOGNE

PORTE
DAUPHINE

av. Victor Hugo

av. Kléber

av. Marceau

av. George V

F.D.
Roosevelt

pl. de la
Concorde

rue de Rivoli

JARDIN
DES TUILERIES

Louvre

PORTE DE
LA MUETTE

pl. du
Trocadéro

av. du Prés. Wilson

Grand
Palais

Petit
Palais

C

Musée
d'Orsay

PORTE DE
PASSY

Palais de
Chaillot

quai d'Orsay

7e

Hôtel des
Invalides

St-Germain

16e

av. de la Bourdonnais

Tour Eiffel

av. de Suffren

bd. Raspail

PORTE
D'AUTEUIL

av. du Prés. Kennedy

bd. de Grenelle

Ecole
Militaire

av. de Breteuil

rue de Sèvres

D

rue de Vaugirard

6e

bd. du Montparnasse

Seine

av. Emile Zola

rue de la Convention

15e

rue Lecourbe

rue de Vaugirard

Gare
Montparnasse

PORTE DE
ST-CLOUD

av. Gén.-Sarrail

bd. Murat

bd. Exelmans

av. Félix Faure

MONTPARNASSE

Cimetière du
Montparnasse

Victor

rue de Vaugirard

bd. Lefebvre

rue d'Alésia

14e

av. du Maine

bd. Brune

PORTE
DE VANVES

bd. Jourdan

MONTROUGE

PORTE
D'ORLÉANS

Paris Map Key

A Paris's Top Attractions;
More Fun Things to Do in Paris;
Paris Shopping

B Light Bites in Montmartre

C Hotels in the Heart of the Right Bank;
Restaurants on the Right Bank;
Light Bites in the Heart of the Right Bank

D Hotels in the Heart of the Left Bank;
Restaurants on the Left Bank;
Light Bites in the Heart of the Left Bank

E Père-Lachaise Cemetery

Taking in All the Spectacular Sights

For most people, the real reason for visiting Paris is to see the quintessentially French attractions for which the city is known. Are the sights really as great as returning travelers say? Yes, yes, and yes. The **Eiffel Tower** graces the city skyline with its lacy presence. The **Louvre** has more exhibits than ever — you can see its primitive art exposition near the Denon Wing until 2004, when the **Musée Branly** is scheduled to open and take over that collection. After a thorough cleaning, **Notre-Dame** cathedral is now the original ivory color its builders intended. Take a tour boat down the Seine and see the towers of Notre-Dame highlighted against the sky as lights from bridges older than the United States cast reflections in the water. Watch the performers on **Pont Saint-Louis** (the bridge connecting Ile Saint-Louis and Ile de la Cité) and then wander away for a *cornet* (cone) of Paris's best ice cream at nearby **Berthillon.** Consult Chapters 16 and 17 for the best sights to see and things to do in Paris.

Wining and Dining, and Wining Some More

Parisians are on an eternal quest for the perfect meal, and what wonderful meals they have to choose from — regional French, 3-star haute cuisine, North African *couscouseries,* tasty crêpes sold from street vendors, and more. During the last decade, the city witnessed the rise of "baby bistros," restaurants opened by celebrity chefs and their talented young apprentices offering simpler and less expensive meals than those served at their deluxe establishments. Also in vogue is a back-to-Grandmère's-kitchen approach featuring chefs turning out homey meals like *blanquette de veau* (veal stew in white sauce), *cassoulet* (meat-and-vegetable casserole), and *confit de canard* (duck preserved and cooked in its own fat until it's so tender that it falls off the bone).

Dine under the stained-glass ceiling at **Bofinger** — Paris's quintessential Belle Époque brasserie — while waiters in long aprons deftly make a fuss over you. Or sip a drink at chic **Café Flore,** where Simone de Beauvoir and Jean-Paul Sartre worked on their theories and met friends by appointment. You soon find that you're not only sitting down to a fine meal but also entering the life of a thriving city. Chapters 13, 14, and 15 give you the lowdown on Paris dining, including the addresses of some of the city's best restaurants, and tell you how to fill up quickly when you don't have time for a three-course meal.

Shopping in the Home of High Fashion

Shopping in Paris is always divine. A recent upswing in France's economy has seen many new stores open and others expand. The city has a well-deserved reputation as a bastion of over-the-top luxury. All you have to do to understand why is head for the 8th *arrondissement* (district, abbreviated 8e). For that matter, more places than ever offer you merchandise at a discount — Chapter 19 gives you the lowdown on *dégriffe* (labels cut out), *stock* (overstock), and *dépot-vente* (resale) shops and tells you everything you need to know about shopping in Paris.

Sampling Culture, Both Day and Night

Paris is *the* place to pursue culture. It boasts more than 100 theaters, competing opera houses, and ballet at the **Opéra Garnier** and chamber music concerts in many churches.

Even if your French is rusty or not up to par, many avant-garde productions and English-language theaters serve as alternatives to French-language plays.

And if you're a movie-lover, you'll have many films from which to choose — Hollywood blockbusters at big cinemas and new independent releases and classics by filmmakers such as Truffaut and Rohmer at art houses. See Chapters 22 and 23 for more info on cultural attractions.

Painting the Town at Clubs and Cabarets

Paris is a perpetual party, and each neighborhood makes a different contribution to the nightlife scene. The **Marais** is central to gay clubs and bars and to some of the best dance clubs. The **Bastille** attracts bohemian types and clubgoers. The side streets of the **Champs-Elysées** are home to upscale bars and discos, and a new generation of trendsetters is turning **Pigalle** into a rock music lovers' paradise. Jazz lovers find it easy to club-hop around **Les Halles** or on the **Left Bank.**

News flash: The people are nice!

Why are the French now so inclined to speak English and be polite? Perhaps they're tired of having a reputation for rudeness. Or perhaps they realized how much their economy depends on tourism. Whatever the reason, the new friendliness only makes a visit to the city more appealing.

It remains to be seen whether Paris dominates the tourism industry in the future as brilliantly as it has in the past. Yet for a city that has survived brutal wars, revolution, occupation, and political disarray (like recent presidential elections that gave a right-wing extremist a shot at the presidency), Paris has demonstrated strength and resiliency that should sustain it well into the next millennium. The fact that Paris is much more friendly and open benefits not only the city but also the country. With 72 million annual visitors, Paris is the world's most visited destination.

The naughty cancan dancers still attract crowds at the **Lido, Crazy Horse Saloon,** and **Moulin Rouge** clubs, though torch singers that made these clubs famous have given way to glitzy light shows, special effects, and recorded music. One thing hasn't changed: Flesh is plentiful and on display everywhere. Chapters 23 and 24 tell you how to dance the night away or catch a show.

Going Green in the Parks and Gardens

From flowers, plants, and city views to puppet shows, pony rides, and museums, Paris has parks for every taste and interest. You can relax in the beauty and serenity of planted gardens, splashing fountains, and arrow-straight paths. Chapter 17 steers you toward the best green spaces in town. Stunning beauty doesn't stop at the city limits, either. In Chapter 21 side trips to Versailles, Fontainebleau, Giverny and the like are highlighted, offering their own brand of sprawling splendor.

A brief history, from Parisii to Parisians

The Parisii tribe on the Ile de la Cité settled Paris in the third century B.C. Peaceful fishermen, they traded with other tribes along the river and with travelers on the main north-south trading road that connected the Mediterranean with northern Europe. Unfortunately, the road made attacking the Parisii all too convenient for invaders. The first and most successful were Romans led by Julius Caesar in 52 B.C. During their 500-year stay, the settlement became known as Lutetia Parisiorum ("Lutèce" in French). You can still see their public baths at the Musée National du Moyen Age/Cluny Museum in the Latin Quarter.

Years of barbarian invasions eventually weakened Rome's hold over the territory. Around 350, Attila the Hun, on his way to sack Paris, changed course at the last minute, purportedly answering the prayers of a young girl named Geneviève. She became the patron saint of Paris. In the 400s, Franks from the east successfully wrested control away from the Romans. In 508, Clovis, king of the Franks, chose Paris as his capital. It was abandoned as a capital 250 years later only to regain that status in 987 when Hugues Capet was proclaimed king of France. Celebrating the city's importance, two Gothic masterpieces, the cathedral of Notre-Dame and Sainte-Chapelle, were built on the Ile de la Cité. Across the river, on the Left Bank, Sorbonne University was born. Under Louis XIV, who ruled for 72 years, the monarchy's power reached its height, supported by heavy taxes. Although he added monuments and splendor to the city, the Sun King moved his court to Versailles, alienating the citizenry and preparing the way for the French Revolution.

On July 14, 1789, a mob stormed the Bastille. Three days later at the Hôtel de Ville, Louis XVI was forced to kiss the new French tricolor. On July 14, 1790, the Festival of the Federation was celebrated on the Champs de Mars, and an estimated 300,000 attended a Mass at which the king swore an oath of loyalty to the constitution. Yet radical factions grew. On August 10, 1792, revolutionary troops joined a Parisian mob storming the Tuileries, taking the king prisoner. In 1793, he and Queen Marie Antoinette were beheaded in the place de la Concorde. Robespierre then presided over the Reign of Terror until his July 27, 1794, arrest. A reaction ushered in the Directory over the next four years, ending with Napoléon's coup. In 1804, at Notre-Dame, Napoléon crowned himself emperor and his wife, Joséphine, empress before embarking on a series of military campaigns against surrounding countries until his defeat at Waterloo in 1815. During his reign, he gave Paris many of its most grandiose monuments, notably the Arc de Triomphe and the Bourse, but his greatest gift was starting the Louvre on course to becoming an art museum, in part, by displaying the art he had "acquired" in his many campaigns, which became the core of the museum's collection.

(continued)

(continued)

The look that most of us associate with Paris was created in the 19th century. Napoléon landscaped the view from the Louvre, extending the perspective past the Tuileries and the place de la Concorde to the Champs-Elysées and the Arc de Triomphe and built fountains, cemeteries, and the arcades along the rue de Rivoli. From 1852 to 1870, Napoléon's nephew, Napoléon III, reshaped Paris with the aid of Baron Haussmann, razing entire neighborhoods in favor of boulevards, avenues, and 24 parks.

The Eiffel Tower (*La Tour Eiffel*), built only as a temporary structure for the 1889 World's Fair, was allowed to remain standing as the tallest structure in the world at the time. Paris opened its first Métro line in 1900, and by the turn of the 20th century, had 27,000 cafés, about 150 café concerts, and thousands of restaurants.

In the 103 years since, Paris witnessed two world wars with more than 10 million military casualties, nearly 1 million Jews losing their lives, and four years of German occupation. Tens of thousands of soldiers died fighting the end of French colonial rule around the world. In 1968, students took to the streets of Paris, rebelling against France's antiquated educational system. The government flirted unsuccessfully with textbook socialism in the 1980s and ended the decade with a great celebration of democracy: the bicentennial of the French Revolution and the centennial of the Eiffel Tower. Former Paris Mayor Jacques Chirac was elected president in 1995 on his promise to jump-start the economy, but growth remained stagnant, and the president was forced to "cohabit" with Prime Minister Lionel Jospin, after the leader of the opposition called for elections in 1997. Facing rising gas prices, escalating crime, anti-Semitic vandalism, and a lack of interest in the 2002 presidential elections, Jospin lost his prime minister's seat, sending extremist Jean-Marie Le Pen into the presidential race against Chirac. French citizens took to the streets in protest, and Chirac won by a landslide. Jospin retired from politics.

Chapter 2

Deciding When to Go

● ●

In This Chapter

▶ Choosing the best season to visit

▶ Finding events that suit your interests

● ●

*I*n this chapter, I provide you with the pros and cons of each season to help you decide when you can make the most of your visit to Paris. I also compile a calendar of the most memorable events in Paris; you may want to consider planning your trip to coincide with one of the festivals, sporting events, or celebrations I list on it.

Uncovering the Secret of the Seasons: What to Expect

Most residents find Paris ideal in spring and autumn, when weather is kind, crowds are reasonably sized, and Parisian life runs at a steady hum. In reality, Paris is great any time of year. In winter, you can find plenty of things to do inside: You can fill an entire trip with visits just to the Louvre, and don't forget the January sales. In summer, you can bask in daylight that lasts until 10 p.m. Just remember that timing your visit to Paris depends on what kind of experience you want to have.

Table 2-1 presents average temperature by month in Paris to help you as you plan your trip. (In Paris, temperatures will be reported in Celsius.)

Table 2-1	Average Daytime Temperatures for Paris											
	Jan	*Feb*	*Mar*	*Apr*	*May*	*June*	*July*	*Aug*	*Sept*	*Oct*	*Nov*	*Dec*
Fahrenheit (F)	38°	39°	46°	51°	58°	64°	74°	76°	61°	53°	45°	40°
Celsius (C)	3°	4°	8°	11°	14°	18°	28°	29°	16°	12°	7°	6°

Singing in spring

Cole Porter wrote "I love Paris in the springtime," and with good reason. Spring in Paris brings some beautifully clear, fresh days. The parks and gardens of Paris (and those at Versailles, Fontainebleau, and at Claude Monet's home, Giverny; see Chapter 21) are at their colorful, fragrant best early in May. Crowds of visitors don't kick in until summer vacation (except during the spring fashion shows in March), so lines are relatively short at the top sightseeing attractions, and airfares have yet to reach their summertime highs.

But keep in mind that April in Paris is *not* as temperate as Porter would have you believe. In fact, Paris weather is very similar to that in London: It's fickle. Pack for warm, cold, wet, dry, and every other eventuality; in other words, bring layers and don't even *think* about coming without an umbrella. Also, nearly every Monday in May is a holiday in France — stores are closed, and other venues may be affected.

Wandering through summer

Wonderfully long and sultry days are summer's hallmark — I'm talking 6 a.m. sunrises and 10 p.m. sunsets — so you're afforded additional hours to wander and discover. You can find discounts of 30% to 50% in most stores during July, one of the two big months for shopping sales (the other is January). Hotel room rates are less expensive during the July and August low season, and during August, parking is free in much of the city.

But remember that an influx of tourists during the summer means long lines at museums and other sites. The weather also is capricious: You may have a week of rain and 55-degree Fahrenheit temperatures, followed by days of cloudless skies and dry heat.

Because most Parisians take their vacations in August, you either find the city wonderfully tranquil or a ghost town. Although the entire city doesn't exactly shut down in August, some shops and restaurants close for the entire month. The city's cultural calendar slows down, and you may have to walk an extra block or two to find an open shop or newsstand. And if you go to Paris in August with thoughts of practicing your French, think again. French may be the language you're least likely to hear in August.

Featuring fall

Paris crackles back to life starting the first week of September, a time typically known as *la rentrée* (the return). This season is one of the most exciting times of the year, when important art exhibitions open along with trendy new restaurants, shops, and cafés. Airfares drop from summertime highs. And with daytime temperatures in the 60s and 70s and nights in the 50s, the weather is pleasant.

Keep in mind, however, that finding a hotel at the last minute in the fall can be difficult due to the number of business conventions and trade shows happening in the city, including the October fashion shows. Be sure to book ahead.

Transportation strikes of varying intensities traditionally occur during the fall. Some go virtually unnoticed by the average traveler, but others can be giant hassles.

Coasting through winter

You can find great airfare deals during the winter; airlines and tour operators often offer unbeatable prices on flights and package tours. Lines at museums and other sights are mercifully short. And, if shopping is your bag, you can save up to 50% during the sales in January.

But remember that although Paris winters may appear mild on paper, in reality, residents know that they are gray (sometimes the sun doesn't shine for weeks), dreary, and bone-chillingly damp. And look out for those wind tunnels that lash up and down the city's grand boulevards. Bring a warm, preferably waterproof, coat.

Hitting the Big Events: A Paris Calendar

When you arrive, check with the **Paris Tourist Office** (☎ 08-92-68-31-12 at a charge of 0.34€ per minute, Internet: www.paris-tourist office.com) and buy *Pariscope* (a weekly guide with an English-language insert from *Time Out Paris*) or *L'Officiel des Spectacles* for dates, places, and other up-to-date information. For a refresher course in the ways and means of Paris addresses, see the Introduction.

January

La Grande Parade de Montmartre. A big, noisy parade on New Year's Day makes even the mildest hangover throb, but grin and bear it for the fun and flash — today Paris is more Rose Bowl than City of Lights. Watch the majorettes, high school bands, and elaborate floats traverse the city streets. The parade begins at 2 p.m. (so you *can* sleep in) in the place Pigalle, 18e (the 18th *arrondissement* or neighborhood), and ends at the place Jules-Joffrin, 18e. January 1.

Fête des Rois. Some folks wear gold paper crowns to celebrate the Feast of the Three Kings. The main object of celebration is a flaky almond-paste-filled pie that conceals a ceramic charm (so watch your teeth). According to custom, whoever finds the charm becomes king or queen for the day, is entitled to wear the crown, and has free reign, as it were, in his or her choice of a consort. The pie with the charm is available at all *pâtisseries* (dessert shops). January 6.

La Mairie de Paris Vous Invite au Concert. This event features a two-week, two-people-for-the-price-of-one special admission to a variety of jazz and classical concerts across the city. Mid-January.

Commemorative Mass for Louis XVI. Yes, Parisians celebrate Mass for a king their ancestors beheaded more than 200 years ago. It attracts a full turnout of aristocrats, royalists, and even some far-right types. At the Chapelle Expiatoire, 29 rue Pasquier, 8e. Sunday closest to January 21.

Chinese New Year Festival. Though Paris's Chinatown in 13e is mostly high-rise apartment buildings, you can easily find good street life and many excellent restaurants. Residents go all out for the parade, featuring dragons, dancers, and fireworks. Depending on the Chinese calendar, the holiday falls between January 21 and February 19.

February

Foire à la Feraille de Paris. This yearly antiques and secondhand fair takes place in the Parc Floral de Paris in the Bois de Vincennes (12e). Contact the Paris Tourist Office for exact dates.

Salon de l'Agriculture. The country fair comes to Paris with hundreds of farmers displaying animals and produce with prizes for the biggest and best. Regional food stands offer tastes from all parts of France, and the atmosphere is friendly and quintessentially French at the Parc des Expositions de Paris, Porte de Versailles, 15e. For more information, call the Parc des Expositions information line at ☎ **01-43-95-37-00** or the Paris Tourist Office. Admission is 10€ adults; 6€ children and students. Last week of February to first week of March.

March

La Passion à Ménilmontant. Professional actors and residents of the neighborhood perform the Passion play (the events leading up to and including the Crucifixion of Christ) for a month around Easter. The play is staged at the Théâtre de Ménilmontant in the 20e. The event is a local tradition that's been observed since 1932. Call ☎ **01-46-36-98-60** or 01-46-36-03-43 for schedule and ticket prices. Mid-March to mid-April.

Foire du Trone. Tacky and fun, this annual carnival has a Ferris wheel, rides and games, hokey souvenirs, and fairground food. At the Pelouse de Reuilly in the Bois de Vincennes. Late March to end of May.

April

Le Chemin de la Croix (Stations of the Cross). Follow the archbishop of Paris from the square Willette in Montmartre up the steps to the basilica of Sacré-Coeur where he leads prayers to commemorate the Passion and Crucifixion of Jesus Christ. Good Friday, 12:30 p.m.

Paris Marathon. One of the most popular athletic events during the year, this race runs past a variety of the city's most beautiful monuments. Run on a Sunday, the marathon attracts enthusiastic crowds. Call the Paris Tourist Office for exact dates. Mid-April.

Foire de Paris. A great place to bargain hunt and people watch, this huge annual fair signals the start of spring with hundreds of stands selling good-priced food and wine, and a variety of clothing and household goods. The fair takes place at the Parc des Expositions, Porte de Versailles. Late April to early May.

Grandes Eaux Musicales and les Fêtes de Nuit de Versailles. The Grandes Eaux Musicales bring the sounds of classical music to life at the magnificent fountains in the gardens of the Château de Versailles every Sunday from mid-April to mid-October, and every Saturday and national holiday from June through August.

Even better are the Grandes Fêtes, spectacular sound and light shows with fireworks that take place one Saturday in June, three Saturdays in July, one Saturday in August, and two Saturdays in September. Château de Versailles, Versailles. Log on to www.chateauversailles.fr for more information.

May

May Day. Banks, post offices, and most museums are closed May 1, the French version of Labor Day, but you can watch a workers' parade that traditionally ends at the place de la Bastille. Call the Paris Tourist Office for more information. May 1.

Vintage Car Rally, Montmartre. Staged annually since 1924, this array of antique cars makes its way through the streets of Montmartre starting at 10 a.m. in rue Lépic and ending at the place du Tertre. Sunday closest to May 15.

Les Cinq Jours Extraordinaire. During five extraordinary days, the shops in the rue du Bac, de Lille, de Beaune, des St-Pères, and de l'Université, and on the quai Voltaire, feature a free open house focusing on a special object that's been chosen according to the annual theme. The whole quarter takes on a festive ambience, red carpets line the streets, and plants and flowers decorate shop fronts. Third week of May.

French Open. Tickets are hard to come by for this tennis tournament, one of the biggest events on Paris's calendar. The French Open is played in the Stade Roland Garros in the Bois de Boulogne on the western edge of the city. Unsold tickets — those not reserved for corporate sponsors — go on sale two weeks before the competition starts. The stadium is at 2 av. Gordon Bennett, 16e. Call the French Federation of Tennis at the stadium for more information (☎ 01-47-43-48-00) or visit the Web site at www.frenchopen.com. Last week in May and first week in June.

June

Festival Chopin à Paris. The Orangerie museum in the beautiful Bagatelle gardens on the edge of the Bois de Boulogne is the backdrop for this much-loved annual series of daily piano recitals. Mid-June to mid-July.

Fête de la Musique. The entire country becomes a concert venue in celebration of the first day of summer, and you can hear everything from classical to hip-hop for free in squares and streets around Paris. A big rock concert usually happens in the place de la République and a fine classical concert generally takes place in the gardens of the Palais-Royal. June 21.

The Paris Air Show. One of the most distinguished aviation events in the world takes place in odd-numbered years at Le Bourget Airport just outside Paris. Visitors can check out the latest aeronautic technology on display. Call the Paris Tourist Office for more information.

Gay Pride. Art exhibits, concerts, and a fantastic parade are staged in the Marais and in other Paris streets, including the boulevard St-Michel. Call the Centre Gai et Lesbien for dates at ☎ 01-43-57-21-47. Late June.

July and August

Bastille Day. Citywide festivities begin on the evening of July 13 with street fairs, pageants, and feasts. Free *bals* (dances) are open to everyone at fire stations all over the city. (Some of the best *bals* are in the fire stations on the rue du Vieux-Colombier near the place St-Sulpice, 6e; the rue Sévigné, 4e; and the rue Blanche, near place Pigalle, 9e.) Although the *bals* are free, drinks cost.

On July 14, a big military parade starts at 10 a.m. on the Champs-Elysées; get there early if you hope to see anything. A sound-and-light show with terrific fireworks can be seen that night at the Trocadéro. Rather than face the crowds, many people watch the fireworks from the Champs de Mars across the river, from hotel rooms with views, or even from the hill on rue Soufflot, in front of the Panthéon. July 13 and 14.

Paris, Quartier d'Été. Contemporary music, dance, and film are the bills of fare at outside venues around the city. The outdoor movies shown on a giant screen at Parc de la Villette are particularly popular. July 14 to August 15.

Tour de France. The most famous bicycle race in the world always ends in Paris on the Champs-Elysées. For a number of years, spectators along the route have watched Texan Lance Armstrong take on the best in the world and toast some incredible victories. You need a special invitation for a seat in the stands near place de la Concorde, but you can see the cyclists further up the Champs-Elysées and, depending on the route (which changes each year), elsewhere in the city, too. Check the newspapers the day before or log on to www.letour.com. Late July or early August.

Fête de l'Assomption. Church services at Notre-Dame are the most popular and colorful on this important French holiday (many stores are closed, and transportation runs on a holiday schedule), and banners are draped over the church's towers to celebrate the day. August 15.

September

Biennale des Antiquaires. One of the largest and most prestigious antiques shows in the world opens to the public in even-numbered years in the Cour Carée du Louvre, the underground exhibition space connected to the museum. For more information, contact the Paris Tourist Office. Early September.

Les Journées de Patrimoine. Off-limits palaces, churches, and other official buildings throw open their doors to the public for two days. Long lines can put a damper on your sightseeing, so plan what you want to see and show up early (with a good book, just in case). Get a list and a map of all the open buildings from the Paris Tourist Office. Weekend closest to September 15.

Festival d'Automne. This arts festival around Paris is recognized throughout Europe for its innovative programming and the high quality of its artists and performers. Obtain programs through the mail so that you can book ahead for events you don't want to miss. Write to the Festival, 56 rue de Rivoli, 75001 Paris, or call ☎ **01-53-45-17-00.** September 15 to December 31.

October

Fêtes des Vendanges à Montmartre. Celebrate the harvest of the wine produced from Montmartre's one remaining vineyard, Clos Montmartre, and watch as the wine is auctioned off at high prices to benefit local charities. (A word of advice: *Don't* bid! The wine isn't very good.) Locals dress in period costumes, and the streets come alive with music. First or second Saturday of October.

FIAC (Foire Internationale d'Art Contemporain). One of the largest contemporary art fairs in the world, the FIAC has stands from more than 150 galleries, half of them foreign. As interesting for browsing as for buying, the fair takes place in Espace Eiffel Branly, near the Eiffel Tower. For more information, call **08-36-68-00-51.** Early October.

November

Mois de la Photo. Many of the city's major museums celebrate the art of photography with shows. Check listings in the weekly guide *Pariscope.* All month.

Armistice Day. The French commemorate those who died fighting in both World Wars with a wreath-laying ceremony at the Arc de Triomphe, and veterans sell poppy corsages in memory. November 11.

Beaujolais Nouveau. The sooner you drink it the better, and wine bars and cafés are packed for the just-after-midnight public release of the fruity red wine. Third Thursday (technically early Friday morning) in November.

Lancement des Illuminations des Champs-Elysées. The annual lighting of the avenue's Christmas lights makes for a festive evening, with jazz concerts and an international star who pushes the button that lights up the avenue. For more information, call the Paris Tourist Office. Late November.

December

La Crèche sur le Parvis. Each year a different foreign city installs a life-sized Christmas manger scene in the plaza in front of the Hôtel de Ville (City Hall). The crèche is open daily from 10 a.m. to 8 p.m. December 1 to January 3.

Chapter 3

Planning Your Budget

*S*ois raisonnable (Be reasonable), the French say, and being reasonable is the key to budgeting a trip to Paris. A good way to figure out a budget is mentally walking through the trip, from the moment you leave to the minute you get back home, and don't forget to figure in your transportation to and from the airport. Then add in the flight cost (see Chapter 5 for tips on how to fly to Paris for less), the price of getting from the Charles-de-Gaulle or Orly airport to your hotel, your hotel rate per day, meals, public transportation costs, admission prices to museums and the theater, and other entertainment expenses. Afterward, add another 15% to 20% for good measure. To help you record your estimates, look for the "yellow pages" (budget worksheets) provided at the end of the book.

In Paris, you pay for things in euro coins and bills. Check out Chapter 12 for information on how to convert your currency.

Adding Up the Elements

Cities rarely are cheap or expensive across the board; Paris tends to be pricey for dining but reasonable for accommodations, so booking a good hotel shouldn't be a problem. The following list offers guidelines for what you're likely to spend while in Paris. Table 3-1 gives you approximate prices for some common expenses.

✔ **Lodging:** Before you start shelling out money for lodging, think about how much time you'll actually spend in your room. For between 50€ and 75€, you can rent a clean, functionally furnished hotel room with a private bathroom and cable TV. These kinds of budget rooms normally are comfortable, have the basic furnishings and decor, but are supplied with thin yet serviceable towels and thin bars of soap.

If you're feeling extravagant and willing to spend 200€ or more to live in luxury, upper-tier hotels offer more services, such as room service, air conditioning, and toiletries.

✔ **Transportation:** The Paris Métro has been the model for subways around the world since its inauguration in 1900. Simply put, the Métro is one of the best transit systems around in terms of price and efficiency. Getting across town in less than a half-hour is no problem, and the cost is lower when you purchase one of several available discount tickets or a *carnet* (booklet) of ten tickets. (See Chapter 11 for options and prices.)

As for cars, well, expect your heart to be in your throat the entire time you drive in Paris — unless, of course, you thrive on labyrinthine one-way streets, a dearth of parking spaces, hellish traffic, and driving among what are statistically the worst drivers in Europe. If you want to rent a car to see other parts of France or make a day-trip outside of Paris, rent on your way out of the city. (See Chapter 9 for addresses and phone numbers of car rental agencies in Paris.)

✔ **Restaurants:** The French consider dining out one of the finer joys in life, and they pay for it. You too can expect to do so. An average Parisian dining experience — a three-course dinner in a popular eatery — runs about 38€ to 45€ per person.

You can find restaurants serving satisfying two-course meals for as little as 18€ and wonderful ethnic food and sandwich shops that help you save even more money. Dining reasonably in Paris isn't impossible when you know where to look. Chapters 14 and 15 help you discover just that.

✔ **Attractions:** Entry fees to museums and other sights also can add up quickly; after referring to the money-saving advice in Chapters 16 and 17, make a list of must-dos to get a feel for how much money to set aside.

✔ **Shopping:** Paris is a shoppers' paradise, and French shopkeepers arrange their wares in such enticing window displays that they'll have you *faites du leche-vitrines* (licking the windows). You can find some great deals during the semiannual sales in January and July, but remember that a steep 20.6% tax (value-added tax, abbreviated VAT or TVA) is added to most goods. If you live outside the European Union, you're usually entitled to get back part of the tax, whenever you meet certain requirements. See Chapter 19 for more information.

✔ **Nightlife:** Don't forego the spectacles at the Lido or Moulin Rouge if you've always wanted to see them — just know beforehand that they charge a small fortune for entry and alcoholic beverages. Plan on seeing the show without dinner, and come out with a wallet that isn't quite as light as it otherwise will be. Budget big, too, especially when you plan to visit clubs and other nightspots; nightclubs and bars are not cheap.

Table 3-1	What Things Cost in Paris
Expense	*Cost in U.S. Dollars*
Taxi from Charles-de-Gaulle Airport to the city center (depending on traffic)	30.00–45.00
Taxi from Orly Airport to the city center	20.00–25.00
Public transportation for an average trip on Métro within the city (from a Métro *carnet* of 10)	1.30
Local telephone call	0.11
Glass of wine	2.50
Coca-Cola (at a café)	4.00
Cup of coffee	2.50
Roll of ASA 100 color film, 36 exposures	9.00
Admission to the Louvre	7.50
Movie ticket	8.00–9.00
Concert ticket (at the Salle Pleyel)	19.50–60.00

Keeping a Lid on Hidden Expenses

Remembering the tipping rules can save you money in Paris. At restaurants, the tip usually is included; on your bill, you'll see the words *service compris* (which means a 15% gratuity for service is already figured into the bill). Although technically unnecessary, a small additional tip (2€ for a moderately priced meal) is considered appropriate for satisfactory service.

Don't tip a bartender for each round of drinks — instead leave 2€ to 5€ at the end of the night. Hotel service personnel should get 2€ per luggage item or service performed, and taxicab drivers generally are tipped 10% of the fare. If an usher shows you to your seat in a cinema or theater, tip 1€.

Don't think a café is a cheaper alternative to a restaurant. A simple meal of *croque monsieur* with *pommes frites* (a toasted ham and cheese sandwich with French fries) accompanied by a beer or soda can set you back 15€ to 20€. You can get a much tastier meal at the same price or less at a restaurant.

Choosing Cash, Credit Cards, or Traveler's Checks

Money makes the world go round, but dealing with an unfamiliar currency can make your head spin. When it comes to getting cash in Paris, should you bring traveler's checks or use ATMs? How easy is it to pay with a credit card? You find the answers in this section.

Using ATMs: They're everywhere

Before you leave, make a note of the following Web sites: www.visaeu.com (Visa) and www.mastercard.com (MasterCard), which identify the locations of cash machines all over Paris. Most of the major banks in Paris, such as Credit Lyonnais, Credit Agricole, Banque Nationale de Paris (BNP), Banque Populaire, Credit Commercial de France (CCF), Credit du Nord, and even some branches of the post office have automatic cash distribution machines. But you won't be able to check your balance or transfer funds, so keep track of your withdrawals while you travel.

Make sure your ATM card has a four-digit personal identification number (PIN). To withdraw cash, your PIN has to be made up of just numbers; French ATMs usually don't have alphanumeric keypads. (If your PIN is a combination of letters and numbers, use a telephone dial to figure out the numeric equivalent.)

Finally, remember that every time you withdraw cash from an ATM, your bank hits you with a fee, sometimes as much as $5. Check how much your bank charges before leaving home. On top of this fee, the bank from which you withdraw cash may also include its own fee. Thus, taking out larger amounts of money every two to three days makes more sense than more frequent withdrawals of smaller denominations. Likewise, remember that your bank places a limit on the amount of money you can take out per day, usually between 300€ and 500€. Again, check with your bank before you leave for the maximum amount.

Paying by credit card

You can use credit cards to buy virtually anything in France. You can also get cash advances from your Visa and MasterCard at any bank. Establishments accepting Eurocard also accept MasterCard.

As is the case in life, expect a downside. American Express and Diner's Club aren't widely accepted at small restaurants, shops, or budget hotels in Paris. You also pay interest on cash advances on your credit card from the moment you receive the cash. And finally, many credit-card companies now are tacking on additional fees for foreign currency transactions — sometimes up to 4%, on top of the 1% service charge that MasterCard and Visa require. Worse yet, according to Lee Dembart, a writer for *The International Herald Tribune,* credit-card companies don't expect you to notice the charge. "Recognizing the additional fee requires that the consumer know what the exchange rate was on the day the charge came through and then do the math," he writes, "steps most people don't take. You can find the official rate for dates in the past at The Currency Site, www.oanda.com."

If you don't know how much your credit card charges for currency conversion, contact a company representative. If the rate isn't acceptable, consider switching cards — **MBNA America** (☎ **800-421-2110**; Internet: www.mbna.com), a Delaware-based credit-card issuer, charges nothing for currency conversion.

Leaving home without traveler's checks

Because most cities now have banks with 24-hour ATMs, traveler's checks, previously one of a globetrotter's best friends, have become less necessary these days. You may find it difficult to find places that cash traveler's checks. And when you do, well, who wants to stand in a line?

Don't expect to use traveler's checks directly at budget establishments; change them for euros at a bank or change outlet and use cash instead. Keep in mind that many establishments don't accept traveler's checks in euros and that places that do accept traveler's checks in U.S. dollars normally offer poor exchange rates.

If you're still interested in purchasing traveler's checks, your best bet is to buy them and some euros — about $50 to $100 worth — before leaving home, unless you don't mind waiting at the exchange offices at the Paris airports. Make sure to keep a record of the serial numbers of your traveler's checks separately from the checks so you're assured of a refund in an emergency. **American Express** offers denominations of

$10, $20, $50, $100, $500, and $1,000. You pay a service charge ranging from 1% to 4%. You also can obtain American Express traveler's checks online (www.americanexpress.com) and over the phone if you're an American Express cardholder (☎ 888-269-6669). American Automobile Association (AAA) members can get checks without a fee at most AAA offices.

Thomas Cook (☎ 800-227-6811) also offers traveler's checks, available online at www.travelex.com. The service charge ranges between 1.5% and 2.0%, and checks come in denominations of $50, $100, $500, and $1,000. **MasterCard** also offers traveler's checks in the same denominations; call ☎ 800-223-9920 for a location near you.

Cutting Costs

Throughout this book, Bargain Alert icons highlight money-saving tips and/or great deals. Here are some additional cost-cutting strategies:

1. **Fly during the week rather than on weekends.**

   You can also save on airfare and dining when you **travel during the off-season,** the period from approximately October to March.

2. **Try a package tour.**

   For many destinations, you can book airfare, hotel, ground transportation, and even some sightseeing just by making one call to a travel agent or searching the Internet, for a lot less than if you tried to put the trip together yourself. (See Chapter 5 for specific companies to call.)

3. **Pack light.**

   You won't need a cart or a taxi to carry your load.

4. **Take the cheapest way into the city from the airport.**

   You can save around $30 by taking a train or bus instead of a cab from Roissy–Charles-de-Gaulle Airport and about $15 from Orly.

5. **Book your hotel room early.**

   Rooms at the best prices fill up quickly.

6. **Negotiate the room price, especially in the low season.**

   Ask for a discount if you're a student or older than 60; ask for a discount when you're staying a certain number of days, say three or more.

7. **Reserve a room with a kitchen.**

   It may not seem like much of a vacation if you cook your own meals and wash your own dishes, but you can save a lot of money by not eating in restaurants three times a day. Even if you make only breakfast and pack an occasional bag lunch, you can save a little extra cash for souvenirs and gifts for your family and friends back home. And you won't need to fret over a hefty room-service bill.

8. **Try renting an apartment.**

   Renting a Paris apartment can be surprisingly cheap, and apartment rental services flourish online. You'll save money by eating more meals in the apartment, and you'll experience a little of what it's like to live like a resident of Paris. (See Chapter 6 for specific rental agencies.)

9. **Make lunch your main meal.**

   Many restaurants offer great deals on a fixed-price (*prix fixe*) lunch. After two or three courses at midday, you won't want a big dinner.

10. **Try the ethnic neighborhoods.**

    You can get terrific Chinese and Vietnamese foods in the 13e arrondissement between the place d'Italie and the Porte de Choisy; and the 10e, 18e, and 20e have restaurants with North African, Turkish, Vietnamese, and Thai menus. Couscous is on the menu at many restaurants and usually is an inexpensive offering.

11. **Remember that the *plat du jour* usually is the cheapest main dish at a budget restaurant.**

12. **Remember that wine is cheaper than soda.**

    Some mineral waters, likewise, are less expensive than others. Ask for tap water (*une carafe d'eau*), which is free.

13. **Know the tipping rules.**

    Most restaurants include the gratuity in the bill; don't double-tip by mistake. Look for *service compris* on your bill, which means 15% has been added already.

14. **If you're just having drinks or coffee, do it standing at the bar.**

    You pay twice as much when you're seated at a table.

15. **Use the bus or Métro, or walk.**

    Buy a *carnet* of 10 Métro tickets at a time — a single ticket costs 1.30€, while a carnet ticket is 0.85€. Better yet, if you know you're going to be in Paris from two to five consecutive days, buy a **Paris Visite pass,** which is good for unlimited subway and bus travel. A one-day Paris Visite card costs 8.35€, two-day 13.70€, three-day 18.25€, and five-day 26.65€.

16. **Whenever you plan to visit two or three museums a day, buy the *Carte Musées et Monuments (Museum and Monuments) Pass.***

    The pass costs 15€ for one day, 30€ for three days, and 42€ for five days.

17. **Take advantage of the reduced admission fees at museums.**

    The reduced prices usually apply after 3 p.m. and all day Sunday. Remember that on the first Sunday of every month, admission to national museums is free.

18. **For discounts on fashion, try the rue St-Placide in the 6e arrondissement.**

    You find plenty of overstock and *dégriffe* (clothes with labels removed) items on this street near the Bon Marché department store. Stylish inexpensive clothes also can be found at Monoprix stores located all over the city.

19. **Buy half-price theater and other performance tickets.**

    You can find same-day half-price tickets at one of the kiosks by the Madeleine or at the Gare Montparnasse. The kiosks are little huts with panels indicating whether the performance is sold out (symbolized by a little red man) or if tickets are still available (a little green man).

20. **Avoid going to clubs on weekends.**

    You can also save money by sitting at the bar instead of at a table. Some clubs are cheaper than others, and some are cheaper during the week.

Finally, in general, **always ask for discount rates.** Membership in AAA, frequent-flyer plans, trade unions, AARP, or other groups may qualify you for savings on car rentals, plane tickets, hotel rooms, even meals. Ask about everything; you may be pleasantly surprised.

Chapter 4

Planning Ahead for Special Travel Needs

F rance ranks among the most visited of all tourist destinations, and more resources than ever make it available — and enjoyable — to all. How-to guides, tour companies for disabled travelers, and English-speaking baby sitters are only some of the ways that travelers with special needs are making the most of Paris these days. In this chapter, I tell you about those resources and others.

Taking the Family Along

Don't let anyone talk you out of taking your kids to Paris. The City of Light is full of attractions worthy of your children's attention, and they only benefit from the experience — probably longer than you do! Parks and playgrounds abound, as do kid-specific sights and museums, interesting boat rides, and bike tours. And, Paris is just as safe, if not safer, than most big American cities.

 If you plan your trip well in advance, your kids may get a kick out of learning the language from one of the many French-language instructional videotapes on the market.

Books like Ludwig Bemelmans's *Madeline* series, Albert Lamorisse's *The Red Balloon,* and Kay Thompson's *Eloise in Paris* are great for kids under 8 years of age. Look for them at your local library or bookstore or order them from the Librairie de France in New York (☎ **212-581-8810;** Fax: 212-265-1094). Older teens may appreciate Ernest

Hemingway's *A Moveable Feast,* Victor Hugo's *Les Misérables,* Mark Twain's *Innocents Abroad,* and Rose Tremain's *The Way I Found Her.*

Preview some of the museums that you want to visit by checking out their Internet sites (see the sidebar "Ten Web sites to browse with your children" later in this chapter). Children younger than 18 are admitted free to France's national museums (although not necessarily to Paris's city museums).

If you stay long enough, consider a day-trip to Disneyland Paris, which is easily accessible by public transportation. (Chapter 21 has more information.)

Some attractions offer a lower rate for families of four or more. When purchasing tickets, ask if there is a family rate or *carte famille nombreuse.*

If your children are younger than 12, and you're traveling by rail through France, check out the **Carte Enfant Plus,** a children's rail pass. Available at any SNCF (French National Railroads) station or online at www.sncf-voyages.com (for an English version of this site, click on the tiny British flag), the pass offers a 50% discount for the child and up to four adult travel companions. The pass costs 44€, and you can reserve it online right before you leave and pick it up at any Paris train station within the time limit (usually two days). The pass is good for a month, but only a limited number of seats are available, and the discounts aren't offered during periods of peak travel or on holidays. Reserve train travel in advance.

Finally, a word of advice: Although the French people love kids and welcome them just about anywhere, they expect them to be well mannered. Proper behavior is expected everywhere, but especially in restaurants and museums. French children are taught at an early age to behave appropriately in these settings, and French adults expect the same from your kids.

Bringing along baby

You can arrange ahead of time for such necessities as a crib, bottle warmer, and, if you're driving, a car seat (small children are prohibited from riding in the front seat). Find out whether your hotel stocks baby food; if not, take some with you for your first day but then plan to buy some. Plenty of choices are available from Nestlé to Naturalia.

Transportation in Paris isn't as stroller friendly as in the United States. Be prepared to lift your child out of the stroller when boarding buses, climbing up and down stairs, and/or walking long distances in some Métro subway stations. The upside of all of this is that you and your child can stroll in some of the world's prettiest parks and gardens.

Ten Web sites to browse with your children

Checking out some of the following Web sites ahead of time with your children is a wonderful way of giving them a preview of what they'll find in Paris. For more information about each of these attractions, check out the chapters in parentheses in the following list.

✔ Centre Georges Pompidou (see Chapter 16), www.centrepompidou.fr

✔ Cité des Sciences et de l'Industrie (see Chapter 17), www.cite-sciences.fr

✔ Disneyland Paris (see Chapter 21), www.disneylandparis.com

✔ Eiffel Tower (see Chapter 16), www.tour-eiffel.fr

✔ Les Catacombes (see Chapter 17), www.multimania.com/houze

✔ Musée d'Orsay (see Chapter 16), www.musee-orsay.fr

✔ Musée du Louvre (see Chapter 16), www.louvre.fr

✔ Palais de la Découverte (see Chapter 17), www.palais-decouverte.fr

✔ Parc de la Villette (see Chapter 17), www.lavillette.com

✔ Parc Zoologique de Paris (see Chapter 17), www.mnhn.fr

Locating some helpful resources

Whenever you need a baby sitter, consider one of the following agencies that employ English-speaking caregivers. **Ababa,** 8 av. du Maine, 15e (☎ 01-45-49-46-46), **Allo Maman Poule,** 7 villa Murat, 16e (☎ 01-45-20-96-96), or **Kid Services,** 17 rue Molière, 9e (☎ 01-42-61-90-00). Specify when calling that you need a sitter who speaks English.

The books *Family Travel* (Lanier Publishing International) and *How to Take Great Trips with Your Kids* (The Harvard Common Press) are full of good, general advice that can apply to travel anywhere. Another reliable tome with a worldwide focus is *Adventuring with Children* (Foghorn Press).

You can also check out *Family Travel Times,* published six times a year by Travel with Your Children, 40 Fifth Ave., Seventh floor, New York, NY 10011 (☎ **888-822-4FTT** or 212-477-5524; Internet: www.familytravel times.com). It includes a weekly call-in service for subscribers. Subscriptions are $39 a year. A free publication list and a sample issue are available on request.

Searching Out Bargains for Seniors

Mention that you're a senior citizen when you first make your travel reservations; you may be entitled to some discounts before you even get to Paris. When you arrive in Paris, don't be shy about asking for senior discounts, and always carry a form of identification that shows your date of birth.

People over the age of 60 qualify for reduced admission to theaters, museums, and other attractions, and for other travel bargains like the **Carte Senior,** which entitles holders to an unlimited number of train rides and reductions of 20% to 50% on train trips (except during holidays and periods of peak travel). The Carte Senior also triggers some discounts on admission to museums and historic sites. It's valid for one year, costs 46€, and you can buy it at any SNCF station. Be prepared to show proof of your age when buying the card.

Membership in certain organizations can qualify you for some discounts. Be sure to bring whatever membership card the organization issues. Some to consider are

- **AARP:** If you're not already a member, join AARP, 601 E St. NW, Washington, DC 20049 (☎ **800-424-3410;** Internet: www.aarp.org) for discounts on hotels, airfares, and car rentals. As a member, you're eligible for a wide range of special benefits, including *Modern Maturity* magazine and a monthly newsletter.

- **Mature Outlook:** Members of Mature Outlook, P.O. Box 9390, Des Moines, IA 50306 (☎ **800-265-3675**), receive discounts on hotels and a bimonthly magazine. Annual membership is $19.99, which includes discounts and coupons for discounted Sears merchandise.

- **National Council of Senior Citizens:** You get discounts on hotel and auto rentals and receive a magazine that's partly devoted to travel tips, when you join the nonprofit National Council of Senior Citizens, 8403 Colesville Rd., Suite 1200, Silver Spring, MD 20910 (☎ **301-578-8800**). Annual dues are $13 per person or couple.

Available by subscription ($30 a year), *The Mature Traveler,* a monthly newsletter about senior citizen travel, is a valuable resource. A free sample can be had by sending a postcard with your name and address to GEM Publishing Group, Box 50400, Reno, NV 89513 or by e-mailing your information to maturetrav@aol.com. *101 Tips for the Mature Traveler* is another useful publication that's available from **Grand Circle Travel,** 347 Congress St., Suite 3A, Boston, MA 02210 (☎ **800-221-2610;** Internet: www.gct.com).

Hundreds of travel agencies specialize in senior travel, one of which is Grand Circle. Although many of the vacations are of the tour-bus variety, which may cramp the style of an independent senior, one bonus is that free trips are often thrown in for organizers of groups of 20 or more. Obtain travel information from **SAGA International Holidays,** 222 Berkeley St., Boston, MA 02116 (☎ **800-343-0273;** Internet: www.sagaholidays.com), which offers inclusive tours and cruises for those 50 and older.

Check at newsstands for the quarterly magazine *Travel 50 & Beyond,* and at bookstores for The *50+ Traveler's Guidebook* (St. Martin's Press), *The Seasoned Traveler* (Country Roads Press), or *Unbelievably Good Deals and Great Adventures That You Absolutely Can't Get Unless You're Over 50* (Contemporary Books).

Accessing Paris: Advice for Travelers with Disabilities

Unfortunately, the features that make Paris so beautiful — uneven cobblestone streets, quaint buildings with high doorsills from the Middle Ages, and twisting lanes too narrow and traffic-clogged to simultaneously admit pedestrians and autos — also make using a walker or a wheelchair a nightmare. According to French law, newer hotels with 3 stars or more are required to have at least one wheelchair-accessible guest room. Unfortunately, most of the city's older, budget hotels, which are exempt from the law, occupy buildings with winding staircases, or elevators smaller than phone booths, and generally aren't good choices for travelers with disabilities.

And, similar to the way it is for people with babies in strollers, Paris's public transportation system isn't the most accessible to folks with mobility problems. Few Métro stations have elevators, most feature long tunnels, and some have wheelchair-unfriendly moving sidewalks and staircases. Escalators often lead to flights of stairs, and many times when you climb a flight of stairs, you're faced with another set of stairs leading down. Currently, wheelchair lifts aren't standard equipment on city buses, and the buses don't "kneel" closer to the curb to make that first step any lower.

However, the newly built line 14 of the Métro is wheelchair accessible, and so are the stations at Nanterre-Université, Vincennes, Noisiel, Saint-Maur-Créteil, Torcy, Auber, Cité-Universitaire, Saint-Germain-en-Laye, Charles-de-Gaulle–Étoile, Nanterre-Ville, and several others. Bus 91, which links the Bastille with Montparnasse, is wheelchair accessible, and so are new buses on order. Some high-speed and intercity trains are equipped for wheelchair access, and a special space is available in first class (at the price of a second-class ticket) for wheelchairs, although you must reserve well in advance.

But don't let these inconveniences change your mind about visiting Paris. Before your trip to Paris, contact the **French Government Tourist Office** for the publication (with an English glossary) *Touristes Quand Même,* which provides an overview of facilities for the disabled in the French transportation system and at monuments and museums in Paris and the provinces.

You can also get a list of hotels in France that meet the needs of disabled travelers by writing to **L'Association des Paralysés de France,** 2217 rue de Père Guérion bd. Auguste-Blanqui, 75013 Paris (☎ 01-40-78-69-00; Internet: www.apf.asso.fr).

You can contact the **Groupement pour l'Insertion des Personnes Handicapées Physiques** (Help for the Physically Handicapped), Paris Office, 98 rue de la Porte Jaune, 92210 St-Cloud (☎ 01-41-83-15-15) and **Les Compagnons du Voyage** of the **RATP** (Paris public transportation) (☎ 01-45-83-67-77; Internet: www.ratp.fr) for help in planning itineraries using public transportation.

A good English-language guide for disabled travelers is *Access in Paris,* which you can obtain by calling ☎ 020-1250-3222 or writing to **RADAR,** Unit 12, City Forum, 250 City Road, London EC1V 8AF. It costs £13.95 (approximately $9.50).

Check out *A World of Options,* a 658-page book of resources for disabled travelers that covers everything from biking trips to scuba outfitters around the world. The book costs $35 and can be ordered from **Mobility International USA,** P.O. Box 10767, Eugene, OR 97440 (☎ 541-343-1284, voice and TYY; Internet: www.miusa.org). Another place to try is **Access-Able Travel Source** (Internet: www.access-able.com), a comprehensive database of travel agents who specialize in disabled travel and a clearinghouse for information about accessible destinations around the world.

Travelers with disabilities may also want to consider joining a tour that caters specifically to them. One of the best operators is **Flying Wheels Travel,** P.O. Box 382, Owatonna, MN 55060 (☎ 507-451-5005; Internet: www.flyingwheelstravel.com). Flying Wheels offers various escorted tours and cruises, and private tours in minivans with lifts. Another good company is **FEDCAP Rehabilitation Services,** 211 W. 14th St., New York, NY 10011. Call ☎ 212-727-4200 or fax FEDCAP at 212-727-4373 for information about membership and summer tours.

Vision-impaired travelers can contact the **American Foundation for the Blind,** 11 Penn Plaza, Suite 300, New York, NY 10001 (☎ 800-232-5463), for information on traveling with Seeing Eye dogs.

If you have trouble walking or tire easily, consider renting a wheelchair to take with you as checked baggage on your flight. If you're in a wheelchair, be sure to have a maintenance check before your trip and take some basic tools and extra parts with you if necessary.

Living the High Life: Tips for Gay and Lesbian Travelers

They don't call it "Gay Paree" for nothing. Everyone from hotel clerks to servers treats same-sex couples with polite indifference. Oscar Wilde and James Baldwin lived here, and Gertrude Stein settled here with Alice B. Toklas. France is one of the world's most tolerant countries toward gays and lesbians. It has no laws that discriminate against them. Technically, sexual relations are legal for consenting partners ages 16 and older.

 Paris's gay center is the Marais, which stretches from the Hôtel de Ville to the place de la Bastille. The biggest concentration of gay bookstores, cafés, bars, and clothing boutiques is here, and so is the best source of information on Parisian gay and lesbian life — the **Centre Gai et Lesbien,** 3 rue Keller, 11e (☎ 01-43-57-21-47; Métro: Bastille). The center is a source of information, and members of its staff coordinate the activities and meetings of gay people around the world. The center is open daily from 2 to 8 p.m.

Another helpful source is **La Maison des Femmes,** 163 rue Charenton, 12e (☎ 01-43-43-41-13; Métro: Charonne), which has a café and a feminist library for lesbians and bisexual women. Meetings about everything from sexism to working rights and informal dinners and get-togethers all take place there. Call Monday, Wednesday, or Friday from 3 to 8 p.m. for more information.

Gay magazines that focus mainly on cultural events include *Illico* (free in gay bars, about 2€ at newsstands) and *e.m≤* (available free at bars and bookstores). *Lesbia* is available for women. You can find these and others at Paris's largest and best-stocked gay bookstore, **Les Mots à la Bouche,** 6 rue Ste-Croix-la-Bretonnerie, 4e (☎ 01-42-78-88-30; Métro: Hôtel-de-Ville). Open 11 a.m. to 11 p.m. Monday through Saturday and 3 to 8 p.m. Sunday, the store carries French- and English-language publications.

For advice on HIV issues, call **F.A.C.T.S.** (☎ 01-44-93-16-69) from 6 to 10 p.m. Monday, Wednesday, and Friday. The acronym stands for Free Aids Counseling Treatment and Support, and the English-speaking staff provides counseling, information, and doctor referrals.

Part II
Ironing Out the Details

The 5th Wave   By Rich Tennant

"And how shall I book your flight to Paris – First Class, Coach, or Medieval?"

In this part . . .

*W*ondering how to get to Paris and where to stay after you're there? Then look no further than these chapters. Chapter 5 helps you get to the city on your own or with the help of a travel agent and discusses the pros and cons of package tours. Chapter 6 breaks down the neighborhoods in the most-central part of Paris where you may want to stay and lets you know just what kind of accommodations you get for your money. In Chapter 7, you discover how to get the best accommodations at the best rate, how to surf the Web for good hotel deals, and where to turn if you arrive without a reservation. Located in Chapter 8 are descriptions and rates for 43 great hotels — cross-indexed by price and location. And in Chapter 9, you get some advice about those last-minute details that can frustrate even the most frequent flyers.

Chapter 5

Getting to Paris

● ●

● ●

*P*lanning a trip abroad used to be a science so exacting that only travel agents, with their numerous contacts and extensive experience, could get you fantastic trips and low prices. These days, the Internet — with its online travel agents, airline, lodging, and car rental Web sites, and plenty of information about your destination — has drastically changed travel planning. Still, don't entirely negate the idea of the travel agent — sometimes an agent can handle your arrangements better than you. That's why you need to ask yourself: What kind of travel best suits you? Are you an independent traveler? Do you prefer the comfort of a tour group where everything is planned for you? In this chapter, I show you how to get to Paris simply and easily — regardless of whether you do it yourself or have someone do it for you.

Using a Travel Agent

A travel agent can help you find a bargain airfare, hotel, or rental car, but these days many people are choosing to forego this route entirely, preferring instead to serve as their own agents by using the Web. However, whenever you have a complicated itinerary with multiple stops and not much time for planning, a travel agent may be your best bet. A good travel agent also knows how to balance price with value, tells you how much time you need to budget for a destination, finds you a cheap direct flight, gets you a better hotel room for the same amount of money you'd otherwise spend, and even recommends restaurants and sights to see.

Making sure that you get the most out of your travel agent takes homework. Read about your destination and pick out some accommodations and attractions that you think you'd like. Visit travel-planning Web sites like Expedia.com and Travelocity.com for the latest airfares and special hotel promotions. Does your travel agent know about them? Let him or her know that you have a good feel for what's out there and what it costs, and ask for further deals and discounts.

Your travel agent still has access to more resources than even the most complete Web travel site (although the Web is quickly catching up) and should be able to get you a better price than you could get on your own. Besides issuing your tickets right on the spot, an agent can also recommend good alternatives when he or she can't get you the hotel or other reservation of choice.

Keep in mind that travel agents work on commission. Although you don't pay it, the airlines, hotels, resorts, and tour companies do, and some travelers have turned to the Web to avoid pushy agents flaunting vacations designed to net them the highest possible commissions. If you have plenty of time — and planning a vacation takes just that — go ahead and explore your Web options. I provide some helpful travel sites to get you on your way in the "Tips for getting the best airfare" and "Booking Your Ticket Online" sections later in this chapter.

Understanding Package and Escorted Tours

What kind of traveler are you? Do you like listening to a tour guide tell you about a city's important sights, or would you rather discover those sights and lesser-known attractions on your own? Do you like avoiding the stress of getting to unfamiliar places, or do you prefer making an adventure of finding your way in a foreign destination? Is meeting people one of your goals, or do you shrink at the idea of sharing so much time with strangers? How you answer these questions clues you in about whether you'd enjoy an escorted tour.

As the most inclusive kind of travel, an *escorted tour* spells out nearly everything in advance: your flights, your hotels, your meals, your sight-seeing itineraries, and your costs. It's the least independent way to travel, but some travelers find escorted tours to be liberating — no hassles with public transportation, no deciphering maps, and the comfort of knowing what you're getting. Others fervently despise escorted group tours, because they feel like they're being herded from one sight to the next, missing the element of surprise and individuality that independent travel affords.

Package tours are a happy medium between hooking up with a group and going it alone, and they're enormously popular because they save you a ton of money. In many cases, a package tour bundles the price of airfare, hotel, and transportation to and from the airport into a "package" that often costs less than the hotel alone, if you'd booked each item separately. That's because packages are sold in bulk to tour operators, who resell them to the public at a cost that drastically undercuts standard rates.

Many travelers confuse the package tour with the escorted tour. On an escorted tour, every detail of your trip is prearranged, from the flight to the hotels, meals, sightseeing, and transportation. Package tours, on the other hand, bundle various elements of the trip — perhaps your flight and hotel, or your flight and a rental car, for example. But after you arrive at your destination, your time is your own.

Packages vary widely. Some offer a better class of hotels than others. Some offer the same hotels for lower prices. Some offer flights on scheduled airlines, and others book charters. In some packages, your choice of accommodations and travel days may be limited. Some packages let you choose between escorted and independent vacations; others enable you to add only a few excursions or escorted day-trips (also at prices lower than you can locate on your own) without booking an entirely escorted tour. Each destination usually has one or two packagers that are cheaper than the rest because they buy in even greater bulk. If you spend time shopping around, you're sure to save in the long run.

The travel section of your local Sunday newspaper is the best place to start your search, and you can check the ads in the back of national travel magazines like *Arthur Frommer's Budget Travel, Travel & Leisure, National Geographic Traveler,* and *Condé Nast Traveler.* **Liberty Travel** (☎ **888-271-1584** to find a travel agent near you; Internet: www.liberty travel.com) is one of the biggest packagers in the Northeast and frequently runs full-page ads in Sunday papers.

Another good resource is the airlines themselves because they often package their flights with accommodations. (See the sections on "Who flies there . . ." later in this chapter for airline Web addresses and phone numbers.)

If money is most certainly an object, **New Frontiers,** 12 E. 33rd St., New York, NY 10016 (☎ **800-366-6387** in the United States or 212-779-0600; Fax: 212-770-1007) offers hard-to-beat deals. New Frontiers has its own airline, Corsair (one of the few that fly direct from the United States into Orly Airport, 8 miles south of Paris), and a recent round-trip flight bought five days in advance in the middle of summer cost just $498 before tax. But there's always a catch: The plane was older, with small, uncomfortable seats; meals were small and poor in quality; and the flight was jam-packed.

The French Experience, 370 Lexington Ave., Suite 812, New York, NY 10017 (☎ 212-986-3800), offers several fly/drive programs through different regions of France (the quoted price includes airfare and a rental car). You can specify the type and price level of hotels you want. The agency arranges the car rental in advance, and the rest is up to you. Some staff can seem unfriendly, but persevere for good deals.

American Express Vacations, P.O. Box 1525, Fort Lauderdale, FL 33302 (☎ 800-241-1700), is perhaps the most instantly recognizable tour operator in the world. Its offerings in Paris and the rest of Europe are probably more comprehensive than those of any other company and include package tours and independent stays.

Making Your Own Arrangements

So you want to plan the trip on your own? This section tells you all you need to know to research and book the perfect flight.

Who flies there from the United States and Canada

Web sites and phone numbers for the major airlines serving Paris are in the list that follows. These sites offer schedules, flight bookings, and package tours; most have Web pages where you can sign up for e-mail alerts that list weekend deals and other late-breaking bargains.

Air Canada (☎ 800-630-3299; Internet: www.aircanada.ca) flies from Halifax, Montréal, Toronto, and Vancouver.

Air France (☎ 800-237-2747; Internet: www.airfrance.com) flies from Atlanta, Boston, Chicago, Cincinnati, Houston, Los Angeles, Miami, New York City, Philadelphia, and Washington, D.C.

American Airlines (☎ 800-433-7300; Internet: www.aa.com) flies from Boston, Chicago, Dallas, Los Angeles, New York City, and Miami.

British Airways (☎ 800-247-9297; Internet: www.ba.com) flies from Atlanta, Baltimore, Boston, Charlotte, Chicago, Cincinnati, Detroit, Houston, Los Angeles, Miami, Orlando, Philadelphia, Phoenix, Newark, New York, San Diego, San Francisco, Tampa, and Washington, D.C.

Continental Airlines (☎ 800-525-0280; Internet: www.continental.com) flies from Houston and Newark.

Delta Air Lines (☎ 800-221-1212; Internet: www.delta.com) flies from Atlanta, Cincinnati, and New York and shares flights with Air France from Los Angeles, Philadelphia, and San Francisco.

Iceland Air (☎ **800-223-5500;** Internet: www.icelandair.com) flies from Baltimore, Boston, Minneapolis, and New York.

Northwest/KLM (☎ **800-225-2525;** Internet: www.nwa.com) flies from Detroit, Memphis, and Minneapolis.

United Airlines (☎ **800-241-6522;** Internet: www.united.com) flies from Chicago, Los Angeles, San Francisco, and Washington, D.C.

US Airways (☎ **800-428-4322;** Internet: www.usairways.com) flies from Charlotte, Philadelphia, and Pittsburgh.

Who flies there from the United Kingdom

These airlines serve Paris from the United Kingdom:

Air France (☎ **0845-0845-111;** Internet: www.airfrance.com) flies from London and Manchester.

British Airways (☎ **0845-7733-377;** Internet: www.ba.com) flies from Edinburgh, Glasgow, London, and Manchester.

British Midland (☎ **0870-6070-555;** Internet: www.britishmidland. com) flies from Leeds, London, and Manchester.

Who flies there from Australia

These airlines fly to Paris from Australia:

AOM (☎ **61-92-23-44-44;** Internet: www.flyaom.com) flies from Sydney.

Qantas (☎ **13-13-13** anywhere in Australia; Internet: www.qantas.com) flies from Sydney.

Tips for getting the best airfare

Passengers within the same cabin on an airplane rarely pay the same fares. Rather, they pay what the market bears. As a leisure traveler, you never, *ever* need to pay full fare. The top price is for business travelers who need fares with unrestricted flexibility. They buy their tickets a few days or a few hours in advance, need to be able to change itineraries at the drop of a hat, and want to be back home for the weekend. Flying unrestricted coach class from New York to Paris on a major airline can cost more than $1,500 during the summer high season. In the middle of winter, unrestricted fares can go for $1,200.

Most vacation travelers can get a great fare by buying a ticket with restrictions. Booking your tickets at least 14 days in advance, traveling Tuesday through Thursday, and staying over one Saturday night can nab the airline's lowest available fare for you: typically about $650 in summer, $400 in winter — a huge savings over the full unrestricted fare.

Periodically airlines lower prices on their most popular routes. Check your newspaper for advertised discounts, check the Web, or call the airlines directly, asking whether any *promotional rates* or *special fares* are available. You almost never see a sale during the peak summer vacation months of July and August, or during the Thanksgiving or Christmas seasons. Note, however, that the lowest-priced fares often are nonrefundable, require advance purchase of one to three weeks and a certain length of stay, and carry penalties for changing dates of travel.

Check airfares from secondary or alternative airports. If you live in a city that's close to more than one international airport, check prices on flights going to Paris from all of them. For example, travelers living in the Philadelphia area need to check out prices not only from Philadelphia International, but also from Newark and Baltimore–Washington International. You may find lower prices or special promotions not offered from the airport you regularly use.

Consolidators, also known as bucket shops, are also good places to find low fares. Consolidators buy seats in bulk from airlines and sell them back to the public at prices below even airline-discounted rates. Their small, boxed ads usually run at the bottom of the pages in the Sunday newspaper travel sections.

Before paying a consolidator, however, be sure to ask for a confirmation number and then call the airline itself to confirm your seat. If the airline can't confirm your reservation, *don't book* with the consolidator. There are plenty of others from which to choose. Likewise, be aware that bucket-shop tickets are usually nonrefundable or carry stiff cancellation penalties often reaching as high as 50% to 75% of the ticket price.

Council Travel (☎ **800-2-COUNCIL;** Internet: www.counciltravel.com) and **STA Travel** (☎ **800-781-4040;** Internet: www.sta-travel.com) are two consolidators that cater especially to young travelers, but their low prices are available to people of all ages. **TravelHUB** (☎ **888-AIR-FARE;** Internet: www.travelhub.com) represents nearly 1,000 travel agencies, many of whom offer consolidator and discount fares. *Rebaters,* such as **Travac** (☎ **877-872-8221** or 212-630-3310), rebate part of their commissions to you.

You can also try booking a seat on a *charter flight* for pretty good savings. Discounted fares have knocked down the number of charters available, but they can still be found. Most charter operators advertise and sell their seats through travel agents. Before deciding to take a charter flight, however, check the restrictions on the ticket. Two well-known operators that sell tickets directly to the public are **Travac** (☎ **877-872-8221** or 212-630-3310) and **Council Charters,** 205 E. 42nd St., New York, NY 10017 (☎ **212-822-2800**).

Finally, try joining a travel club, such as **Moment's Notice** (☎ **718-234-6295;** Internet: www.moments-notice.com) or **Travelers Advantage** (☎ **877-259-2691**), to get discounted prices on airfares. You pay an annual membership fee to get the club's hotline number. Of course, you're limited to what's available, so you have to be flexible.

Booking Your Ticket Online

Online travel sites are among the most visited on the Web. The top agencies, including Expedia.com and Travelocity.com, offer an array of tools that are valuable even if you don't book online. You can check flight schedules, hotel availability, car rental prices, or even receive a page when your flight is delayed. For each of them, the drill is basically the same: You enter your departure city, destination, and travel dates, and the site generates a list of flights, noting the lowest fare. Some sites even search for lower fares leaving from different airports or on different days.

Most online travel sites now have extensive security policies and protect against credit-card theft with the most advanced encryption technologies. To be assured you're in secure mode when purchasing with a credit card, look for an icon (such as padlocks in Netscape or Internet Explorer) at the bottom of your Web browser. Most sites also offer toll-free numbers if you prefer booking over the phone.

If the thought of all that comparison shopping gives you a headache, then two options await you. Head for **Smarter Living**'s newsletter service (www.smarterliving.com), where every week you get a customized e-mail summarizing the discount fares available from your departure city. They track more than 15 different airlines, so it's a worthwhile timesaver (but keep in mind that the majority of low fares quoted are for travel available the weekend immediately following the e-mail). If you prefer to let the computer do the work for you, bring up **Qixo.com** (www.qixo.com), an airfare search engine that checks almost a dozen separate travel sites, (including the biggies like Expedia.com and Travelocity.com) to find the lowest fares for the dates you have in mind.

Here's the lowdown on what you can expect from the top online sites for discount travel fares:

✔ **Expedia.com** (www.expedia.com) enables you to book flights, hotels, and rental cars on one itinerary. Its hotel search offers crisp maps pinpointing most hotel properties, and you can click on the camera icon to see images of many rooms and facilities. Expedia also offers a service similar to that of Priceline — you name the price for a flight or a hotel room and submit your credit-card information. If your price is matched, Expedia makes the reservation and charges your card. Keep in mind, however, that like many online databases, Expedia focuses on the major airlines and hotel chains, so you may not get the lowest prices out there.

✔ **Travelocity.com** (www.travelocity.com) features international flight, hotel, and rental car bookings; airfare sales; deals on cruises and vacation packages; multimedia "visits" to destinations; and a Fare Watcher that alerts you by e-mail whenever the fare to the city of your choice changes by $25 or more. It also has a Best Fare Finder feature that, after it finds the lowest fare you've requested, searches for better deals by plugging in times that are a little earlier or a little later than those on your itinerary.

✔ **Priceline** (www.priceline.com) lets you name your price for domestic and international airline tickets. Select a route, dates, and a preferred rate; make a bid for what you're willing to pay; and guarantee with a credit card. If the hotels and airlines in Priceline's database have a fare that's lower than your bid, your credit card is automatically charged. You can't say what time you want to fly; you must accept any flight leaving between 6 a.m. and 10 p.m. on the dates you choose, and you may have to make one stopover. No frequent flyer miles are awarded, and tickets are non-refundable and can't be exchanged for other flights. So, if your plans change, you're out of luck. Priceline can be good for travelers who have to take off on short notice (and who, therfore, don't qualify for advance-purchase discounts).

Be sure to shop around first — if you make a bid and then discover that your flight is available elsewhere for a lower price, you're still required to purchase the ticket from Priceline, and Priceline pockets the difference between what it pays for a ticket and what you bid.

✔ **Cheap Tickets** (www.cheaptickets.com), **Lowestfare.com** (www.lowestfare.com), and **Last Minute Travel** (www.lastminutetravel.com) are only three of the sites that sometimes offer exclusive deals not available through more mainstream channels.

Chapter 6

Deciding Where to Stay

If this is your first trip to Paris, your expectations about what a hotel room should look like may be based on what you see in your own country. However, one important thing to know is that rooms tend to be smaller than they are in hotels in North America, even in expensive places (unless you opt for a modern chain hotel, which can be charmless). Parisian doubles are almost never big enough to hold two queen-sized beds, and the space around the bed probably won't be big enough for more than a desk and perhaps a chest of drawers. Welcome to Europe; the story is the same in London, Rome, and most other continental capitals where buildings date back two, three, four, or more centuries, when dimensions — and people! — were smaller.

Parisian hotels also vary widely in their plumbing arrangements. That's a veiled way of telling you that some units come equipped with only a sink; others may also have a toilet and either a shower or tub. Private bathrooms with tubs often have handheld shower devices, and some shower stalls don't have curtains — so pay attention where you aim. The trend is toward renovating small hotels by installing a small shower, toilet, and sink in each room, but you can't count on having all these amenities in your room.

Acoustics tend to be unpredictable in old Parisian hotels. Your quarreling neighbors may compete with street noise for the prize of most annoying, so bring earplugs for the neighbors, or ask for a room in the rear of the hotel to avoid the street noise. Another point to remember: Most budget hotels in Paris don't have air conditioning, but fortunately, their solid stone walls tend to keep out the summer heat and winter cold.

Picking the Place That Suits Your Style

More than 2,200 hotels are located in Paris — chain hotels, deluxe palace-like accommodations, hotels that cater to business travelers, budget hotels, and mom-and-pop establishments. Chapter 8 gives you the details on some of each type.

To find the hotel that's right for you, you need to weigh five variables: price, location, room size, amenities, and — the least tangible, but perhaps most desired of them all — a charming Parisian ambience. If the first variable, price, poses no problem, then you can have it all: great location, huge room, super perks, and sumptuous surroundings. Most travelers, however, need to make some compromises.

Before committing to a hotel, however, keep in mind that Paris offers additional options for lodging — renting an apartment, for example.

Nothing beats living in Paris as a Parisian. In your own apartment, you can conduct cooking experiments, taste fine wines that would be too expensive in a restaurant, and entertain new friends. Although the daily rate can be higher than a budget hotel, the room will be larger, you can save money on meals, and in the end, you may end up paying the same rate you would for room and board at a hotel — or less.

The most practical way to rent an apartment is through an agency. Most agencies require a seven-day minimum stay and offer discounts for longer stays. I've found that apartments vary quite a bit in size, location, and amenities. At the bottom end — for about 100€ per day — you'll find yourself in either a small, centrally located studio, or a larger studio in an *arrondissement* (neighborhood) a bit far from the center of Paris. Studio apartments usually feature a convertible couch, an armchair or two, a bathroom with a tub or shower, and a tiny kitchenette with a refrigerator, stove, coffeemaker, and maybe a microwave. Dishes, cutlery, pots and pans, telephone, TV, iron, vacuum cleaner, linen, and sometimes a washing machine are also provided. Pay a bit more — 100€ to 125€ per day — and you get a more centrally located one-bedroom apartment. As with anything else, higher prices pay for larger, more luxurious spaces.

You can find many rental agencies online and comparison shop among them. Companies offering attractive apartments at reasonable prices are **Apartment Living in Paris** (Internet: www.apartment-living.com), which is run by two French real estate brokers, and Lodgis Solutions (Internet: www.lodgis.com). **Paris Vacation Rentals** (Internet: www.rentals-paris.com) is an agency that deals in short-term rental of upscale apartments at very good prices. More expensive is **New York Habitats** (Internet: www.newyorkhabitat.com), a New York real estate brokerage that rents Paris flats as a sideline. The free e-mail newsletter from **International Living** often has listings for Paris apartment rentals; visit its Web site at www.international living.com to sign up.

Keep in mind that this is a short-term apartment rental. You have to sign a contract and put down a security deposit, which may not be refunded if you damage the apartment in any way.

If the agency offers optional gift baskets or transportation to and from the airport, you're better off refusing. The gift basket usually contains items you can buy more cheaply at the grocery store, and the transportation is usually twice as much as a cab.

If you bring the kids with you to Paris, your best option may be the *aparthotel,* a hybrid between an apartment and a hotel where you can have the autonomy of an apartment with some of the amenities of a hotel. Like hotels, they have 24-hour reception desks, satellite TV, housekeeping services, kitchenettes, and laundry. For a family of four, a one-bedroom apartment is a good-value alternative to two double rooms in a cheap hotel. And if you use your kitchenette to prepare even half of your own meals in Paris, you can reap huge savings on your dining bill.

And don't write off *home exchanges.* The money that you save by swapping can be substantial. Contact **Trading Homes** (Internet: www.trading-homes.com) or check out **FUSAC** (France USA Contacts, P.O. Box 115, Cooper Station, New York, NY 100276; ☎ **212-777-5553**; Fax: 212-777-5554), a Paris-based publication that contains listings of apartments in Paris available for rental and exchange. The magazine is available in the United States for $10 an issue or $90 a year.

Finding the Perfect Location

You're coming to Paris to see the city, and you need accommodations that put you in the middle of everything — not a short Métro ride away, but smack dab in the center. You want to be within walking distance of at least two major sights. The river should be a short stroll away. Therefore, you absolutely need a hotel in one of the first eight districts. Period. Chapter 8 has already done the hard work for you because every single one of the recommended hotels is located in arrondissements 1 through 8. Pick one of them, and you're guaranteed a decent address. (I explain Paris's layout and the arrondissement system in Chapter 10.)

With the field narrowed to central Paris, you next have to decide which neighborhood you want. The city is made up of a patchwork of districts, and each has a distinctive style and character. Your Paris experience is determined greatly by the neighborhood you choose. (See Chapter 10 for more information.) The following sections run through the various neighborhoods and their main attractions.

Right Bank

The Right Bank of the Seine is home to the **Marais** and **Opéra** neighborhoods, the **Louvre, Champs-Elysées,** and technically, the two islands that sit in the middle of the Seine, **Ile de la Cité** and **Ile St-Louis.**

Louvre (1er)

You can't get any more central than the first arrondissement, unless you want to spend the night in the river. The **Louvre, Tuileries Gardens, Place de la Concorde,** and **Palais Royal** are within a five-minute walk of each other. The opulent Ritz Hotel is here on **Place Vendôme,** and *haute couture* shopping abounds nearby on **rue Faubourg St-Honoré.** The area is well connected by buses, and the Métro and is an ideal location in terms of convenience, although it is more crowded with tourists and less atmospheric than the nearby Marais. So if you plan to stay in the Louvre neighborhood, keep in mind that:

- ✔ The Louvre and other major sights are close, and the rest of Paris is easily accessible.
- ✔ You may meet more tourists than Parisians.
- ✔ The area isn't known for its cheap hotels, so you may have to sacrifice ambience if you're on a budget.
- ✔ Restaurants tend to cater to the tourist crowd and may be more expensive, or of lesser quality, than elsewhere.

Bourse (2e)

Home to the **Bourse** (stock exchange), this district lies mainly between the ninth arrondissement's Grands Boulevards, dominated by the newly renovated **Opéra Garnier** and the big department stores (**Galéries Lafayette, Au Printemps**), and rue Etienne Marcel. Some of the historic covered shopping arcades are in this neighborhood. Check out the most beautiful of all of them, the **Galerie Vivienne** on 6 rue Vivienne or 5 rue de la Banque.

Much of the garment trade is here in an area called the Sentier, and so are some prostitution and sex shops. The area is more business-oriented, and you get fewer glimpses of essential Parisian daily life (such as outdoor food markets and neighborhood shops) than in the more residential districts. So, if you plan to stay here, keep these things in mind:

✔ If you're a shopping addict, you're close to big department stores and shopping arcades.

✔ If you like ballet and opera, you're in the right place.

✔ Métro stations are plentiful.

✔ You see fewer slices of French life than in residential neighborhoods.

✔ Parts of the Sentier area are seedy.

✔ Cafés, restaurants, and snack bars tend to be higher priced.

Le Marais (3e, 4e)

One of the hippest neighborhoods in Paris, **Le Marais** (translated as "the swamp") fell into decay for years after its 17th-century aristocratic heyday. The neighborhood was revived with the construction of the wonderful **Centre Georges Pompidou** modern art museum, but as a result, the traditional working-class neighborhood of Beaubourg, to the west, was largely destroyed. Paris's old Jewish neighborhood is in the Marais around the **rue des Rosiers,** and the **rue Vieille-du-Temple** is home to numerous gay bars and trendy boutiques. Attractions include the **Musée Picasso,** stuffed with treasures that the artist's estate had to turn over to the French government in lieu of astronomical inheritance taxes, and the beautiful **place des Vosges,** a former royal residence. So if you plan to stay in Le Marais, keep these things in mind:

✔ Stores are open, and the neighborhood is hopping on Sundays.

✔ Some of the best Jewish food in the city can be found here.

✔ If you're a light sleeper, Le Marais may be too loud.

✔ The narrow sidewalks and cobblestone streets are difficult for travelers with limited mobility.

The Islands (1er, 4e)

Paris has two islands that lay side-by-side in the middle of the Seine: Ile de la Cité and Ile St-Louis. Although Ile de la Cité seems to have it all — **Notre-Dame, Sainte-Chapelle,** and the **Conciergerie,** where Queen Marie Antoinette was sentenced to death in 1793 — it has all the tourists, too. The tiny Ile St-Louis, on the other hand, is more peaceful. Gorgeous town houses, leafy courtyards, and tiny shops that deal in antiques provide atmosphere galore. The location is superb, with the **Marais** directly across the river on the Right Bank, and the **Latin Quarter** on the Left. The Islands are the costliest arrondissement in which to rent or buy an apartment in Paris. So if you plan to stay here, keep these things in mind:

✔ Every spot is picture-postcard perfect.

✔ Notre-Dame, Sainte-Chapelle, the Latin Quarter, and the Marais are within easy walking distance.

✔ Paris's best ice-cream shop, **Berthillon,** is located on the Ile St-Louis.

✔ The islands often are overrun with visitors — especially in spring and summer.

✔ Prices are higher at cafés, shops, and restaurants.

✔ Few hotels are located here.

Champs-Elysées (8e)

The 8e is the heart of the Right Bank, and its prime showcase is the Champs-Elysées. In this neighborhood, you find the **triangle d'or** (golden triangle) formed by av. Champs-Elysées, av. Montaigne, and av. George V over which the most fashionably attired Parisians stride into *haute couture* houses, the most elegant hotels, and expensive restaurants and shops. The 8e features many of the city's best, grandest, and most impressive places and attractions. It has the most splendid square in all of France (**place de la Concorde**), the grandest hotel in France (**the Crillon**), the most impressive triumphal arch (**L'Arc de Triomphe**), the world's most expensive residential street (**avenue Montaigne**), the city's oldest Métro station (**Franklin-D-Roosevelt**), the most ancient monument in Paris (the 3,300-year-old **Obelisk of Luxor**), and the biggest stores (which you can probably find at home). So if you plan to stay in the Champs-Elysées, keep these things in mind:

✔ You're never at a loss for something to do or see.

✔ Many stores are open on Sunday.

✔ Budget hotels and eateries (besides fast-food establishments) are scarce.

✔ The neighborhood can be impersonal because of its rampant commercialism.

✔ Some stores and fast-food places are the same as those you'd expect to find in your hometown mall.

Left Bank

The Left Bank is home to that eternal symbol of Paris, the **Eiffel Tower,** and to the **Latin Quarter** and **St-Germain-des-Prés** neighborhoods.

Latin Quarter (5e)

The Latin Quarter is the intellectual heart and soul of Paris. Bookstores, schools, churches, nightclubs, student dives, Roman ruins, *bouquinistes* (outdoor booksellers), and low-end boutiques characterize the district. The famous university, the **Sorbonne,** is also located within the Latin Quarter. The quarter is actually called "Latin" because Sorbonne students and professors once spoke Latin together here. The

Latin Quarter of the past is gone forever now. Changing times have brought Greek, Moroccan, and Vietnamese immigrants, among others, hawking souvlaki, couscous, and spring rolls, or selling American-influenced fashion along bd. St-Michel. Sights include the **Panthéon,** the **Jardin du Luxembourg,** and the **Musée de Cluny.** So if you plan to stay in the area, keep these things in mind:

✔ Students help keep restaurant prices down.

✔ You're close to the Seine, the Jardin du Luxembourg, and the Roman ruins.

✔ Room sizes are often tighter than in other neighborhoods.

✔ Eateries are mediocre (and on rues de la Huchette and Harpe just plain bad deals).

St-Germain-des-Prés (6e)

The heart of Paris publishing, and home to the famous **École des Beaux-Arts (School of Fine Arts),** St-Germain-des-Prés encompasses everything anyone can love about the Left Bank. Strolling the boulevards of the 6e, including St-Germain, you can window shop some of the chicest designers and art galleries around — but the secret of the district lies in discovering its narrow streets and hidden squares. Nearby main attractions include the Jardin du Luxembourg, and the fabled (and you pay for it) **Café de Flore, Brasserie Lipp,** and **Les Deux Magots.** So if you plan to stay in the area, keep these things in mind:

✔ You're in the middle of the Left Bank's best cafés and shops.

✔ You're near the Jardin du Luxembourg and the Seine.

✔ Establishments of all kinds are pricier than those in the nearby Latin Quarter.

✔ Comparatively few major sightseeing attractions are at your doorstep.

Eiffel Tower and Invalides (7e)

The city's most famous symbol, the Eiffel Tower, dominates the 7e, a district of stately government buildings (including the Prime Minister's residence), traditional bourgeois shops, and some of the most magnificent mansions in Paris. Even visitors with no time to thoroughly explore the 7e take the time to at least rush to its second major attraction, the **Musée d'Orsay,** the world's premier showcase of 19th-century French art and culture. **Les Invalides,** which houses **Napoléon's Tomb** and the **Musée de l'Armée** are also in the 7e, and so is the **Musée Rodin,** housed where the sculptor lived until his death in 1917. Overall, the 7e makes a great base if you want to be central but still favor peace and quiet at night. On the other hand, it can feel rather dull if you want to go out on the town, and Métro stations are far apart. So if you plan to stay here, keep these things in mind:

✔ You're near the Eiffel Tower, the Musée d'Orsay, and Invalides.

✔ The area is quiet at night, meaning nightlife is practically nonexistent.

✔ Métro stations are farther apart than those in other neighborhoods.

Getting the Most for Your Money

Prices for the hotels recommended in Chapter 8 are designated with dollar signs — the more you see, the more expensive the hotel. The number of dollar signs corresponds to the hotel's rack rates (full rate) from the cheapest double room in low season to the most expensive in high season. The most noticeable difference between hotels in the budget bracket and the most expensive hotels is better amenities and services, followed by a more luxurious decor. None of the recommended hotels listed in Chapter 8 is a dump; the places are decent and reputable. Naturally, the luxury level in a 1,000€ room is substantially higher than in a 100€ one.

Here's how the dollar-sign system works:

$ (less than 100€) — The low end of the scale represents the true budget hotels. Don't expect a lot of space or extras: You won't get room service, and though you may get a TV, it may only receive French channels. You can expect a clean, private bathroom with shower or tub and thin towels, and the room will offer a basic level of comfort. Low price aside, the decor can evoke true Parisian charm — though it may be slightly dated or old-fashioned.

$$ (100€ to 150€) — Moving up a level, the rooms are roughly the same size as those in the first category. The decor is a big step up, however, and the overall comfort is substantially higher. Although you won't have access to a concierge, the front desk usually helps you make dinner reservations if you ask. Some creature comforts — air conditioning, satellite TV, and in-room hair dryers — can be expected. A step above budget, the loving care that hoteliers put into their properties is clearly visible here. You can find many real bargains for a reasonable price.

$$$ (150€ to 215€) — The middle-range hotels offer rooms that are slightly larger than those in the first two categories. The decor tends to be more luxurious, often featuring at least some antique furnishings, and more amenities (better toiletries, perhaps more English-language channels on TV). The amenities of these hotels probably won't include an adjoining restaurant or a concierge, but limited room service is probably available, and the front desk can help you make reservations for dinner or entertainment.

$$$$ (215€ to 300€) — These hotels feel like luxury hotels, although not the sky's-the-limit kind. Room size is much bigger than in the less expensive hotels, concierges are on hand to assist you, 24-hour room service is available, and decor is much more luxurious, with antiques and quality fabrics the norm. Expect a restaurant or other in-house facilities, but probably no fitness center.

$$$$$ (more than 300€) — Here you get much more than a room: You get an experience. Service is impeccable, decor features quality down to the last knick-knack, and rooms are enormous compared to the typical European standard. A 1- or 2-star Michelin chef may oversee the hotel's restaurant, and the fare is often excellent and pricey. Usually a fitness center and/or pool is available for guest use. These hotels do everything with more style than their less-expensive counterparts.

Chapter 7

Booking Your Room

* *

In This Chapter

▶ Beating the rack rates

▶ Getting the best room at the best rate

▶ Surfing the Net for hotel deals

▶ Landing a room if you arrive without a reservation

* *

*A*fter you decide on the type of lodging that's best for you and the neighborhood where you'd like to stay (see Chapter 6), you need to get down to the nitty-gritty of paying the least amount possible for accommodations. Paris tends to have reasonable hotel rates, and many of its hotels offer additional special deals; in this chapter, I show you how to find them. You can use the money saved on your room for dinners in quality restaurants, spectacular entertainment, and perhaps a day-trip or two out of the city (see Chapter 21).

Uncovering the Truth about Rack Rates

The *rack rate* is the maximum rate that a hotel charges for a room. It's the rate you'd get if you walked in off the street and asked for a room for the night. You sometimes see the rate printed on the fire/emergency exit diagrams posted on the back of your door.

Hotels are happy to charge you the rack rate, but you don't have to pay it! At chain hotels and at other luxury hotels, you can often get a good deal by simply asking for a discounted rate. Your odds improve drastically if you're staying for more than just a few nights.

Keep in mind, however, that bartering for a cheaper room isn't the norm at Paris's budget hotels. Most establishments are small and privately owned; they post their rates in the reception area and may not be willing to negotiate. To be fair, they may not be able to afford to let rooms go for less.

Getting the Best Room at the Best Rate

In all but the smallest accommodations, the rate you pay for a room depends on many factors — chief among them being how you make your reservation. A travel agent may be able to negotiate a better price with certain hotels than you can get by yourself. (That's because often the hotel gives the agent a discount in exchange for steering his or her business toward that hotel.)

Reserving a room through the hotel's toll-free number may also result in a lower rate than if you called the hotel directly. On the other hand, the central reservations number may not know about discount rates at specific locations. For example, local franchises may offer special group rates for a wedding or family reunion, but they may neglect to tell the central booking line. Your best bet is calling both the local and the toll-free numbers to which one gives you a better deal.

Room rates also change with the seasons as occupancy rates rise and fall. If a hotel is close to full, it's less likely to extend discount rates; if it's close to empty, it may be willing to negotiate. Room prices are subject to change without notice, so the rates quoted in this book may be different than the actual rate you receive when you make your reservation. Be sure to mention membership in AAA, AARP, frequent-flyer programs, and any other corporate rewards programs you belong to when making your reservation. You never know when it may be worth a few dollars off your room rate (although in truth, this usually works only at chain hotels; family-run establishments rarely have arrangements with large organizations).

The best room in the house, please

After you've made your reservation, asking one or two more pointed questions can go a long way toward making sure that you have the best room in the house.

Always ask for a *corner room*. They're usually larger, quieter, closer to the elevator, and have more windows and light than standard rooms, and they don't always cost more. Likewise, be sure to ask whether the hotel is renovating; if it is, request a room *away from the renovation work*. If you're sensitive to street noise, ask for a room in the back of the hotel, but remember that you may be sacrificing a good view. And if you aren't happy with your room when you arrive, talk to the front desk. If another room is available, your hotel probably will be happy to accommodate you, within reason.

Here's some advice to keep in mind when you're trying to save money on a room:

✔ Ask about **corporate discounts** when you'll be staying in one of the chains.

✔ A **travel agent** may be able to negotiate a better price at top hotels than you can get yourself. (The hotel gives the agent a discount for steering business its way.)

✔ Always ask if the hotel offers any **weekend specials,** which typically require you to stay two nights (either Friday and Saturday, or Saturday and Sunday). In Paris, you can find this kind of deal from September through March at almost all price levels.

✔ A *forfait* (*fohr*-feh) is a discount that requires you to stay a certain number of nights — perhaps a minimum of three or five. Sometimes something else is thrown in — like a bottle of champagne — to sweeten the deal. If you're going to be in Paris for more than three days, always ask if there's a *forfait* and then pick the hotel with the best deal.

✔ Visit during the **summer low season** (see Chapter 2). That's no typo. Room rates tend to be lower in July and August, which, though big tourist months, are considered low season by Paris hoteliers. November and December are also low season, but early fall is high season, with October, in particular, heavy on conventioneers, making it difficult to find a room.

✔ Don't forget about **package deals** (see Chapter 5) that include airfare, hotel, and transportation to and from the airport.

✔ Look on the **Internet** for deals (see "Surfing the Web for Hotel Deals" later in this chapter).

✔ If you're a risk taker, go without a reservation. During the slow seasons of July and August or November and December, you can get a good deal at the **Office de Tourisme de Paris,** 127 av. des Champs-Elysées, 8e. Hotels with unsold rooms offer them through the Office de Tourisme at rock-bottom prices, so you may get a 3-star hotel at a 2-star price. During the summer slow season, however, you'll have to wait in a long line, and you aren't necessarily guaranteed a room. The Office de Tourisme also charges a small fee for the service (see "Arriving without a Reservation" later in this chapter).

Surfing the Web for Hotel Deals

Although the major travel booking sites (such as Travelocity, Orbitz, Expedia, and Cheap Tickets; see Chapter 5 for details) offer hotel booking, using a site devoted primarily to lodging can be best, because you may find properties that aren't listed on more general online travel agencies. **The Office de Tourisme de Paris** (www.paris-tourist office.com) gives detailed information on hotels and other lodging sanctioned by the Paris Convention and Visitor's Bureau and provides links to accommodation reservation centers (but the Web site doesn't tell you about special rates). Some lodging sites specialize in a particular type of accommodation, such as bed-and-breakfast accommodations, which you won't find on the more mainstream booking services. Others offer weekend deals on major chain properties that cater to business travelers and have more empty rooms on weekends. Therefore, checking out some of the online lodging sites, many of which offer discounts, is in your best interest.

Hotel Discounts (www.hoteldiscounts.com), a service of the Hotel Reservations Network (HRN), offers bargain room rates at hotels in more than two-dozen U.S. and international cities. HRN prebooks blocks of rooms in advance, so sometimes it has rooms — at discount rates — at hotels that otherwise are considered "sold out." **TravelWeb** (www.travelweb.com) lists more than 16,000 hotels worldwide, focusing on chains such as Hyatt and Hilton, and you can book almost 90% of these online. Find weekend deals at many leading hotel chains on TravelWeb's Click-It Weekends. **France Hotels Online** (www.france-hotel-online.com) offers detailed listings of independent hotels, apartments, and bed-and-breakfasts according to budget and neighborhood. **All Hotels on the Web** (www.all-hotels.com) lists tens of thousands of lodgings throughout the world. (The hotels on this site pay a fee to be listed.) **Places to Stay** (www.placestostay.com) lists inns, B&Bs, resorts, hotels, and properties you may not find anywhere else.

Arriving without a Reservation

If you arrive in Paris without a reservation, you have two choices. You can pick up a phone and start dialing (after you've purchased a phone card at the nearest *tabac,* a café or kiosk that sells tobacco products). Or you can let the multilingual staff at one of the branches of the **Office de Tourisme de Paris** (127 av. des Champs-Elysées, 8e, ☎ **08-92-68-31-12** — 0.34€/min.; Fax: 01-49-52-53-00; Internet: www.paris-tourist office.com; E-mail: info@paris-touristoffice.com; Métro: Charles-de-Gaulle–Étoile, or George V) do it for you. The office is open daily from 9 a.m. to 8 p.m. (November to April Sunday 11 a.m. to 6 p.m.). For a fee, the staff will make an accommodations reservation for you on the same day that you want a room. The charge is 1.20€ for hostels and *foyers* ("homes"), and beyond that depends on the French government's star ratings. This system is based on factors like room size, facilities, plumbing, and dining options, with 4 stars being the best rating a hotel can receive. The tourism office charges 3.05€, for 1-star hotels, 3.80€ for 2-star hotels, and 6.10€ for 3-star hotels. Small information offices are located at the airports; their staffs can help you make a hotel reservation, but they work only with hotels that charge more than 53.35€ a night.

 During slow periods, hotels with unsold rooms often sell to the tourist office at a huge discount, providing you with a good way to stay in a 3-star hotel at a 2-star price. The office is very busy in summer, with lines sometimes stretching outside.

The Office de Tourisme has an auxiliary office at the Eiffel Tower (open May through September only, daily 11a.m. to 6 p.m.) and at the Gare de Lyon (Monday to Saturday 8 a.m. to 8 p.m.).

Confirming Your Reservation

In Paris, as in many major world cities, hotels routinely overbook, so booking by credit card doesn't automatically hold your room if you arrive later than expected, or after 6 p.m. To protect against losing your room, be sure to call your hotel immediately when you find that you're going to arrive later than expected.

 Hotels in Paris usually ask at what time you expect to arrive, so always pad your arrival time by a few hours to be safe. If you've made a reservation very far in advance, confirm within 24 hours of your expected arrival. If you're experiencing a major delay, alert the hotel as soon as you can.

Chapter 8

Paris's Best Hotels

· ·

In This Chapter

▶ Reviewing a list of Paris favorites

▶ Finding other great places to stay

▶ Locating hotels by neighborhood and by price

· ·

*P*aris has more than 2,200 hotels, but only 43 are described here. The reason? You don't need an overwhelming, encyclopedic list of all the hotels, just ones that are right for you, and an equally right backup in case your first choice is booked solid. In compiling this list, the first step was considering the typical traveler's wish list. And for most of you, the main priority is location. Thus, the first criterion, though ruthless, was simple: If the hotel isn't located in the first eight arrondissements, it isn't recommended in this book. The second concern was price. The most expensive category listed here, $$$$$, contains hotels that cost more than 300€ a night, which is expensive by nearly anyone's standards. Only two hotels described here fall into the $$$$$ category because, seriously, why waste your time? (For a complete rundown on the $ system, check out Chapter 6.) Three quarters of the hotels in this chapter rent doubles for less than 150€ night but nevertheless give you comfort, some nice amenities, and that *frisson* of Parisian character for which the city's hotels are known. And none of the hotels listed here is a dive.

Finally, a variety of neighborhoods is represented here with a nice range of styles from conservative to trendy. The aim? I want to make sure that everyone is accounted for, regardless of budget, taste, or style of travel. The two maps in this chapter pinpoint the locations of the hotels I describe — one map for "Hotels in the Heart of the Right Bank" and one for "Hotels in the Heart of the Left Bank." Reviews are arranged alphabetically for easy reference. Hotels that are especially good for families are designated with the kid-friendly icon. Listed immediately beneath the name of the hotel is the neighborhood in which it's located and the number of dollar signs corresponding to the hotel's rack rates, from the cheapest double room in low season to the most expensive in high season; Chapter 6 lists the corresponding price ranges. Breakfast is continental, unless otherwise stated.

Hotels in the Heart of the Right Bank

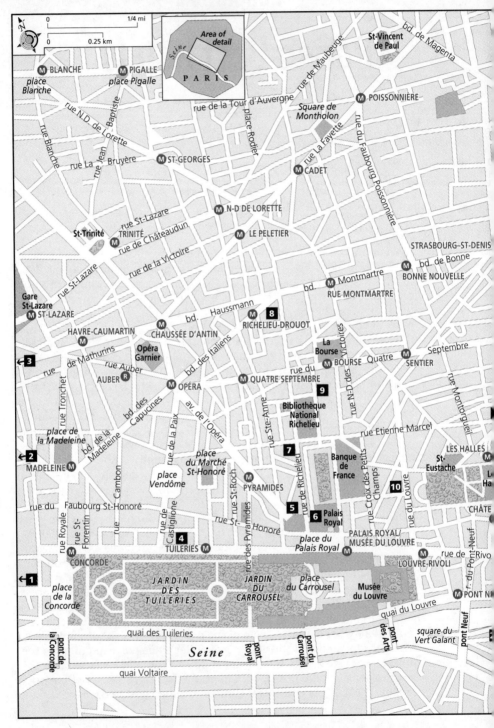

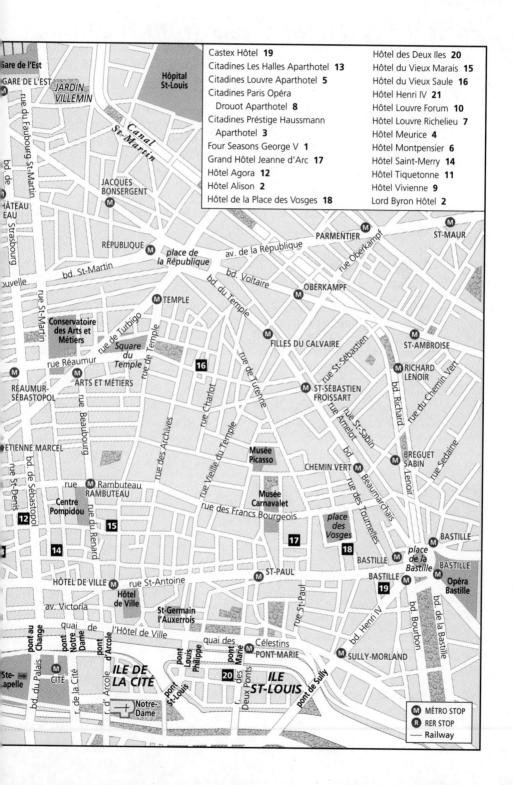

Castex Hôtel **19**
Citadines Les Halles Aparthotel **13**
Citadines Louvre Aparthotel **5**
Citadines Paris Opéra
  Drouot Aparthotel **8**
Citadines Préstige Haussmann
  Aparthotel **3**
Four Seasons George V **1**
Grand Hôtel Jeanne d'Arc **17**
Hôtel Agora **12**
Hôtel Alison **2**
Hôtel de la Place des Vosges **18**

Hôtel des Deux Iles **20**
Hôtel du Vieux Marais **15**
Hôtel du Vieux Saule **16**
Hôtel Henri IV **21**
Hôtel Louvre Forum **10**
Hôtel Louvre Richelieu **7**
Hôtel Meurice **4**
Hôtel Montpensier **6**
Hôtel Saint-Merry **14**
Hôtel Tiquetonne **11**
Hôtel Vivienne **9**
Lord Byron Hôtel **2**

Paris's Top Hotel Picks from A to Z

Castex Hôtel

$ Le Marais (4e)

The Castex is a popular budget classic, near *everything* in the Marais. Each large room has a writing table or a desk and chair; some have views overlooking the courtyard. The staff is friendly and accommodating. Rooms don't have televisions, but you can watch TV or read the papers in the TV salon. Reserve at least a month in advance.

5 rue Castex. ☎ *01-42-72-31-52. Fax: 01-42-72-57-91. Métro: Bastille or Sully-Morland. Rates: 45€–53€ single; 55€–61€ double; 70€–75€ triple; 91€ quad. AE, DC, MC, V.*

Citadines Les Halles Aparthotel

$$–$$$ Louvre (1er)

Staying here is like living in your own high-rise apartment in Paris. Studios and one-bedrooms have fully equipped kitchenettes, and services include a 24-hour reception desk, satellite TV, air conditioning, housekeeping, baby equipment rental, and laundry facilities. The Les Halles neighborhood is a bit rough at night, so if you're a single traveler, this hotel might not be the best bet.

4 rue des Innocents (100 yards from the Forum des Halles). ☎ *01-40-39-26-50. Internet:* www.citadines.com. *Métro: Les Halles. Rates: 141€–160€ for 1–6 days, 127€–144€ 7–29 days 2-person studio; 212€–245€ for 1–6 days, 191€–220€ 7–29 days 4-person (1 bedroom) apt. AE, MC, V.*

Citadines Louvre Aparthotel

$$$ Louvre (1er)

This seven-story aparthotel is in a terrific location in an upscale and pretty neighborhood just opposite the Comédie-Française and next to the Jardin du Palais-Royal. It has several studios and apartments equipped for travelers with disabilities. Studios and one-bedrooms have fully equipped kitchenettes, and services include a 24-hour reception desk, satellite TV, air conditioning, housekeeping, baby equipment rental, and laundry facilities. Rent well in advance.

8 rue de Richelieu (1 block north of the Louvre). ☎ *01-55-35-28-00. Internet:* www.citadines.com. *Métro: Palais-Royal or Pyramides. Rates: 160€–180€ for 1–6 days, 144€–166€ 7–29 days 2-person studio; 261€–297€ 1–6 days, 235€–267€ 7–29 days 4-person (1 bedroom) apt. AE, MC, V.*

Citadines Paris Opéra Drouot Aparthotel
$$$–$$$$ Opéra (2e)

Around the corner from the Opéra Comique and the Comédie Française and near the Grands Boulevards, this five-story aparthotel is the most centrally located in the Citadines chain. It's located in a peaceful passage, and rooms come with fully equipped kitchenettes; available services include a 24-hour reception desk, satellite TV, air conditioning, baby equipment rental, dry cleaning, laundry facilities, housekeeping, bar, billiards table, and fitness center. A one-bedroom apartment here is a good alternative to renting two rooms in a cheap hotel.

18 rue Favart. ☎ *01-40-15-14-00. Internet:* www.citadines.fr. *Métro: Richelieu-Drouot. Rates: 160€–228€ 1–6 days, 144€–206€ 7–29 days 2-person studio; 250€–269€ 1–6 days, 225€–236€ 7–29 days 3-person duplex (1 bedroom) apt.; 261€–297€ 1–6 days, 235€–267€ 7–29 days 4-person (1 bedroom) apt. AE, MC, V.*

Citadines Préstige Haussmann Aparthotel
$$$ Champs-Elysées (8e)

Located near Galeries Lafayette and Au Printemps and in walking distance of the Champs-Elysées, the Madeleine church, and parc Monceau, this seven-story aparthotel is one of Citadines chain's most luxurious. Studios and apartments are more expensive but also more spacious and luxurious — featuring rare wood furnishings and granite bathrooms. Services and amenities include a 24-hour reception desk, satellite TV, air conditioning, baby equipment rental, dry cleaning, laundry facilities, housekeeping, bar, and fitness center.

129–131 bd. Haussmann. ☎ *01-56-88-61-00. Internet:* www.citadines.fr. *Métro: Miromesnil. Rates: 197€–227€ 1–6 days, 177€–197€ 7–29 days 2-person studio; 298€–388€ 1–6 days, 267€–345€ 7–29 days 4-person apt. AE, MC, V.*

Familia Hôtel
$ Latin Quarter (5e)

You can tell that this hotel is a labor of love for owners, the Gaucherons; they've made it the prettiest it can be. Flowers spill out of window boxes; the stone walls in some of the bedrooms have been painstakingly restored or have had toile de Jouy wallpaper added. In other rooms, artists from l'École des Beaux-Arts have painted sepia-toned murals of Parisian scenes. The cozy lobby exudes the atmosphere of a tiny castle with rich tapestries, a winding staircase and frescoed walls. Some rooms have balconies (numbers 22, 23, 52, and 53) with enchanting views of the Latin Quarter. From the fifth and sixth floors, you can see Notre-Dame. Bathrooms are small but modern and tiled. All rooms have cable TV and hair dryers. The staff understands what it's like to travel with children and tries to provide kid-friendly services (such as bottle heating) and larger rooms for the weary traveler who requests ahead. Take note that most rooms in the hotel are on the small side, and the least expensive doubles in the corners are tiny. No air conditioning is provided, and remember that it can get hot in Paris heat waves. The Jardin des Plantes is down the street, and the Seine is across the street from the garden's front entrance.

11 rue des Écoles. ☎ *01-43-54-55-27. Fax: 01-43-29-61-77. Internet:* www.hotel-paris-familia.com. *Métro: Jussieu. Rates: 64€–95€ single; 75€–95€ double; 160€ quad; 106€ single or double with balcony. Breakfast 5.50€. AE, DC, MC, V.*

Four Seasons George V
$$$$$ **Champs-Elysées (8e)**

If palatial splendor is business as usual for you, then you can't do much better than the Four Seasons George V. From the elegant light-wood-and-marble lobby opening onto an outside marble courtyard decorated with bright blue awnings and umbrellas, to the cascading displays of fresh flowers, to the friendly welcome of the team of concierges, you feel good about staying here. And that's *before* you reach your room, the size of which starts at 450 square feet. Separated from the public corridors by their own hallways for more peace and quiet, rooms are decorated in Louis XVI–style furniture and enjoy the latest technology, including dual phone lines, a modem line, 51-channel TV, stereo system, and VCR. Kids will love the Sony PlayStation console, a room standard. Internet access is also available via a wireless infrared keyboard on the television. Views from the upper floors are truly remarkable, with some rooms offering a stone's throw view of the Eiffel Tower — from their bathtubs. Other amenities include the signature Four Season mattresses (930 coils instead of the industry-standard 800), a spa (with its own elevator) offering 24-hour massages and a huge pool, an American bar, and a 2-star gourmet restaurant.

31 av. George V, 1½ blocks from the Champs-Elysées. ☎ *01-49-52-70-00. Fax: 01-49-52-70-10. Métro: George V. Rates: 700€–1,200€ double; 1,500€–1,900€ 1-bedroom suite. AE, DC, MC, V.*

Grand Hôtel des Balcons
$–$$ **St-Germain-des-Prés (6e)**

If you'll be celebrating your birthday while in Paris, treat yourself to a stay here; the breakfast buffet (which includes sausage and eggs) is free for the birthday boy or girl. Denise and Pierre Corroyer are proud of their gracious and comfortable hotel with its balconied rooms, modern light oak furnishings, bright fabrics, new beds, 19th-century stained-glass windows and Art Nouveau lobby furnishings (look for the voluptuous statue of Venus in the breakfast room). Although most rooms and their wrought-iron balconies are small, clever use of space has allowed for large closets and full-length mirrors. Bathrooms are also small but well designed and come equipped with a clothesline. The higher-priced doubles, triples, and quads are big and luxurious; some have double-sink bathrooms. Free tea and coffee are available in the lounge. The Théâtre de l'Odéon is steps away.

3 rue Casimir Delavigne. ☎ *01-46-34-78-50. Fax: 01-46-34-06-27. Internet:* www.balcons.com. *Métro: Odéon. RER: Luxembourg. Rates70€–110€ single; 90€–140€ double; 180€ triple. Buffet breakfast 10€, free on your birthday. AE, DC, MC, V.*

Grand Hôtel de Suez
$ **Latin Quarter (5e)**

Guests return for the hotel's many good-sized, quiet rooms at great prices. Beds are firm, storage space is ample, and the modern bathrooms have hair dryers. But don't even think of opening the windows to the streetside balconies — the Boulevard St-Michel is as noisy as a carnival. The hotel is in a great location near Musée de Cluny, Jardin du Luxembourg and the Panthéon. The Seine and Notre-Dame are a 10-minute walk away.

31 bd. St-Michel. ☎ *01-53-10-34-00. Fax: 01-40-51-79-44. Métro: St-Michel. Rates: 65€–70€ single or double with toilet and shower; 70€ single or twin with full bathroom; 70€–85€ twin beds with shower and toilet; 85€ twin beds with full bathroom; 85€–95€ triple with toilet and shower, 95€ triple with full bathroom. Breakfast 6€. AE, DC, MC, V.*

Grand Hôtel Jeanne d'Arc
$ **Le Marais (4e)**

Reserve well in advance for this great budget hotel on a pretty little street just off the place St-Catherine. It's in an 18th-century building where contemporary artists have brightly hand-painted the walls of the breakfast and sitting rooms, adding their own surrealistic touches. (You can't miss one artist's explosive mosaic mirror, a tribute to French pride.) The decent-sized rooms have large windows, card-key access, and large bathrooms, but storage space is a bit cramped. Other room features include direct-dial telephones, satellite TV, and bedside tables. If a view is important, make sure you request one because some rooms don't have views. The hotel is in the center of the Marais, and it can be a little noisy, but you're near the Musée Picasso, place des Vosges, and the Bastille, and the wonderful Au Bistro de la Place café is in the square next door.

3 rue de Jarente. ☎ *01-48-87-62-11. Fax: 01-48-87-37-31. Internet:* www.hotel jeannedarc.com. *Métro: St-Paul or Bastille. Rates: 64€ single; 67€–73€ double; 107€ triple; 122€ quad. Breakfast 5.80€. MC, V.*

Grand Hôtel Lévêque
$ Eiffel Tower (7e)

The 1930s–era Grand Hôtel Lévêque is 3 blocks from the Eiffel Tower on a colorful pedestrian street with a vivid marketplace, bakeries, restaurants, wine shops, and florists. The lobby has a comfortable lounge area with plush circular sofas, a drink- and ice-dispenser, and the daily newspaper. Rooms are snug, with just enough space to be comfortable, and have been renovated with new, if not inspired, decorations. The bathrooms are small but in excellent condition, and each room has a satellite TV, hair dryer, and ceiling fan. Staff members are very friendly and helpful, and if you ask, they may be able to give you a higher-priced room on the fifth floor with a balcony and partial view of the Eiffel Tower. This hotel fills up fast, so book well in advance.

29 rue Cler. ☎ *01-47-05-49-15. Fax: 01-45-50-49-36. Internet:* www.hotel-leveque.com. *Métro: École-Militaire or Latour-Maubourg. Rates: 53€ single room without bathroom; 84€ double bed with bathroom; 91€ twin beds with bathroom; 114€ triple with bathroom. Breakfast 7€. AE, MC, V.*

Hôtel Agora
$–$$ Louvre (1er)

This 2-star hotel on a very busy pedestrian street near Les Halles has a traditional French air once you take the small elevator or climb a curved staircase to its eclectic lobby (the ugly entryway disguises a good find). Rooms have antique furniture, marble mantlepieces, floral prints, and old-fashioned wallpapers. The windows are double-glazed, thankfully, which helps muffle the outside noise. Fifth-floor rooms have balconies with views of the impressive St-Eustache Church. European film crews often stay here because of the location and reasonable prices.

7 rue de la Cossonnerie. ☎ *01-42-33-46-02. Fax: 01-42-33-80-99. Métro: Châtelet. Rates: 75.65€ –91.65€ single; 90.30€ –117.30€ double. Breakfast 7.50€. AE, MC, V.*

Hôtel Alison
$–$$ Madeleine (8e)

Located between the Madeleine and the Elysée Palace and near the Champs-Elysées and rue Faubourg St-Honoré, this hotel has a sleek, upscale ambience perfectly in tune with the classy neighborhood. The large, well-appointed rooms are furnished in modern style, with black furniture and light walls. Inside the rooms are plenty of storage space, a safe, trouser presses, and double-glazed windows. Hair dryers and Roger & Gallet toiletries grace gleaming, tiled bathrooms with wall-mounted showers. You can relax in the plush lobby or enjoy a drink in the hotel bar.

21 rue de Surène. ☎ *01-42-65-54-00. Fax: 01-42-65-08-17. Métro: Madeleine or Concorde. Rates: 75€–135€ single; 89€–135€ double; 120€–135€ twin beds. Breakfast 7€. AE, DC, MC, V.*

Hôtel Amélie
$ Eiffel Tower (7e)

The pretty Hôtel Amélie has flower pots brimming with bouquets at each window. The interior is more modest, with small renovated rooms and small closets, but the white-tiled bathrooms offer hair dryers and good-quality toiletries. Despite the central location (between the Champs de Mars, the lawn surrounding the Eiffel Tower, and the Esplanade des Invalides, the lawn surrounding Invalides and Napoleon's Tomb), the atmosphere is peaceful, almost serene. There is no elevator.

5 rue Amélie. ☎ *01-45-51-74-75. Fax: 01-45-56-93-55. Métro: Latour-Maubourg. Rates: 65€–72€ single; 77€–82€ double with shower; 80€–90€ double with bath; 84€–92€ twin beds. Breakfast: 6.10€, free for stays in Aug after 4 nights. AE, DC, MC, V.*

Hôtel Claude-Bernard
$$–$$$ Latin Quarter (5e)

Evident from the moment you enter the lobby, the 3-star Hôtel Claude-Bernard keeps very high standards. The congenial, spacious rooms have tasteful wallpaper, sleek bathrooms, decorative balconies with flowers, and often a charming piece of antique furniture, such as a writing desk. Some particularly attractive suites come with couches and armchairs. A sauna is available for guests to use, and all rooms are air-conditioned. Don't miss the nearby free garden at the Cluny Museum; its plants are featured in the museum's Lady and the Unicorn tapestries.

43 rue des Écoles. ☎ *01-43-26-32-52. Fax: 01-43-26-80-56. Internet:* www.hotel claudebernard.com. *Métro: Maubert-Mutualité. Rates: 89€–129€ single; 115€–169€ double; 135€–198€ triple; 269€ suite for 1–4 persons. Continental breakfast 8€. AE, DC, MC, V.*

Hôtel de Fleurie
$$$–$$$$ St-Germain-des-Prés (6e)

Just off place Odéon on a pretty side street, the Fleurie has all the comforts, including air conditioning, marble bathrooms with heated towel racks, quality toiletries, Oriental carpets, and fresh flowers. The rooms are on the small side, but all are furnished in a modern or classic style. Book at least six weeks in advance for one of the *chambres familiales —* connecting rooms with two large beds. Rooms have data ports, or you can check your e-mail on the hotel computer in the lobby for 0.30€ per minute. Breakfast is served in the cozy vaulted stone cellar dining room. The staff is friendly, and the hotel is in a superb location near the church of St-Germain-des-Prés; the historic Café de Flore, Café les Deux Magots, and Brasserie Lipp; and a few blocks from the Seine and the Jardin du Luxembourg. If you book for more than seven nights, the hotel throws in a free three-day museum pass (*Carte Musées et Monuments*).

32–34 rue de Grégoire-de-Tours. ☎ *01-53-73-70-00. Fax: 01-53-73-70-20. Internet:* www.hotel-de-fleurie.tm.fr. *Métro: Odéon. Rates: 145€ single; 167€– 198€ double with queen-size bed; 244€–274€ deluxe rooms (large room with twin beds or king-size beds); 297€–343€ chambre familiale (family suite). Breakfast 9€. AE, DC, MC, V.*

Hôtel de l'Abbaye Saint-Germain
$$$ **St-Germain-des-Prés (6e)**

It began as a convent, became a prison during the Revolution, and was a residence for Asian students during World War II. Now this is one of the Left Bank's most delightful and cozy hotels — a popular stop for travelers who have a taste for chic surroundings on a budget. You enter through a courtyard and check in at the reception desk, which is in the convent's original vault. Some of the rooms have their original oak ceiling beams, and all are air-conditioned, sporting 19th-century–style furnishings and damask upholstery. The standard rooms are a good size by Paris standards, and the duplex suites are absolutely spacious. Some first-floor rooms open onto a vine-covered terrace; late Italian actor Marcello Mastroianni preferred Room 3. Rooftop suites have terraces. In summer you can eat breakfast — included in the price of your room — in the flower-filled courtyard; in winter, you can lounge in front of the lobby fireplace.

10 rue Cassette, 4 short blocks from the northwest corner of the Jardin du Luxembourg. ☎ *01-45-44-38-11. Fax: 01-45-48-07-86. Internet:* www.hotel-abbaye.com. *Métro: St-Sulpice. Rates: 185€–292€ double room; 345€–373€ suites; 380€–427 duplex suite. AE, MC, V.*

Hôtel de la Place des Vosges
$$ **Le Marais (4e)**

King Henri IV once kept his horses here, but you'd never know this hotel was a former stable by its plush, antiques-filled lobby. Many of the small but well-maintained rooms have beamed ceilings, and the bathrooms are tiled. Most beds are firm, but storage space is lacking. All rooms have TVs (suspended by a chain from the ceiling), desks, and hair dryers. The larger top-floor room has a pretty view over the Right Bank, but the elevator stops a floor down, a consideration when you have a bunch of luggage. The entrance to the place des Vosges is only steps away.

12 rue de Birague. ☎ *01-42-72-60-46. Fax: 01-42-72-02-64. Métro: Bastille. Rates: 76€–84€ single with shower and toilet; 101€–120€ single or double with bathroom; 106€–120€ twin with bathroom; 140€ top-floor room with bathroom. Breakfast 6€. MC, V.*

Hôtel de Nevers
$ St-Germain-des-Prés (7e)

Tucked away in the St-Germain-des-Prés premier shopping area, this renovated 17th-century house provides simple rooms at reasonable prices. After entering the charming wood-beamed lobby, thick with North African rugs and amber-toned wall coverings, where friendly staff check you in, you're escorted up a quaint, tapestry adorned winding staircase to a very clean room with wooden bureaus and wood-framed mirrors. Bathrooms are spotless and well maintained, if not brand new. Although you must pay in cash, you can save your credit cards for more shopping in nearby stores. There is no elevator.

83 rue de Bac. ☎ *01-45-44-61-30. Fax: 01-42-22-29-47. Métro: Rue du Bac. Rates: 86€ single with terrace; 81€ double with shower; 91€ twin beds with bathroom; 90€ double with bathroom and terrace. Continental breakfast 6€; 18€ for extra bed. MC, V for making reservations, cash or traveler's checks only for payment.*

Hôtel des Deux-Îles
$$$ Île St-Louis (4e)

With only 17 double rooms, this charming hotel is intimate and superbly located on the Île St-Louis (practically in Notre-Dame's backyard). The owners are interior decorators, and it shows; the rooms have exposed oak ceiling beams and provincial upholstery, and the lobby is a warm and cozy gem with fresh flowers and bamboo furniture. Off the lobby is a garden that some of the rooms overlook and a basement breakfast room with a fireplace. Although amenities include bathrooms, hair dryers, satellite TV, and air conditioning, rooms run from tiny to small, so if you have a large amount of luggage, you may want to look elsewhere. Paris's best ice cream shop, Berthillon (closed in August), is just around the corner, and you can find ice cream in nearby brasseries, too. So much is nearby — the Memorial de la Déportation commemorating the French Jews sent to Auschwitz, the bird and flower markets on Île de la Cité, and the Conciergerie — you may not know where to begin. *Hint:* Start early in the morning with Notre-Dame.

59 rue St-Louis-en-l'Île. ☎ *01-43-26-13-35. Fax: 01-43-29-60-25. Métro: Pont Marie. Rates: 139€ double. Breakfast 9€. AE, DC, MC, V.*

Hotels in the Heart of the Left Bank

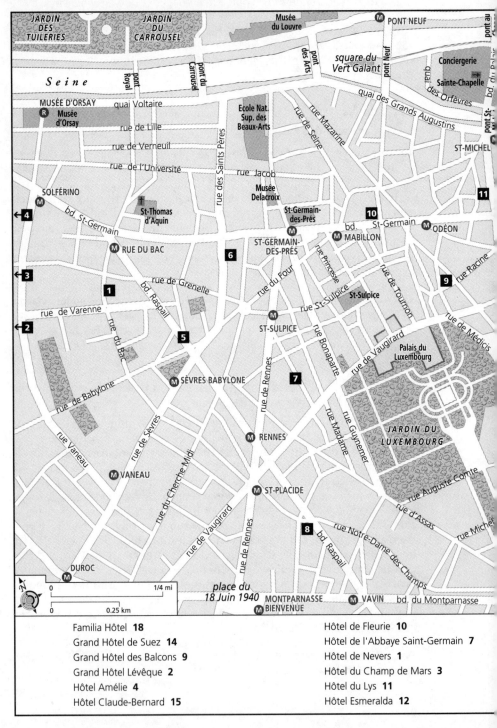

Familia Hôtel **18**
Grand Hôtel de Suez **14**
Grand Hôtel des Balcons **9**
Grand Hôtel Lévêque **2**
Hôtel Amélie **4**
Hôtel Claude-Bernard **15**

Hôtel de Fleurie **10**
Hôtel de l'Abbaye Saint-Germain **7**
Hôtel de Nevers **1**
Hôtel du Champ de Mars **3**
Hôtel du Lys **11**
Hôtel Esmeralda **12**

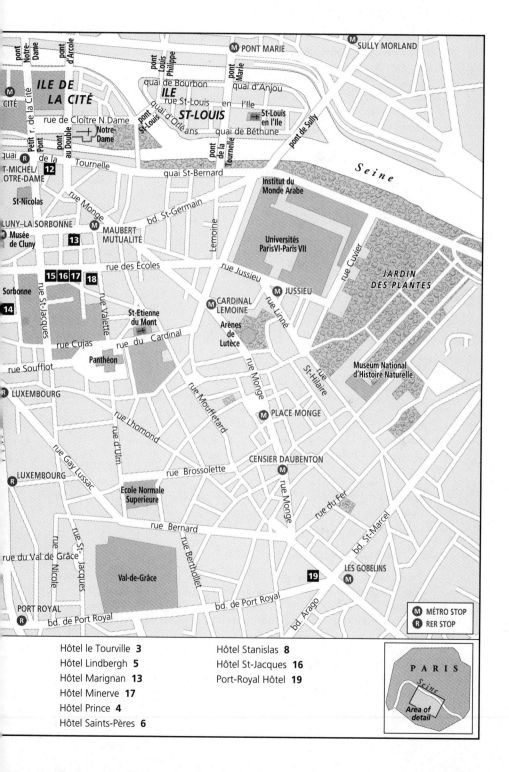

Hôtel le Tourville **3**
Hôtel Lindbergh **5**
Hôtel Marignan **13**
Hôtel Minerve **17**
Hôtel Prince **4**
Hôtel Saints-Pères **6**

Hôtel Stanislas **8**
Hôtel St-Jacques **16**
Port-Royal Hôtel **19**

Hôtel du Champ de Mars
$ **Eiffel Tower (7e)**

Like a country house tucked away on a colorful street near the Eiffel Tower, the Champ de Mars is a bargain that's hard to beat. Its 20 rooms have flowing curtains, fabric-covered headboards, throw pillows, and cushioned high-backed seats. Bathrooms are in mint condition with hair dryers, large towels, and good lighting, and those with tubs have wall-mounted showers. A cozy breakfast room is located in the remodeled basement. Reserve at least four months in advance. In the summer, the two best rooms are on the ground floor and open onto the leafy courtyard; they stay cool despite the lack of air conditioning. A Franprix grocery store is two doors down for travelers needing provisions.

7 rue du Champ de Mars. ☎ 01-45-51-52-30. Fax: 01-45-51-64-36. E-mail: reservation@hotel-du-champ-de-mars.com. Internet: www.hotel-du-Champ-de-mars.com. Métro: École-Militaire. RER: Pont de l'Alma. Rates: 66€ single; 72€ double; 76€ twin beds; 92€ triple. Breakfast 6.50€. AE, MC, V.

Hôtel du Lys
$–$$ **Latin Quarter (6e)**

Housed in a 17th-century mansion with original tall casement windows, Hôtel du Lys is the perfect place for a romantic tryst on a budget. The homey, intimate rooms are decorated in floral wallpaper with exposed-beam high ceilings. Rooms feature double glazing to keep out the noise, and rooms 19 and 22 have balconies. People with disabilities need to heed the lack of an elevator, and the staircase, although historic, is narrow. The Lys is right in the heart of the Latin Quarter, just a few blocks from the Seine and Notre-Dame in an area that gets quite crowded in summer; fortunately, a room here is a haven.

23 rue Serpente. ☎ 01-43-26-97-57. Fax: 01-44-07-34-90. Métro: St-Michel or Odéon. Rates: 93€ single; 93–105€ double; 120€ triple. Rates include breakfast. MC, V.

Hôtel du Vieux Marais
$$ **Le Marais (4e)**

This hotel is totally renovated and now has a sparkling elegant lobby, air-conditioned rooms, a lighted garden, new wardrobes, and tiled bathrooms with a Mexican-inspired design. Rooms are average size, are spotless, and have faux leather upholstery; some overlook the garden. The service is impeccable, and the staff is friendly and helpful. The Pompidou Center modern art museum is a two-minute walk away, and all the wonderful shops and restaurants of the Marais are within walking distance. If you have enough time, visit the nearby Musée Picasso or Musée Carnavalet, and don't miss the place des Vosges down rue des Francs Bourgeois.

8 rue du Plâtre. ☎ *01-42-78-47-22.* *Fax: 01-42-78-34-32. Métro: Hôtel-de-Ville. Rates: 92€–103€ single with shower; 106€–122€ twin or double with shower or bath. Breakfast 7€. MC, V.*

Hôtel du Vieux Saule

$–$$ Le Marais/Bastille (3e)

This hotel in the Marais near place de la République offers not only air conditioning but a free sauna, too. The cheerful small rooms have tiled bathrooms, hair dryers, safes, double-glazed windows, luggage racks, satellite TV, trouser presses, and even small irons and ironing boards. The rooms on the fifth floor tend to be bigger. Breakfast is a buffet served in the original 16th-century cozy vaulted cellar accessed by a winding staircase (no elevator).

6 rue Picardie. ☎ *01-42-72-01-14.* *Fax: 01-40-27-88-21. Internet:* www.hotel vieuxsaule.com. *Métro: République. Rates: 76€–91€ single with shower; 91€–121€ double with shower or tub; 121€–136€ deluxe double. Buffet breakfast 9€. AE, DC, MC, V.*

Hôtel Esmeralda

$ Latin Quarter (5e)

This hotel is a favorite of many travelers, and you may have to book at least two months in advance. The Esmeralda is funky and ramshackle with an old, winding wooden staircase and outstanding views of Notre-Dame and the Seine from its front rooms. East rooms overlook St-Julien-le-Pauvre and square Viviani. Shabby-chic velvet coverings and antique furniture create a homey warmth that almost makes up for the disappointingly dark rear rooms. The front rooms with a view have modern bathrooms with tubs, and some are exceptionally large, making them perfect for travelers with children. The location — in the center of everything, and just steps away from the Shakespeare and Company bookstore — couldn't be better for parents accompanying little ones who tend to tire quickly. Sadly, the hotel's pet cats, permanent lobby residents and a favorite of visiting kids, recently checked out.

4 rue St-Julien-le-Pauvre. ☎ *01-43-54-19-20. Fax: 01-40-51-00-68. Métro: St-Michel. Rates: 30€ single with sink; 60€–85€ double with bathroom; 95€ triple; 105€ quad. Breakfast 6€. Shower 2€ per person. No credit cards.*

Hôtel Henri IV

$ Louvre (1er)

This hotel is old. It doesn't have an elevator; only five rooms have showers or baths, only two have toilets, and none have phones. But this super-budget hotel is one of Europe's most famous and nearly always is full. It occupies a dramatic location on place Dauphine — the northenmost tip of Ile de la Cité, across the river from St-Germain and the Louvre and a few steps from Pont-Neuf. The 17th-century building houses cozy rooms that are past their prime, though many find them romantically evocative (others think they're just run-down). Each room has a sink, but guests share the spotless toilets and showers on each of the five floors. One of the communal bathrooms has an enormous tub, and a few rooms have beautiful views of place Dauphine. Manager François Balitrand is a wealth of knowledge about the hotel and place Dauphine. All in all, staying here is an adventure. Book far in advance.

25 place Dauphine. ☎ *01-43-54-44-53. Métro: Pont Neuf. Rates: 22€–23€ single with sink; 29€–35€ double with sink; 41.50€–44.50€ double with shower but no toilet; 55€–69€ double with toilet and bath or shower. Breakfast is included.*

Hôtel le Tourville
$$ Eiffel Tower (7e)

This splendid restored mansion, located just steps behind Les Invalides, can be addictive. You receive almost all the amenities of a pricier hotel — Roger & Gallet toiletries, hair dryers, air conditioning, chic decor with antiques — for prices that are manageable. Rooms are decorated in soft yellows, pink or sand, with crisp white damask upholsteries, antique bureaus and lamps, fabulously mismatched old mirrors, and marble bathrooms. Rooms also have satellite TV, hair dryers, and 24-hour room service. You may want to ask for one of the four wonderful rooms with walk-out vine-draped terraces or a junior suite with whirlpool bath. The staff is wonderfully helpful. A grocery store a few doors down is open until 10 p.m., and a tabac is right next door.

16 av. de Tourville. ☎ *01-47-05-62-62. Fax: 01-47-05-43-90. Métro: École-Militaire. Rates: 145€ standard double; 215€ superior double; 240€ double with private terrace; 310€ junior suite. Breakfast 12€. AE, DC.*

Hôtel Lindbergh
$ St-Germain-des-Prés (7e)

Aviation-themed photos add a tasteful touch to the decor at this pretty hotel named for the American aviator. The rooms range from simple and charming, with colorful bedspreads and matching bathrooms, to refined and elegant, with classic touches — graceful floor-length curtains, fabric headboards, and color-coordinated cushioned seats. The garnet-toned lobby is inviting; you can chat there with the friendly owners who like to talk about their collections of photos that include Charles Lindbergh in his plane, Lindbergh standing with Blériot (the first man to fly across the English Channel), and Lindbergh with Antoine de Saint-Exupéry, the pilot author of *Le Petit Prince*. The hotel is right at the edge of the

St-Germain-des-Prés shopping district, and Au Bon Marché department store, with its terrific L'Épicerie supermarket, is only a few short blocks away. The Musée Rodin is within walking distance. Those with energy can hoof the long blocks over to the Eiffel Tower; otherwise catch bus number 69 from nearby rue du Bac to the Champ du Mars.

5 rue Chomel. ☎ *01-45-48-35-53. Fax: 01-45-49-31-48. Internet:* www.hotel lindbergh.com. *Métro: Sévres-Babylone. Rates: 91€ double with shower; 91€–104€ double (or twin beds) with shower and bath; 108€–152€ larger double for 1–4 people. Breakfast 8€. AE, MC, V.*

Hôtel Louvre Forum
$ Louvre (1er)

For a truly central, reasonably priced hotel just steps from the Louvre, this comfortable modern hotel is difficult to beat. The brightly colored rooms all are newly renovated with tiled bathrooms (with hair dryers) and furniture that includes writing tables, lamps, and chairs. Each room has a small armoire with hanging space and shelves; however, the rooms on the lower floors are a bit cramped. The staff is a bit chilly, but that's a small price for such a great location. The lobby features a mural of the neighborhood, which is only a short walk from the elegant Palais Royal, once the garden of Cardinal Richelieu and the young Louis XIV, later used for gambling and illicit trysts, and now a showcase for outdoor sculpture, including nearly 300 permanent prison-striped columns by Daniel Buren.

25 rue du Bouloi. ☎ *01-42-36-54-19. Fax: 01-42-36-66-31. Métro: Louvre-Rivoli. Rates: 68.60€ single; 77.75€ double with shower; 86.10€ double with full bath. Discounts (around 20%) available for stays of more than 5 nights and in July and Aug. Continental breakfast 8€. AE, DC, MC, V.*

Hôtel Louvre Richelieu
$ Louvre (1er)

The rooms in this hotel are a good size, and the location is terrific — halfway between the Louvre and the Opéra. Enter through a corridor with restored stone walls; the pleasant reception area and lobby are on the second floor. The two-bed double rooms are dark, but spacious with high ceilings. Each room has a writing table, a small closet, and a luggage rack. The lack of an elevator here means that you may want to pack light. Reserve at least two weeks in advance for summer. A bakery is right next door.

51 rue de Richelieu. ☎ *01-42-97-46-20. Fax: 01-47-03-94-13. Métro: Palais-Royal– Musée du Louvre, Pyramides. Rates: 45€ single with toilet; 60€ single with bath- room; 55€ double with toilet; 76€ double with bathroom; 92€ triple with bathroom. Breakfast 6€ MC, V.*

Hôtel Marignan

$ Latin Quarter (5e)

It's plain and unassuming on the outside, but owners Paul and Linda Keniger have invested much time and energy in renovating this hotel. They have retained much of the building's architectural detailing, such as the stucco ceiling moldings, tiled the bathrooms, and added new beds. They welcome families, don't mind if you bring your own food into the dining room, and they even make the kitchen available during the low season. You also have a washer-dryer and iron at your disposal. Signs in English recommend neighborhoods to visit and tours to take, and you can always ask one of the Kenigers for recommendations. The hotel is very close to the Sorbonne — it's around the corner from the Panthéon, near the marché Mouffetard — and its good rates attract students. Rooms fill up quickly in July and August, so if you plan to travel then, book well in advance. Credit cards are not accepted.

13 rue du Sommerard. ☎ *01-43-54-63-81. Fax: 01-42-78-14-15. Métro: Maubert-Mutualité or St-Michel. Rates: 42€–45€ single with shower on floor, 64€ in-room shower; 60€ double with shower on floor, 86€–92€ in-room shower; 85€–105€ triple with shower in hall, 100€–110€ in-room shower; 95€–110€ quad with shower in hall, 120€–130 in-room shower. Breakfast 3€. No credit cards.*

Hôtel Meurice

$$$$$ Louvre (1er)

When Parisians speak about palace hotels, they mean this one. The Meurice is positively awe-inspiring from your first step onto its mosaic and marble floors to its towering ceilings with chandeliers, gold-leafed walls, hand-painted friezes, and its 18th-century furnished grand lobby. You'll think you're staying at Versailles, and, indeed, royalty stays here (the hotel's slogan is "The Hotel of Kings"). Each floor corresponds to a particular period of decor. Rooms are spacious, soundproofed, air-conditioned, and have ornate molded ceilings. They lack nothing in the way of luxuries, from fresh flowers and antique furnishings to walk-in closets, satellite television, and computer ports. On-site restaurants include the Meurice, for a true French gastronomic experience, and the lighter-fare Winter Garden — go if only to see the splendid, newly restored Art Nouveau glass roof. Amenities include an on-site health club and spa with Jacuzzi, Turkish baths, and massage; a laundry and dry cleaners; office and translation services; and round-the-clock maid service. The hotel faces the Jardin des Tuileries and is around the corner from the couture houses of the Faubourg St-Honoré and the elegant place Vendôme. The Louvre is about 7 blocks east on rue Rivoli. Rooms in the upper price categories have Tuileries views.

228 rue Rivoli. ☎ *01-44-58-10-10. Fax: 01-44-58-10-19. Internet: www.meurice hotel.com. Métro: Tuileries, but if you're going to stay here, you want to arrive* by limo or taxi, at the very least. Rates: 490€–650€ singles; 650€–800€ doubles; 950€–2,600€ suites; prices for apartments and royal suite with private terrace available on request. Continental breakfast 32€, American breakfast 42€. AE, DC, MC, V.

Hôtel Minerve

$–$$ Latin Quarter (5e)

Owners of the Familia Hotel, Eric and Sylvie Gaucheron, have purchased and renovated the Hotel Minerve next door. More upscale than the Familia, rooms are larger and have wood-beamed ceilings, exposed stone walls, carved mahogany wood furnishings, and expensive wallpapers. Pretty hand-painted sepia frescos can be found in several of the rooms, and ten rooms have large balconies with a table and chairs overlooking the street. The Minerve is as welcoming to kids as the Familia.

13 rue des Ecoles. ☎ 01-43-26-26-04. Fax: 01-44-07-01-96. Métro: Cardinal Lemoine or Jussieu. Rates: 69€–115€ single; 83€ double with shower, 99€–115€ double with shower and tub; 83€–115€ twin; 135€ triple; 115€ large double with balcony, patio, or cathedral ceiling. Breakfast 7€. AE, MC, V.

Hôtel Montpensier

$ Louvre (1er)

Supposedly the former residence of Mademoiselle de Montpensier, cousin of Louis XIV, this hotel's high ceilings and windows, the stained-glass ceiling in its lounge and its grand staircase create a sense of faded grandeur. Many rooms on the first two floors, which date from the 17th century, are either drab or have a faded elegance (depending on your point of view), while rooms on the fifth floor (an elevator is available) have attractive slanted ceilings and good views over the rooftops. Most rooms are comfortably outfitted with easy chairs, ample closet space, and modern bathrooms with hair dryers, but in-room tubs have no shower curtains. Reserve at least a month in advance for July. The prices are terrific for this location, just 2 blocks from the Jardin du Palais Royal and right down the street from the Louvre and the Jardin des Tuileries.

12 rue Richelieu. ☎ 01-42-96-28-50. Fax: 01-42-86-02-70. Internet: www.hotel-paris-montpensier.com. Métro: Palais-Royal–Musée du Louvre. Rates: 51€–56€ single with toilet and sink; 74€ double with sink, 87€ double with bath-room; 101€ triple; 113€ quad; 122€ quintuple. Shower 4€ per person. Breakfast 7€. AE, MC, V.

Hôtel Prince

$ Eiffel Tower (7e)

Just a ten-minute walk from the Eiffel Tower, the Prince is a good value for the location. Rooms are modern, soundproofed, and have exposed brick walls, matching curtains and bedspreads, and big bathrooms with fluffy towels. Although they vary in size, all rooms are pleasant, comfortable, and well kept, with double-glazed windows, luggage racks, TV, minifridges, and ample closets; some have hair dryers and safes. If you're too worn out from sightseeing to stagger out the door to the two down-stairs cafés (not a part of the hotel), the hotel can arrange for a local restaurant to deliver a meal. A ground-floor room is available with facilities for travelers with disabilities.

66 av. Bosquet. ☎ *01-47-05-40-90. Fax: 01-47-53-06-62. Internet:* www.hotel-paris-prince.com. *Métro: École-Militaire. Rates: 67€ single with shower; 78€ double with shower, 87€ double with tub; 87€ twin with shower, 99.90€ twin with tub; 109€ triple. Buffet breakfast 6.86€. AE, DC, MC, V.*

Hôtel Saint-Merry
$$$ Le Marais (4e)

On a pedestrian-only street in the Marais, this hotel is formerly the 17th-century presbytery of the Church of Saint-Merri next door, and it retains a medieval, if eccentric, atmosphere. Beds have wood screens for head-boards, except for Room 9, where the bed has flying buttresses on either side that make you feel like you're sleeping in Notre-Dame. If you prefer sunny rooms, then this place is not for you; the rooms are dark with beamed ceilings, stone walls, wrought-iron chandeliers, sconces, and can-delabras. Fabrics are sumptuous; rugs are Oriental; and bathrooms are pleasantly modern, fully tiled, and equipped with hair dryers. Higher prices are for larger rooms with views. In keeping with its medieval churchlike feeling, the phone in the lobby is in a confessional, and you won't find an elevator in the building. TVs are in suites only. The hotel location is only a few short blocks from the Seine and Hôtel de Ville. The Louvre is about a 15-minute walk down nearby rue de Rivoli.

78 rue de la Verrerie. ☎ *01-42-78-14-15. Fax: 01-40-29-06-82. Métro: Hôtel-de-Ville or Châtelet. Rates: 146€–210€ double; 146€–210€ room with twin beds; 186€–250€ triple; 305€–370€ suites. In-room breakfast10€. AE, V.*

Hôtel Saints-Pères
$$ St-Germain-des-Prés (6e)

The late poet Edna St. Vincent Millay loved the garden filled with camel-lias, and travelers make this romantic hotel one of the Left Bank's most popular. Designed in the 17th century by Louis XIV's architect, the hotel is furnished with antiques, old paintings, tapestries, and gilt mirrors, but its 39 rooms have modern amenities such as TVs and minibars. The most requested room is the *chambre à la fresque,* which has a 17th-century painted ceiling. Breakfast is served in the garden when the weather is good. The hotel is a stone's throw from Brasserie Lipp, Café de Flore, and the Deux Magots.

65 rue des St-Pères. ☎ *01-45-44-50-00. Fax: 01-45-44-90-83. Métro: St-Germain-des-Prés or Sèvres-Babylone. Rates: 105€ double; 275€ suites. Breakfast 9.20€. AE, DC, MC, V.*

Hôtel Stanislas

$$ St-Germain-des-Prés (6e)

This family-owned hotel has some of the friendliest staff in Paris, a small café open until midnight, and larger-sized rooms in good condition. Just around the corner from the bd. du Montparnasse and its Lost Generation cafés Rotonde, Coupole, Select, and Dôme, down the street from St-Germain-des-Prés shopping, and a short walk from the Jardin du Luxembourg, the hotel is an excellent value. Rooms have satellite TV and double-glazed windows.

5 rue du Montparnasse. ☎ *01-45-48-37-05. Fax: 01-45-44-54-43. Métro: Notre-Dame des Champs. Rates: 55€ single with toilet; 58.65€ double with bathroom; 64€ twin with bathroom; 72€ triple with bathroom. Breakfast is 5.70€.*

Hôtel St-Jacques

$$ Latin Quarter (5e)

This hotel could serve as a set for a movie about a 19th-century romance. Several rooms have restored 19th-century ceiling murals, and most of the high ceilings have elaborate plasterwork, giving the decor an old-Paris feel that is accentuated with traditional furniture and fabric-covered walls. The owners have added their own touches in the hallways, with stenciling on the walls and *trompe l'oeil* painting (a clever technique in which architectural elements are added to a room by painting them in to appear real) around the doors and walls and ceiling murals in the breakfast room and lounge. Modern comforts include generally spacious rooms, an elevator, immaculate tiled bathrooms with hair dryers and toiletries, double-glazed windows, and ample closet space. Although they aren't accessible by elevator, the rooms on the top floor are less expensive and have great views. The hotel is in a good location near the Sorbonne, Panthéon, and the Musée de Cluny, and not far from bd. St-Germain, rue Mouffetard, and the Arènes de Lutèce.

35 rue des Écoles (at rue des Carmes). ☎ *01-44-07-45-45. Fax: 01-43-25-65-50. Métro: Maubert-Mutualité. Rates: 68€ single; 102€ double; 114.50€ triple. Breakfast 8€. AE, DC, MC, V.*

Hôtel Tiquetonne

$ Opéra (2e)

If a view is more important than room space, ask the owner, Madame Sirvain, to give you one of the top rooms at this welcoming budget hotel. Rooms at the top boast views of the Eiffel Tower or Sacré-Coeur. Although all rooms are in need of updating (the furniture is old and wallpaper faded), they nevertheless are spotless, with firm beds and adequate storage space. Each room has the basics: a bed, table, and comfortable chairs. The Tiquetonne is located just off a busy pedestrian street containing body piercing establishments, food stores, and artsy jewelry shops, and is not too far from the red-light rue St-Denis. Still, it manages to be a haven from the outside world. Ask for rooms facing the quieter rue Tiquetonne. The hotel is closed during August.

6 rue Tiquetonne. ☎ *01-42-36-94-58. Fax: 01-42-36-02-94. Métro: Etienne Marcel or Réamur-Sébastopol. Rates: 23€ single with toilet, 35€ single with shower; 41€ double with shower or bath. Shower 5€ per person. V only.*

Hôtel Vivienne
$ Opéra (2e)

Hôtel Vivienne is well located between the Louvre and the Opéra and offers comfortable, if not the most luxurious, rooms at a good price. Rooms and bathrooms vary in size from adequate to huge, and all are in good shape. Some rooms have adjoining doors, perfect for families, others have small terraces. The newly renovated bathrooms have hair dryers and wall-mounted showers in the tubs, and some rooms have views of the Eiffel Tower. Children under 10 stay free. Before venturing from the neighborhood, explore the Galeries Vivienne and Colbert, gorgeous historic covered passageways with pretty shops, intimate restaurants, and art galleries with an entrance at 6 rue Vivienne down the street.

40 rue Vivienne. ☎ *01-42-33-13-26. Fax : 01-40-41-98-19. E-mail:* paris@hotel-vivienne.com. *Métro: Bourse, Richelieu-Drouot, Grands Boulevards. Rates: 48€–63€ single; 75€–78€ double, 84€ twin. Breakfast 6€. MC, V.*

Lord Byron Hôtel
$ Champs-Elysées (8e)

Located just off the Champs-Elysées on a narrow street lined with town houses, the Lord Byron is one of the best values in the neighborhood. Exuding a sense of luxury and peacefulness, draperies filter the sun in the Lord Byron's lobby, the reception desk is under an arch, and a charming little garden makes guests feel miles away from the busy Champs-Elysées. Rooms are furnished with antique reproductions, Provençal and classic French fabrics, and framed landscapes. They also feature mini-bars, satellite TV, hair dryers, and full bathrooms. Near the Arc de Triomphe, this is a good hotel to stay in during the Tour de France or the Bastille Day military parade; you're close enough to walk to the action early on a side street so that crowds won't interfere.

5 rue de Chateaubrand. ☎ *01-43-59-89-98. Fax: 42-89-46-04. Métro: George V, then rue Washington for 1 block, turn left. Rates: 148€ single with bathroom; 160€–175€ double or twin; 229€ suite. Breakfast is included.*

Port-Royal Hôtel
$ Latin Quarter (5e)

Located down the (long) av. des Gobelins from hilly rue Mouffetard, which passes behind the Panthéon, this hotel is the farthest away of the centrally located options in this chapter. However, with the rates of a super-budget motel but the look of a high-class hotel, this hotel is a budget traveler's dream. Halls are freshly painted, the elevator is super-sized, and all the rooms are decorated with flowery pastel wallpaper. The front rooms have double-glazed windows for peace and quiet, and many rooms have decorative fireplaces. (Don't try to light them, though; they don't work.) A breakfast/TV room and small courtyard for outside dining are located on the premises. The hotel has been run by the same family for more than 60 years. Note that the hotel does not accept credit cards, but a Credit Lyonnais bank with an outdoor ATM is located a few doors down.

8 bd. Port-Royal. ☎ *01-43-31-70-06. Fax: 01-43-31-33-67. Métro: Gobelins. Rates: 51€ single with sink, 76€ single with bathroom; 56€ double with sink, 81€ double with bathroom. Shower 2.50€ per person. Continental breakfast is included. No credit cards.*

Paris's Runner-Up Hotels

What if you've browsed the list of hotels, chosen the ones you think would suit you, and everything is booked? Don't despair, the staff at one of the branches of the **Office de Tourisme de Paris** (127 av. des Champs-Elysées, 8e; ☎ **08-36-68-31-12** or 01-49-52-53-35; Fax: 01-49-52-53-00; Internet: www.paris-touristoffice.com; E-mail: info@paristourist office.com; Métro: Charles-de-Gaulle–Étoile or George V) can make a hotel reservation for you. Keep in mind, however, that you need to arrive in person at the office or at one of its branches. The main office is open daily 9 a.m. to 8 p.m. (Sunday 11 a.m. to 7 p.m., Novevember through April). For a fee, the staff makes a reservation for you on the same day you want a room (see Chapter 7).

You can also try the following very good hotels — there just wasn't enough space to include a full listing!

Atelier Montparnasse
$$ St-Germain-des-Prés (6e) Here you'll find Art Deco–inspired elegance within shouting distance of three cafés favored by 1920s artists — Le Dôme, Le Select, and La Coupole. *49 rue Vavin.* ☎ *01-46-33-60-00. Fax: 01-40-51-04-21.*

Hyatt Regency Paris Madeleine
$$$$–$$$$$ Champs-Elysées (8e) This hotel provides good-sized rooms with all the amenities of the Hyatt hotel chain. 24 bd. Malesherbes.

☎ **888-591-1234** in the U.S., or 01-55-27-12-34 in Paris. Fax: 01-55-27-12-35. Internet: www.hyatt.com.

La Sanguine

$$ *Champs-Elysées (8e)* Just steps away from the Madeleine and the rue du Faubourg St-Honoré. *6 rue de Surène.* ☎ **01-42-65-71-61.** Fax: 01-42-66-96-77.

L'Astor Sofitel Demeure

$$$$ *Champs-Elysées (8e)* A reliable hotel with large rooms Ωfor families who want to stay near the chain-store madness of the Champs. *11 rue d'Astorg.* ☎ **01-53-05-05-05** in Paris. Fax: 01-53-05-05.

Paris Marriott Champs-Elysées

$$$$$ *Champs-Elysées (8e)* Chic 19th-century decor, a fabulous location, soundproofing, business services, and all the amenities the Marriott chain provides can be found here. *70 av. des Champs-Elysées.* ☎ **888-236-2427** in the U.S., or 01-53-93-55-00 in Paris. Fax: 01-53-93-55-01. Internet: www.marriott hotels.com.

Pavillon de la Reine

$$$$ *Le Marais (3e)* Each room is unique here; some even have sleeping lofts above cozy salons. Featured in the Demi Moore movie Passion of the Mind. *28 place des Vosges.* ☎ **01-40-29-19-19** in Paris. Fax: 01-40-29-19-20.

Index of Accommodations by Neighborhood

Hôtel St-Jacques $$
Port-Royal Hôtel $

St-Germain-des-Prés (6e)

Grand Hôtel des Balcons $–$$
Hôtel de Fleurie $$$–$$$$
Hôtel de l'Abbaye Saint-Germain $$$
Hôtel du Lys $–$$
Hôtel Saints-Pères $$
Hôtel Stanislas $$

Eiffel Tower (7e)

Grand Hôtel Lévêque $
Hôtel Amélie $$$
Hotel de Nevers $

Hôtel du Champ de Mars $
Hôtel le Tourville $$
Hôtel Lindbergh $
Hôtel Prince $

Champs-Elysées–Madeleine (8e)

Citadines Préstige Haussmann
    Aparthotel $$$
Four Seasons George V $$$$$
Hôtel Alison $$
Lord Byron Hôtel $

Index of Accommodations by Price

Chapter 9

Taking Care of the Remaining Details

*S*ometimes it seems that the planning for a trip abroad lasts longer than the actual trip itself. This chapter advises and helps you organize those innumerable loose ends and last-minute tasks that can frustrate the most seasoned travelers.

Getting a Passport

The only legal form of identification recognized around the world is a valid passport. You cannot cross an international border without one. Besides clothing, a passport is the only item you absolutely *must* have to travel in other countries. In the United States, you're used to your driver's license being the all-purpose ID card. Abroad, it proves only that some American state lets you drive. Getting a passport is easy, but completing the process takes some time.

When applying for a passport for the first time in the United States, you need to go in person to one of 13 passport offices throughout the country or to one of the many federal, state, or probate courts, or major post offices (not all accept applications; call the number listed later in the chapter to find out which ones do). When you go, you need to take along proof of citizenship, which means a certified birth certificate. You also need to take your driver's license, state or military ID, and any other identifying documents. More important, you need two *identical* passport-sized photos (2 inches x 2 inches) that you've had taken within the last six months. You can obtain the photos at almost any corner photo shop that has a special camera used to make the pictures identical. You *cannot* use the strip photos from one of those photo vending machines.

When you have your passport photos taken, ask the photo shop to make up six or eight total. You may need extra photos to apply for an International Driving Permit, a student or teacher ID, or for a *Carte Orange* transportation pass (see Chapter 11). Take the extras with you. You never know when you may need one, and if you ever happen to lose your passport, you can use one as a replacement photo.

For people 16 years old and older, a passport is valid for 10 years and costs $85 ($55 plus a $30 handling fee); for those younger than 15 years of age, passports are valid for five years and cost $70 total. If you're older than 15 and have an undamaged passport issued fewer than 12 years ago, you can renew it by mail by filling out an application, which is available online at http://travel.state.gov (click on the "Passport Information" link). By mail, you can bypass the $30 handling fee, and it therefore costs only $55.

Allow plenty of time — at least six weeks, preferably longer — before your trip to apply. The processing takes four weeks on average but can run somewhat longer during busy periods (especially in the spring). Writing a departure date within the next three weeks helps speed things along. Visiting an agency directly, or going through the court or post office and having them overnight your application can help you obtain your passport more quickly — in two weeks — but you'll probably have to pay an additional $35 fee. For more information, such as finding your regional passport office, visit the State Department Web site at http://travel.state.gov (click on the "Passport Information" link) or call the **National Passport Information Center** (☎ **900-225-5674** or 888-362-8668 to pay with credit card; 55¢ a minute for automated service; $1.50 a minute to speak with an operator).

Keep your passport with you at all times. The only times to give it up are at the bank for changing traveler's checks (they photocopy it), at borders for the guards to peruse, for the conductor on overnight train rides, whenever any police or military personnel ask for it, and *briefly* to the concierge when you check in at your hotel.

A valid passport is the only documentation you need as an American to visit France. When you enter the country, your passport is stamped with a temporary tourist **visa** that's good for 90 days of travel within France. If you plan to stay longer, contact any French consulate in the

United States before you leave to get a specific visa, or any U.S. consulate once you are abroad.

If you're a resident of Canada, you can pick up a passport application at one of 33 regional passport offices, most travel agencies, and online at www.dfait-maeci.gc.ca/passport. The Canadian passport is valid for 5 years and costs C$85. Children younger than 16 must have their own passports; however, if you hold a valid Canadian passport issued before December 11, 2001, that bears the name of your child, the passport remains valid for you and your child until it expires. Applications must be accompanied by two identical passport-sized photographs and proof of Canadian citizenship. You can also get your passport from the central **Passport Office,** Department of Foreign Affairs and International Trade, Ottawa, Canada K1A 0G3 (☎ **800-567-6868**). Processing takes ten days if you apply in person, about four weeks by mail.

Residents of the United Kingdom and Ireland need only an identity card, not a passport, to travel to other European Union member countries. However, if you have a passport, you can't go wrong by carrying it.

Australian residents can pick up a passport application at a post office or download one from the government Web site at www.passports. gov.au. You must schedule an interview at the passport office to present your application materials; call the **Australian Passport Information Service** at ☎ **131-232** for more information. Passports for adults are A$144, and for seniors and those younger than 18 years of age, A$72. A $60 processing fee is added to guarantee issue of a passport in 48 hours.

New Zealand citizens can download a passport application form from the site www.passports.govt.nz, pick up an application at any travel agency, or apply through the **Passports Office** at ☎ **0800-225-050.** Passports for adults are NZ$80; for children younger than 16 years old, NZ$40. It takes 10 days to process a standard application, three days and NZ$160 adult, NZ$120 child, for an urgent passport.

Always keep a photocopy of the inside page of your passport with your picture packed separately from your wallet or purse. In the event your passport is lost or stolen, the photocopy can help speed up the replacement process. When traveling in a group, never let one person carry all the passports. If the passports are stolen, obtaining new ones can be much more difficult, because at least one person in a group needs to be able to prove his or her identity to identify the others.

If you're a U.S. citizen and either lose or have your passport stolen in Paris, go to the Consulate of the American Embassy at 2 rue St. Florentin, 1er (☎ **01-43-12-22-22;** Métro: Concorde). Canadians in the same circumstances need to visit the Consulate of the Canadian Embassy, 35 av. Montaigne, 8e (☎ **01-44-43-29-00;** Métro: Franklin-D-Roosevelt or Alma Marceau). Australians must go to the Ambassade d'Australie at 4 rue Jean-Rey, 15e (☎ **01-40-59-33-00;** Métro: Bir-Hakeim). New Zealanders need to visit the New Zealand Embassy, 7*Ter* rue Léonard de Vinci, 16e (☎ **01-45-01-43-43,** ext. 280, from 9 a.m. to 1 p.m.; Métro: Victor-Hugo).

Playing It Safe with Travel and Medical Insurance

Considering three primary kinds of travel insurance — trip cancellation, medical, and lost luggage insurance — is a good idea.

Trip cancellation insurance is always a good idea whenever you pay a large portion of your vacation expenses upfront, but medical insurance and lost luggage insurance aren't really necessary for most travelers. Your existing health insurance should cover you if you get sick while you're on vacation, but be sure to check your policy before leaving home to find out exactly what it promises. Similarly, homeowner's insurance should cover stolen luggage whenever you have off-premises theft. Check your existing policies thoroughly or contact your insurance agent before buying any additional coverage. If you're a renter, remember that renter's insurance doesn't typically cover property that has left the premises, but you can buy insurance with one of the recommended companies in the listing that follows. The airlines are responsible for $2,500 on domestic flights (and $9.07 per pound, up to $640, on international flights), if they lose your luggage. If you plan to carry anything more valuable than that, keep it in your carry-on bag. Some credit cards (American Express and certain gold and platinum Visa and MasterCards, for example) offer automatic flight insurance against death or dismemberment in case of an airplane crash.

If you still think you need more insurance, try one of the following reputable issuers of travel insurance:

- ✔ **Access America: ☎ 866-807-3982;** Fax: 800-346-9265; Internet: www.accessamerica.com; E-mail: service@accessamerica.com

- ✔ **Travelex Insurance Services:** Internet in the United States, www.travelex-insurance.com; in Australia, www.travelex.com.au; in the United Kingdom, www.travelex.co.uk; and in New Zealand, www.travelex.co.nz

- ✔ **Travel Guard International: ☎ 800-826-4919;** Internet: www.travel-guard.com

✓ **Travel Insured International, Inc.:** ☎ **800-243-3174;** Internet: www.travelinsured.com

Don't pay for more insurance than you need. For example, if you only need trip cancellation insurance, don't purchase coverage for lost or stolen property. Trip cancellation insurance costs approximately 6% to 8% of the total value of your vacation.

Staying Healthy When You Travel

Apart from how getting sick can ruin your vacation, finding a doctor you trust when you're away from home can be difficult. Bring all your medications with you and a prescription for more if you're worried that you may run out. If you wear contact lenses, bring an extra pair in case you lose one. And don't forget remedies for common travelers' ailments like upset stomach or diarrhea.

If you already have health insurance, check with your provider to find out the extent of your coverage outside your home area. Be sure to carry your identification card in your wallet. And if you're worried that your existing policy won't be sufficient, purchase medical insurance for more comprehensive coverage (see previous "Playing It Safe with Travel and Medical Insurance" section).

If you suffer from a chronic illness, talk to your doctor before taking the trip. For certain conditions, such as epilepsy, diabetes, or a heart condition, wearing a *Medic Alert identification tag* immediately alerts any doctor to your condition and gives the doctor access to your medical records through Medic Alert's 24-hour hotline. Membership is $35, with an annual renewal fee of $20. Contact the Medic Alert Foundation at ☎ **888-633-4298** or the Web site at www.medicalert.org.

The French government pays 70% of the cost of doctor visits, and its national health insurance covers 99% of France's population. Visitors needing medical care in France find that same-day appointments are easily made, and patient fees are relatively inexpensive. Patients almost always have to pay upfront, unless they're citizens of European Union countries with reciprocal medical arrangements. U.S. health insurance companies usually reimburse most of the cost of treating illnesses in foreign countries; make sure to keep all your receipts.

If you do get sick, ask the concierge at your hotel to recommend a local doctor — even his or her own doctor, if necessary. You can also call SOS Medecins (☎ **01-43-37-77-77**), a 24-hour service. Ask for an English-speaking doctor. The **Centre Médicale Europe,** 44 rue d'Amsterdam, 9e (☎ **01-42-81-93-33**), is another good and efficient option. It has a host of specialists, and foreigners pay only about 20€

for a consultation. If you're in urgent need of a dentist, try **SOS Urgences Stomatologique Dentaire,** 87 bd. Port-Royal (☎ **01-43-36-36-00**).

Renting a Car in Paris (Extreme Sports Aficionados, This Is for You)

In the Robert DeNiro movie, *Ronin,* the bad guys in a BMW are fleeing from the good guys in a Mercedes through the center of Paris. The BMW speeds through traffic the wrong way with the Mercedes in hot pursuit, and after nearly ten nail-biting minutes, one of the cars flips over (I won't tell you which one) in a flaming crash. To the uninitiated, simply driving a car in Paris makes you feel like you're in this Paris chase. Why? Parisian drivers are ruthlessly aggressive. Traffic is dense. Roundabouts pop up everywhere, and cars seem to hurtle at you from the left — no better example than the circle called Étoile that surrounds the Arc de Triomphe, where cars enter and exit from *12 different locations* at high speeds. Parking is difficult, both in terms of finding a space and the size of the spaces available. Most hotels, except luxury ones, don't have garages, and if you drive to Paris from somewhere else, you'll find that a limited-access roadway called the *périphérique* circles the city, and its exits aren't numbered. Because the Paris Métro is one of the world's best urban transportation systems, having a car in Paris seems highly unnecessary. Even day-trips described in Chapter 21 are easily accessible by public transportation.

If you must drive in Paris, make sure that you have a copilot helping you navigate the streets. Children, by law, are required to sit in the back, and backseat passengers must wear seat belts. And remember that the majority of rentals available in France (and, indeed, most of Europe) have manual (stick shift) transmissions. In fact, you'll probably end up paying more for a car whenever you request an automatic transmission. The major highways (*autoroutes*) to Paris are the **A1** from the north (UK and Belgium); the **A13** from Normandy and other points in northwest France; the **A109** from Spain and the southwest; the **A7** from the Alps, the Riviera, and Italy; and the **A4** from eastern France. At the beginning and end of long weekends, school breaks, and August summer vacations, these roads become parking lots.

When you rent a car, try doing so for three days or more, because the cost usually works out to be less per day than renting for one day, with unlimited mileage thrown in. Reserve before you leave home (make sure to print out your reservation!), and keep in mind that government taxes are calculated at an eye-popping 20.6% of the total contract, collision damage insurance tacks on 15€ to 20€ per day, gas is very expensive, and a surcharge of about 15€ is assessed when you pick up the car at the airport.

Car rental agencies in Paris include

- ✔ **Avis,** gare d'Austerlitz, 13e (☎ **01-45-84-22-10;** Internet: www. avis.com). A compact car, such as a Renault Megane, that seats four runs about 86€ per day before tax and other related costs.

- ✔ **Hertz France,** gare de l'Est, 10e (☎ **01-42-05-50-43;** Internet: www.hertz.com). A Ford Focus costs about 113€ per day with all taxes and related costs.

- ✔ **National,** gare de Lyon, 12e (☎ **01-40-04-90-04;** Internet: www.nationalcar.com). A compact four-door car that seats four, such as an Opel Astra, costs about 74.25€ per day before tax.

Making Reservations and Getting Tickets in Advance

Paris's cultural and entertainment scene is hot, and you need to book early for opera and ballet performances, classical music concerts, and some museum exhibitions. You also need make reservations ahead of time when you want to dine at sought-after restaurants (see Chapter 14 for the ones that require early bookings). The most popular walking tours (see Chapter 18) also need to be booked in advance, because waiting until you arrive in the city may mean you get shut out.

For information on major cultural events, begin from home on the Web with the **French Government Tourist Office** (www.francetourism. com), the **Office de Tourisme et de Congrès de Paris** (www.paris-touristoffice.com), and the **Maison de la France** (www.france guide.com). You can also try **Culture Kiosque** (www.culturekiosque. com) for excellent magazine-style sites in English about opera, dance, and major museum exhibits around the world, including schedules, reviews, and phone numbers for ordering tickets. Culture Kiosque also features an online magazine in English, *JazzNet,* which includes a calendar of upcoming jazz club dates in Paris. A free monthly English-language magazine published in Paris, the *Paris Free Voice* (http://parisvoice. com), features an events calendar and reviews of current opera, dance, and theater. **Bonjour Paris** (www.bonjourparis.com) also lists the week's top events.

You can also try these strategies to secure hard-to-get tickets to music, dance, and opera performances:

- ✔ **Call the box office.** Call the venue's box office directly and pay over the phone with your credit card to purchase tickets. Tickets can be sent to your hotel in your name, or held at the box office. See Chapters 22 and 23 for phone numbers to specific venues.

✔ **Contact your hotel's concierge.** If you're planning to stay at a hotel with a staff concierge, phone or fax ahead and ask him or her to obtain tickets for the productions you desire as early as possible, specifying your preferred date with a couple of backup dates, and the maximum amount you're willing to spend. Expect to pay handsomely for hard-to-land tickets, and don't forget to tip the concierge for his or her efforts (20€ discreetly slipped into an envelope that you present to him or her upon receipt of your tickets is appropriate).

✔ **Try a ticket broker.** One of the most respected international ticket agencies is **Keith Prowse,** 234 West 44th St., Suite 1000, New York, NY 10036 (☎ **800-669-8687;** 212-398-4175 in New York, Fax: 212-302-4251; Internet: www.keithprowse.com, E-mail: tickets@ keithprowse.com). Prowse almost always has excellent seats to upcoming musical concerts, ballets, operas, and some sports events. You can also prepurchase city tours, museum passes, and transportation discounts through Prowse.

✔ **Check the Web.** Find out what's going on in Paris. You can get box office phone numbers, and in some cases, you may be able to link to sites and buy tickets directly. *Time Out's* Paris Web site (www. timeout.com) lists events in English and updates them weekly. If you can read French, have a look at the online version of Paris's weekly entertainment guide, *Pariscope* (www.pariscope.fr).

After you're in Paris, you can find several local publications providing up-to-the-minute listings of performances and other evening entertainment. Foremost among these is ***Pariscope: Une Semaine de Paris*** (0.40€), a weekly guide with thorough listings of movies, plays, ballet, art exhibits, clubs, and more. It contains an English-language insert written by staff in *Time Out's* Paris office and can be found at any newsstand. ***L'Officiel des Spectacles*** (0.35€), also a weekly guide, and the major newspapers, *Le Monde* and *Le Figaro,* contain good articles and listings, although they don't provide information in English. Costs for events vary depending on who is performing what on which day of the week. Call the theaters for information, or consult *Pariscope* and the other entertainment listings.

Many concert, theater, and dance tickets are sold through **FNAC** stores and at the box office. FNAC outlets number more than a dozen throughout Paris; the most prominent is 74 av. des Champs-Elysées (Métro: George V). You can also reserve by phone (☎ **08-92-68-36-22**) Monday through Friday from 9 a.m. to 8 p.m., Saturday 10 a.m. to 5 p.m. **Virgin Megastore,** 52 av. des Champs-Elysées (Métro: Franklin-D-Roosevelt), is another reputable ticket seller. The store is open Monday through Saturday from 10 a.m. to midnight, Sunday noon to midnight, and its tickets-by-phone number is ☎ **01-49-53-50-00.**

Packing It Up

Start by taking everything you think you need and laying it out on the bed. Then get rid of half of it; you won't have space in your suitcase or your hotel room for that much.

The trick to packing light is bringing items that are versatile — to which you can add a jacket, scarf, or jewelry. This technique yields more mileage from your wardrobe. French women who are so elegantly put together dress in such a way all the time. If you bring separates in neutral colors that can make several outfits, you never need worry about something to wear, and you always look smart.

To conserve baggage space, limit yourself to two pairs of shoes. No exceptions! One pair needs to be for walking. Keep in mind that Paris is a more formal city where sneakers are looked down upon in many places (nothing screams tourist more than a pair of bright white sneakers). Try for a "casual Fridays at work" look.

The same holds true for evenings. Think a notch dressier than what you normally wear out to dinner (even more if your normal evening out attire usually consists of sweats and a Yankees cap). Even at casual neighborhood bistros, most men wear sport jackets, and women wear skirts or smart pants at dinner.

Don't forget those handy resealable plastic sandwich bags — they make great toiletry cases, solve the problems of leaky items, and if you have small kids, you can put a damp washcloth in one to clean up little messes. You can also save space by buying travel-sized plastic bottles at the drugstore to fill with shampoo, conditioner, and other liquid beauty essentials.

When packing your suitcase, remember that filling your shoes with small items like socks and underwear can help save space. Fit the rest of your small items around your shoes, and pack breakable items between several layers of clothing. Dry cleaners' plastic bags are great for protecting items that wrinkle easily.

In addition to sneakers, leave your cellphone at home — unless you have one of the phones that adapt to the GSM norm on which the European cellphone system works. And as for appliances, not only are they clumsy to carry around, you need an electrical adapter to use them — European current runs on 210–220V, while American current is 110V, 60 cycles — and a transformer to bring the voltage down and the cycles up. If you must bring an appliance, be sure that it runs on dual voltage.

Blending in: Dressing like a local

Male tourists usually find it easy to look like a local. The staple casual look for Parisian men is a blazer over a button-down shirt and khakis (or sometimes nicely pressed Levis) with loafers or other casual shoes that don't fall into the sneaker category. The tie is optional. Men with more formal careers wear beautifully tailored suits and often carry small leather briefcases that one *Seinfeld* episode jokingly referred to as "the male handbag."

For women, obtaining that *Parisienne* look is a bit harder. In the first place, it seems French women are born understanding how to put outfits together with that *je ne sais quoi* that few foreigners can imitate. Accessorizing is the key. For nights out, bring feminine clothes in neutral colors and accessorize with a pretty scarf or piece of jewelry. For the big nights out, you can never go wrong with a little black dress and pearls. For walking during the day, avoid being instantly picked out as a tourist by investing in a pair of comfortable walking shoes that are dressy enough to wear with a casual skirt. (Many American stores carry comfortable, casual skirts that are perfect for a visit to a park and lunch at a restaurant afterward.) Wear a small purse with long straps diagonally across your body for a fashionable and safe way to carry your belongings.

Leave the sneakers, T-shirts, fanny packs, shorts, sweat suits, and tennis visors at home. I recently saw an elderly Parisienne stare disapprovingly at two American women wearing shorts on the Métro, proving that in the most visited (and fashionable) city in the world, clothes matter.

And, finally, if you have room, fold an empty carry-on bag into your luggage. Paris is a shopper's paradise, and you may be surprised at how much you have to bring home.

For more tips on packing, consult **Travelite** (www.travelite.org), which gives advice on packing light, choosing luggage, and selecting appropriate travel wear. Its printable packing lists are very helpful.

Part III
Settling into Paris

WHILE ON VACATION IN PARIS, SYLVIA FINDS HERSELF MYSTERIOUSLY DRAWN TO A FELLOW TRAVELER ON THE TRAIN.

In this part . . .

This section helps you go from point A to point B without wasting time and money. Chapter 10 guides you from the airport to your hotel, describes the most popular neighborhoods, and tells you where to go for information after you're in Paris. Need to know how to get around by subway, taxi, bus, and on foot? Read Chapter 11 and prepare to start zipping around the city in no time. Chapter 12 helps you make sense of the euro, tells you where you can get cash in Paris, and gives you emergency phone numbers to call if your wallet or purse is lost or stolen.

Chapter 10

Arriving and Getting Oriented

● ●

In This Chapter

▶ Navigating passport control and Customs

▶ Securing transportation to your hotel

▶ Getting to know Paris by neighborhood

▶ Finding info after you arrive

● ●

*T*he Paris experience begins as soon as your plane lands at the airport — all the sights and sounds are unmistakably French. The smell of strong coffee and fresh croissants wafts out of airport cafés. Luggage carts are free! Little dogs peek out of bags or prance at the end of leashes. People dress more formally than at home. And, yes, that harsh burning scent is the unmistakable odor of black tobacco — people smoke in the airport terminal at Charles-de-Gaulle (but not at Orly Airport). It all may seem a little astonishing, especially when you arrive at the spaceship-looking Charles-de-Gaulle Aérogare 1 — and that's because you've probably landed at some ungodly early morning hour. But, the important thing is you've arrived! Now you can move on to the first item of the day — getting from the airport to your hotel.

Navigating Your Way through Passport Control and Customs

Most visitors to Paris land at Charles-de-Gaulle Airport, the larger, busier, and more modern airport, commonly known as CDG and some- times called Roissy–Charles-de-Gaulle. It's located 14½ miles (23km) northeast of downtown Paris. Nearly all direct flights from North America land at Charles-de-Gaulle. Bilevel Terminal 1 (Aérogare 1) is the older and smaller of the two terminals and is used by foreign air- lines. Narrow escalators and moving sidewalks connect its podlike glass terminals. The bright and spacious Terminal 2 (Aérogare 2) is divided into halls A through F and used by Air France, domestic and intra-European airlines, and some foreign airlines, including Air Canada. A free shuttle bus (*navette*) connects the two terminals.

Signs in French and English in both terminals direct you to Customs, baggage claim, and transportation to the city. Staff at information desks also are on hand to answer questions.

Two lines are set up for passport control, one for European Union nationals and the other for everyone else. These lines can move quite fast or horrendously slow; it usually depends on the clerk checking your passport and riffling through your luggage.

When passing through Customs, keep in mind that restrictions are different for citizens of the European Union than they are for citizens of non-EU countries. As a non-EU national, you can bring in 200 cigarettes or 100 cigarillos or 50 cigars or 250 grams of smoking tobacco duty-free. You can also bring in 2 liters of wine and 1 liter of alcohol of more than 38.80 proof. In addition, you can bring in 50 grams of perfume, ¼ liter of toilet water, 500 grams of coffee, and 100 grams of tea. Travelers 15 years old and older can also bring in 171€ in other goods; for those 14 years of age and younger, the limit is 85.75€. (See Chapter 19 for what you're allowed to bring home.) Because you probably aren't going to need to make a claim, you should be waved through by an officer pretty quickly. Customs officers do, however, pull random travelers over to check luggage. Whenever that happens to you, don't be offended; be polite and as helpful as you can, and if you don't speak French, let them know.

Regardless of the terminal, you need euros to get from the airport into Paris. You can find ATMs in the arrivals areas of the airports and *bureaux de change,* where you can exchange dollars for euros, but you're better off buying and bringing 100 euros from your bank at home. Airport ATMs are notorious for being broken when you need them most, and the airport bureaux de change are just as notorious for their bad rates of exchange.

Getting from Charles-de-Gaulle Airport to Your Hotel

You can travel to and from the airport by several different means, and the amount of text here notwithstanding, they're all easy.

Taking a taxi

Probably the easiest, but certainly not the cheapest, mode of transportation to your hotel from the airport is by **taxi.** A cab into town from Charles-de-Gaulle takes 40 to 50 minutes, depending on traffic, and costs about 40€ from 7 a.m. to 8 p.m., and about 40% more at other times. Taxi drivers are required to turn the meter on and charge the price indicated plus 0.90€ for each piece of luggage stowed in the trunk. If your French is poor or nonexistent, writing down the name and full address of your hotel is a good idea. The five-digit postal code is the most important morsel of information, because, it tells the driver to which arrondissement to drive you. Check the meter before you pay — rip-offs of arriving tourists are not uncommon. Whenever you strongly think that you may have been overcharged, demand a receipt (which drivers are obligated to provide) and contact the Paris Préfecture of Police (☎ **01-53-73-53-73** or 01-53-71-53-71).

Here's where you find the taxi stands at Charles-de-Gaulle:

- ✔ **CDG Terminal 1:** Exit 16, arrivals level
- ✔ **CDG Terminals 2A and 2C:** 2A Exit 6, 2C Exit 6
- ✔ **CDG Terminals 2B and 2D:** 2B Exit 8, 2D Exit 8
- ✔ **CDG Terminal 2F:** Exit 0.10, arrivals level

Taking a shuttle

If you don't want to schlep your bags through Paris's streets and Métro stations, taking an airport shuttle is definitely the way to go. Although more expensive than airport buses and trains, shuttles are much cheaper and roomier than taxis. And you can reserve a seat in advance and pay by credit card. **World Shuttle,** 13 rue Voltaire, 94400 Vitry-sur-Seine (☎ **01-46-80-14-67** or 06-83-85-23-45; Fax: 01-49-62-78-79) costs 23€ for one person, 14€ per person for two or more, and 90€ set price for a group of seven or eight people from Charles-de-Gaulle and Orly.

PariShuttle, 128 bis av Paris, 94800 Villejuif (☎ **01-43-90-91-91;** Fax: 01-43-90-91-10; Internet: www.parishuttle.com) offers a similar serv-ice. While you wait for your bags, call PariShuttle's toll-free number to confirm pickup (☎ **08-00-63-34-40**). You're picked up in a minivan at Orly or Charles-de-Gaulle and taken to your hotel for 23€ for one person, 17€ per person for groups of two to five people, and 15€ per person for six to eight people. Book ten days in advance and pay only 13€ per person.

Both companies accept Visa and MasterCard.

Riding the rails

A good option when you're not overloaded with baggage and you want to keep down your expenses is to take the suburban commuter train to the Métro. **RER** (Réseau Express Régional) **Line B** stops near Terminals 1 and 2. Easy, cheap, and convenient, you can ride both to and from the airport from 5 a.m. to midnight Monday through Friday, and 7 a.m. to 9 p.m. weekends.

Free shuttle buses connect terminals CDG 1 and CDG 2 to the RER train station. You can pick up the free shuttle bus at:

- ✔ **CDG Terminal 1:** Follow RER signs to exit on arrivals level
- ✔ **CDG Terminal 2A:** Exit A8
- ✔ **CDG Terminal 2B:** Exit B6
- ✔ **CDG Terminal 2C:** Exit C8
- ✔ **CDG Terminal 2D:** Exit D6
- ✔ **CDG Terminal 2F:** Exit 2.06

You can also take a walkway to the RER station — ask an airport employee or look for the round RER logo. (RER is pronounced "air-uh-air" in French.)

Buy the **RER plus Métro** ticket, which costs 7.60€, at the RER ticket counter and hang onto it in case of ticket inspection. (You can be fined if you can't produce your ticket for an inspector.) In any case, you need your ticket later to get off the RER system and onto the Métro.

Depending where your hotel is located, you'll exit either on the Right or the Left Bank. From the airport station, trains depart about every 15 minutes for the half-hour trip into town and stop on the **Right Bank** at Gare du Nord and Châtelet–Les Halles, and on the **Left Bank** at St-Michel, Luxembourg, Port-Royal, and Denfert-Rochereau, before heading south out of the city.

Boarding the bus

A bus is better than the RER if

- ✔ You're heading into Paris during off-peak driving hours.
- ✔ Your hotel is located near one of the drop-off points. *Note:* From the Charles-de-Gaulle Airport, this option won't work for most of the accommodations I recommend in this book. I suggest hotels only within the first eight arrondissements. Of those, the bus is convenient only for the 2e and 8e arrondissements. Nevertheless, if you're staying in those areas, or if you happen to be staying farther out from the center of town, the bus may be the right option for you. If a bus isn't convenient, check out the door-to-door airport shuttle services in the earlier "Taking a shuttle" section.

If your hotel is located on the **Right Bank,** in the **8e, 16e,** or **17e** arrondissements, take **Air France coach Line 2,** which stops at rue Gouvion Saint-Cyr at Porte Maillot before ending up at 1 av. Carnot at place Charles-de-Gaulle–Étoile, the name for the huge traffic roundabout at the Arc de Triomphe. The bus costs 10€ one-way and runs every 15 minutes from 5:40 a.m. to 11:00 p.m. (from 6 a.m. to 11 p.m.

back to the airport). You needn't have flown on an Air France flight to use the service, and tickets are available right on the bus. The trip from the airport into the city and vice versa takes about 40 minutes in light traffic, such as on weekend mornings. During weekday morning rush hour, however, the same trip can take twice as long, if not longer. Pick up the coach from:

- ✔ **CDG Terminal 1:** Exit 34, arrivals level

- ✔ **CDG Terminals 2A and 2C:** Exit 5

- ✔ **CDG Terminals 2B and 2D:** Exit 6

- ✔ **CDG Terminal 2F:** Exit 0.07, arrivals level

If your hotel is located on the **Right Bank** near the **Bastille (11e** or **12e)** or on the **Left Bank** in **Montparnasse (14e),** take the **Air France Line 4** coach, which stops at bd. Diderot in front of the Gare de Lyon before ending up on rue du Commandant Mouchotte near the back of the Gare de Montparnasse. The bus costs 11.50€ one-way and runs every 30 minutes from 7:00 a.m. to 9:30 p.m. both to and from the airport. It takes about 50 minutes to get from the airport into the city in light traffic. Catch this coach from:

- ✔ **CDG Terminal 1:** Exit 34, arrivals level

- ✔ **CDG Terminals 2A and 2C:** Exit 2 from Terminal 2C

- ✔ **CDG Terminals 2B and 2D:** Exit 2 from Terminal 2B

- ✔ **CDG Terminal 2F:** Exit 0.07, arrivals level

Take the **Roissybus** if your hotel is on the **Right Bank** near the **Opéra** (2e or 9e). It costs 8€ and leaves every 15 minutes from the airport between 6 a.m. and 11 p.m. (from 5:45 a.m. to 11:00 p.m. back to the airport). The drop-off point is on rue Scribe, a block from the **Opéra Garnier** near American Express. You can get to your destination in 45 to 50 minutes in regular traffic. Buy your tickets in the small office next to where the bus is parked. Pick up this coach from:

- ✔ **CDG Terminal 1:** Exit 30, arrivals level

- ✔ **CDG Terminals 2A and 2C:** Exit 9 from Terminal 2A

- ✔ **CDG Terminals 2B and 2D:** Exit 11 from Terminal 2D

- ✔ **CDG Terminal 2F:** Exit 0.08, arrivals level

If You Fly into Orly

Orly Airport, 8½ miles (14km) south of the city, has two terminals — **Ouest** (West) and **Sud** (South) — and English speakers find the terminals easy to navigate: French domestic flights land at Orly Ouest, and intra-European and intercontinental flights land at Orly Sud.

Shuttle buses connect these terminals, and other shuttles connect them to Charles-de-Gaulle every 30 minutes or so. A tourist information desk is conveniently located on the arrivals level of both terminals.

Like Charles-de-Gaulle Airport, two lines are set up for passport control; one for European Union nationals, one for visitors carrying passports from all other countries, and you should be waved through Customs. (See the previous section, "Navigating Your Way through Passport Control and Customs" for information about what you can bring into France.) If an official asks to inspect your luggage, be courteous and helpful, and let him or her know if you don't speak French.

Taking a taxi

A cab from Orly into Paris costs about 20€ to 25€, depending on traffic, and takes anywhere from 25 minutes to an hour. The taxi stand at Orly Sud is just outside Exit L; at Orly Ouest it's at Exit I. The same advice as when taking a taxi from Charles-de-Gaulle holds true here: Write down the full name and address of your hotel for the driver. And remember that cabs charge 0.90€ for each piece of luggage put in the trunk.

Busing is best — sometimes

Take the **Air France coach Line 1** if your hotel is located on the **Left Bank** near Les Invalides (7e). Buses leave Orly Sud at Exit K, Platform 6 and Orly Ouest at Exit D, arrivals level every 12 to 15 minutes. The trip takes 30 minutes and costs 5.50€. You can request that the bus stop at Montparnasse-Duroc (14e).

The cheapest trip into town is on the **Jetbus.** You take this bus from Orly to Métro station Villejuif–Louis Aragon in south Paris (13e). It costs 4.80€ for the 15-minute journey. Beginning at 6:34 a.m., the bus leaves every 15 minutes from Orly Sud, Exit H, and Platform 2 and from Orly Quest at Exit C on the arrivals level. The bus departs Paris for Orly from 6:15 a.m. to 10:15 p.m. An **Orly bus** also operates from 6 a.m. to 11:30 p.m. from Exit J, arrivals level at Orly Ouest, and from Exit H Platform 4 at Orly Sud to the Left Bank's Denfert-Rochereau station. It costs 5.50€ for the 25-minute journey. It departs Paris for Orly from 5:35 a.m. to 11:00 p.m.

Taking the train

You can also take the **RER C line,** which is a bit of a hassle. You catch a free shuttle bus from Exit G, Platform 1 at Orly Sud and Exit G on the arrivals level at Orly Ouest to the **Rungis** station, where RER C trains leave every 15 minutes for **Gare d'Austerlitz** (13e). A one-way fare is 5.15€, and the trip into the city takes 30 minutes, making various stops along the Seine on the **Left Bank.**

If you're staying on the **Right Bank,** you can take the **RER B line** to **Châtelet** Métro station. From Orly Sud, it departs from Exit K near the baggage-claim area; from Orly Ouest, it leaves from Exit W on the departures level. You connect at the **Antony** RER station where you board the RER B train to Paris. Hold onto the ticket because you will need it to get into the Métro/RER system. A trip to the Châtelet station on the Right Bank takes about 30 minutes and 8.65€. Once in Paris, the train stops at **Denfert-Rochereau, Port-Royal, Luxembourg,** and **St-Michel** on the Left Bank, and then crosses to the Right Bank for stops at **Châtelet** and **Gare du Nord.**

You can avoid lines by buying your tickets from a machine if you have euro coins with you.

Figuring Out the Neighborhoods

You arrive at your hotel, check in, and maybe unpack a little. But taking a nap prolongs your jet lag. So, go out and act like a Parisian by having a cup of coffee at a café before getting ready to explore. *Note:* Those little shots of espresso you get in Paris cafés have less caffeine than a mug of American-style coffee or a cup of tea!

The Seine River divides Paris into two halves: the **Right Bank** (*Rive Droite*) on the north side of the river and the **Left Bank** (*Rive Gauche*) on the south side of the river. The larger Right Bank is where you find the city's business sector, stately monuments, and high-fashion industry. The Left Bank has the publishing houses, universities, and a reputation as bohemian because students, philosophers, and creative types have been congregating there for centuries. Two of the city's tallest monuments are on the Left Bank — the **Tour Montparnasse** (that lonely tall black building hovering on the edge of the city) and the **Eiffel Tower. Sacré Coeur,** the white wedding-cake of a basilica (church) on the hill overlooking Paris, is on the Right Bank, and so are Notre-Dame and St-Chapelle, although neither is technically on any bank. They're actually on an island in the Seine.

The city is divided into 20 numbered *arrondissements* (municipal districts). And although visitors tend to think of Paris in terms of neighborhood names, Parisians think of the city in terms of arrondissement numbers. For example, ask a hometowner where he works, and he's more likely to say "in the 5th" and not "in the Latin Quarter." The layout of these districts follows a distinct pattern. The first (abbreviated 1er for *premiere*) arrondissement is the dead center of Paris, comprising an area around the Louvre. From there, the rest of the districts spiral outward, clockwise, in ascending order. The lower the arrondissement number, the more central the location. To get a better idea of what I'm talking about, consult the nearby "Paris Neighborhoods" map.

Paris Neighborhoods

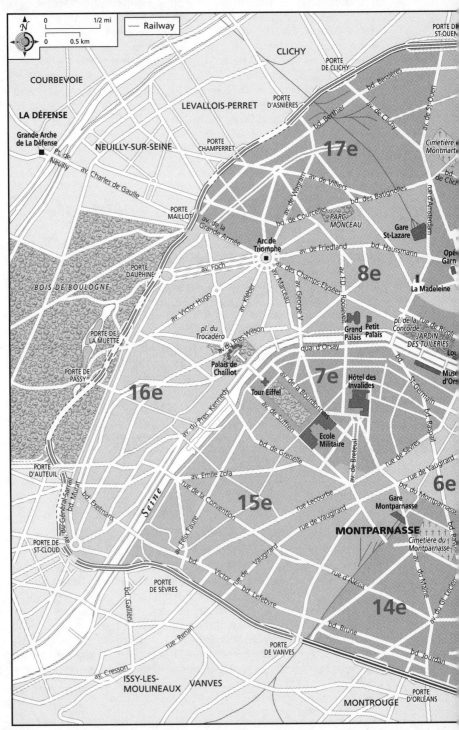

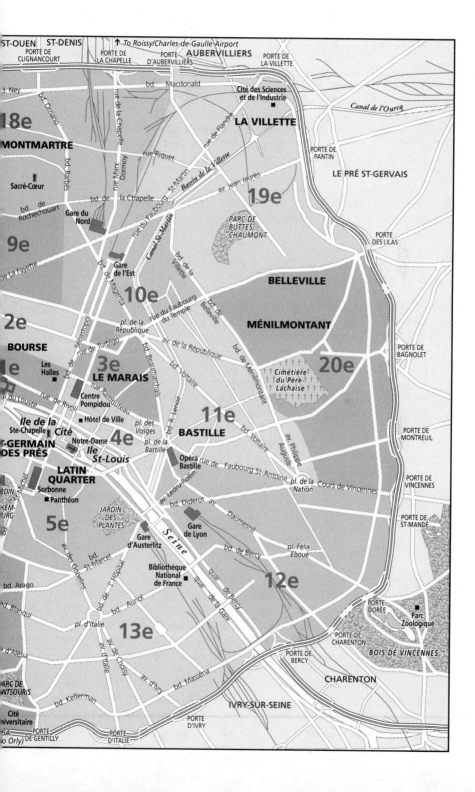

Arrondissement numbers are key to locating an address in Paris. And this book lists addresses the way they appear in Paris, with the arrondissement number following the specific street address (for instance, 29 rue de Rivoli, 4e, would be in the fourth arrondissement). Arrondissement numbers are on street signs and are indicated by the last two digits of the postal code. For instance, an address with a postal code of 75007 would be located in the seventh arrondissement. Once you know in which arrondissement an address is located, finding that spot is much easier. Numbers on buildings running parallel to the Seine usually follow the course of the river east to west. On north-south streets, numbering begins at the river.

Neighborhoods in the following sections are listed first by arrondissement, and then by neighborhood name. Only the better-known arrondissements — meaning the ones that you're most likely to stay in or visit — are mentioned.

On the Right Bank

The following are the neighborhoods you're likely to visit on the Right Bank.

1er Arr.: Musée du Louvre/Palais-Royal/Les Halles

One of the world's greatest art museums (some say *the* greatest), the **Louvre** still lures all visitors to Paris to the 1er arrondissement. You can see the contrast between many of the city's elegant addresses along the rue de Rivoli and arched arcades under which all kinds of touristy junk is sold. Walk through the **Jardin des Tuileries,** the most formal garden of Paris, and take in the classic beauty, opulence, and wealth of the **place Vendôme,** which is home to the Ritz Hotel. Browse the arcaded shops and view the striped columns and seasonal art on display in the garden of the **Palais Royal,** once the home to Cardinal Richelieu. The slightly seedy **Forum des Halles,** an above- and below-ground shopping and entertainment center, is also here. This arrondissement tends to be crowded, and hotel prices are higher during Paris's high tourist season (in early fall) because the area is so convenient.

2e Arr.: La Bourse

Often overlooked by tourists, the 2e houses the **Bourse** (stock exchange), and some of the pretty 19th-century covered shopping passageways. The district, lying between the Grands Boulevards and the rue Etienne Marcel, is also home to the Sentier area, where the garment trade is located, and wholesale fashion outlets abound. Sex shops and prostitutes line parts of the rue St-Denis.

3e Arr.: Le Marais

Le Marais (translated as "the swamp") is one of Paris's hippest neighborhoods, and one of the city's most popular attractions, the **Musée**

Picasso, and one of the more interesting museums, **Musée Carnavalet,** are located here. Paris's old Jewish neighborhood is located around the rue des Rosiers, and the rue Vieille-du-Temple is home to numerous gay bars and boutiques.

4e Arr.: Ile de la Cité/Ile St-Louis/Centre Pompidou

Aristocratic town houses, courtyards, and antiques shops, flower markets, the **Palais de Justice, Notre-Dame cathedral** and **Sainte-Chapelle,** the **Centre Georges Pompidou museum,** and the **place des Vosges** are on the two islands of the 4e, the Ile de la Cité and the Ile St-Louis — or very close by. The islands located in the middle of the Seine compose one of the prettiest, and most crowded, of Paris's arrondissements. The area around the Centre Pompidou is one of Paris's more eclectic; you see everyone from pierced and goth-style art students to chic Parisians sipping coffee at Café Beaubourg to tourists buying football shirts from one of the many souvenir stores.

8e Arr.: Champs-Elysées/Madeleine

The 8e is the heart of the Right Bank, and its showcase is the **Champs-Elysées.** The fashion houses, the most elegant hotels, expensive restaurants and shops, and the most fashionably attired Parisians are here. The Champs stretches from the **Arc de Triomphe** to the city's oldest monument, the Egyptian obelisk on **place de la Concorde.**

9e Arr.: Opéra Garnier/Pigalle

Everything, from the **Quartier de l'Opéra** to the strip joints of **Pigalle,** falls within the 9e, which was radically altered by Baron Haussmann's 19th-century redevelopment projects; his Grands Boulevards radiate through the district. You'll probably pay a visit to the 9e to shop at its famous department stores **Au Printemps** and **Galeries Lafayette.** Try to visit the **Opéra Garnier** (Paris Opera House), which recently reopened after an expensive restoration.

10e Arr.: Gare du Nord/Gare de l'Est

In the movie *Amélie,* the young heroine likes to skip stones on the Canal St-Martin, which is located here. Though most of this arrondissement is dreary (**Gare du Nord** and **Gare de l'Est** are two of the city's four main train stations), the canal's **quai de Valmy** and **quai de Jemmapes** are scenic, tree-lined promenades. The classic movie *Hotel du Nord* was also filmed here.

11e Arr.: Opéra Bastille

The 11e has few landmarks or famous museums, but the area has become a mecca for hordes of young Parisians looking for casual, inexpensive nightlife. Always crowded on weekends and in summer, the overflow retires to the steps of the **Opéra Bastille,** where inline skaters and skateboarders skate, and teens flirt.

16e Arr.: Trocadéro/Bois de Boulogne

This area of Paris is where the moneyed people live. Highlights include the **Bois de Boulogne,** the **Jardin du Trocadéro,** the **Musée de Balzac,** the **Musée Guimet** (famous for its Asian collections), and the **Cimetière de Passy,** resting place of Manet, Talleyrand, Giraudoux, and Debussy. One of the largest arrondissements, the 16e is known today for its exclusivity, its BCBG residents (*bon chic bon genre,* or yuppie), its upscale rents, and some rather posh (and, according to its critics, rather smug) residential boulevards. The arrondissement includes what some visitors consider the best place in Paris from which to view the Eiffel Tower, the **place du Trocadéro.**

18e Arr.: Montmartre

Montmartre, the **Moulin Rouge,** the **Basilica of Sacré-Coeur,** and the **place du Tertre** are only some of the attractions in this outer arrondissement. Take a walk through the winding old streets here, and you feel transported into another era. The city's most famous flea market, **Marché aux Puces de la Porte de St-Ouen,** on the arrondissement's outskirts, is another landmark, and so is the **Bateau-Lavoir,** where Picasso kept his studio.

On the Left Bank

The following are neighborhoods you're likely to visit on the Left Bank.

5e Arr.: Latin Quarter

Bookstores, schools, churches, nightclubs, student dives, Roman ruins, publishing houses, and expensive boutiques characterize this district, which is called "Latin" because students and professors at the Sorbonne, located here, once spoke Latin. Stroll along **quai de Montebello,** inspecting the inventories of the *bouquinistes* (booksellers), and wander the shops in the old streets of rue de la Huchette and rue de la Harpe (but don't eat here; you can find much better places). The 5e also stretches down to the **Panthéon,** and to the steep cobblestone rue Mouffetard behind it, where you can visit one of the city's best produce markets, eat at a variety of ethnic restaurants, or raise a glass in très cool Café Contrescarpe.

6e Arr.: St-Germain and the Luxembourg Gardens

The art school that turned away Rodin, the **École des Beaux-Arts,** is here, and so are some of the chicest designers around. But the secret of the district lies in discovering its narrow streets and hidden squares. Everywhere you turn in the district, you encounter famous historical and literary associations. For instance, the restaurant **Brasserie Lipp,** located here, is where Hemingway lovingly recalls eating potato salad in *A Moveable Feast,* and the **Café les Deux Magots** is depicted in the movie adaptation of Hemingway's *The Sun Also Rises.* The 6e takes in the **rue de Fleurus** where Gertrude Stein lived with Alice B. Toklas, and down the street, is the wonderful **Luxembourg Gardens,** probably local residents' most loved park. (Try to find the Statue of Liberty in the garden.)

7e Arr.: Near the Eiffel Tower and Musée d'Orsay

The city's most famous symbol, the **Eiffel Tower,** dominates the 7e, and part of the **St-Germain** neighborhood is here, too. The **Hôtel des Invalides,** which contains **Napoléon's Tomb** and the **Musée de l'Armée,** is also in the 7e, in addition to the **Musée Rodin** and the **Musée d'Orsay,** the world's premier showcase of 19th-century French art and culture. The Left Bank's only department store **Le Bon Marché** is also located here, and so is a warren of streets along which beautiful shoes, clothing, and objects for the home are sold.

13e Arr.: Butte-aux-Cailles and Chinatown

Although high rises dominate much of 13e, a nightlife scene is emerging on the dance barges along the **quai Tolbiac** (where the new Bibliothèque François Mitterand sits) and in the cozy network of winding streets that make up the **Butte-aux-Cailles** (literally hill of pebbles) neighborhood. The 13e has also become a lively hub for Paris's Asian community with Vietnamese and Chinese restaurants along **av. d'Ivry** and **av. de Choisy** next to stores selling all kinds of items from France's former colonies in Southeast Asia. The Chinese New Year Parade takes place here in late January or February.

14e Arr.: Montparnasse

Montparnasse is the former stomping ground of the "lost generation": Writers Gertrude Stein, Ernest Hemingway, Edna St. Vincent Millay, Ford Madox Ford, and other expatriates gathered here in the 1920s. After World War II, it ceased to be the center of intellectual life in Paris, but the memories linger in its cafés. Some of the world's most famous literary cafés, including **La Rotonde, Le Select, Le Dôme,** and **La Coupole,** are in the northern end of this large arrondissement, near the Rodin statue of Balzac at the junction of boulevard Montparnasse and boulevard Raspail. Some of those same literary giants (most notably Jean-Paul Sartre and Simone de Beauvoir) are buried nearby, in the Cimitière du Montparnasse. At its southern end, the arrondissement contains pleasant residential neighborhoods filled with well-designed apartment buildings, many built between 1910 and 1940.

Where to Get Information After You Arrive

The prime source of information is the **Office de Tourisme de Paris,** 127 av. des Champs-Elysées, 8e (☎ **08-92-68-31-12;** Fax: 01-49-52-53-00; Internet: www.paris-touristoffice.com; E-mail: info@paris-touristoffice.com; Métro: Charles-de-Gaulle–Étoile or George V).

The office is open daily from 9 a.m. to 8 p.m. (Sunday 11 a.m. to 7 p.m. November through April).

The Office de Tourisme has an auxiliary office at the Eiffel Tower (open May through September only, daily from 11 a.m. to 6 p.m.) and at the Gare de Lyon (Monday through Saturday from 8 a.m. to 8 p.m.). At the main and auxiliary offices, you can also reserve concert, theater, or cabaret tickets without an extra fee.

Chapter 11

Getting around Paris

• •

• •

You've arrived in Paris; now start exploring! How you get around depends on how much ground you need to cover in a given time frame, but you can use several modes of transportation during your trip. This chapter gives you pointers on how to master the public transportation system, how to find a cab when you need one most, and what to watch out for while walking.

Probably your best introduction to Paris, and to the way the city is laid out, is from the north tower at Notre-Dame. You can see the magnificent cathedral from many parts of the city, and a visit helps you get oriented. You will see that the river Seine is actually Paris's most important "street."

Getting Around by Métro

The best way to get around Paris is to walk, but for longer distances the Métro, or subway, rules.

The **Métropolitain** is fast, safe, and easy to navigate — pretty spry for a 103-year-old! Open from 5:45 a.m. to 12:45 a.m., it's an efficient and cheap way to get around. The only times you may want to avoid it are the hours between 7 to 10 a.m. and 6 to 8 p.m. — in other words, rush hour. Operated by the RATP (Régie Autonome des Transports Parisiens), the Métro has a total of 16 lines and more than 360 stations, making it likely that one is near your destination. The Métro is connected to the suburban commuter train, the **Réseau Express Régional (RER),** which connects downtown Paris with its airports and suburbs.

Navigating the Métro is easy, and you'll be a pro in no time. Here's what you do:

Using this book, figure out what station is the closest to where you are. For example, if you want to go to the Louvre and are in your hotel in the Latin Quarter, say the Familia, check the listing in this book for your hotel. Your nearest Métro station, or your starting point, is Jussieu. Look at the Métro map on the Cheat Sheet at the front of the book for the line that the Jussieu station is on. (Each end of the lines on the Métro map is marked with the number of the line.) The Jussieu station is on Line 7.

Then look for your destination station, the Louvre. You see that the Louvre has two stops: the Palais Royal-Musée du Louvre station on Line 7 and the Louvre Rivoli station on Line 14. Choose the Palais-Royal Musée du Louvre station, and you won't have to change trains.

Walk to the Métro station; you can recognize it either by an elegant Art Nouveau gateway reading MÉTROPOLITAIN or by a big yellow M sign. Unless otherwise marked, all Métro stations have a ticket booth, where you purchase from an attendant a single ticket (1.30†) or a group of 10 tickets called a carnet (kar-nay; 9.60†). Most stations also have machines where you can purchase tickets (bills and coins only). Every Métro stop has maps of the system; you can get portable maps by asking at the ticket booths. Near the exits, you usually can find a plan du quartier, a very detailed pictorial map of the streets and buildings surrounding the station, with all exits marked. A good idea is to consult the plan du quartier before you exit the system, especially at very large stations. You may want to use a different exit to reach the other side of a busy street or wind up closer to your destination.

After you get beyond the ticket booths, you enter the Métro system through a turnstile with two ticket slots. With the magnetic strip facing down, insert your ticket into the nearer slot. Your ticket pops out of the second slot. Remove it, and you either walk through a set of rubberized doors that briskly open on each side, or you push through a turnstile. Keep your ticket with you until you exit the station. At any point while in you're the Métro, an inspector may ask to see your ticket again. If you fail to produce it, you're subject to a steep fine. When you ride the RER, you must keep your ticket because you have to insert it in a turnstile when you exit the station.

After you're past the entrance, you need to make sure you're going in the right direction. Look at your subway map and trace the line past your destination to its end. The station's name at the end of the line is the name of the subway train on which you'll be traveling; in the case of Line 7 the train is LA CORNEUVE. To get back to your hotel from the Louvre, you take the train marked VILLEJUIF LOUIS ARAGON and exit at the Jussieu station.

See? Pretty easy!

Suppose, however, that the Métro line nearest to you doesn't directly go to your destination. For example, you want to go to the Arc de Triomphe from Jussieu, and the stop is Charles-de-Gaulle–Étoile. Find the Charles-de-Gaulle–Étoile stop on the Métro map. You see that you can reach Charles-de-Gaulle–Étoile on Line 6 or Line 1. But you're on Line 7. You have to change trains. Changing trains is called a *correspondance,* or transfer.

On your map, you may notice blank white circles where a number of lines intersect. These circles are transfer stations, where you can change subway trains. To figure out where you need to change trains in order to get on Line 1 or Line 6, use the map to see where Line 7 and Line 1 or Line 7 and Line 6 intersect. Line 7 and Line 6 intersect at Stalingrad, opposite from where you want to go. But Line 7 and Line 1 intersect at Concorde, very close to Charles-de-Gaulle–Étoile. To make sure you go in the right direction on Line 1, look on your map for the name of the station at the very end past Charles-de-Gaulle–Étoile. Make sure you ride the train marked Grande Arche de la Défense.

You get out at Concorde and look for the bright orange CORRESPONDANCE sign above the platform and the white sign that shows the number 1 in a circle. This sign refers to the line you want, so go in the direction the sign indicates. You eventually come to two stairwells leading to the platforms. Navy blue signs mark this area, indicating the train's direction. These signs also list all the stops the train makes. Make sure you choose the stairwell leading to the train going in the direction of Grande Arche de la Défense. Then board the train and exit at Charles-de-Gaulle–Étoile. Blue signs reading SORTIE mark all exits.

The distances between platforms at the *correspondance* (transfer) stations can be very long. You may climb stairs, walk a short distance, only to descend stairs to walk some more. Châtelet is particularly long. Some lines are connected by moving sidewalks that seem to do nothing but make a very long walk less long. For those with limited mobility, take the bus or a cab.

The Métro connects with the suburban commuter train, the RER, in several stations in the city. The RER operates on a zone fare system, but Métro tickets are valid on it in the city. You probably won't go past the first two zones, unless you visit Disneyland on the A4 or Versailles on the C5. When you ride the RER, keep your ticket because you need to insert it into a turnstile to leave the station.

The doors on most Métro cars don't open automatically. You must lift a door handle or press a button to get on and off.

Anyone who has ever been crushed on a Paris subway at rush hour can attest that commuters don't easily give up their places. If you step out of the train to let someone off, you may just be giving others on the platform the chance to squeeze in before you. Be polite, but stand your ground.

Buying the best travel pass

The RATP (Paris's public transportation agency) offers a variety of travel cards that you can purchase in larger Métro stations. You simply show these cards to bus conductors and Métro ticket booth personnel, who will let you by.

Mobilis

This pass is good for unlimited travel on subway and bus lines (except to and from the airports) for one day. The cost is 5€. If you will be hopping on and off subways for more than one day, you may want to try one of the following passes.

Carte Orange

The weekly (*coupon hebdomadaire*) or monthly (*coupon mensuel*) passes are inexpensive — 13.75€ for a week's unlimited travel or 46.05€ for a month's pass. Bring a photo of yourself to a Métro ticket booth in one of the larger stations, such as Châtelet, Monday through Wednesday mornings when the carte is on sale. The monthly card is only sold the first two days of the month.

Paris Visite

This pass is good for unlimited travel for one, two, three or five days. Though it has discounts for some museums and monuments, make sure you want to see the listed sites (you receive a brochure listing discounted sites). Otherwise, the Paris Visite card turns out to be more expensive than a Carte Orange or a one-day Mobilis pass. A one-day Paris Visite card costs 8.35€, two-day 13.70€, three-day 18.25€, and five-day 26.65€.

Paris l'Open Tour

This pass is good for one or two days of unlimited travel around Paris on special open-air buses. You can get on and off whenever you like. It's a bit pricey at 24€ for one day and 26€ for two days, but it's a good way to get to know Paris.

After the subway shuts down, the RATP operates **Noctambuses** that run on the hour from 1:30 a.m. to 5:30 a.m. from Châtelet-Hôtel de Ville, but they don't cover every arrondissement. Check the maps at the entrance to Métro stations to determine if a Noctambus services your destination. (If your hotel isn't in a Noctambus zone, consult the sidebar "Top taxi stands" later in this chapter for the one nearest you and queue up with all the others who are trying to get home.) The bus has a distinctive yellow-and-black owl symbol, and tickets cost 2.50€.

A dozen stations enjoyed a recent centenary makeover. Based on themes, the newly designed stations include Bonne Nouvelle, which now resembles a film set and displays film screens showing various old movies.

A ten-ticket *carnet* good for the Métro and on buses is a good deal for 9.60€ because a single ticket costs 1.30€. You can purchase *carnets* at all Métro stations as well as *tabacs* (cafés and kiosks that sell tobacco products). The heavily publicized **Paris Visite** card, which starts at 8.35€ a day offers free or reduced entry to some attractions in addition to unlimited travel on Métro and buses, but make sure the attractions that interest you are included on the list.

How long do you plan to be in Paris? If you plan to use public transportation frequently, consider buying the **Carte Orange.** The weekly or monthly pass is inexpensive — 13.75€ for a week's unlimited travel (*coupon hebdomadaire*) or 46.05€ for a month's pass (*coupon mensuel*) covering the first 20 arrondissements.

The only catch is that you must supply a passport-sized photo of yourself. Bring one from home, or visit a photo booth at one of the many Monoprix stores, major Métro stations, department stores, or train stations, where you can get four black-and-white pictures for less than 5€. The weekly Carte Orange is on sale Monday through Wednesday morning and is valid through Sunday, but the monthly card is only sold the first two days of the month.

For more information on the city's public transportation, call the RATP's English information line (0.34€/minute, ☎ 08-92-68-41-14; Internet: www.ratp.fr).

Riding the Bus

The bus system is convenient and can be an inexpensive way to sightsee without wearing out your feet. Most Parisian buses run from 6:30 a.m. to 8:30 p.m.; a few run until 12:30 a.m. Each bus shelter has a route map, which you want to check carefully. Because of the number of one-way streets, the bus is likely to make different stops depending on its direction. Main stops are written on the side of the buses with the endpoint shown on the front above the driver. Furthermore, the back of every bus shelter has posted large bus maps and smaller maps inside the shelter showing the specific bus route. Métro tickets are valid for bus travel, and although you can buy single tickets from the conductor, you can't buy ticket packages *(carnets)* on the bus.

Board at the front of the bus. If you have a single-trip ticket, insert it into the slot in the small machine right behind the driver. The machine punches your ticket and pops it back out. If you have a pass, show it to the driver. To get off at the next stop, press one of the red buttons on the safety poles; the *arrêt demandé* (stop requested) sign will light up above the driver.

Keeping the picks out of your pockets

Over the past few years, petty crime has been making a comeback in Paris, a city that is otherwise relatively safe. Anywhere where you find a high concentration of tourists, you also find pickpockets — including in the Métro, hovering around the lines outside the Eiffel Tower and Notre-Dame, and in the church and its bell tower. Keep an eye out for little bands of scruffy children, who often surround you, distract you, and make off with your belongings.

Your best bet is to use common sense. Be aware of the people around you at all times. Get a money belt. Women wear purses diagonally across the body with the flap facing the body. Make sure zipper purses are closed at all times. (In fact, zippered purses aren't recommended.)

The downside of taking the bus is that it often gets mired in heavy Parisian traffic, so it's not recommended if you're in a hurry. And, like the Métro, avoid the bus during rush hours when it seems *le monde* (the world) is sharing the bus with you.

Bus routes great for sightseeing include:

- ✔ **Bus 69:** Eiffel Tower, Invalides, Louvre, Hôtel de Ville, place des Vosges, Bastille, Père-Lachaise Cemetery

- ✔ **Bus 80:** Department stores on bd. Haussmann, Champs-Elysées, Ave. Montaigne *haute couture* shopping, Eiffel Tower

- ✔ **Bus 96:** St-Germain-des-Prés, Musée de Cluny, Hôtel de Ville, place des Vosges

Touring by Taxi

You have three ways to get a taxi in Paris, and they're ranked here in order of how successful they are. The best way to find a cab is by phoning **Taxis Bleues** (☎ **08-25-16-10-10**), **Alpha Taxis** (☎ **01-45-85-85-85**), or **G7** (☎ **01-47-39-47-39**). Keep in mind, however, that phoning ahead is more expensive because the meter starts running as soon as the driver commences the journey to get you. You can also wait at a taxi stand (*station de taxis;* see the "Top taxi stands" sidebar in this chapter); a blue Taxi sign denote the stands. Depending on the time of day, however, you may wait in a long line of people, or a very limited number of cabs stop. Finally, you can hail a cab, as long as you're not within 200 feet of a taxi stand. Look for a taxi with its white light illuminated, which means the cab is available. An orange light means the cab is occupied or on the way to a pickup. You may get a cab driver who refuses to take you to your destination; by law, he or she can only do this during his or her last half-hour at work. Be prepared, as well, for the selective vision of drivers, especially when you hail a cab. Don't be surprised to see a free taxi or two pass you by.

Top taxi stands

Go to the following locations within each arrondissement to find the most convenient taxi stands. *Place* indicates a square, *pont* is a bridge, and *hôpital* is a hospital.

1er Arrondissement

Métro Concorde

Place André Malraux

Place du Châtelet

2e Arrondissement

Place de l'Opéra

3e Arrondissement

Métro Rambuteau

Square du Temple

4e Arrondissement

Métro St-Paul

5e Arrondissement

Place des Gobelins

Place Maubert

Place Monge

Place St-Michel

Pont de la Tournelle

6e Arrondissement

Métro Mabillon

Métro Port-Royal

Métro St-Germain

7e Arrondissement

Métro Bac

27 bd. La Tour-Maubourg

Métro La Tour-Maurbourg

Métro Solferino

Place de l'Ecole Militaire

Tour Eiffel (Eiffel Tower)

8e Arrondissement

Av. de Friedland

Place de l'Alma

Place de la Madeleine

Place des Ternes

Rond Point des Champs-Elysées

9e Arrondissement

Métro Richelieu-Drouout

Place d'Estienne d'Orves

Square de Montholon

10e Arrondissement

Métro Goncourt

11e Arrondissement

Métro Faidherbe-Chaligny

Métro Goncourt

Place de la Bastille

Place de la Nation

Place de la République

Place Léon Blum

(continued)

(continued)

12e Arrondissement

Hôpital Trousseau

Château de Vincennes (Bois de Vincennes)

Porte Dorée

13e Arrondissement

Métro Glacière

Porte d'Italie

Hôpital Pitié-Salpétrière (bd. de l'Hôpital)

14e Arrondissement

Métro Plaisance

Porte d'Orléans

Place Denfert-Rochereau

Porte de Vanves

15e Arrondissement

Métro Bir-Hakeim

Métro LaMotte-Piquet Grenelle

Métro Convention

Place Balard

Place de Breteuil

16e Arrondissement

Métro Muette

Métro Passy

Maison de la Radio

Place d'Iéna

Place du Trocadero

12 place Victor Hugo

Gare Henri Martin

17e Arrondissement

Métro Brochant

Métro Villiers

Place Charles de Gaulle

Porte de Clichy

Porte de Saint-Ouen

18e Arrondissement

Métro Lamarck-Calaincourt

Métro Porte de la Chapelle

Place Blanche

Place de la Clichy

Place Jules Joffrin

Place du Tertre

Porte de Clignancourt

19e Arrondissement

Métro Stalingrad

Métro Botzaris

Porte de Lilas

Porte de Pantin

Porte de la Villette

Église de Belleville

20e Arrondissement

Métro Ménilmontant

Métro Père-Lachaise

Métro Porte de Montreuil

Métro Pyrénées

For one to three people, the fare in Paris proper is 2€; the rate per kilometer is 0.60€ from 7 a.m. to 7 p.m. Monday through Saturday; otherwise, it's 1€. You will pay 0.70€ supplements for taxi stands at train stations and at the Air France shuttle-bus terminals, as well as 0.90€ for each piece of luggage weighing more than 5kg. If the driver agrees to do so, it's 1.50€ for transporting a fourth person. Common practice is to tip your driver 10% to 15% on longer journeys when the fare exceeds 15€; otherwise round up the charge and give the driver the change.

Check the meter carefully, especially if you're coming in from an airport; rip-offs are very common. If you feel that you may have been overcharged, demand a receipt (which drivers are obligated to provide) and contact the **Préfecture of Police** (☎ **01-53-73-53-73**; Internet: www.prefecture-police-paris.interieur.gouv.fr).

Driving a Car

Streets are narrow, parking is next to impossible, and nerve, skill, ruthlessness, and a knowledgeable copilot are required if you insist on driving in Paris. I *strongly* recommend that you don't. (If you must drive in Paris, do it in August when Parisians are away on vacation, and traffic is lighter.)

A few tips: Get an excellent street map and ride with another person; traffic moves so lightning-fast you don't have time to think at intersections. For the most part, you must pay to park in Paris. Depending on the neighborhood, expect to pay 1.80€ to 2.30€ an hour for a maximum of two hours. Place coins in the nearest meter, which issues you a ticket to place on your dashboard. You can also buy parking cards at the nearest tabac for meters that accept only parking cards. Parking is free on Sundays, holidays, and for the entire month of August.

Drivers and all passengers must wear seat belts. Children under 12 must ride in the back seat. Drivers are supposed to yield to the car on the right, except where signs indicate otherwise, as at traffic circles.

Watch for the *gendarmes* (police officers), who lack patience and who consistently contradict the traffic lights. Horn blowing is frowned upon except in emergencies. Flash your headlights instead.

Hopping on a Bicycle

City planners have been trying to encourage more cycling by setting aside 62 miles of bicycle lanes throughout Paris. The main routes run north-south from the Bassin de La Villette along the Canal St-Martin through the Left Bank and east-west from Château de Vincennes to the Bois de Boulogne and its miles of bike lanes. For more information and a bike map, pick up the *Plan Vert* from the tourist office. (For bike tours of the city, see Chapter 18.)

In addition, the banks of the Seine are closed to cars and opened to pedestrians and cyclists March to November each Sunday from 10 a.m. to 5 p.m. It may not make much of a dent in the air quality, but bicycling is a fun and healthy way to spend a Sunday afternoon.

To rent a bicycle, contact **Paris À Vélo C'est Sympa!,** 37 bd. Bourdon, 4e (☎ **01-48-87-60-01;** Métro: Bastille). The price is 12.50€ a day, 9.50€ per half-day, 24€ for a weekend. A 200€ deposit on a credit card is required.

Strolling around Paris à Pied (on Foot)

Paris is one of the prettiest cities in the world for strolling, and getting around on foot is probably the best way to really appreciate the city's character. The best walking neighborhoods are **St-Germain-des-Prés** on the Left Bank and the **Marais** on the Right Bank, both of which are filled with romantic little courtyards, wonderful boutiques, and congenial cafés and watering holes. The **quays of the Seine,** as well as its bridges, are also lovely, especially at sunset when the sun fills the sky with a pink glow that's reflected on the water. And try not to miss the pretty **Canal St-Martin** with its arched bridges and locks in the 10e, featured in the movies *Amélie* and *Hôtel du Nord.*

A word to the wise: Take special care when crossing streets, even when you have the right of way. The number one rule of the road in France is that whoever is coming from the right side has the right of way. Drivers often make right turns without looking, even when faced with pedestrians at crosswalks. And don't ever attempt to cross a traffic circle if you're not on a crosswalk. The larger roundabouts, such as the one at the Arc de Triomphe, have pedestrian tunnels.

Chapter 12

Managing Your Money

● ●

In This Chapter

▶ Understanding the euro

▶ Finding out where to get cash in Paris

▶ Getting the last word on taxes

● ●

So how expensive is Paris, really? The introduction of the euro in early 2002 made many costs skyrocket as merchants rounded up their prices and profited from the conversion. And euro or no, a whopping 20.6% *détaxe* on purchases (otherwise known as the value-added tax, abbreviated TVA or VAT) still is tacked on.

But all is not lost. Historic monuments commemorating the events that created Paris are free. Many museums offer reduced entrance fees at certain times, and admission to the national museums is free on the first Sunday of every month. The parks are free, and you can load up on provisions for picnics at local grocery stores. You can linger over one glass of wine in a café, walk to your heart's content among floodlit monuments, or stroll the banks and bridges of the Seine.

And fortunately, you have plenty of ways to keep your travel costs down. Consider this chapter to be a toolkit for helping you do just that.

Getting to Know the Euro

Imagine traveling through Europe without standing in line at exchange counters. On January 1, 2002, that became reality in Austria, Belgium, Finland, France, Germany, Greece, Ireland, Italy, Luxembourg, the Netherlands, Portugal, and Spain, when the euro was introduced. Of course, the move had been planned long before that. In 1999, those 12 European Union (EU) members adopted the euro, officially locking their respective exchange rates together and switching most banking and credit-card operations to the euro. Euro bills and coins were issued December 15, 2001, with a great deal of publicity. In France, news stories featured merchants and consumers trying to get used to the new currency and exchange rate. France removed the franc for good in February 2002, although you still find many prices marked in euros and francs, thus easing residents into the transition. After some highs and significant lows, the euro seems to have reached stability and is pretty much equal to the dollar.

Euro banknotes come in denominations of 5 (light blue/gray), 10 (pink), 20 (darker blue), 50 (orange), 100 (green), 200 (gold), and 500 (fuschia). The back of each banknote is emblazoned with an image of bridges found throughout the 12 EU countries, while 12 stars and windows and gateways of famous EU monuments grace the front.

The copper-colored 0.01€ piece is the smallest euro coin (smaller but thicker than a U.S. dime). The copper-colored 0.02€ coin is about the size of a U.S. penny; the copper-colored 0.05€ piece is the same size as a U.S. nickel, but it's thinner. The gold-colored 0.10€ piece is the size of a U.S. penny with ridged edges. The gold-colored 0.20€ piece is a little bigger than a U.S. nickel and is notched in seven places. And, the gold 0.50€ coin is about the size of a U.S. quarter and has ridged edges. The 1€ coin is a little smaller than a U.S. quarter; however, it is thicker and is gold around its circumference, silver within. The 2€ is a little bigger than the 1€ and silver around its circumference, gold inside. The backs of the euro coins have symbols relating to one of the 12 European Union countries; in France it's Marianne (the French Revolution-era female symbol of a strong republic) or a tree with RF for République Française.

For a look at the most recent rates of exchange (updated each minute), log on to www.xe.net/currency, or check the exchange rate in the financial pages of your local newspaper.

Finding a Bank

You can find a bank on nearly every corner in Paris, but if you're nervous about finding one, pay a visit to the Web sites for Visa (www.visaeu.com) and MasterCard (www.mastercard.com), which identify the locations of cash machines all over Paris. Most of the major banks in Paris, such as Credit Lyonnais, Credit Agricole, Banque Nationale de Paris (BNP), Banque Populaire, Credit Commercial de France (CCF), Credit du Nord, and even some branches of the post office have automated teller machines (ATMs). But you won't be able to check your balance or transfer funds, so keep track of your withdrawals while you travel. For more about using your ATM card in France, see Chapter 3.

You can exchange traveler's checks for euros at any of the following banks:

▮ ✔ **American Express,** 11 rue Scribe, 9e (☎ **01-47-14-50-00;** Métro: Opéra Chaussée-d'Antin or Havre-Caumartin; RER: Auber)

- ✔ **Barclays,** 24Bis av. de l'Opéra, 1er (☎ **01-44-86-00-00;** Métro: Pyramides), or 96 rue Turenne, 3e (☎ **01-42-77-24-70;** Métro: St-Paul)

- ✔ **Citibank,** 125 av. Champs-Elysées, 8e (☎ **01-53-23-33-60;** Métro: Charles de Gaulle Étoile), or 17 av. Montaigne (☎ **01-44-43-45-00;** Métro: Alma-Marceau)

- ✔ **Lloyd's Bank,** 15 av. d'Iéna, 16e (☎ **01-44-43-42-41;** Métro: Iéna)

- ✔ **Thomas Cook,** 194 rue de Rivoli, 1er (☎ **01-42-60-37-61;** Metro: Tuileries), or 25 bd. des Capucines, 2e (☎ **01-42-96-26-78;** Metro: place de l' Opéra), and 18 other locations around Paris

Handling Loss or Theft

In the unlikely event that your wallet or purse is lost or stolen, be sure to block charges against your credit-card account immediately. Almost every credit-card company has an emergency international number that you can call if your wallet or purse is stolen. The company may be able to wire you a cash advance off your credit card immediately, and in many places, can deliver an emergency credit card in a day or two. Call ☎ **0800-90-11-79** if you've lost or had your **Visa** card stolen. **American Express** card and traveler's check holders in France can call ☎ **336-393-1111** for money and lost card emergencies. For **MasterCard,** call ☎ **0800-90-13-87**.

If your traveler's checks are lost or stolen, you need to be able to report exactly which checks are gone in order to get them replaced. The check issuer can tell you where to pick up the new checks.

If your purse or wallet is gone, the police aren't likely to recover it for you. However, contact the police anyway and file a police report — you may need it for credit-card or insurance purposes later.

Taxing Matters

As noted earlier in the chapter, the price of all goods in Paris includes a 20.6% sales tax called the *détaxe,* abbreviated *TVA.* If you live outside the European Union, you can be reimbursed for part of the TVA that you pay, but as always, a catch is involved: You must spend at least 175€ in the same store *in the same day.* The amount of the refund varies from store to store, but generally comes out to about 13% of the tax you paid on the item. The department stores **Au Printemps** and **Galeries Lafayette** have special *détaxe* desks where clerks prepare your sales invoices, but small shops don't always have the necessary paperwork. (For information about how to obtain a TVA refund, see Chapter 19.)

Part IV
Dining in Paris

The 5th Wave
By Rich Tennant

"Now THAT was a great meal! Beautiful presentation, an imaginative use of ingredients, and a sauce with nuance and depth. The French really know how to make a 'Happy Meal'."

In this part . . .

With many of the world's best chefs — and best restaurants — dining in Paris can be a wonderful experience to which travelers greatly look forward. Though dining out can be the highlight of your trip, it can also cause plenty of confusion if you're not familiar with the language, the regional specialties, the order in which the food is served, and tipping. Forget your worries — this section tells you all you need to know about French dining so that you can soon be chorusing *"Bon appetit!"* as though you were born eating this way.

Chapter 13 presents an overview of French dining — what's hot now in Paris, where locals eat, how to dress to dine — and gives you tips for saving money, and a glossary that covers everything from cuts of meat to how dishes are prepared. Chapter 14 contains an alphabetical list of some of my favorite places to eat in Paris, with lots of low-to-moderate-priced restaurants and only two true haute cuisine establishments. The restaurants are indexed by type of cuisine, price, and location for reader-friendliness. Chapter 15 provides options for those times when you just don't want to sit down to a full-course meal; everything's covered, from street food and sandwich shops to tea salons, cafés, wine bars, and ice cream places.

Chapter 13

The Lowdown on Paris's Dining Scene

Paris is restaurant heaven — but unless you grew up in France, it can be quite intimidating to translate a menu and figure out what to eat when. (Salad before the meal and cheese after? Cheese before dessert or instead of it?) This chapter is designed to make you feel comfortable about dining in Parisian restaurants, so that your experiences dining *a la française* are pleasant and memorable, as well as delicious. Here, you find the differences between bistros, brasseries, cafés, and restaurants, in addition to money-saving tips and suggestions on how to dress. And, oh, yes, we need to address the matter of tipping — don't worry about tipping in France because a 15% service charge (it appears on the bill as *service compris*) is added to the bill. Etiquette dictates leaving a token sum — 2€ for a moderately priced dinner — to let the waiter know you enjoyed your meal.

Now is probably a good time to mention that in France, as anywhere, you should never underestimate the importance of good manners. Your meal will be much smoother if you remember essential but basic phrases such as *"Bonjour, monsieur"* (hello, sir) and *"Merci, madame"* (thank you, madam). Keep in mind, too, that French table manners require that all food, even fruit, be eaten with a knife and fork.

Contrary to what you may have seen in the movies, never, *ever* refer to the waiter as *"garcon,"* (boy) and don't snap your fingers at him or her. Instead, say, *"Monsieur, s'il vous plaît!"* or *"Madame/Mademoiselle, s'il vous plaît!"* (Sir/Madam/Miss, if you please!).

Catching Up on the Latest Trends

Parisians take dining very seriously. They expect the same freshness and quality in their meals that their ancestors had, and newspapers are full of outrage that American fast-food chains have made inroads into their country. They worry about the consequences of genetically altered fruits and vegetables, and though mad cow disease hasn't been as prevalent in France as it has been in England, each new case merits mention on the national news. But all this turmoil doesn't stop Parisians from dining out. They're on an eternal quest for the perfect meal, and they make a pastime of sharing *les bonnes addresses* (the right addresses) with their friends.

And how many *bonnes addresses* there are! In the last decade, the city has seen celebrity chefs open *baby bistros* — restaurants offering simpler and less expensive meals than served at their deluxe establishments. The gifted apprentices of these celebrity chefs have also been opening their own restaurants. Also in vogue is a back-to-grandmère's kitchen approach that has chefs turning out homey dishes like *pot-au-feu, brandade,* and *cassoulet* — dishes that evoke an earlier era in France. (Check out the "Salivating over French cooking" sidebar in this chapter for descriptions of each dish.)

The best baby bistros, like Spoon, Food & Wine from the seasoned chef Alain Ducasse, are still going strong, and well-prepared home-style food, such as that served by La Bastide Odéon, has become a trend everyone appreciates. (Check out Chapter 14 for more on these restaurants.)

Searching Out Where the Locals Eat

Eateries go by various names in France, and in theory at least, these labels give you some clue to how much a meal costs. From most expensive to least expensive, the lineup generally goes like this: restaurant, bistro, brasserie, and café. The key word is *generally.* Never rely on the name of an establishment as the sole price indicator; some of the city's most expensive eateries call themselves cafés. Furthermore, the awnings above quintessential cafés often claim the labels of restaurant, café, brasserie, or some other combination. The only way to be sure of the price is to read the menu, which by law must be posted outside. Here are some short descriptions of the eateries of Paris:

- **Restaurants** are where you go to savor French cuisine in all its glory. At their best, classic dishes are excellent, and new dishes are inventive. Dining is usually more formal than in bistros or brasseries, and service is slower. You may also have more than one server. Like bistros, restaurants serve lunch between noon and 2:30 p.m. and dinner between 7:00 and 10:00 p.m. Generally, you must be seated for lunch no later than 2 p.m. if you want a full meal.

Between 3 and 7 p.m., you may find it nearly impossible to have a sit-down meal in a Paris restaurant or bistro. During this swing shift, your best bet is to head to a café, tearoom, or wine bar. Dining at 7 p.m. is considered very early for dinner in Paris; most Parisians wouldn't think about sitting down before 8 p.m. But starting too late — 10 p.m. is getting dangerous — can also leave you without too many options.

Restaurant critics are divided about the *menu dégustation* (sampler, or tasting, menu; meh-noo day-goo-stah-seeown), featured in many of the city's top restaurants. Made up of small portions of the chef's signature dishes, it offers tremendous value because you have the opportunity to try more dishes. But some say the dish has too many portions for a customer to get a sense of the chef's artistry, and the mixture of so many flavors just confuses, instead of enriches, the palate.

- The typical **bistro** used to be a mom-and-pop operation with a menu confined to Parisian standbys like *boeuf bourguignon* (braised beef in red wine sauce), and *tarte Tatin* (caramelized upside-down apple pie). Today many bistros have expanded upon the old classics but retain the tradition of offering hearty, relatively low-priced dishes in a convivial, intimate atmosphere. Think crush of elbows and the sounds of corks popping, glasses clinking, and people having a good time. Bistros are where Parisians come to dine the most often.

- Literally, the word **brasserie** means "brewery" and refers to the Alsatian menu specialties that include staples, such as beer, Riesling wine, and *choucroute* (sauerkraut, usually topped by cuts of ham). Most brasseries are large, cheerful, brightly lit places that open early and close late (some are open 24 hours a day), and have an immense selection of dishes on the menu, although many no longer specialize in Alsatian fare. At brasseries, you can usually get a meal at any time of day, even in hours when restaurants and bistros are closed, and the food is relatively inexpensive.

Sadly, brasseries began to fall to corporate acquisition in the 1970s, and today are part of one all-encompassing chain (with the exception of Brasserie Ile St-Louis in the 1er; see Chapter 14). Although this fact shouldn't stop you from visiting some of Paris's legendary eateries, look out for places with mundane and repetitive food — they're more numerous than you think. Your best bet is to get a look at the menus of brasseries that interest you and compare costs, as well as listings. If _poulet rôti_ (rotisserie chicken), _steak frites_ (steak and fries), and omelets seem to be highlights, you may want to try eating somewhere else.

✔ **Cafés** are typically open from about 8 to 1 a.m. They serve drinks and food all day from a short menu that often includes salads, sandwiches, mussels, and French fries. Prime locations or famous literary cafés carry higher price tags. Most cafés offer reasonably priced omelets, sandwiches, soups, or salads. Omelets come plain with just a sprinkling of herbs or filled with cheese, ham, or other hearty additions. Onion soup (_soupe à l'oignon_) is a traditional Parisian dish, and you may see _soupe de poisson_ (fish soup) on the menu. Another café favorite is _croque monsieur,_ a grilled ham sandwich covered with melted cheese, or a _croque madame,_ the same dish topped with an egg. Or try a _salade Niçoise,_ a huge bowl filled with lettuce, boiled potatoes, tuna, hard-boiled eggs, capers, tomatoes, olives, and anchovies or a _salade de chèvre chaude,_ fresh greens topped with warm goat cheese on croutons. These dishes make a light, pleasant meal for 6€ to 12€.

Parisians use cafés the way the British use pubs — as extensions of their living rooms. They're places you meet friends before heading to the movies or a party, read your newspaper, write in your journal, or just hang out and people watch. Regardless of whether you order a cup of coffee or the most expensive cognac in the house, no one will ask you to leave. Coffee, of course, is the chief drink. It comes black in a small cup, often with a thin wrapped square of chocolate, unless you order a _café crème_ or _café au lait_ (coffee with steamed milk, which Parisians usually have at breakfast). _Thé_ (tay; tea) is also fairly popular but generally isn't high quality. _Chocolat chaud_ (shock-o-_lah_-shohl; hot chocolate), on the other hand, is absolutely superb and made from real ground chocolate.

✔ **Tearooms,** or _salons de thé,_ usually open mid-morning and close by early evening. Some serve light lunches, but most are at their best in the afternoon for desserts with coffee or tea.

✔ **Wine bars** operate from mid-morning to late evening when you can order wine by the glass and munch on snacks such as _tartines_ (open-face sandwiches), olives, and cheese. Some offer simple lunch menus, but like cafés and tearooms, they're generally better for light bites. I recommend some of the city's best cafés, tearooms, and wine bars in Chapter 15.

Salivating over French cooking

Even with English translations, confronting a French menu can be a daunting experience. Dishes that have been familiar to French people since childhood are often unknown to outsiders. The following list is a user's guide to typically French dishes that you're likely to encounter.

Andouillette (ahn-dwee-*et*): A sausage of pork organs encased in intestines. Andouillette has a strong flavor with a distinct aftertaste and is usually grilled and served with mustard and French fries. Look for the A.A.A.A.A. label — the Association Amicale des Authentiques Amateurs d'Andouillettes (Association of Real Andouillette Lovers) stamps it on the best andouillettes.

Blanquette de veau (blahn-*ket* duh voe): Veal cooked in a white stew that includes eggs and cream.

Boeuf Bourguignon (buhf bor-gee-*nyon*): Beef cooked with red burgundy wine, mushrooms, and onions.

Boudin (boo-*dan*): A rich sausage made from pig's blood, usually combined with *créme fraîche,* onions, and eggs. More elaborate versions may feature a touch of garlic or chestnuts. The dish is often served with sautéed apples or mashed potatoes, which enhance the slightly sweet taste of the sausage.

Boudin Blanc (boo-*dan* blahn): A white sausage made from veal, chicken, or pork.

Bouillabaisse (*bwee*-ah-bess): A fish stew from the Mediterranean that includes assorted shellfish and white fish accompanied by croutons, grated cheese, and *rouille,* a mayonnaise made with garlic.

Brandade (brahn-*dahd*): Salt cod (*morue*) soaked in cold water, shredded, and cooked with garlic, olive oil, milk, and potato. It has the look and consistency of mashed potatoes but tastes like salted fish. A green salad makes a good accompaniment.

Carpaccio (car-*pahsh*-shyow): Thinly sliced, cured raw beef or tuna.

Cassoulet (cass-oo-*lay*): A rich stew made of white beans, dry sausage, onion, duck, prosciutto, herbs, carrots, and tomatoes. It's cooked slowly and usually served in a ceramic bowl or pot. Absolutely delicious, but heavy; don't plan any serious physical exertions after eating — digestion will be enough.

Cervelles (suhr-vel): Pork or sheep brains.

Cheval (sheh-vahl): Horse meat.

Choucroute (shoo-*kroot*): Sauerkraut cooked with juniper berries and wine, served with an assortment of pork cuts, usually including brisket, pork shoulder, ham, frankfurters, or spicy sausage. It goes well with boiled potatoes and is served with mustard.

Confit de Canard (con-*fee* duh can-*ahr*): A duck leg cooked and preserved in its own fat. The fatty skin is usually salty, but the meat underneath is tender and juicy. Mashed potatoes make a good side dish.

(continued)

(continued)

Cuisses des Grenouilles (cwees day gren-*wee*): Frogs' legs.

Escargots (es-car-*go*): Snails.

Foie (fwah): Liver.

Gesiers (jeh-*zyay*): Gizzards; very good in salads.

Lapin à la Moutarde (la-*pan* ah la moo-*tard*): Rabbit cooked with mustard, crème fraîche, and sometimes white wine. The mustard perks up the rabbit meat, which has a mild flavor.

Lièvre (lee-*yevr*): Hare.

Magret de Canard (mah-gret duh can-*ahr*): The sliced breast of a fattened duck, sautéed and sometimes served with a green peppercorn sauce. The result more closely resembles red meat than poultry. As with any meat, specify how you want it cooked — *bleu* (very rare), *saignant* (rare), *à point* (medium), or *bien cuit* (well done).

Pieds de cochon (pyay duh coh-*shon*): Pig's feet.

Plateau de Fruits de Mer (plah-*toe* duh free duh mair): A variety of raw and cooked seafood served on ice. You usually find two kinds of oysters — flat, round *belon*, and larger, crinkly *creuse*. Both types are cultivated, not harvested. The oysters are eaten with lemon or red-wine vinegar and accompanied by thin slices of buttered rye bread. In addition to various kinds of shrimp, clams, and mussels, you also see periwinkles (*bulots*), which are eaten with mayonnaise.

Pot-au-Feu (*pot*-oh-fuh): A hearty dish of boiled vegetables and beef that sometimes includes the marrow bone. Scrape out the marrow, spread it on toast, and sprinkle it with salt. Sometimes the broth is served first, followed by the vegetables and beef. Mustard is the preferred condiment.

Ris de Veau (ree duh voe): The thymus gland of a calf (a white meat) sautéed in a butter and cream sauce. It has a delicate, pleasant taste but is high in cholesterol.

Rognons (*ron*-yawn): Kidneys.

Tête de Veau (tet duh voe): Calf's head.

Finding Ethnic Eateries

Even the French need a break from French food every once in a while, and you may find your taste buds craving something different and perhaps highly spiced. If you want an ethnic cuisine, take advantage of the Chinese, Thai, Vietnamese, Indian, Tex-Mex, and Russian restaurants that are popular with residents, although not necessarily cheaper (or tastier) than French restaurants. Try the 10e or 18e for North African, Turkish, Vietnamese, and Thai. Probably the most popular ethnic dish in France is couscous from North Africa — steamed semolina garnished with broth, stewed vegetables, and meat. You can find at least one restaurant or *couscouserie* on nearly every street in the capital.

Eating Out without Losing Your Shirt: Tips for Cutting Costs

If you're watching your pocketbook when it comes to dining out, following a few of these simple tips can go a long way toward making the bill as appealing as the food.

- ✔ **Order prix-fixe (set-price) meals.** These set-price meals are up to 30% cheaper than ordering the same dishes a la carte. What's the trade-off? Your options are more limited than if you order from the main menu. Review the prix-fixe option carefully to determine what you're getting at that price. Does it come with wine, and if so, how much — a glass or a half bottle? Is dessert or coffee included?

- ✔ **Make lunch your main meal.** Many restaurants offer great deals on a fixed-price lunch. You probably won't be hungry for a full meal after two or three courses at lunch.

- ✔ **Try the crêperies.** Crêperies (many are off the bd. du Montparnasse around the Square Délambre) offer a great value. Try savory meat- or vegetable-filled crêpes called *galettes* with a bowl of cider for your main meal and honey, jam, *chantilly* (whipped cream), chocolate, or fruit-filled crêpes for dessert. Surroundings are usually Brittany-inspired with red-checked tablecloths, wooden beams, maritime souvenirs, and pictures of Bretagnons in native dress.

- ✔ **Try chain restaurants or sandwich shops.** Batifol, Hippopotamus, Léon de Bruxelles, and l'Écluse offer some good-value, though not inspired, meals. Pomme de Pain and Lina's have fresh and tasty sandwiches.

- ✔ **Pay attention to the menu's details.** On most menus, the cheaper dishes are made of cheaper cuts of meat or the organs of animals, like brains, tripe, and the like.

- ✔ **Don't eat breakfast at your hotel.** Doing so will add at least $5 more per person to your hotel bill. Grab a croissant or a *pain au chocolat* (chocolate-filled pastry) from a *boulangerie* (bakery).

- ✔ **Know the tipping rules.** Service is usually included at restaurants; don't double-tip by mistake. If service is excellent, however, you may want to round up the price with one or two euros.

Dining Details

The majority of French restaurants are very small establishments where you may feel like all eyes are upon you. To feel more comfortable, follow the advice set out in this section, and you can dine in Paris like a local.

Understanding the order of a meal

Be aware of the traditional way that French restaurants serve food:

✔ An *apéritif* is a drink that precedes the meal, but the French don't like to start a meal by numbing the palate with strong liquor. Try a *kir,* a mixture of white wine and *crème de cassis* (black currant liqueur), which is light and the most common pre-meal drink.

✔ You're always served bread with your meal, but you must request butter.

✔ Water isn't placed on the table automatically — you must ask for it. To get regular tap water (which is perfectly fine to drink), as opposed to the pricey equivalent in a bottle, simply ask for *une carafe d'eau.*

✔ Many times, salads are served after meals, though salad as an appetizer is becoming more common.

✔ Cheese comes after the main course and is usually accompanied by red wine.

✔ Dessert comes after the cheese course, but dessert and cheese can be served at the same time if diners at the same table wish it.

✔ Diners traditionally don't drink coffee during the meal. Black coffee is served after dessert in a demitasse cup with sugar cubes on the side. If you want milk with your coffee, you must ask for a *café au lait* or *café crème.*

✔ Although a proper meal consists of three or sometimes four courses, portions are usually moderate.

✔ If you have food left on your plate, don't ask for a doggie bag.

✔ The *menu du jour* at many establishments includes red or white wine. The standard measure is *un quart* (a quarter-liter carafe), sometimes served in *un pot* or *un pichet* (a pitcher). If wine isn't included, you can order *vin ordinaire* (house wine) or a Beaujolais (a light, fruity red wine), a Côtes du Rhône (a dry red wine), or a Chardonnay (a light white wine), which are very reasonably priced. And you can always opt for soda, juice, or water instead (*l'eau plat* is still water; *l'eau gazeuse* is carbonated water). Cocktails are available but discouraged because they're thought to numb the palate.

Making reservations for dinner

The vast majority of French restaurants are very small establishments with limited seating, and tables are scrupulously saved for folks who book. Always try to make at least a same-day reservation, even for a modest neighborhood bistro. Some top restaurants require several weeks' notice. Remember to call if you're going to be more than 20 minutes late. Showing up late is considered bad form.

If you're staying at a hotel with a staff concierge, phone or fax ahead and ask the concierge to make a reservation at the sought-after restaurant where you'd like to eat. Make the call as early as possible, specifying your preferred date with a back-up date or two. Don't forget to tip him or her (slip 10€ discreetly into an envelope that you present when checking out).

Dressing to dine

Only the most expensive restaurants enforce dress codes (suit and tie), and in theory, you can dress up or down as you like. Realize, however, that Parisians are a pretty stylish lot, even when dressing informally. Relaxed dressing doesn't mean sloppy jeans and sneakers — *especially* sneakers. The look to aim for is casual Fridays at work. You can't go wrong if you dress in neutral colors — think black, beige, cream, navy, and chocolate. Go a notch dressier than what you'd wear at home. Even at neighborhood bistros, most men wear sports jackets, and women wear skirts or smart pants suits and the ever-present scarf.

A Glossary That's Good Enough to Eat

Use this helpful guide when you're trying to decide what to order and how you want it cooked.

General Terms

Compris (comb-*pree;* included)
Déjeuner (*day*-zhu-nay; lunch)
Dîner (*dee*-nay; dinner)
Petit Déjeuner (pet-*tee day*-zhu-nay; breakfast)
Ménu Dégustation (meh-noo day-goo-stah-sion; sampler, or tasting, menu)
Prix-Fixe (pree-feeks; set-price)
Supplément (sup-play-*mahn;* extra charge)

Les Entrées (layz ahn-trays; appetizers)

Charcuterie (shar-koot-*ree;* assorted cold cuts)
Crudités (kroo-dee-*tay;* assorted raw vegetables)
Foie gras (fwah grah; goose liver paté)
Saumon fumé (soh-*moh foo*-may; smoked salmon)
Soupe à l'oignon (soop-ah-lowh-*yon;* onion soup)
Soupe à pistou (soop-ah-pees-*too;* vegetable soup with pesto)

Velouté (vay-loot-*ay;* cream-based soup)

Vichyssoise (vee-shee-*swahz;* cold leek and potato soup)

Salade composée (sa-*lad com*-poh-zay; mixed salad)

Salade de chèvre chaud (sa-*lad* deh-shev-rah-*sho;* salad with warm goat cheese on croutons)

Salade gesiers (sa-*lad* zeh-shee-*air;* salad with sautéed chicken gizzards)

Salade landaise (sa-*lad* lahn-*dehs;* salad containing duck breast, duck liver, and duck gizzards)

Salade de Niçoise (sa-*lad* nee-*shwahz;* salad with tuna, canned corn, anchovies, and potato)

Boeuf (buhf; beef)

á point (a pwahn; medium)

Bavette (bah-*vet;* flank steak)

Bien cuit (byen kwee; well done)

Bleu (bluh; very rare)

Chateaubriand (cha-tow-bree-*ahn;* porterhouse)

Contre-filet (*kahn*-trah-fee-lay; filet steak)

Côte de boeuf (cote dah boof; T-bone)

Entrecôte (ahn-trah-*cote;* rib-eye)

Faux-filet (foe-fee-*lay;* sirloin)

Filet mignon (fee-*lay* mee-*nyahn;* tenderloin)

Langue de boeuf (lahng dah boof; tongue)

Onglet (ahn-*glay;* hanger steak)

Pavé (pah-*vay;* thick steak; *Literally:* paving stone)

Queue de boeuf (kyew dah boof; oxtail)

Rôti de boeuf (*roe*-tee dah boof; roast beef)

Saignant (sen-*yahn;* rare)

Steack haché (stake *ha*-shay; minced meat or hamburger)

Steak tartare (stake tar-*tar;* a lean cut of beef that is minced and served raw — a high-quality dish prepared by experts, people rarely get sick from eating this)

Tournedo (*tor*-nay-doe; small tender filet usually grilled or sautéed)

Veau (voe; veal)

Other Meats

Agneau (ah-*nyoe;* lamb)

Gigot (*gee*-joe; leg — usually of lamb)

Jambon (zhahm-*bon;* ham)

Médaillon (meh-dah-ee-*on;* medallions — beef, veal, lamb)

Merguez (mare-*gay;* spicy sausage)

Porc (pork; pork)

Saucisses/saucisson (soh-*sees,* soh-see-*sohn;* sausage/little sausage)

Volailles (voe-lie; fowl)

Blanc de volaille (blahn dah voe-*lai;* chicken breast)

Caille (kaih; quail)

Canard (kah-*nahr;* duck)

Dinde (dand; turkey)

Magret de canard (mah-*gret* dah kah-*nahr;* duck breast)

Oie (wah; goose)

Pigéon (pee-jee-*ohn;* game pigeon)

Pintade (pan-*tahd;* guinea fowl)

Poulet (*poo*-lay; chicken)

Fruits de Mer (free duh mair; seafood)

Bar (bar; bass)

Coquilles St-Jacques (*koe*-kee san-*jahk;* scallops)

Crevettes (kreh-*vet;* shrimp)

Daurade (doe-*rahd;* sea bream)

Homard (oe-*mahr;* lobster)

Huîtres (wee-*tra;* oysters)

Langoustine (lang-oo-*steen;* crayfish)

Morue/Cabillaud (moh-roo/ka-bee-*oh;* cod)

Moules (mool; mussels)

Poissons (pwah-*son;* fish)

Raie (ray; skate)

Rascasse (ras-*kass;* scorpion fish)

Rouget (roo-*zhay;* red mullet)

Saumon (soh-*moh;* salmon)

Thon (than; tuna)

Truite (trweet; trout)

Les Légumes (lay lay-goom; vegetables)

Artichault (ar-tee-*show;* artichoke)
Asperge (as-*pearzh;* asparagus)
Aubergine (oe-bur-*zheen;* eggplant)
Champignons/Cèpes/Truffes/Girolles (sham-pee-*nyahn*/sep/troof/*gee*-roll; mushrooms)
Choucroute (shoo-*kroot;* sauerkraut)
Choux (shoo; cabbage)
Choux de Bruxelles (shoo dah broo-*zells;* Brussels sprouts)
Courgette (kore-*zhette;* zucchini)
Épinard (ay-pee-*nahr;* spinach)
Haricots (ahr-ee-*koe;* beans)
Haricots verts (*ahr*-ee-koe-vair; string beans)
Oignons (wah-*nyoh;* onions)
Petits pois (*pet*-tee pwah; peas)
Poireaux (pwah-*roe;* leeks)
Poivron rouge (pwah-vrah-*roozh;* red pepper)
Poivron vert(pwah-vrah-*vair;* green pepper)
Pomme de terre (pum-dah-*tair;* potato)
Pommes frites (pum freet; French fries)
Riz (ree; rice)
Tomate (toe-*maht;* tomato)

Les Fruits (lay free; fruit)

Abricot (*ah*-bree-koh; apricot)
Ananas (a-*na*-nas; pineapple)
Banane (bah-*nan;* banana)
Cerise (sair-*ees;* cherry)
Citron (sec-*troh;* lemon)
Citron vert (see-troh-*vair;* lime)
Fraise (frayz; strawberry)
Framboise (frahm-*bwahz;* raspberry)
Myrtille (meer-*teel;* blueberry)
Pamplemousse (pahm-pull-*moos;* grapefruit)
Pêche (pehsh; peach)
Poire (pwahr; pear)
Pomme (pum; apple)
Prune (proon; plum)
Pruneau (proo-*noh;* prune)
Raisin (rah-*zeen;* grape)
Raisin sec (rah-zeen-*sek;* raisin)

Les Desserts (lay day-sair; desserts)

Charlotte (shar-*lote;* molded cream ringed with a biscuit)
Clafoutis (clah-foo-*tee;* thick batter filled with fruit and fried)
Crème brûlée (krem broo-*lay;* creamy custard with caramel topping)
Fromage blanc (froe-*mahzh* blahn; smooth cream cheese)
Gâteau (gah-*toe;* cake)
Glace (glahs; ice cream)
Marquise (mar-*keez;* light, mousse-like cake)
Mousse au chocolat (moos oh shok-*lah;* chocolate mousse)
Tarte aux (tart oh; pie)
Tarte tatin (tart ta-*ta;* caramelized upside-down apple pie)
Vacherin (*vahsh*-reh; cake of layered meringue, fruit, and ice cream)

How Dishes Are Prepared

À l'ail (ah lai; with garlic)
Au four (oh fore; baked)
Béarnaise (bare-*nayse;* Hollandaise sauce with tarragon, vinegar, and shallots)
Bechamel (beh-sha-*mel;* white sauce made with onions and nutmeg)
Beurre blanc (bur blahn; white sauce made with butter, white wine, and shallots)
Bordelaise (bore-dah-*lays;* brown meat stock made with red wine, mushrooms, shallots, and beef marrow)
Bouilli (bwee-*ee;* boiled)
Bourguignon (bore-gee-*nyoh;* brown meat stock flavored with red wine, mushrooms, and onions)
Confit (kahn-*fee;* meat — usually duck or goose — cooked in its own fat)
Consommé (kahn-soe-*may;* clear broth)
Coulis (koo-*lee;* any nonflour sauce, purée, or juice)
En croûte (ahn *kroot;* in a pastry crust)
Cru (kroo; raw)

Diable (dee-*ah*-blah; brown sauce flavored with cayenne pepper, white wine, and shallots)

Estouffade (ay-too-*fahd;* meat that has been marinated, fried, and braised)

Farci (fahr-*see;* stuffed)

Feuilleté (fwee-eh-*tay;* in puff pastry)

Fumé (*foo*-may; smoked)

Gratiné (*grah*-tee-nay; topped with browned bread crumbs or cheese)

Grillé (*gree*-ay; grilled)

Hollandaise (ahl-lan-*dehs;* white sauce with butter, egg yolks, and lemon juice)

Lyonnais (lee-ohn-*nay;* with onions)

Marinière (mar-ee-*nyair;* steamed in garlicky wine stock)

Meunière (moo-*nyur;* fish rolled in flour and sautéed)

En papillote (ohn pah-pee-*oat;* cooked in parchment and opened at the table — usually fish)

Parmentier (pahr-men-tee-*ay;* with potato)

Provençal (pro-ven-*saw;* tomato-based sauce, with garlic, olives, and onions)

Rôti (*roe*-tee roasted)

Terrine (tuh-*reen;* cooked in an earthenware dish)

Chapter 14

Paris's Best Restaurants

· ·

In This Chapter

▶ Reviewing my favorite Paris restaurants

▶ Finding a restaurant by location, cuisine, and price

· ·

*O*ne of the best things about visiting Paris is finding out for yourself what a high-quality meal really is. You may want to experience a true French meal that stretches blissfully over several courses, and you can do just that at the establishments listed in this chapter. Each establishment has all the ingredients of an excellent dining spot — fantastic cooking, reasonable prices, and great atmosphere — and creates the kind of experience that lingers on in your memory after the last dishes are cleared away. When you're in the mood for just a light bite, turn to Chapter 15 for cafes, tearooms, wine bars, family chains, and sandwich shops.

The list here concentrates on moderately priced establishments from homey neighborhood favorites to chic "in" spots. Also included are some bargain eateries and a few of the city's most sumptuous restaurants where haute cuisine is an art form. Use the two maps in this chapter, "Restaurants on the Right Bank" and "Restaurants on the Left Bank," to locate the restaurants of your choice.

What the $ Symbols Mean

Restaurants are listed alphabetically for easy reference, followed by price ranges, neighborhoods, and types of cuisine. Price ranges reflect the cost of a three-course meal for one person ordered à la carte, featuring an appetizer, main dish, dessert, and coffee:

$	Less than 20€
$$	20€–30€
$$$	30€–50€
$$$$	50€–75€
$$$$$	More than 75€

The number of dollar signs used to describe each restaurant gives you a general idea of how much a meal costs at dinner, but don't make price your only criteria for choosing a restaurant. Most establishments offer fixed-price menus (also called *formules* or *prix fixe*) that can bring the cost down one whole price category. Likewise, if you're dying to try a place that's above your budget, visit it at lunch when meals are cheaper.

Paris Restaurants from A to Z

Au Bascou
$–$$ **Le Marais (3e)** **BASQUE/SOUTHWEST**

Specializing in dishes from the Basque country, the corner of southwestern France resting along the Spanish border, Au Bascou offers excellent meals and fills up fast. Start with *piperade*, a delicious concoction of sautéed peppers and onions on salad leaves topped with ham; then try superb seasonal fish or *agneau de lait des Pyrénées rôti* (roasted milk-fed lamb). Finish up with *gâteau Basque*, a cake made of ground almonds and jam. A bottle of Basque's Irrouleguy, a smooth red wine, makes a nice accompaniment to meals, and the service is friendly without being condescending.

38 rue Réaumur. ☎ *01-42-72-69-25. Métro: Arts et Métiers. (Exit the station at rue de Turbigo and cross over it to rue Réamur. Head east 1 block; the restaurant is on the corner of rue Réamur and rue Volta.) Main courses: 13€. AE, MC, V. Open: Tues–Fri noon to 2 p.m.; Mon–Sat 8–11 p.m.*

Ooh la la! Sampling the regional French cuisines

French cuisine is deservedly famous, and it's the various parts — the regional specialties — that add up to the wondrous and delicious whole.

Alsatian/Brasserie

Alsatian refers to the specialties from the Alsace region of France, which lies close to Germany. Most notable among these specialties are beer, Riesling wine, and *choucroute* (sauerkraut cooked in wine, topped with tender morsels of beef or pork, and accompanied by potatoes). Most Alsatian restaurants in Paris are brasseries (breweries).

Auvergne

This rugged region in the center of southern France is known for hearty peasant cooking with generous portions. *Potée,* a thick soup from this region, filled with cabbage, turnips, potatoes, leeks, and morsels of pork, is especially rich.

Basque/Southwest

This beautiful area bordering Spain is home to the spiciest cuisine of the French regions. Menus may include *cassoulet basquaise,* made with red beans and duck, and the very spicy *boudin noir* (blood sausages).

Breton

You'll know that a place is Breton when the menu consists of oysters, crêpes, and cider. Breton refers to the Brittany region on France's west coast, and Breton restaurants often boast low-beamed ceilings, checkered tablecloths, wildflowers in jugs, and an open stove.

Classic French

The meals of traditional French cooking have been enjoyed in France for centuries. French cooking is rich; dishes are made with butter, cream, and eggs, and organ meats often are used. Menus may include *cuisses de grenouilles* (frog's legs), *confit de canard* (duck leg preserved and cooked in its own fat), *blanquette de veau* (veal cooked in a whitish stew that includes eggs and cream), *pot-au-feu* (a hearty dish of boiled vegetables and beef that may include bone marrow), and *tarte tatin* (carmelized upside down apple pie).

Corsican

The earthy regional specialties from this island off the southern coast of France are not to be missed. Corsican livestock eat the herb-filled underbrush known as *maquis* that spicily infuses meats (*sanglier,* or wild boar, is a particular specialty) and cheeses (try the *brébis* in the cheesecake-like *fiadone,* a dessert from the island). Italian-influenced sauces and pasta are also on the menus; Corsica was once part of Italy.

Lyonnaise

Lyon, in central France, is home to celebrated chef Paul Bocuse, and sophisticated gastronomy is one of the city's chief attractions. A restaurant claiming to be Lyonnaise will have classic French dishes cooked to perfection and Lyonnaise specialties that may include *Jésus* (sausage with truffles) and *tablier de sapeur* (tripe, or the lining of a calf's stomach).

Provençal

The dishes in this southeastern region of France rely heavily on tomatoes, herbs, garlic, and olive oil, with olives and anchovies also figuring prominently. *Bouillabaisse,* a stew made with three kinds of fresh fish, saffron, onions, tomatoes, and herbs, is the region's most famous dish.

Restaurants on the Right Bank

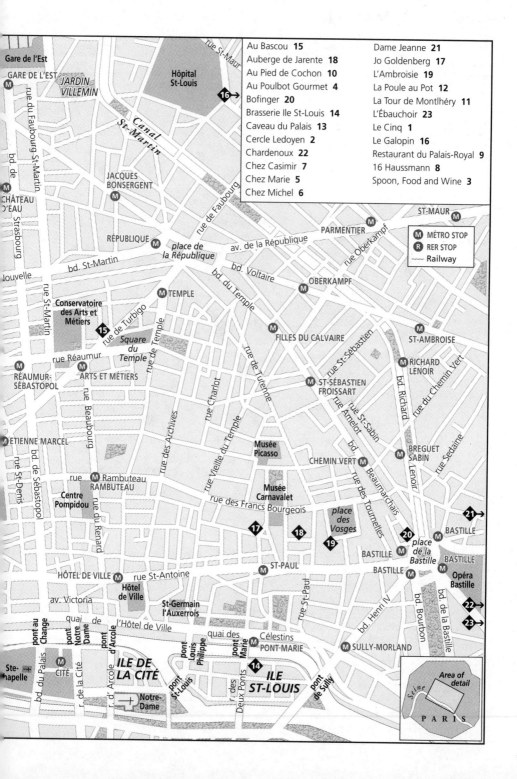

Au Bascou **15**
Auberge de Jarente **18**
Au Pied de Cochon **10**
Au Poulbot Gourmet **4**
Bofinger **20**
Brasserie Ile St-Louis **14**
Caveau du Palais **13**
Cercle Ledoyen **2**
Chardenoux **22**
Chez Casimir **7**
Chez Marie **5**
Chez Michel **6**

Dame Jeanne **21**
Jo Goldenberg **17**
L'Ambroisie **19**
La Poule au Pot **12**
La Tour de Montlhéry **11**
L'Ébauchoir **23**
Le Cinq **1**
Le Galopin **16**
Restaurant du Palais-Royal **9**
16 Haussmann **8**
Spoon, Food and Wine **3**

Ⓜ MÉTRO STOP
Ⓡ RER STOP
—— Railway

Restaurants on the Left Bank

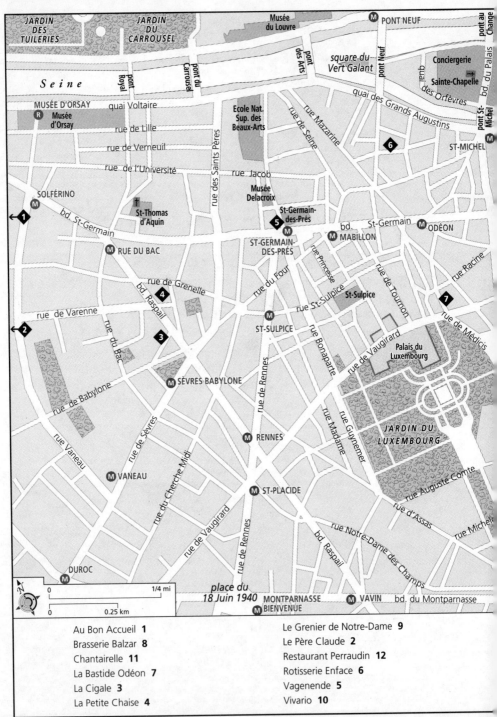

JARDIN DES TUILERIES

JARDIN DU CARROUSEL

Musée du Louvre

M PONT NEUF

pont au Change

pont Royal

pont du Carrousel

pont des Arts

square du Vert Galant

pont Neuf

Conciergerie

Sainte-Chapelle

quai du Palais

bd. du Palais

Seine

MUSÉE D'ORSAY

R Musée d'Orsay

quai Voltaire

Ecole Nat. Sup. des Beaux-Arts

quai des Grands Augustins

quai des Orfèvres

pont St-Michel

M ST-MICHEL

rue de Lille

rue de Verneuil

rue de l'Université

rue des Saints Pères

rue Jacob

rue de Seine

rue Mazarine

◆ 6

SOLFÉRINO

M

rue Jacob

Musée Delacroix

St-Germain-des-Prés

ODÉON M

◀ 1

bd. St-Germain

St-Thomas d'Aquin

◆ 5

ST-GERMAIN-DES-PRÉS

bd. St-Germain

M MABILLON

M RUE DU BAC

rue de Grenelle

bd. Raspail

◆ 4

rue du Four

rue Princesse

rue St-Sulpice

St-Sulpice

rue de Tournon

rue Racine

◆ 7

rue de Médicis

rue de Varenne

◀ 2

rue du Bac

◆ 3

ST-SULPICE

rue Bonaparte

Palais du Luxembourg

rue de Babylone

M SÈVRES BABYLONE

rue de Rennes

rue de Vaugirard

rue de Sèvres

rue Vaneau

rue du Cherche Midi

M RENNES

rue Madame

rue Guynemer

JARDIN DU LUXEMBOURG

M VANEAU

M ST-PLACIDE

rue d'Assas

rue Auguste Comte

rue Michelet

DUROC

M

place du 18 Juin 1940

MONTPARNASSE

M VAVIN

bd. du Montparnasse

M BIENVENUE

rue de Vaugirard

rue de Rennes

bd. Raspail

rue Notre-Dame des Champs

N

0   1/4 mi

0   0.25 km

Au Bon Accueil **1**	Le Grenier de Notre-Dame **9**
Brasserie Balzar **8**	Le Père Claude **2**
Chantairelle **11**	Restaurant Perraudin **12**
La Bastide Odéon **7**	Rotisserie Enface **6**
La Cigale **3**	Vagenende **5**
La Petite Chaise **4**	Vivario **10**

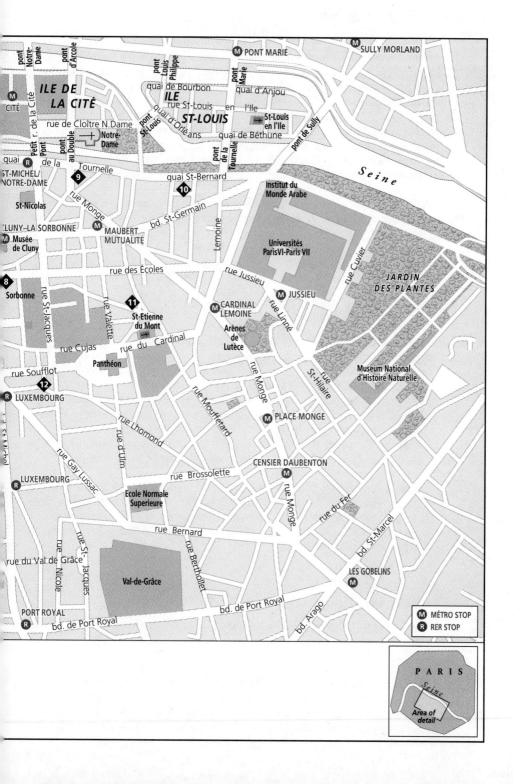

Auberge de Jarente

$$$ Le Marais (4e) BASQUE

When you've had enough of cream sauces, come here for the taste of southwest France where cooks use olive oil, tomatoes, and all kinds of peppers. The 39€ prix-fixe menu may include starters of *charcuterie, les chipirons au piment d'Espelette* (squid with a type of hot Basque pepper), or *la soupe des poissons* (fish soup), and for a main course, such Basque-influenced dishes as red fish with coriander and garlic, or duck breast with oyster mushrooms and sautéed apples. Choose from smooth Basque wines like irouleguy, tursan, and madiran. The rustic decor includes a cave-like cozy downstairs, and service is friendly.

7 rue de Jarente (between rue de Sevigné and rue de Turenne, just west of place des Vosges). ☎ 01-42-77-49-35. Métro: Bastille or St-Paul. (Take rue de Turenne and follow it 1 block to rue de Jarente.) 39€ prix fixe. AE, V. Open: Tues–Sat noon to 2:30 p.m. and 7:30–10:30 p.m. Closed three weeks in Aug.

Au Bon Accueil

$$–$$$ Eiffel Tower (7e) MODERN BISTRO

The menu here is simply amazing. It changes daily according to what owner Jacques Lacipière finds in the markets. If you're ordering from the prix-fixe menu, you may start with *filets de sardines mi-cuites à l'huile et romarin méli mélo de legumes provencaux* (sardines lightly grilled in oil with a blend of vegetables from Provence), followed by *steack de thon poélé et son caviar d'aubergine aux olives* (seared tuna steak with eggplant, caviar, and olives). Main dishes are divine and can include scallops with asparagus or whole lobster from Brittany roasted in herbs and tomatoes. Fantastic desserts include fig tart and crème brûlée made with walnuts. The place is nearly always full, so reserve in advance.

14 rue de Monttessuy. ☎ 01-47-05-46-11. Métro: Alma Marceau. (Exit the station, cross the Pont l'Alma and the quai Branly, and turn onto av. Rapp; follow av. Rapp 2 blocks to rue de Monttessuy and turn right.) Reservations strongly recommended. Main courses 9.50–54€; three-course prix fixe 29€. MC, V. Open: Mon–Fri noon to 2:30 p.m. and 7:30–10:30 p.m.

Au Pied de Cochon

$–$$$ Les Halles (1er) CLASSIC FRENCH

The welcoming gardenia-bedecked restaurant on a side street in Les Halles is Au Pied de Cochon, which opened in 1946 and has played a vibrant part of the history of this old market neighborhood. With marble, murals, elaborate sconces, chandeliers, and plenty of tourists, the restaurant provides great fun at manageable prices. You can have a plate of a half-dozen oysters or onion soup to start. Follow with grilled salmon or an *entrecôte maître d'hôtel* (rib steak in rich red-wine sauce) or their specialty and namesake, *pied de cochon* (pigs feet). Or, if you're daring —

and hungry — have the 43€ *plateau rouge:* ½ a Canadian lobster, langoustines, shrimp, crabs, and other red fish served on a towering pile of shaved ice. Finish with mouth-watering *profiteroles* (cream puffs).

6 rue Coquillière (between rue du Jour and rue Jean-Jacques Rousseau on the northwest side of the garden of the Forum des Halles shopping center). ☎ *01-40-13-77-00. Métro: Châtelet–Les Halles. Main courses: 13.50€–33.40€. AE, DC, V. Open: Daily 24 hours.*

Au Poulbot Gourmet
$$$ Montmartre (18e)   CLASSIC FRENCH

Photos of old Montmartre and original drawings by illustrator Francisque Poulbot adorn the walls, and chic burgundy leather banquettes are usually filled with a local crowd savoring moderately priced classic cuisine. Chef Jean-Paul Langevin brings tremendous finesse to the preparation and presentation of dishes such as *noisette d'agneau* (lamb slices) served with delicate splashes of mashed potatoes and spinach, and *marmite de poissons,* assorted fresh fish in a light saffron sauce. As an appetizer, the *oeufs pochés* (poached eggs) with smoked salmon is a standout. For dessert, try the *charlotte glacée,* a concoction made with ladyfingers and ice cream.

39 rue Lamarck. ☎ *01-46-06-86-00. Métro: Lamarck-Caulincourt. (Follow rue Lamarck from Sacré-Coeur; the resturant is about a third of the way down the hill.) Three-course prix-fixe 30€. MC, V. Open: Mon–Sat noon to 1:30 p.m. and 7:30–10:00 p.m.; Oct–May only Sun noon to 1:30 p.m.*

Bofinger
$$ Le Marais (4e)   ALSATIAN/BRASSERIE

Bofinger is one of Paris's best-loved restaurants with its dark wood, gleaming brass, bright lights, curved and painted glass ceiling, and waiters with long white aprons delivering good food. It's owned by the Flo brasserie chain, which means that you'll see similar menus in the chain's other restaurants, which include Julien and Brasserie Flo. The downstairs dining room is ornately decorated with Art Nouveau flourishes and a glass-domed ceiling. Upstairs is cozier with wood paneling and separate rooms for smokers. The menu features many Alsatian specialties, such as *choucroute* (sauerkraut with smoked ham), and oysters and foie gras for which the restaurant is renowned. Best of all: The prices are actually quite moderate for Paris.

5–7 rue de la Bastille. ☎ *01-42-72-87-82. Métro: Bastille. (Exit the station at bd. Beaumarchais and turn left at rue de la Bastille.) Main courses 12€–25€; lunch and dinner prix-fixe including a half-bottle of wine 20€ and 30€, respectively. AE, MC, V. Open: Mon–Fri noon to 3:00 p.m. and 6:30 p.m.–1:00 a.m; Sat–Sun noon to 1 a.m.*

Brasserie Balzar
$–$$ Latin Quarter (5e)   ALSATIAN/BRASSERIE

Brasserie Balzar has played host to some of France's most famous intellectuals, including Jean-Paul Sartre. It's always full of rich yuppies, even during off hours. The brasserie was the center of a controversy a few years ago when a group of regulars, including Adam Gopnik of the *New Yorker,* fought but ultimately failed to keep a chain from buying it. Nothing obvious has changed, however. People still stop here for coffee and pastries between lunch and dinner and drop in for drinks in the evening. Regulars go for *poulet rôti avec frites* (roast chicken with french fries) or *choucroute garni,* but you can also get a good veal liver (*foie de veau*), *steak au poivre,* and a few fresh fish dishes. Portions are copious. For dessert, try the *gâteau au chocolate amère* (bittersweet chocolate cake).

49 rue des Écoles (on the corner of rue de la Sorbonne and rue des Écoles, 1 block south of the Musee de Cluny). ☎ *01-43-54-13-67. Métro: Cluny-Sorbonne. Main courses: 12€–20€. AE, MC, V. Open: Daily noon to midnight. Closed Aug.*

Brasserie Ile St-Louis
$–$$ Ile St-Louis (4e)   ALSATIAN/BRASSERIE

Brasserie Ile St-Louis is loud and bustling, and is one of my favorite places for comfort food. It's also the last remaining independent brasserie in Paris, owned by the same family for more than 60 years. Once the favorite haunt of writer James Jones (*The Thin Red Line*), who kept a mug at the bar, its location is perfect: It's situated directly off the footbridge from Ile de la Cité to Ile St-Louis with an unparalleled view of the eastern tip of Ile de la Cité (including the back of Notre-Dame). The food is quintessentially Alsatian — *choucroute* with heaps of tender, biting sauerkraut and meaty slices of ham; the hearty cassoulet, laden with rich beans and tender pieces of lamb and pork; and ham shank atop a bed of lentils.

55 quai de Bourbon. ☎ *01-43-54-02-59. Métro: Pont Marie. Main courses: 11€–24€ lunch and dinner. V. Open: Fri–Tues noon to 1 a.m.; Thurs 6 p.m.–1 a.m.*

Caveau du Palais
$$ Ile de la Cité (4e)   CLASSIC FRENCH

Located in the heart of the charming, tree-lined place Dauphine, a secluded little park nestled off Pont Neuf near the tip of Isle de la Cité, is this pretty little restaurant serving excellent food at reasonable prices. Try the house's special *côte de boeuf,* grilled giant ribs, which are prepared for two. The *confit de canard et pommes Sarladaise,* duck served with crispy potato bits sauteed in goose liver drippings, is another must. Have a look at the original art on the walls — the owners display the work of up-and-coming artists.

19 place Dauphine. ☎ *01-43-26-04-28. Métro: Pont Neuf. Main courses: 14€–25€. AE, DC, MC, V. Open: Mon–Sat 12:15–2:30 p.m. and 7:15–10:30 p.m.*

Cercle Ledoyen

$$$$$ Champs-Elysées (8e)   CLASSIC FRENCH

The less expensive sister of 2-star Ledoyen restaurant, Cercle Ledoyen is a haven of greenery and gourmet pleasures off the noisy Champs-Elysées. It's also pricey (desserts start at 22€), but oh, is it worth it! Ledoyen's chef, Ghislaine Arabian (one of Paris's few female French chefs), offers light, classic cooking of French and Flemish dishes. The menu varies but may include *dos de cabillaud aux pousses d'épinards* (cod filet with baby spinach) or *carré d'agneau roti au romarin* (roasted lamb with rosemary). Desserts, such as pear tart, are wonderful, too. Although a meal for two here with wine runs more than 100€, this place is well worth the splurge. The restaurant may look familiar to you if you've seen Robert Altman's film *Prêt-à-Porter . . .* (also known as *Ready to Wear*).

1 av. Dutuit. ☎ *01-53-05-10-02. Métro: Franklin D. Roosevelt. (Exit the station, walk 1 block to the Champs-Elysées, and make a left; the restaurant is about 75 feet away.) Main courses: 49€–109€. AE, DC, MC, V. Open: Mon–Sat noon to 2:30 p.m. and 7:30–10:30 p.m.*

Chantairelle

$–$$ Latin Quarter (5e)   AUVERGNE

This charming little place has a backyard garden that children will love, while parents can appreciate the atmosphere that literally reeks of the Auvergne, the rugged south-central region of France. (Tiny bottles of essential oils made from native plants provide you with the scents of the region.) An old church door and a tiny fountain are incorporated into the decor, and a sound system plays bird songs and church bells. Order an appetizer — maybe some of the famous *charcuterie* (cold sliced meats) — only if you're ravenous; the delicious peasant food is presented in enormous portions. Main courses like *yssingeaux* (cabbage stuffed with beef, mushrooms, and sausage and wrapped in layered pastry) or *potée* (a tureen filled with pork, cabbage, potatoes, turnips, and leeks in broth) are substantial. Although most dishes use ham or pork, vegetarians enjoy the *croustade forestière* of assorted mushrooms and eggs poached with Fourme d'Ambert cheese. The best Auvergne wine is the Chateaugay, a fine fruity red.

17 rue Laplace. ☎ *01-46-33-18-59. Métro: Maubert-Mutualité. (Take the street behind the Panthéon, rue Valette, and turn right onto rue Laplace.) Main courses: 12€–18€. MC, V. Open: Mon–Fri noon to 2 p.m.; daily 7:00–10:30 p.m.*

Chardenoux

$$ Bastille (11e)   CLASSIC BISTRO

This small, charming place is at the top of the list of Parisians' favorite bistros. From the etched plate-glass windows to the swirling stucco decorations on the walls and ceiling and the lacy curtains in the windows, its turn-of-the-20th-century decor is the very essence of old Paris. (It has been appointed a Monument Historique.) Service is friendly and English-speaking. A variety of French regional dishes appears on the menu — try the *oeufs en meurette,* a Burgundian dish of poached eggs in a sauce of red wine and bacon, and the *boeuf en daube,* braised beef Provençal style. Wash it all down with a Château d'Ardennes (26€). Desserts are pure comfort food, especially the fruit tarts and the nougat in raspberry sauce.

1 rue Jules-Valles. ☎ *01-43-71-49-52. Métro: Charonne. (Exit the station on rue Charonne and walk 1 block to rue Jules-Valles. Turn left and walk to the end of the street. The restaurant is on the corner of rue Jules-Valles and rue Chanzy.) Main courses: 12€–20€. AE, MC, V. Open: Mon–Fri noon to 2 p.m.; Mon–Sat 8:00–11:30 p.m.*

Chez Casimir

$ Gare du Nord (10e)   CLASSIC FRENCH

The trip is worth it from almost anywhere to experience this hidden delight near the Gare du Nord, far from the more touristy sides of Paris. Chef Philippe Tredgeu works magic in his kitchen, cooking with ingredients he finds at the market that morning or the night before. Start with the refreshing *crème de petit pois au Parmesan,* a cold green pea soup with slices of Parmesan cheese served with toasted bread (take as much soup as you want from the pot placed on your table), then have *filet de rascasse avec des spaguetti de courgettes,* a scorpionfish filet served with spaghetti-style cooked zucchini, fresh-cut tomatoes, and a touch of vinegar, or leg of lamb cooked on the bone with aromatic juices and fresh peas. For dessert, indulge in homemade pastry topped with raspberries and vanilla cream, or *pain perdu* (French toast) and cherries cooked with honey. The wine list is highly affordable with prices starting at 7.50€ for half a bottle.

Beware the barkers

The 5e arrondissement's **rue de la Huchette** and **rue de la Harpe** are quaint and scenic, and the barkers shouting about the good food are unusual, to say the least. But beware of dining in these establishments: Your bill will be padded with all kinds of extras, from overpriced drinks to extra bread. For another scenic street in the 5e with much better food minus the bill padding, try **rue Mouffetard** behind the Panthéon (Métro: Cardinal Lemoine or Maubert Mutualité).

6 rue Belzunce. ☎ *01-48-78-28-80. Métro: Gare du Nord. (Exit the station on rue de Dunkerque and look for rue de Compiegne. Follow rue de Compiegne across bd. Magenta. Rue de Compiegne turns into rue Belzunce. The restaurant will be on your right.) Reservations recommended for dinner. Main courses: 13€–14€. No credit cards. Open: Mon–Fri noon to 2:00 p.m. and 7:00–11:30 p.m.; Sat 7:00–11:30 p.m.*

Chez Marie
$–$$ Montmartre (18e)   CLASSIC FRENCH

At the base of the steps heading to the place de Tertre, you can find some of the cheapest eats in this neighborhood, which isn't exactly known for bargain dining. Food is hearty, the owners are charming and friendly, and they welcome children in their humbly decorated, cozy dining room with wood benches, red and white picnic tablecloths, and wallpaper in the style of Toulouse Lautrec. Stick to the basics like lamb and frites or duck *confit* (duck cooked and preserved in its own fat), and you're guaranteed to leave full and content with money in your wallet.

27 rue Gabrielle. ☎ *01-42-62-06-26. Métro: Abbesses. Main courses 5.80€–20.70€; three-course menus (including apéritif) 9.90€, 17€, 21.20€. AE, DC, MC, V. Open: Daily noon to 3:30 p.m. and 6:00 p.m.–1:30 a.m. Closed Jan.*

Chez Michel
$$$ Gare du Nord (10e)   BRETON

Crowds of Parisians come here for excellent, unusual food at very fair prices. Chef Thierry Breton, the chef at the Presidential Palace during François Mitterand's tenure, puts old-fashioned Breton dishes on his menu; look for succulent scallops, hand picked by scuba divers, that are served with truffles in the winter. The menu might include *crème d'homard Bréton* (cream of lobster soup) or a side of home-style farm-raised pig roasted in butter. For the cheaper menu, sit in the cellar at wooden tables and eat all the shellfish, patés, and salads you can fit into your stomach — which is stretched by the end of the night. Choose from more than 100 different wines at retail cost, a truly dizzying experience.

10 rue Belzunce. ☎ *01-44-53-06-20. Métro: Gare du Nord. (Exit the station onto rue de Dunkerque and look for rue de Compiegne. Follow rue de Compiegne across bd. Magenta. Rue de Compiegne turns into rue Belzunce. Walk up rue Belzunce to the corner of rue Belzunce and rue St-Vincent de Paul, where you'll find the restaurant.) Three-course menu 30€, menu dégustation homard (lobster menu, reserve 2 days in advance) 60€. MC, V. Open: Tues–Sat noon to 2 p.m. and 7 p.m. to midnight. Closed last week of July and first three weeks of Aug.*

Dame Jeanne
$$ Bastille (11e)   MODERN BISTRO

Dame Jeanne is a bit of a hike from the Lédru-Rollin Métro stop but well worth the walk. Chef Francis Lévêque loves to cook (he conducts cooking classes here), and he creates memorable dishes at fair prices at this restaurant decorated in autumnal colors illuminated by soft lighting. The seasonal fruit and vegetable menu may have dishes like *fricassée de légumes au lard et à l'estragon* (sauteed vegetables served with cured ham and terragon) and desserts like carmelized brioche topped with sweetened banana. Main dishes may be duck breast sautéed with black olives or salmon roasted with spices. The reasonably priced wine list begins with Dame Jeanne's discoveries — lesser-known wines — for 14€ a bottle. Service is friendly.

60 rue de Charonne. ☎ *01-47-00-37-40. Métro: Lédru-Rollin. (Exit the station on rue du Faubourg-St-Antoine and walk east to the next street, passage de la Main d'Or. Follow this street about ¼-mile until you reach rue de Charonne. The restaurant is on the corner.) Reservations required. Main courses 15€; seasonal fruit and vegetable menu 20€. MC, V. Open: Tues–Sat noon to 2 p.m.; Tues–Thurs 7:30–11:00 p.m.; Fri–Sat 7:30–11:30 p.m.*

Jo Goldenberg

$ Le Marais (4e)   CENTRAL EUROPEAN

The atmosphere at Jo Goldenberg is convivial amid its long red banquettes surrounded by photographs of famous patrons, including former French President Mitterand, and original paintings of up-and-coming artists. Eastern specialties abound, such as poulet paprika, goulash, bagels, and Wienerschnitzel, and typical deli offerings like pastrami and corned beef — allegedly invented right here by Goldenberg senior in the 1920s. Adding to the festive air are the Gypsy musicians who begin playing around 9 p.m.

7 rue des Rosiers. ☎ *01-48-87-20-16. Métro: St-Paul. (Exit the station and cross over rue de Rivoli to rue Pavée. Follow rue Pavée to rue des Rosiers, about 800 feet. Turn left onto rue des Rosiers and walk about 350 feet.) Main courses: 10€–14€. AE, DC, MC, V. Open: Daily 9 a.m. to midnight.*

La Bastide Odéon

$$$ St-Germain-des-Prés   (6e) PROVENÇAL

After an evening stroll in the Jardin du Luxembourg head across the street for some delicious Provençal cooking in a lovely dining room. The menu changes regularly, but Chef Gilles Ajuelos's dynamic creations include cold omelet stuffed with eggpplant and basil in a red pepper sauce, or leek and goat cheese terrine with balsamic caramel, and for dessert, roasted pear and ricotta with gingerbread and cottage cheese ice cream. You can also savor an iced tomato soup with *grappa* (a strong, colorless brandy) or olives from the chef's *cuisine du marché* (from the market).

7 rue Corneille. ☎ *01-43-26-03-65. Métro: Odéon. (Exit the station and take rue de l'Odéon south to pl. de l'Odéon, where the Théâtre de l'Odéon is located. To the left of the theater is rue Corneille; take this about 150 feet to the restaurant.)*

Two-course menu: 20.34€ lunch, 30.34€ dinner. AE, MC, V. Open: Tues–Sat noon to 3:00 p.m. and 7:30–11:00 p.m. Closed Aug.

La Cigale

$–$$ Eiffel Tower (7e)   CLASSIC BISTRO

La Cigale serves delicious soufflés (among other specialties) to a sophisticated and high-spirited clientele in an intimate space of soft lighting and cozy tables. The food is simply some of the best you can get in Paris for these prices. The delicate soufflés are beaten high and brim with Camembert, sauteed spinach, or tarragon cream. They melt in your mouth. If you're not in the mood for a soufflé, other tempting entrées include a rump roast and succulent lamb chops. And dessert offers — you got it — soufflés of heavenly lemon and sinful chocolate.

11 rue Chomel. ☎ 01-45-48-87-87. Métro: Sèvres-Babylone. (Exit the station at bd. Raspail and head north, turning left onto rue Chomel; the restaurant is about 80 feet down.) Reservations recommended. Main dishes: 9€–17€. MC, DC, V. Open: Mon–Fri noon to 2:00 p.m.; Mon–Sat 7:30–11:00 p.m.

L'Ambroisie

$$$$$ Le Marais (4e)   HAUTE CUISINE

This is the place to take someone you *really* want to impress. Chef Bernard Pacaud creates exquisite food in this gorgeous 17th-century mansion on the place des Vosges. Specialties may include fricasée of lobster in wine sauce, roasted free-range chicken with black truffles, and an award-winning *tarte fine,* a chocolate pie served with bitter chocolate and mocha ice cream. The restaurant is made up of two high-ceilinged Renaissance-inspired salons, a cozy back room, and terrace dining in the summer. It calls out for marriage proposals, anniversaries, and other special and romantic events.

9 place des Vosges. ☎ 01-42-78-51-45. Métro: St. Paul. (Exit the station on rue St-Antoine and head east to rue de Birague, which leads into the place des Vosges. Turn left in the place des Vosges, follow the arcade around the corner to the restaurant.) Reserve at least four weeks ahead. Jacket and tie advised. No prix fixe; expect to spend at least 200€ per person per meal. AE, MC, V. Open: Tues–Sat noon to 1:30 p.m. and 8:00–9:30 p.m. Closed two weeks in Feb and three weeks in Aug.

La Petite Chaise

$$ St-Germain-des-Prés (7e)   CLASSIC FRENCH

Originally built in the mid-17th century, this small gem is alleged to be the oldest restaurant in Paris. The entranceway, adorned with a smoky antique mirror from the early 18th century, leads to a softly illuminated, cozy dining room reminiscent of an old country inn. Start with *escargots bourguignon* (snails in garlic and butter) or the homemade *foie gras de canard* (duck liver paté). As a main dish, the *magret de canard pomme et miel* (duck breast cooked with apples and honey) melts away your appetite. A piece of chocolate cake with English cream tops off your meal with the elegance the nobility used to enjoy in their visits to the restaurant some 300 years ago. The old maxim holds true: The best things in life never change.

36 rue de Grenelle. ☎ 01-42-22-13-35. Métro: Sèvres-Babylone. (Exit the station on bd. Raspail and walk 1 block north to rue de la Chaise. Follow the street to the end, where it intersects rue de Grenelle.) Main courses (with a half-bottle wine): 19.05€. AE, MC, V. Open: Daily noon to 2:00 p.m. and 7:00–10:45 p.m.

Fast French food zones

When you're short on time or money, the following streets have many restaurants with fast service at low prices.

Avenue d'Ivry and **Avenue de Choisy,** 13e. Far off the tourist track, the Vietnamese, Chinese, and Thai restaurants along these wide avenues cater to the local southeast Asian population. Prices are low and quality is high, and you can eat like the locals.

Bd. de Belleville, 11e. This street of features many *couscouseries* (couscous restaurants) that are reasonably priced and satisfactory, if not outstanding. Middle Eastern snacks, pastries, and a glass of mint tea make an exotic and inexpensive meal.

Bd. du Montparnasse, 14e. The 1 block between rue Vavin and bd. Raspail has four cafes with literary associations (early 20th-century writers such as Hemingway and Fitzgerald, Joyce and St-Vincent Millay spent a lot of time at La Coupole, Le Dôme, Le Select, and La Rotonde), high and moderately priced seafood restaurants, creperies, sandwich shops, and ethnic specialties.

Métro Belleville, 11e. The streets radiating out from this station are the northern headquarters for Asian cuisine. You can usually slurp down noodle soup at any hour of the day and well into the night.

Rue des Rosiers, in the Marais, 3e. People have been known to trudge across town for the huge pita-bread sandwiches sold on this street. Stuffed with falafel (deepfried chickpea balls), eggplant, and salad, and then topped with your choice of sauce, this must be the best 4€ meal in town.

Rue du Montparnasse, 14e. The street between boulevard Edgar Quinet and boulevard du Montparnasse is a Crêperie Row of inexpensive Breton eateries. Whether the *crêpes* are sugared up with syrups and jam or stuffed with vegetables and meat (these are often called *galettes*), they make a tasty light meal for less than 9€.

Rue Sainte-Anne, 9e. Sushi usually is expensive in Paris, but because this street lies within the same neighborhood as many Japanese businesses, you find the freshest fish and most authentic Japanese dishes at moderate prices.

La Poule au Pot
$$ **Les Halles (1er)** **CLASSIC BISTRO**

Poule au pot, an old French recipe of chicken stewed with broth and vegetables, has been served here since 1935 with much success if the *livre d'or* (a gold book filled with the names of visiting celebrities) means anything. When Les Halles still was Paris's marketplace, its workers came to La Poule au Pot here to share a bowl of poule au pot. After the market's demise, visits from such celebrities as Maurice Chevalier, Miou Miou, the Rolling Stones, and Prince kept this Parisian bistro on the map. The atmosphere created by the long zinc bar, *pots* of wine, red leather banquettes, wood paneling, and waiters in long aprons transports you back to another era. How can the menu serve anything other than traditional French fare? Begin with *foie gras maison* (house goose liver paté), or *œufs cocotte à la crème* (eggs baked with cream), then try the *rognons de veau à la graine de moutarde* (veal kidneys cooked with mustard grains), or the succulent house poule au pot (28€) with a tureen of the broth on the side. Finish with a velvety crème brûlée.

9 rue Vauvilliers. ☎ *01-42-36-32-96. Métro: Louvre-Rivoli. (Exit the station on rue de Rivoli and cross the street to rue du Louvre. Walk 2 blocks to rue St-Honoré and make a right. Proceed 2 blocks to rue Vauvilliers. The restaurant is near the end of the street, close to the gardens of the Forum des Halles.) Main courses: 28€–40€. MC, V. Open: Mon–Sat 7 p.m.–5 a.m.*

La Tour de Montlhéry
$$ **Les Halles (1er)** **CLASSIC FRENCH**

With barrels of wine, a zinc bar, and a homey dining room with hams and sausages dangling from its beams, this is a true Parisian restaurant. It's also a meat lover's place. The less expensive items on the menu tend to be dishes like tripe Calvados and stuffed cabbage and kidneys. Other typical dishes are grilled lamb chops and, for those who want to try truly authentic, reputably delicious French fare, *cervelles d'agneau* (sauteed lamb's brain). *Bon courage!*

5 rue des Prouvaires. ☎ *01-42-36-21-82. Métro: Louvre-Rivoli. (Exit the station on rue de Rivoli and head east to rue du Roule. Follow rue du Roule to rue St-Honoré, where Roule becomes rue des Prouvaires. The restaurant is near the corner of Prouvaires and St-Honoré.) Reservations required. Main courses: 13.70€–19.80€. V. Open: Mon–Fri 24 hours. Closed July 10–Aug 15.*

L'Ébauchoir
$$ **Bastille (12e)** **CLASSIC BISTRO**

Tucked into a part of the Bastille often overlooked by tourists, this restaurant is well worth the visit. A mural pays homage to the working class roots of the neighborhood, and the space is just large enough to render dining here a bit noisy. Friendly waiters rush to show diners seated at the first-come, first served tables the day's offerings written on a tall chalkboard, and once you've sampled lunch or dinner, you find the superb food more than makes up for the decibel level. Diners may be offered appetizers of warm foie gras or stuffed ravioli followed by mouth-watering red label filet of bass with a saffron cream or steak in a red-wine Bordelaise sauce. For dessert, the *mille feuille* (a flaky multilayered pastry) is divine. On one visit, the waiter recommended mountain honey they had received that day from an *apiculteur* (bee keeper) to accompany dessert.

45 rue de Citeaux. ☎ *01-43-42-49-31. Métro: Faidherbe-Chaligny. (Exit the station on rue du Faubourg St-Antoine. Walk 1 block to rue de Citeaux and turn left. The restaurant is next to a small alley called the Impasse Druinot.) Reservations not accepted. Main courses: 11€–18.50€. MC, V. Open: Mon–Thu noon to 2:30 p.m. and 8:00–10:30 p.m. (Fri–Sat till 11 p.m.).*

Le Cinq

$$$$$ Champs-Elysées (8e)   HAUTE CUISINE

Chef Phillippe Legendre has earned high acclaim for Le Cinq, a heavenly bastion of elegance. Every element is in place, from the stately yet serene dining room with its high ceilings and overstuffed chairs to the Limoges porcelain and Riedel stemware created for the restaurant and the perfect waitstaff. The sumptuous and inventive cuisine includes *crème de cresson de source glacée au caviar Sevruga* (chilled watercress cream with Sevruga caviar), *blanc manger au caviar d'Aquitaine, avocat mariné à l'huile de noisette* (sole mousse with French caviar and avocado marinated in hazelnut oil), and for dessert, the delightful *autour de la fraise,* a whimsical assortment of strawberry confections ranging from strawberry tiramisu to sorbet of strawberry and green tomato. Dining here is truly a special experience.

31 av. George V (in the Four Seasons George V Hotel). ☎ *01-49-52-71-54. Métro: George V. Reservations required. Gourmet tasting menu 190€; main courses 38€–60€. AE, MC, V. Open: Daily 5:30–10:30 p.m.*

Le Galopin

$ Belleville (10e)   ALSATIAN/BRASSERIE

Yes, it's off the beaten track, but it's worth the jouney for tasty inexpensive traditional French food in a homey, casual atmosphere. Le Galopin overlooks the tree-lined pl. St-Marthe. Appetizers may include a moist and delicate *terrine campagne* (country-style casserole with vegetables) or fresh mushrooms in a light cream sauce, followed by entrees of tuna steak in an herb-sprinkled sauce Provençal, and a delicious *rôti de veau* (roast veal). Fresh ratatouille (a southern French dish made from tomatoes, eggplant, onions, zucchini, peppers, and garlic) and a tasty carrot salad garnish many of the dishes. And you must try the ice cream, which is made on the premises and features flavors like honey nut, cinnamon, and lavender. Traditional French music is performed on weekends, and patrons are encouraged to sing along (dinner costs 10% more at these times to cover the costs of the musicians).

34 rue Sainte Marthe. ☎ *01-53-19-19-55. Métro: Belleville. (Exit the station on the west side of bd. de la Villette. Turn left onto rue de Sambre et Meuse, and take the first left onto rue St-Marthe. The restaurant will be on your left in front of the little square.) Two- and three-course dinner menus 9.90€ and 15€, respectively. AE, DC, MC, V. Open: Tues–Sat noon to 2:30 p.m. and 8:00–11:00 p.m. (Sat till midnight); Sun brunch noon to 2:30 (except summer), dinner 8:00–11:00 p.m.*

Le Grenier de Notre-Dame
$ Latin Quarter (5e)   VEGETARIAN

Le Grenier is GREEN, from the walls and tablecloths to the outdoor patio under a balcony of hanging plants, as if to prove that, yes, this is a vegetarian restaurant. The food is good; especially recommended is the *cassoulet végétarien,* with white beans, onions, tomatoes, and soy sausage. The couscous and the cauliflower *au gratin* are also delicious. Le Grenier has a well-deserved reputation for desserts, such as *tarte de tofu.* The wine list includes a variety of organic offerings.

18 rue de la Bûcherie. ☎ *01-43-29-98-29. RER: St-Michel/Notre-Dame. (Exit onto quai de Montebello; turn right onto rue d'Arcole, then left onto rue de la Bûcherie.) Three courses 12.04€, main courses 9.61€–11.37€. MC, V. Open: Mon–Thurs 12:30–3:00 p.m. and 7:00–10:30 p.m.; Fri–Sat noon to 2:30 p.m. and 7:00–11:00 p.m.; Sun noon to 3:00 p.m. and 7:00–10:30 p.m.*

Le Père Claude
$$ Eiffel Tower (15e)   CLASSIC BISTRO

The rotisserie behind the bar signals that the house specialty here is roasted meat, and that's an understatement: Le Père Claude is known for its enormous portions of red meat dishes. Starters include warm sausage with pistachio and apples, or *terrine de gibier et foie gras de canard* (game terrine with duck liver). The *panaché de viandes* is an assortment of perfectly roasted meats served with a comforting heap of mashed potatoes. Make sure you specify how you want the beef cooked, or it will be served the way the French like it — *bleue,* which means very, very rare. Seafood lovers won't be disappointed in the mussel soup with saffron or the *assiette de pecheur aux pates fraiches* (fisherman's plate with fresh terrine). President Jacques Chirac and Don King have been spotted (separately) chowing down here, but it's usually home to families and, to a lesser extent, tourists with big appetites. After dinner, you can stroll up the avenue de La-Motte-Picquet and take in a view of the spectacular illuminated Eiffel Tower.

51 av. de La Motte-Picquet. ☎ *01-47-34-03-05. Métro: La-Motte-Picquet–Grenelle. (Exit the station on av. de La Motte-Picquet and head northeast about ¼-mile, toward the Champ de Mars.) Main courses: 15€–24€. AE, MC, V. Open: Daily 11:30am–2:30 p.m. and 7:00 p.m. to midnight.*

Restaurant du Palais-Royal

$$$ Louvre (1er)   CLASSIC FRENCH

The elegant arcade that encircles the gardens inside the Palais-Royal also surrounds this restaurant, making it one of the most romantic locations in Paris. Sit at the terrace on warm, sun-filled days and begin your meal with starters such as marinated leeks in a beet-juice vinaigrette or scallop salad. Main dishes vary with the season but may include grilled tuna steak with a Basque relish, or filet mignon and *frites* (french fries). The desserts are delicious, and the good house red wine is served Lyonnaise-style in thick-bottomed bottles. The dining room was recently renovated and shines in tones of gold, silver, and warm red whenever dining outside just isn't an option.

43 rue Valois (on the northeast side of the Palais-Royal arcade). ☎ *01-40-20-00-27. Métro: Palais-Royal-Musée du Louvre. Main courses: 18€–31.50€. AE, DC, MC, V. Open: Mon–Fri 12:15–2:15 p.m. and Mon–Sat 7:15–9:30 p.m. Closed from the end of Dec to the end of Jan.*

Restaurant Perraudin

$–$$ Latin Quarter (5e)   CLASSIC BISTRO

People say that Ernest Hemingway went to the Closerie des Lilas when rich, and Perraudin was his favorite spot when broke. Professors and students from the nearby Sorbonne, and families and tourists enjoy this historic bistro, with its red-checked tablecloths and lace lampshades, jolly atmosphere, and staff that welcomes kids. A bargain lunch menu offers a choice of three appetizers, two main courses, and cheese or dessert. You may start with tomatoes and mozzarella, or *flammekueche* (square, thin-crusted pizzas topped with cream, herbs, or cheese), then have ham with endive or roast beef, followed by *tarte tatin*. Classic dishes like duck confit and *gigot d'agneau* (leg of lamb) with *gratin Dauphinois* (cheese-topped potatoes) are on the à la carte menu. At lunch, Madame Perraudin offers a quarter-liter of red wine for 2€. Arrive early for a table, because reservations aren't accepted here.

157 rue St-Jacques (on the west side of the Panthéon, take rue Soufflot to rue St-Jacques and turn left). ☎ *01-46-33-15-75. RER: Luxembourg. Reservations not accepted. Main courses around 10€; three-course gastronomic menu 22€. No credit cards. Open: Tues–Fri noon to 2:30 p.m.; Mon–Sat 7:30–10:00 p.m.*

Rotisserie En Face

$$$ St-Germain-des-Prés (6e)   MODERN BISTRO

This baby bistro is across the street (*en face*) from Jacques Cagna's first huge Parisian success, Restaurant Jacques Cagna. It's the first of four bistros he subsequently opened. The decor is cozy and subdued, yet a bit eclectic — the focus of the room is on the figurine of a woman in a striped bathing suit, her arm slung companiably over a fish. Cagna's modern approach to hearty bistro dishes draws crowds of publishing people for lunch, and the local elegant set for dinner. Everything's delicious, and may even warrant a return trip before you go back home! Freshly baked warm bread accompanies starters like the _quenelles de brochet, sauce Nantua aux crustacés_ (poached pike dumplings filled with mousse in a creamy crustacean sauce), or a dozen wild Burgundy snails. Main courses include _cuisse de lapin à la sauge et légumes grillés à l'huile d'olive_ (spit-roasted rabbit leg served with gravy and vegetables grilled in olive oil) or _aïoli de morue fraîche, bulots, laitue de mer et légumes de saison à la vapeur_ (cod fish filet served with sea snails, braised seaweed, steamed vegetables, and garlic mayonnaise). Finish up with a caramel and walnut ice cream cake, or raspberry and redcurrant flan.

2 rue Christine. ☎ _01-43-26-40-98. Métro: Odéon. (Exit the station on bd. St-Germain and make a left onto rue l'Éperon. Follow it to rue St-André des Arts and make a left. Follow and make a right onto rue des Grands Augustins; the restaurant is up the street on the left at the corner of rue des Grands Augustins and rue Christine.) Three-course menu 39€. AE, DC, MC, V. Open: Mon–Fri noon to 2:30 p.m. and Mon–Sat 7:00–11:00 p.m. (Fri and Sat till 11:30 p.m.)._

16 Haussmann

$$$ Opéra (9e)   CLASSIC FRENCH

Bold concoctions are the hallmarks of this restaurant. _Oeufs coques à la crème d'épices et caramel de xérés_ (soft-boiled eggs in sherry cream sauce with spices) is a good dish to start off your meal, while the cod roasted with truffle oil and basil is a delicious main course. Even with a tureen of salmon spread as an hors d'oeuvre, the two-course menu may not satisfy a large appetite, so plan on sampling one of the luscious desserts. A good selection of wines is available by the glass.

In the Hôtel Ambassador, 16 bd. Haussmann. ☎ _01-48-00-06-38. Métro: Chausée d'Antin or Richelieu-Drouot. Two-course menu 30€; three-course menu 37€. AE, DC, MC, V. Open: Mon–Fri noon to 2:30 p.m. and 7:00–10:30 p.m._

Spoon, Food and Wine

$$–$$$ Champs-Elysées (8e)   MODERN BISTRO

Many-starred chef Alain Ducasse has reinvented the joy of dining out in this restaurant designed to celebrate dining "freedom." A variety of international dishes are presented through a menu of mixing and matching; the customer chooses the condiment, side dishes, and vegetables from the menu shown in columns numbered 1, 2, and 3. For example, say you decide you want fish. Choose the type of fish you want from column 1 (pan-seared tuna and pan-seared scallops are among the choices), then decide which sauce you want from column 2 (spicy citrus and satay are among sauces listed). Column 3 lists the side dishes, like Thai rice, or caramelized chicory. It's an interesting concept that doesn't always work, but it's plenty of fun all the same. Spoon has one of the most international wine lists in Paris, with 120 from South Africa, Argentina, and New Zealand. Desserts are delicious; the only oddity is the bubble gum ice cream. Opt for the oozing warm chocolate "pizza"; it's simply heaven.

14 rue de Marignan. ☎ *01-40-76-34-44. Métro: Franklin-D-Roosevelt. (Exit the station on the west side of the Champs-Elysées and head west. Take a left at the passage Marignan, then take another left onto rue de Marignan. The restaurant is about 100 feet away.) Reservations recommended one month in advance. Main courses: 14.48€–38.11€. AE, MC, V. Open: Mon–Fri 11:45 a.m.–2:30 p.m. and 6:30–11:30 p.m.*

Vagenende
$$ St-Germian-des-Prés (6e)   ALSATIAN/BRASSERIE

M. Chartier, of the 9e arrondissement restaurant of the same name, founded Vagenende in 1904 as a *bouillon* (a workers' canteen or soup kitchen). The restaurant evolved into a brasserie that is now classified as a Monument Historique. The Art Nouveau decor is authentic — mirrors, frescoes, and swirling floral patterns abound within walls of dark wood. Lace curtains, globe lights, and spacious booths enhance the classic atmosphere. The dishes are equally classic: You may start out with a half-dozen Fine des Claires oysters or soup of rockfish served with red pepper mayonnaise. Main courses include *confit de canard* (duck confit), suckling pig with carmelized onions and Indian spices, or *pavé de morue sauce vierge* (cod with lemon-flavored sauce). Finish up with a vanilla- and bourbon-flavored crème brûlée.

142 bd. St-Germain. ☎ *01-43-26-68-18. Métro: Odéon. Main courses 11€–23.17€; prix fixe 23.17€. AE, DC, MC, V. Open: Daily noon to 1 a.m.*

Vivario
$$ Latin Quarter (5e)   CORSICAN

You'll want to see Corsica after you eat at Vivario, an excellent spot to sample the hearty flavors of the Belle Isle, Napoléon's birthplace. Many of the products used in Vivario's dishes come straight from sunny Corsica to the dim, cavelike restaurant, with ceiling beams and stone walls. To start, opt for the rich traditional Corsican soup, teeming with beans, vegetables, and generous pieces of dried prosciutto. Or try the charcuterie plate served with a Mason jar of spicy cornichons (small pickles). Follow with *cabri rôti à la Corse* (roast goat) or eggplant with cheese and spicy tomato sauce. Chewy whole-wheat baguettes accompany the meal, which may end with a selection of Corsican cheeses or the Corsican dessert *fiadone,* a cheesecake made with mild *bruccio,* the island's famous, pungent cheese.

6 rue Cochin. ☎ *01-43-25-08-19. Métro: Maubert-Mutualité. (Cross the pont de l'Archeveque behind Notre-Dame to the Left Bank and turn left onto the quai de la Tournelle. Make a right onto rue de Pontoise and the first left onto rue Cochin. The restaurant is about 100 feet away.) Main courses: 9.40€–19.30€. AE, MC, V. Open: Tues–Fri noon to 2 p.m.; Mon–Sat 7:30–10:00 p.m.*

Index of Restaurants by Neighborhood

Louvre, Les Halles (1er)
Au Pied de Cochon $–$$$
Caveau du Palais $$
La Poule au Pot $$
La Tour de Montlhéry $$
Restaurant du Palais-Royal $$$

Le Marais, Ile St-Louis/ Ile de la Cité (3e, 4e)
Au Bascou $–$$
Auberge de Jarente $$$
Bofinger $$
Brasserie Ile St-Louis $–$$
Jo Goldenberg $
L'Ambroisie $$$$$

Latin Quarter (5e)
Brasserie Balzar $–$$
Chantairelle $–$$
Le Grenier de Notre-Dame $
Restaurant Perraudin $–$$
Vivario $$

St-Germain-des-Prés (6e)
La Bastide Odéon $$$
La Petite Chaise $$
Rotisserie En Face $$$
Vagenende $$

Eiffel Tower and Invalides (7e, 15e)
Au Bon Accueil $$–$$$
La Cigale $–$$
Le Père Claude $$

Champs-Elysées (8e)
Cercle Ledoyen $$$$$
Le Cinq $$$$$
Spoon, Food and Wine $$–$$$

Opéra (9e)
16 Haussmann $$$

Gare du Nord, Belleville (10e)
Chez Casimir $
Chez Michel $$$
Le Galopin $

Bastille (11e)
Chardenoux $$
Dame Jeanne $$
L'Ébauchoir $$

Montmartre (18e)
Au Poulbot Gourmet $$$
Chez Marie $–$$

Index of Restaurants by Cuisine

Alsatian/Brasserie
Bofinger ($$, Le Marais)
Brasserie Balzar ($–$$, Latin Quarter)
Brasserie Ile St-Louis ($–$$, Ile St-Louis)
Le Galopin ($, Belleville)
Vagenende ($$, St-Germain-des-Prés)

Auvergne
Chantairelle ($–$$, Latin Quarter)

Basque/Southwest
Au Bascou ($–$$, Le Marais)
Auberge de Jarente ($$$, Le Marais)

Breton
Chez Michel ($$$, Gare du Nord)

Central European
Jo Goldenberg ($, Le Marais)

Classic Bistro
Chardenoux ($$, Bastille)
La Cigale ($–$$, Eiffel Tower)
La Poule au Pot ($$, Les Halles)
L'Ébauchoir ($$, Bastille)
Le Père Claude ($$, Eiffel Tower)
Restaurant Perraudin ($–$$, Latin Quarter)

Classic French
Au Pied de Cochon ($–$$$, Les Halles)
Au Poulbot Gourmet ($$$, Montmartre)
Caveau du Palais ($$, Ile de la Cité)
Cercle Ledoyen ($$$$$, Champs-Elysées)
Chez Casimir ($, Gare du Nord)
Chez Marie ($–$$, Montmartre)
La Petite Chaise ($$, St-Germain-des-Prés)
La Tour de Montlhéry ($$, Les Halles)

Restaurant du Palais-Royal ($$$, Louvre)
16 Haussmann ($$–$$$, Opéra)

Corsican
Vivario ($$, Latin Quarter)

Haute Cuisine
L'Ambroisie ($$$$$, Le Marais)
Le Cinq ($$$$$, Champs-Elysées)

Modern Bistro
Au Bon Accueil ($$–$$$, Eiffel Tower)
Dame Jeanne ($$, Bastille)
Rotisserie En Face ($$$, St-Germain-des-Prés)
Spoon, Food and Wine ($$–$$$, Champs-Elysées)

Provençal
La Bastide Odéon ($$$, St-Germain-des-Prés)

Vegetarian
Le Grenier de Notre-Dame ($, Latin Quarter)

Index of Restaurants by Price

$
Au Bascou (Le Marais)
Au Pied de Cochon (Les Halles)
Brasserie Balzar (Latin Quarter)
Brasserie Ile St-Louis (Ile-St-Louis)
Chantairelle (Latin Quarter)
Chez Casimir (Gare du Nord)
Chez Marie (Montmartre)
Jo Goldenberg (Le Marais)
La Cigale (Eiffel Tower)
Le Galopin (Belleville)
Le Grenier de Notre-Dame (Latin Quarter)
Restaurant Perraudin (Latin Quarter)

$$
Au Bon Accueil (Eiffel Tower)
Bofinger (Le Marais)
Caveau du Palais (Ile de la Cité)
Chardenoux (Bastille)
Dame Jeanne (Bastille)
La Petite Chaise (St-Germain-des-Prés)
La Poule au Pot (Les Halles)
La Tour de Montlhéry (Les Halles)
L'Ébauchoir (Bastille)
Le Père Claude (Eiffel Tower)
Spoon, Food and Wine (Champs-Elysées)
Vagenende (St-Germain-des-Prés)
Vivario (Latin Quarter)

$$$

Auberge de Jarente (Le Marais)
Au Poulbot Gourmet (Montmartre)
Chez Michel (Gare du Nord)
La Bastide Odéon (St-Germain-
    des-Prés)
Restaurant du Palais-Royal (Louvre)
Rotisserie en Face (St-Germain-
    des-Prés)
16 Haussmann (Opéra)

$$$$–$$$$$

Cercle Ledoyen (Champs-Elysées)
L'Ambroisie (Le Marais)
Le Cinq (Champs-Elysées)

Chapter 15

On the Lighter Side: Snacks and Meals on the Go

● ●

In This Chapter

▶ Tracking down the best street food

▶ Grabbing a sandwich

▶ Filling up in a caféteria

▶ Finding the fixings for a great picnic

▶ Lounging in the hippest cafés, tea salons, and wine bars

▶ Screaming for ice cream

● ●

*F*ace it: Who can sit down to multiple-course meals every day —
even if they are cooked by legendary chefs? Fortunately, many
alternatives to a full meal are available. You can choose from street
food and sandwiches to cafeterias and tea salons, and if your stay is
blessed with fabulous weather, you definitely want to have a picnic.
(Find the best places to get picnic fare here, and then check out
Chapter 25 for the ten best places to take that picnic grub.)

No, I haven't forgotten that Parisian institution, the café. This chapter
fills you in on some of the best cafés and their more sophisticated sis-
ters, the wine bars — visit both and join in the great French art of
people watching!

Partaking of Paris Street Food

Some street vendors sell Belgian waffles, called *gaufres,* served warm
with powdered sugar or chocolate sauce, but the Parisian street food
you'll see the most is the *crêpe* — a thin wheat pancake stuffed with a

filling that's either salty or sweet. When served with savory fillings, like cheese or mushrooms, the crêpe becomes a *galette*. Sweet crêpe fillings include plain powdered sugar, chocolate-hazelnut spread, ice cream, or jam (called *compote*). Talk about a sugar rush!

You can find stalls or carts selling crêpes near most of the major attractions, in the parks and bigger gardens, and along the rue de Rivoli between the Marais and the place de la Concorde. When you buy a crêpe from a street vendor, you won't have much of a choice of sweet fillings; for a more extensive menu visit a crêperie.

Make a meal of crêpes at one of the many good establishments on rue du Montparnasse, where you can settle down in a peaceful atmosphere with a bowl of cider (a Breton specialty), a galette for a main course, and a crêpe for dessert — usually under 12€ a person (Métro: Edgar Quinet or Montparnasse-Bienvenüe).

The other typical Parisian street food, *panini,* is also sold just about anywhere. Named for the Italian-style bread they're made with, panini can be almost any filling stuck between two slices of bread, then flattened and grilled between two hot plates. The most common fillings are mozzarella, basil, and sun-dried tomatoes (a pizza sandwich, if you will). Panini are cheap, tasty, and easy to eat on the run.

Snacking on Sandwiches

Even sandwiches are yummy in France. Sandwich (and more) shops Lina's, Cosi, and Le Pain Quotidien make their own breads. See the "Light Meals in the Heart of the Right Bank" and "Light Meals in the Heart of the Left Bank" maps for locations.

- If nothing will do but a bagel, try **The Bagel Place,** 51 pass Choiseul, 2e (☎ 01-42-86-07-36; Métro: Pyramides), a mecca for homesick Yanks, offering a baker's dozen of New York-style bagels and a blackboard full of bagel sandwich specials.

- **Cosi,** 54 rue de Seine, 6e (☎ 01-46-33-35-36; Métro: St-Germain-des-Prés), serves its sandwiches on delicious homemade flat bread, and fillings are plentiful and delicious. You can choose from an assortment of specialties, including mozzarella, Parmesan, Italian ham, roast tomatoes, and tapenade (olive spread). Another branch is at 95 rue Réamur, 2e (☎ 01-40-26-13-30).

- **Le Pain Quotidien,** 18 Marché-St-Honoré, 1er (☎ 01-42-96-31-70; Métro: Tuileries), is one of the best bakeries in Paris, and you can order one of the delicious tartines (open-faced sandwiches) made with combinations like country ham and Gruyère cheese, or goat cheese and honey; or beef, basil, and Parmesan. Locations are popping up all over; another is in the Marais at 18 rue des Archives, 4e (☎ 01-44-54-03-07).

✔ **Lina's,** 22 rue St-Pères, 7e (☎ 01-40-20-42-78; Métro: St-Germain-des-Prés), packs an assortment of fillings onto whole-meal bread and rolls, American deli-style. Add a soup or salad and finish with a brownie for a quick meal. Another location is at 7 av. de l'Opéra, 1er (☎ 01-47-03-30-29).

✔ **Pomme de Pain,** 76 rue de Rivoli, 4e (☎ 01-42-74-64-93; Métro: Châtelet), boasts a fast-food–style counter where members of the staff slice baguettes (French bread) in half and put on the top-pings of your choice. You can try the Lyonnaise, with slices of *saucisson sec* (dry sausage) and cornichon pickles, or a hot moz-zarella and tomato special. The drink and sandwich combinations are usually good buys. Branches are located all across the city, including one at 2 bd. Haussmann, 9e (☎ 01-48-24-20-60).

Choosing Cafétérias and Restaurant Chains

You can fill up cheaply at cafétérias and restaurant chains, and the offerings can be quite tasty. They're also kid-friendly. My personal favorite is the cafétéria at the department store Galeries Lafayette — the food is fresh and the surroundings sleek and modern — the perfect pick-me-up after a morning spent shopping for gifts.

✔ **Cafétéria Monoprix,** 23 av. Opéra, 1er; ☎ 01-42-96-34-96; Métro: Palais Royal-Musée du Louvre.

✔ **Chez Clément,** 9 pl. St-Andre des Arts, 6e; ☎ 01-56-81-32-00; Métro: St-Michel. Specialties include spit-roasted meats. You'll know them by their copper pots.

✔ **Hippopotamus,** 6 av Champs-Elysées, 8e; ☎ 01-42-24-77-96; Métro: Franklin D. Roosevelt. Their red awnings are all across town. You can get a hot meal here when most other places are closed.

✔ **Le Relais des Galeries** (6th floor, Galeries Lafayette), 40 bd. Haussmann, 9e; ☎ 01-42-82-34-56 (information desk); Métro: Havre-Caumartin.

✔ **Oh! Poivrier!,** 25 quai des Grands Augustins; ☎ 01-43-29-41-77; Métro: St-Michel. Light fare, moderate prices, long hours. This one is right on a quay of the Seine.

✔ **Universal Restaurant** (in the Carrousel du Louvre), 99 rue de Rivoli, 1er; ☎ 01-47-03-96-58; Métro: Palais Royal-Musée du Louvre.

Light Meals in the Heart of the Right Bank

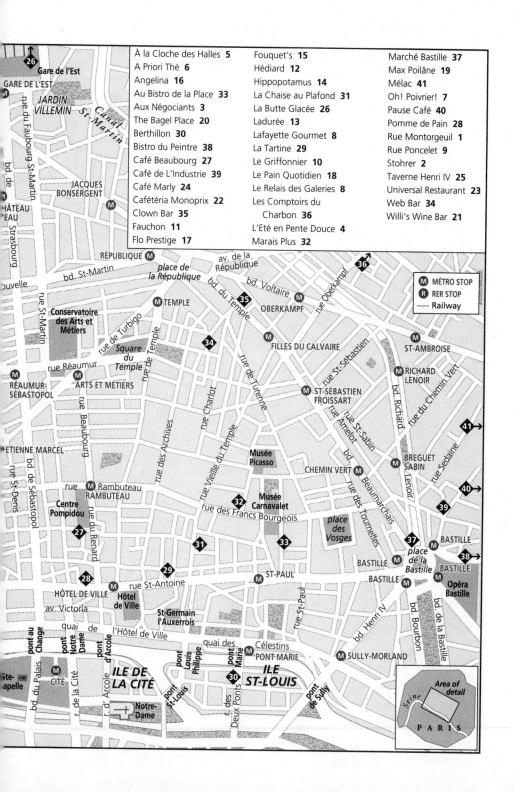

À la Cloche des Halles **5**
A Priori Thé **6**
Angelina **16**
Au Bistro de la Place **33**
Aux Négociants **3**
The Bagel Place **20**
Berthillon **30**
Bistro du Peintre **38**
Café Beaubourg **27**
Café de L'Industrie **39**
Café Marly **24**
Cafétéria Monoprix **22**
Clown Bar **35**
Fauchon **11**
Flo Prestige **17**

Fouquet's **15**
Hédiard **12**
Hippopotamus **14**
La Chaise au Plafond **31**
La Butte Glacée **26**
Ladurée **13**
Lafayette Gourmet **8**
La Tartine **29**
Le Griffonnier **10**
Le Pain Quotidien **18**
Le Relais des Galeries **8**
Les Comptoirs du
   Charbon **36**
L'Eté en Pente Douce **4**
Marais Plus **32**

Marché Bastille **37**
Max Poilâne **19**
Mélac **41**
Oh! Poivrier! **7**
Pause Café **40**
Pomme de Pain **28**
Rue Montorgueil **1**
Rue Poncelet **9**
Stohrer **2**
Taverne Henri IV **25**
Universal Restaurant **23**
Web Bar **34**
Willi's Wine Bar **21**

M MÉTRO STOP
R RER STOP
—— Railway

Light Meals in the Heart of the Left Bank

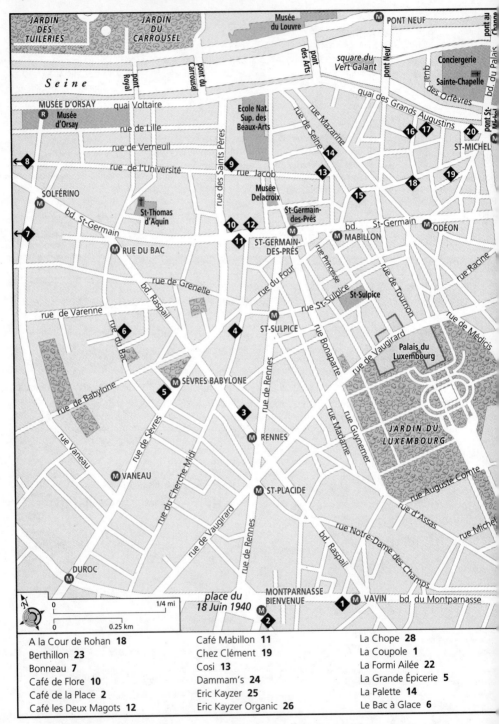

A la Cour de Rohan **18**
Berthillon **23**
Bonneau **7**
Café de Flore **10**
Café de la Place **2**
Café les Deux Magots **12**

Café Mabillon **11**
Chez Clément **19**
Cosi **13**
Dammam's **24**
Eric Kayzer **25**
Eric Kayzer Organic **26**

La Chope **28**
La Coupole **1**
La Formi Ailée **22**
La Grande Épicerie **5**
La Palette **14**
Le Bac à Glace **6**

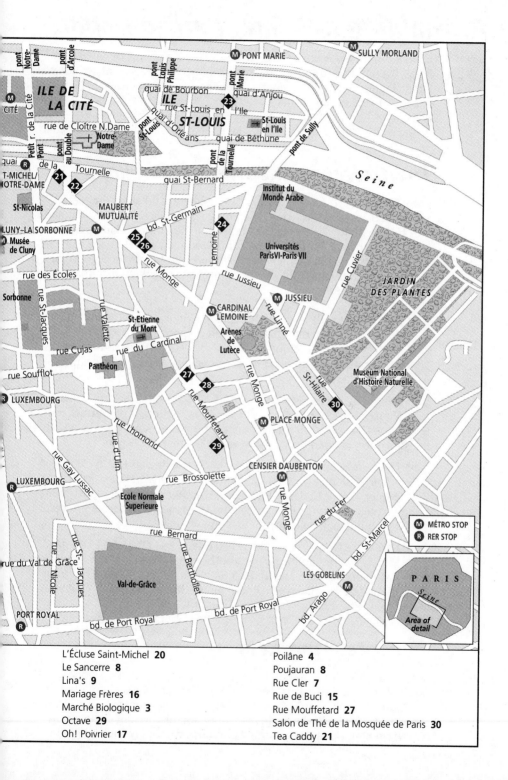

Assembling a Picnic, Parisian Style

Grab a crusty baguette or two, dried sausage, a wedge of cheese, and some fruit and head to the nearest park or to a garden that strikes your fancy. Picnicking in Paris can be as fun and as unforgettable as a meal in a 3-star restaurant at just a fraction of the cost. In this section, you discover where to stock up on provisions. (*Note:* Picnic fixings can also be assembled cheaply from Parisian supermarkets all across the city.)

The traiteurs (gourmet food shops)

Look for the word *traiteur,* which designates a food shop that sells ready-made meat, pasta, and salad dishes. The most famous, **Fauchon** and **Hédiard,** are at place de la Madeleine, 8e (Métro: Madeleine), but many grocery stores sell Fauchon products, and Hédiard has branches all across Paris. Every neighborhood has several good *traiteurs,* so be on the lookout and don't hesitate to ask your hotel staff for recommendations.

- **Flo Prestige,** 42 place du Marché-St-Honoré, 1er (☎ 01-42-61-45-46; Métro: Pyramides), is a well-respected food shop and caterer with everything from foie gras and Norwegian smoked salmon to fancy breads and cheeses. Open daily with branches around the city.

- **Hédiard,** 118 rue Monge, 5e (☎ 01-43-31-88-94; Métro: Censier-Daubenton), mentioned earlier in this section, is a gourmet food shop that sells upscale products and ready-made food to go. This location is open every day from 9:30 a.m. to 9:30 p.m.

- **La Grande Épicerie,** Bon Marché, 38 rue de Sèvres, 7e (☎ 01-44-39-80-00; Métro: Sèvres-Babylone), is simply the most wonderful grocery store in Paris. It has large *traiteur* and wine departments and sells everything from cleaning supplies to gourmet chocolate to fresh fish. Open Mon–Sat 10:00 a.m.–8:30 p.m.

- **Lafayette Gourmet,** 52 bd. Haussmann, 9e (☎ 01-48-74-46-06; Métro: Havre-Caumartin), is another wonderful grocery store that has everything you need for a picnic, located smack in the middle of the Galeries Lafayette complex (in the men's store). Open Mon–Sat 9:30 a.m.–7:00 p.m., Thurs till 9:00 p.m.

The street markets

Every neighborhood in Paris has its street market, and it's probably the best place to find the freshest produce, cheeses of excellent quality, and other picnic supplies. Even when you don't buy anything, visiting one or two is worth the authentic reflection of Parisian society you encounter. Markets are generally open from Tuesday through Saturday,

Light Bites in Montmartre

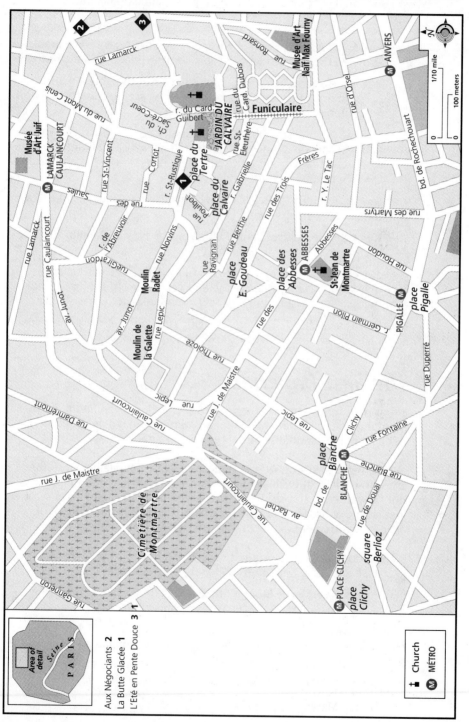

from 8 a.m. to 1 p.m., and of course, the pickings are better the earlier you go. The ones that are open Sundays are indicated. Some of the more well known include:

- **Rue Montorgueil,** 1er (Métro: Les Halles/Châtelet): Have breakfast at one of the many sidewalk cafés before choosing your produce.

- **Rue Mouffetard,** 5e (Métro: Monge): One of the oldest markets in Paris on one of the city's more interesting streets. Sing along with accordion players on Sunday mornings.

- **Marché Biologique,** boulevard Raspail between rue du Cherche-Midi and rue de Rennes, 6e (Métro: Rennes): This all-organic market features green grocers, winemakers, butchers, and bakers. Open Sun 8:30 a.m.–1:30 p.m.

- **Rue de Buci,** 6e (Métro: Odéon): This lively market is close to all the Latin Quarter action.

- **Rue Cler,** 7e (Métro: Ecole-Militaire): See how diplomats shop for their dinner in this "chic" market.

- **Marché Bastille,** 11e (Métro: Bastille): This huge market sells everything from game, cheese and vegetables to fish and condiments. Open Thurs and Sun 8:30 a.m.–1:30 p.m.

- **Rue Poncelet,** 17e (Métro: Ternes): The Poncelet market is especially renowned for its fresh fruit stalls.

The best bakeries

You want a fresh baguette for your picnic, and you can find bakeries (*boulangeries*) on nearly every corner in residential neighborhoods. Keep in mind that quality of the breads vary considerably.

Long lines of locals on weekend mornings or evenings before dinner give away the best bakeries. You can get a sandwich or a quiche to go, but be warned that most bakeries make very plain sandwiches — often just a slice of bread or cheese on a baguette with no condiment or other accoutrement. Some of the best bakeries are

- **Bonneau,** 75 rue d'Auteuil, 16e; ☎ 01-46-51-12-25. Tues–Sun 6:30 a.m.–8:30 p.m. Métro: Michel–Ange–Auteuil.

- **Eric Kayzer,** 8 rue Monge, 5e; ☎ ☎ 01-44-07-17-81. Wed–Mon 6:30 a.m.–8:30 p.m. Métro: Maubert Mutualité.

- **Eric Kayzer Organic,** 14 rue Monge, 5e; ☎ 01-44-07-17-81. Tues–Sun 8 a.m.–8 p.m. Métro: Maubert Mutualité.

- **Max Poilâne,** 42 Marché St-Honore, 1er; ☎ 01-42-61-10-53. Mon–Sat 7:30 a.m.–8:00 p.m. Métro: Porte de Vanves.

✔ **Poilâne,** 8 rue du Cherche-midi, 6e; ☎ **01-45-48-42-59.** Mon–Sat 7:15 a.m.–8:15 p.m. Métro: St-Sulpice or Sèvres Babylone.

✔ **Poujauran,** 20 rue Jean Nicot, 7e; ☎ **01-47-05-80-88.** Mon–Sat 8:00 a.m.–8:30 p.m. Métro: Latour Maubourg.

✔ **Stohrer,** 51 rue Montorgeuil, 2e; ☎ **01-42-33-38-20.** Open daily 7 a.m.–7 p.m. Métro: Châtelet.

Watching the World Go By at a Café

In this section, I dish up some of Paris's best places to read the paper, write postcards, watch people, soak up the city's atmosphere, and relax with a cup of coffee or a glass of wine or beer, or grab a sandwich, salad, or traditional French specialty like *pot-au-feu* (beef boiled with vegetables). Full listings are given for the cafés. Cafés are generally open from about 8 a.m. until 1 a.m. See the "Light Bites in Montmartre" map for Montmartre locations.

Au Bistro de la Place

This square on the place du Marché Sainte-Catherine is a pedestrian zone on the site of an 18th-century market, and this is the prettiest of all the bistros on the outdoor terrace here. The food is also the best; you may find fresh vegetable soup served hot or cold or fresh goat cheese marinated in olive oil with salad. Even if you don't come here for a meal, visit after the lunch hour (noon to 2:30 p.m.) to enjoy a leisurely drink or pastry on the terrace.

2 place du Marché Sainte-Catherine, 4e. ☎ *01-42-78-21-32. Métro: St-Paul.*

Café Beaubourg

This hip but dark bilevel café is cool and elegant with large circular columns that soar to an illuminated ceiling. The walls are filled with books, and a small wooden bridge spans the upper part of the café and leads to quieter, artistically designed tables. The bathrooms are attractions in themselves; they have the serenity of Zen gardens. Simple food may include a smooth gazpacho, salmon club sandwich, or goat cheese salad. The outside terrace is in a strategic spot overlooking the Pompidou Center, and you'll become a main attraction yourself as passersby cast curious glances at the people chic enough to eat here.

43 rue St-Merri, 4e. ☎ *01-48-87-63-96. Métro: Rambuteau or Hôtel-de-Ville.*

Café de Flore

In the heart of St-Germain-des-Prés, this café is still going strong, even though the famous writers have moved on, and you now pay high prices. Sartre is said to have written *Les Chemins de la Liberté* (*The Roads to*

Freedom) at his table here, and he and Simone de Beauvoir saw people by appointment here. Other regulars included André Malraux and Guillaume Apollinaire. Paris's leading intellectual bookstore, La Hune, is right next door.

172 bd. St-Germain, 6e. ☎ *01-45-48-55-26. Métro: St-Germain-des-Prés.*

Café de la Place

This old-fashioned café overlooking small, tree-lined place Edgar Quinet, has become a popular spot for young neighborhood residents. Browse the menu of inexpensive bistro specialties, or opt for a simple sandwich and a glass of wine. If you're lucky, there will be a *brocante* (like a garage sale) or crafts fair in the square. The Café de la Place is also a good place to stop before any trips from the Gare du Montparnasse, which is around the corner and just down the street.

23 rue d'Odessa, 14e. ☎ *01-42-18-01-55. Métro: Edgar-Quinet.*

Café de L'Industrie

This popular bar and café is young, friendly, and casual. Plants, wood floors, and wood Venetian blinds lend the two spacious rooms a vaguely colonial flavor. Hip Bastille denizens drift in and out all day, and after 9:30 p.m., the place is mobbed. Bartenders specialize in rum drinks. Closed Saturdays.

16 rue St-Sabin, 11e. ☎ *01-47-00-13-53. Métro: Bastille.*

Café les Deux Magots

Like its neighbor, Café de Flore, Café les Deux Magots was a hangout for Sartre and Simone de Beauvoir. The intellectuals met here in the 1950s, and Sartre wrote at his table every morning. With prices that start at 4€ for coffee and 2.50€ for a croissant, the café is an expensive place for literary-intellectual pilgrims, but a great spot to watch the nightly promenade on the boulevard St-Germain. Service can be snippy.

6 place St-Germain-des-Prés, 6e. ☎ *01-45-48-55-25. Métro: St-Germain-des-Prés.*

Café Mabillon

Welcome the dawn at Café Mabillon, which stays open all night. During the day, contemporary rock music draws a young, hip crowd to relax on the outdoor terrace or in the ultramodern interior. At night the music changes to techno, and the bordello-red banquettes fill with a wide assortment of night owls. As dawn approaches, the sound drops to a level just loud enough to keep you from dozing off in your seat.

164 bd. St-Germain, 6e. ☎ *01-43-26-62-93. Métro: Mabillon.*

Café Marly

This stunning café at the Louvre has a gorgeous view of the glass pyramid that is the museum's main entrance. With high ceilings, warmly painted pastel walls and luxurious red sofa chairs, the rooms could house the museum's latest art collection. Don't let the elegant ambience intimidate you, there is good food to be had. Choose from the lovely wine list, sit on the balcony, and enjoy the exquisite lighting on the pyramid and surrounding 18th-century facades. After 8 p.m., seating is for dinner only.

93 rue de Rivoli, cour Napoléon du Louvre, 1er. ☎ *01-49-26-06-60. Métro: Palais-Royal–Musée du Louvre.*

Fouquet's

Not far from the Arc de Triomphe, the turn-of-the-20th-century Fouquet's is a Champs-Elysées institution. Patrons have included James Joyce, Charlie Chaplin, Marlene Dietrich, Winston Churchill, and Franklin D. Roosevelt. You pay dearly for the glitzy associations and nostalgia, however.

99 av. des Champs-Elysées, 8e. ☎ *01-47-23-50-00. Métro: George V.*

La Chaise au Plafond

Tucked away on a pedestrians-only sidestreet in the heart of the Marais, this friendly, stylish place is a perfect spot for a timeout after visiting the Musée Picasso. It serves enormous salads, imaginative sandwiches, and thick tartes. A weekend brunch (about 16€) is served, but the tiny café tables aren't designed to hold the assortment of dishes, so you may feel squeezed.

10 rue Trésor, 4e. ☎ *01-42-76-03-22. Métro: Hôtel-de-Ville.*

La Chope

This café is worth a stop for its location on top of rue Mouffetard, right on place de la Contrescarpe. The square centers on four lilac trees and a fountain. It can get rowdy at night.

2–4 place de la Contrescarpe, 5e. ☎ *01-43-26-57-26. Métro: Cardinal Lemoine.*

La Coupole

La Coupole has been packing them in since Henry Miller came here for his morning porridge. The cavernous interior is always jammed and bristling with energy. Japanese business people, French yuppies, models, tourists, and neighborhood regulars keep the frenzied waiters running until 2 a.m. You won't know which is more interesting, the scene on the street, or the parade that passes through the revolving doors. The food is good, too. Prices are high.

102 bd. Montparnasse, 14e. ☎ *01-43-20-14-20. Métro: Vavin.*

La Palette

Students from the nearby Ecole des Beaux-Arts, artists and gallery owners linger and watch the life of the Left Bank flow by. The interior is decorated with colorful murals, and a palette hangs above the bar. The fare is open-faced sandwiches and salads at reasonable prices. Service can be snippy.

43 rue de Seine, 6e. ☎ *01-43-26-68-15. Métro: Mabillon.*

Les Comptoirs du Charbon

In the heart of the soon-to-be-too-trendy rue Oberkampf, this turn-of-the-20th-century dance hall is one of the hottest spots in Paris for people who like people and don't mind being crowded. The stunning Art Nouveau interior has high ceilings, hanging lamps, and walls covered with mirrors, wood, and hand-painted murals — which you can barely perceive through the bustle and haze. During the day or early evening you can relax, hang out, chat, or read a newspaper. After about 9 p.m., the music gets louder, the long wood bar and banquettes fill up, and you're lucky to get in, let alone get a seat.

109 rue Oberkampf, 11e. ☎ *01-43-57-55-13. Métro: Parmentier.*

L'Eté en Pente Douce

To escape the shoulder-to-shoulder tourists on place du Tertre, head down the eastern steps under Sacré-Coeur, where you find yourself on a leafy square, popular with a local crowd. The terrace here faces the stairs and iron lamps painted by Utrillo, and someone always is performing for the captive audience. The interior is brightly decorated with mosaics, unusual *objets d'art,* and a lovely painted ceiling. Between lunch and dinner, the restaurant serves a tempting array of pastries and sandwiches.

23 rue Muller, 18e. ☎ *01-42-64-02-67. Métro: Chateau-Rouge.*

Pause Café

Featured in the French film *Chacun Cherche Son Chat* (released in the U.S. as *When the Cat's Away*), this café has become one of Paris's hottest. Its hip clientele are denizens of the club scene (flyers inside give dates for upcoming events) or cool residents of the neighborhood. A groovy distressed interior features paintings of big-eyed worried women, while outdoors is made tropical with cloth and bamboo umbrellas and potted palms. You can get a tasty 8€ quiche of the day or bowl of soup made with fresh ingredients for 5€, and beer and other drinks.

41 rue de Charonne, 11e. ☎ *01-48-06-80-33. Métro: Lédru-Rollin.*

Web Bar

The "Factory" of cyber-bars, this cool, three-level bar is in the Marais, and it's also home to art exhibits, experimental music, and short films, and features storytelling, fashion shows, and even an occasional chess tournament. A casual crowd of locals creates a warm mood in contrast to the rather stark décor, which features iron railings and an old skylight. Fees for the use of one of the 18 computers are 1€ for 1 to 15 minutes, 2€ for 15 to 30 minutes, 3€ for 30 to 45 minutes, and 4€ for 45 to 60 minutes. Avoid weekdays between 5 and 7 p.m., or you may have to wait to use a computer.

32 rue de Picardie, 3e. ☎ *01-42-72-66-55. Internet:* www.webbar.fr. *Métro: République.*

Steeping and Sipping at a Tea Salon (Salons de Thés)

If you're tired of all those short blasts of French coffee, tea's your alternative. Paris tea salons have a wide range of blends, steeped to perfection in refined and, often, elegant settings. The pastry selections in these places are usually excellent, but save your full meals for a restaurant — tea salons tend to be expensive.

- ✔ **A la Cour de Rohan,** 59–61 rue St-André-des-Arts (actually a passageway off of rue St-André-des-Arts), 6e; ☎ **01-43-25-79-67.** Open Sun–Thurs noon to 7:30 p.m.; Fri–Sat noon to 11:30 p.m. Métro: Odéon or St-Michel.

- ✔ **Angelina,** 226 rue de Rivoli, 1er; ☎ **01-42-60-82-00.** Open daily 9:00 a.m.–5:45 p.m. (lunch served 11:45 a.m.–3:00 p.m.). Métro: Concorde or Tuileries.

- ✔ **A Priori Thé,** 35–37 Galerie Vivienne (enter at 6 rue Vivienne, 4 rue des Petits-Champs, or 5 rue de la Banque), 2e; ☎ **01-42-97-48-75.** Open Mon–Fri 9 a.m.–6 p.m.; Sat 9:00 a.m.–6:30 p.m.; Sun 12:30–6:30 p.m. Métro: Bourse, Palais-Royal–Musée du Louvre, or Pyramides.

- ✔ **Ladurée,** 16 rue Royale, 8e; ☎ **01-42-60-21-79.** Open Mon–Sat 8:30 a.m.–7:30 p.m. Métro: Concorde or the Champs-Elysées at number 75. ☎ **01-40-75-08-75.** Métro: Franklin-D-Roosevelt.

✔ **La Formi Ailée,** 8 rue du Fouarre, 5e; ☎ **01-43-29-40-99.** Open daily noon to 1 a.m. Métro: Maubert-Mutualité.

✔ **Marais Plus,** 20 rue des Francs-Bourgeois, 3e; ☎ **01-48-87-01-40.** Open daily 11 a.m.–7 p.m. Métro: St-Paul.

✔ **Mariage Frères,** 13 rue Grands Augustins, 6e; ☎ **01-40-51-82-50.** Open daily noon to 7 p.m. Métro: Hôtel-de-Ville.

✔ **Salon de Thé de la Mosquée de Paris,** 39 rue Geoffroy-St-Hilaire, 5e; ☎ **01-45-35-97-33.** Open daily 10 a.m.–10 p.m. Métro: Monge.

✔ **Tea Caddy,** 14 rue St-Julien-le-Pauvre, 5e; ☎ **01-43-54-15-56.** Open daily noon to 7 p.m. Métro: St-Michel.

Combing the Streets for a Heady Mix of Wine Bars

With good selections of wines by the glass, and tasty light meals served all day in pleasant surroundings, the Paris wine bar is often a cozy and sophisticated alternative to the café.

À la Cloche des Halles

This tiny bar and café is crowded at lunchtime with people dining on plates of ham or quiche, accompanied by a bottle of wine. It's convivial and fun, but very noisy and crowded. If you can't find a seat, you can usually stand at the bar and eat. Look closely at the exterior for the bell that once tolled the opening and closing of the vast food market for which this neighborhood was named.

28 rue Coquillière, 1er. ☎ *01-42-36-93-89. Mon–Fri 8 a.m.–10 p.m.; Sat 10 a.m.– 5 p.m. Métro: Les Halles or Palais-Royal–Musée du Louvre.*

Aux Négociants

The photographer Robert Doisneau came here often (his picture is on the wall), but today a discerning crowd of regulars keep this tiny, unpretentious wine bar near Montmartre humming. The excellent pâtés and terrines are homemade and served with fresh, chewy bread.

27 rue Lambert, 18e. ☎ *01-46-06-15-11. Mon–Fri noon to 3 p.m.; Tues–Thurs 6:30–10:30 p.m. Métro: Château-Rouge or Lamarck-Caulincourt.*

Bistro du Peintre

Painters, actors, and night crawlers hang out here nightly. The zinc bar, wood paneling, large terrace, and superb Belle Époque style make this wine bar a highlight even if the wine selection wasn't as reasonably priced as it is.

116 av. Ledru-Rollin, 11e. ☎ 01-47-00-34-39. Daily 7 a.m. to midnight. Métro: Ledru-Rollin.

Clown Bar

You may just stand shoulder-to-shoulder with a real clown from the nearby Cirque d'Hiver. The bar is decorated with a mélange of circus posters and circus-themed ceramic tiles. The wine list features an extensive selection of French offerings.

114 rue Amelot, 11e. ☎ 01-43-55-87-35. Mon–Sat noon to 2:30 p.m. and 7:00 p.m.–1:00 a.m. Métro: Filles du Calvaire.

La Tartine

This wine bar is the one that time forgot — pure pre-World War II Paris, from the nicotine-browned walls and frosted globe chandeliers, to the worn wood furniture. The ambience is funky and working-class, but a broad segment of society savors glasses of wine at the bar or linges over a newspaper and a tartine (open face sandwich) in the high-ceilinged room. This is one of the few wine bars in Paris open on Sunday.

24 rue de Rivoli, 4e. ☎ 01-42-72-76-85. Wed–Mon noon to 10 p.m. Métro: St-Paul.

L'Écluse Saint-Michel

This location originally was home to a small chain of wine bars. L'Écluse is casually chic and authentic. Have one of its 20 wines by the glass and a light bites like *carpaccio*, salad, or soup.

15 quai des Grands-Augustins, 6e. ☎ 01-46-33-58-74. Daily 11:30 a.m.–1:30 a.m. Métro: St-Michel.

Le Griffonnier

The kitchen at Le Griffonnier is a first-rate, and the wine cellar is terrific. Sample bistro specialties such as *confit de canard maison,* or try a hearty plate of charcuterie, terrines, and cheese, usually from the Auvergne region of central France, and ask your waiter to recommend the wine. Hot meals are served only at lunchtime and Thursday evenings.

8 rue des Saussaies, 8e. ☎ 01-42-65-17-17. Mon–Fri 7:30 a.m.–9:00 p.m. Métro: Champs-Elysées–Clemenceau.

Le Sancerre

Le Sancerre is a quiet place to relax for a light meal or glass of wine after visiting the Eiffel Tower. Loire wines are the specialty here, including, of course, Sancerre. La Sancerre serves typically French items, such as omelettes of all varieties with a side of fried potatoes, and duck liver terrine. The more adventurous can sample the ubiquitous *andouillette*, the sausage that is decidedly an acquired taste.

22 av. Rapp, 7e. ☎ *01-45-51-75-91. Mon–Fri 8 a.m.–10 p.m.; Sat 8 a.m.–4 p.m. Métro: Alma Marceau.*

Mélac

Owner Jacques Mélac has an excellent selection of wine from nearly all the regions of France, which he dispenses to a lively crowd of regulars. He's happy to give you recommendations. Usually a hot *plat du jour* is available for lunch, but you can feast on a selection of first-rate pâtés, terrines, charcuterie, and cheeses all day.

42 rue Léon Frot, 11e. ☎ *01-43-70-59-27. Mon 9 a.m.–2 p.m.; Tues–Sat 9:00 a.m.– 10:30 p.m. Métro: Charonne.*

Taverne Henri IV

Although on the expensive side, the wine and food are excellent at this authentic, old-fashioned bar, where regulars, mostly male, read newspapers, discuss the news of the day, and smoke nonstop. The variety of wines by the glass can accompany open-faced sandwiches (including warm goat cheese), patés, and such cheeses as Cantal and Auvergne blue.

13 place du Pont Neuf, 1er. ☎ *01-43-54-27-90. Mon–Fri noon to 10 p.m.; Sat noon to 4 p.m. Métro: Pont-Neuf.*

Willi's Wine Bar

Willi's has become a Paris institution since it opened in 1980. You can sample any of 250 different varieties of wine while seated at the polished oak bar or dine in the high-ceilinged oak-beamed dining room from a full menu of main courses costing just 15€. Each year the owners commission an image relating to wine from an artist, and the colorful paintings are available for sale as prints for around 200€.

13 rue des Petits-Champs, 1er. ☎ *01-42-61-05-09. Mon–Sat noon to 2:30 p.m., and 7:00–11:00 p.m..; bar open Mon–Sat noon to midnight.*

Getting the Scoop on Paris Ice Cream

Rhubarb, plum, cassis, honey nut. . . . If Paris doesn't have the best ice cream in the world, it must run a close second. Such flavors, such creaminess! Ask for a *cornet seule* (kor-*nay* sul; single-scoop cone) or *cornet double* (kor-*nay* doobl; double scoop) — even the cone is yummy. Prices range from 2€ for a single to 4€ for a double-scoop cone. Most places open daily around 10:30 a.m. and close around 8:00 p.m. *Note:* Sitting down when ordering ice cream is always more expensive — sometimes twice as much as ordering your cone to go. You find the best ice cream at **Berthillon,** 31 rue St-Louis-en-l'Ile, 4e (☎ 01-43-54-31-61; Métro: Cité), but the following establishments also put soft-serve to shame. Although Berthillon closes from July 15 through the first week in September, a note on the door directs customers to other nearby shops that sell its ice cream.

- ✔ **Dammam's,** 20 rue Cardinal Lemoine, 5e; ☎ 01-46-33-61-30; Métro: Cardinal Lemoine.

- ✔ **La Butte Glacée,** 14 rue Norvins, 18e; ☎ 01-42-23-91-58; Métro: Abbesses.

- ✔ **Le Bac à Glaces,** 109 rue du Bac, 7e; ☎ 01-45-48-87-65; Métro: Rue du Bac.

- ✔ **Octave,** 138 rue Mouffetard, 5e; ☎ 01-45-35-20-56; Métro: Monge.

Part V
Exploring Paris

In this part . . .

So many things to see in Paris . . . what do you do first? Chapter 16 tells you a bit about what's worth seeing, with an alphabetical list of the city's top sights, described and indexed by neighborhood and type of attraction. Chapter 17 lists some more cool things to see and do for kids, teens, history buffs, and art and literature lovers, and it lists gardens and parks to relax in after visiting all those museums! Chapter 18 provides you with guided tour options, from buses to bicycles, while Chapter 19 describes today's shopping scene in Paris, previews four great shopping neighborhoods, covers the outdoor markets, and provides an A to Z review of local shops of interest. In Chapter 20, you have the chance to discover Paris in three itineraries and on a walking tour. And just when you're getting used to Paris, Chapter 21 sends you away on one of five great day-trips in the Ile-de-France region.

Chapter 16

Paris's Top Sights

. . . .

In This Chapter

▶ Reviewing Paris's top attractions

▶ Listing the sights by neighborhood and type

. . . .

*T*his chapter starts off with a succinct review of each of Paris's top sights, giving you the lowdown on when to go, how to get there, and why you should visit it in the first place. The list of sites is followed by indexes that point to the city's top 20 sights by location and by type, plus its most popular tour (a river cruise).

Saving on seeing the sights

One of the best bargains for tourists visiting Paris is the Carte Musées et Monuments, which offers free and unlimited admission to 70 of the top sights of Paris and the Ile-de-France. The card also promises no waiting in admission lines, but you still have to stand in line for security checkpoints at the museums that have them. **Note:** The pass is *not* accepted at the Eiffel Tower.

A one-day pass is 15€, a three-consecutive-day pass costs 30€, and a five-consecutive-day pass is 45€. Your best bet is to jot down a list of all the museums and monuments you want to see and use this book to add up their costs. For example, say that you decide to visit attractions in the 7e on a designated day. It would cost 18€ to see the Musée d'Orsay (7€), Invalides (6€) and the Musée Rodin (5€). Using the one-day Carte Musées et Monuments (15€) saves you 3€. You're better off, however, buying a three-day pass so you aren't rushing to fit in all those attractions in one day.

You can buy the pass at the Office de Tourisme de Paris, 127 av. des Champs-Elysées, in principal Métro stations, at the 70 museums and monuments that accept it, and at FNAC ticket branches.

Paris's Top Attractions

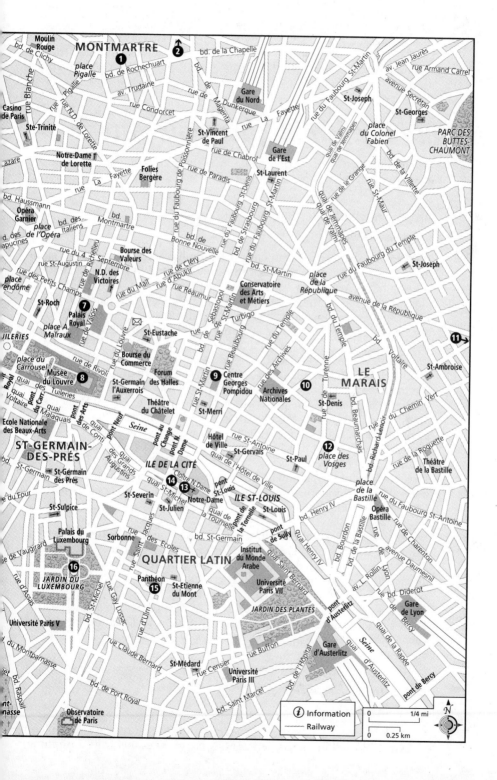

Even after whittling down Paris's many attractions, these 20 sites are still probably more than you can see in a single trip (the "Paris's Top Attractions" map shows you where my choices are). At the end of this book is a worksheet you can use to plot the top sights according to how much you want to see them. Chapter 20 also outlines very doable itineraries that take in several top sights.

Hitting the Highlights from A to Z

The highlights in this section range from the standard historical tourist attractions to the newest art museum.

Arc de Triomphe
Champs-Elysées

The Arc de Triomphe is the largest triumphal arch in the world, commissioned by Napoléon to honor his army and its 128 victorious battles. Although the Arc has witnessed the agony of defeat, as in 1871 when Paris was seized by the Prussians during the Franco-Prussian War, and in 1940 when Nazi armies marched victoriously through the arch and down the Champs-Elysées, it better symbolizes the thrill of victory; De Gaulle striding through the Arc to symbolize Paris's liberation in 1944 is one of the country's most cherished memories, and the racers in the Tour de France riding up the Champs and around the Arc on the last day, when the victor is declared. Today the Arc houses the Tomb of the Unknown Soldier, which was dedicated in 1921 to honor the 1,500,000 French soldiers who died during World War 1; every evening at 6:30 the flame is symbolically relit. The panoramic view, however, is the real attraction for visitors. From the top, 162 feet up, you can see in a straight line the Champs-Elysées, the obelisk in the place de la Concorde, and the Louvre. That big cube at the far end is the Grande Arche de la Défense in St-Denis, built to be the modern equivalent to this arch. Allow an hour to visit, an hour and a half in high summer.

To reach the stairs and elevators that climb the arch, take the underpass using the white Métro entrances. Please don't try to cross on surface streets! Attempting to dodge the warp-speed traffic zooming around the circle will likely get you seriously hurt.

Place Charles-de-Gaulle, 8e. ☎ *01-55-37-73-77. Métro: Charles-de-Gaulle–Étoile. Bus: 22, 30, 31, 52, 73, 92. Admission: 7€ adults, 4.50€ ages 12–25, free for children younger than 12. Open: Apr–Sept 10 a.m.–11 p.m.; Oct–March 10:00 a.m.–10:30 p.m. Closed major holidays.*

Cathédral de Notre-Dame
Ile de la Cité

Crusaders prayed here before leaving for the holy wars. Napoléon crowned himself emperor here, and then crowned his wife, Josephine,

Notre-Dame de Paris

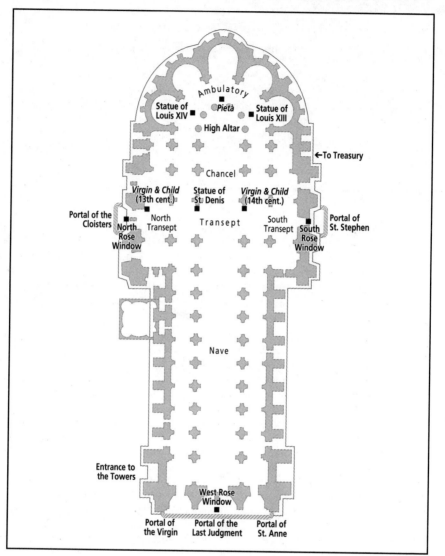

empress. When Paris was liberated during World War II, General de Gaulle rushed to this cathedral to give thanks. (See the nearby "Notre-Dame de Paris" map.)

Construction of Notre-Dame started in 1163 when Pope Alexander III laid the cornerstone and was completed in the 14th century. Built in an age of illiteracy, the cathedral windows tell the stories of the Bible in its portals, paintings, and stained glass. Angry citizens pillaged Notre-Dame during the French Revolution, mistaking religious statues above the portals on the west front for representations of kings and beheading them.

Keeping an eye on your wallet while eyeing the goods

You won't be able to avoid pesky (and illegal) vendors trying to cajole you into buying everything from Eiffel Tower key chains to postcards to mechanical butterflies; they constantly approach tourists standing in line for Eiffel Tower admission tickets. Be very attentive — some of these vendors work in tandem with pickpockets who will rip you off while you're busy looking at the displays. As for the quality of the merchandise — it's pretty bad. Buy your souvenirs from shops and licensed vendors.

Nearly 100 years later, when Notre-Dame had been turned into a barn, writer Victor Hugo and other artists called attention to Notre-Dame's dangerous state of disrepair and architect Viollet-le-Duc began the much-needed restoration. He designed Notre-Dame's spire, a new feature, and Baron Haussmann (Napoléon III's urban planner) evicted the residents of the houses that cluttered the cathedral's vicinity and tore down the houses for better views of the cathedral.

Before entering, walk around to the east end of the church to appreciate the spectacular flying buttresses. Visit on a sunny morning to catch the giant rose windows — which retain some of their 13th-century stained glass — in all their glory. The highlight for kids will undoubtedly be climbing the 387 narrow and winding steps to the top of one of the towers for a fabulously Quasimodo view of the gargoyles and of Paris. My advice: If you plan to visit the tower, go early in the morning! Lines stretch down the square in front of the cathedral during the summer.

6 Parvis Notre-Dame, Ile de la Cité, 4e. ☎ *01-42-34-56-10. Métro: Cité or St-Michel. RER: St-Michel. Bus: 21, 38, 85, 96. Admission: Church free; tower 5.49€ adults, 3.51€ ages 18–26 and seniors, free for youth younger than 18. Open: Cathedral daily 8:00 a.m.–6:45 p.m. (closed Sat 12:30–2:00 p.m.); treasury Mon–Sat 9:30 a.m.–5:30 p.m. Six masses celebrated on Sun, four on weekdays, one on Sat. Free guided visits in English Wed and Thurs at noon.*

Centre Georges Pompidou
Le Marais

British architect Richard Rogers and Italian architect Renzo Piano designed this building in the late 1960s as part of a redevelopment plan for the Beaubourg neighborhood. Since its opening in 1966, the Centre National d'Art et de Culture Georges Pompidou has been a surprisingly popular attraction. So popular that the wear and tear of about 160 million visitors caused the building to begin crumbling. It closed for three years in 1997, undergoing a renovation that cost more than $100 million. Its reopening January 1, 2000, was planned to coincide with the new century. The renovation didn't change at all the brightly colored escalators, elevators, air conditioning, and tubular passages resembling a giant gerbil habitat, running along the building's outside, but the inside is more of a spacious haven in which to view, touch, or listen to modern art and artists. The newer of Paris's two modern art museums, the Centre Georges Pompidou includes two floors of work from the Musée National d'Art Moderne, France's national collection of modern art. The Centre Pompidou also houses a cinema, a huge public library, spaces for modern dance and music, temporary exhibits that often include video and computer works, and nearly 150 drawings, paintings, and other works by Romanian sculptor Constantin Brancusi in the Brancusi Atelier, a small building near the Pompidou's entrance.

Sadly, taking a free escalator ride to the top for the breathtaking panoramic view of Paris is no more; you must purchase admission to the museum. However, if all you're interested in is the view, consider stopping at the Pompidou's ultrahip top-floor restaurant Georges. For the same price as an adult's full-package admission to the museum (10€), you can relax with a glass of wine and enjoy the view from indoors.

As a bonus, visit the nearby Igor Stravinsky fountain, which is free. Its fun sculptures by Tinguely and Niki de Saint Phalle include red lips spitting water, a mermaid squirting water from "strategic" body parts, and a twirling grinning skull. Dedicate at least two hours to viewing the works and slipping upstairs for the view.

Place Georges-Pompidou, 4e. ☎ *01-44-78-12-33. Internet:* www.centrepompidou. fr. *Métro: Rambuteau, Hôtel-de-Ville, or Châtelet–Les Halles. Bus: 21, 29, 38, 47, 58, 69, 70, 72, 74, 75, 76, 81, 85, 86. Admission: A one-day package to all exhibits, the Brancusi Atelier, and the National Museum of Modern Art costs 10€ adults, 8€ ages 18–26, free for children younger than 18; admission to only exhibits is 8.50€ adults, 6.50€ ages18–26, free for children younger than 13; admission to National Museum of Modern Art and Brancusi Atelier is 5.50€ adults, 3.50€ ages 18–26. Free the first Sun of the month. Open: Daily 11 a.m.–10 p.m.*

Champs-Elysées
Champs-Elysées

If you were in Paris when the French won the World and Euro Cup soccer championships (1998 and 2000, respectively), you understand what the Champs-Elysées means to the French. When close to a million singing, flag-waving Parisians spilled into the avenue, it was said that the country hadn't experienced such group euphoria since the days following the Liberation of Paris by the Allies in 1944. The Champs also overlooked the city's biggest New Year's party; in 2000, crowds of people gathered here to watch astonishing fireworks and cheer in the new century. The Champs is the avenue where the military march on Bastille Day and where the Tour de France ends. The scene on France's most famous street is liveliest at night, with people lining up for the numerous cinemas (see English-language films here by looking for "v.o." for *version originale* on schedules and movie posters), and floodlights illuminating the Arc de Triomphe and place de la Concorde. Restaurants consist mainly of standard chain cafes (Chez Clément, Hippo) and American-style fast food (McDonald's, Planet Hollywood, ChiChi's), although good restaurants abound on the streets surrounding the avenue (see Chapter 14). You can shop at reasonably priced stores, such as Zara, the very luxe (Louis Vuitton), and chain stores that you'd see in any American mall (the Disney Store, Quiksilver). Many of the stores are open on Sunday. Allow an hour to walk from top to bottom, longer if you want to shop, eat, or dawdle.

Champs-Elysées, 8e. Métro: Concorde, Champs-Elysées Clémenceau, Franklin-D-Roosevelt, George V, Charles-de-Gaulle-Étoile. Bus: Many lines cross it, but only the 73 travels its entire length.

Eiffel Tower (La Tour Eiffel)
Eiffel Tour/Les Invalides

Gustave Eiffel beat out 699 others in a contest to design what was supposed to be a temporary monument for the 1889 Exposition Universelle (World's Fair). His designs for the tower spanned 6,000 square yards of paper. Praised by some and criticized by others, the tower created as much controversy in its time as did I.M. Pei's pyramid at the Louvre 100 years later. Upon completion, the Eiffel Tower was the tallest human-built structure in the world, and the Prince of Wales (later Edward VII) and his family were invited to ascend it first. People have climbed it, bungee-jumped from it, and cycled down the tower's steps. In 1989, the tower's centennial was celebrated with 89 minutes of music and fireworks, and in the 1990s it counted down the days and then the minutes until the start of the new millenium.

Did you know the Eiffel Tower has its own post office? Whenever you mail anything from the town, it is postmarked with an Eiffel Tower stamp. Did you know the Tower is lit up at night by 336 projectors with bulbs ranging in wattages from 150 to 1,000? You can fill an entire page with trivia about Paris's most famous symbol, which weighs 7,000 tons, soars 1,056 feet, and is held together with 2.5 million rivets. But what you really want to know are the practicalities: *Do I have to climb stairs? Do elevators go to the top? Are there bathrooms? Snacks? Can I ascend in a wheelchair?* The answers: The Tower has three levels that all are accessible by elevator. No elevator goes directly from ground level to the top; you must change elevators at the second level. Although you can take stairs from the ground to the first and second levels, you can't take stairs from the second level to the top. Most likely you'll wait for elevators on the first and second levels in specially roped-off lines. In high season, the wait sometimes is as long an hour — for each line. Restrooms are located on each level, and snack bars and souvenir stands are on the first and second levels. The tower is wheelchair accessible to the second level but not to the top.

Taking a Seine river cruise

One of the most romantic and beautiful ways to see Paris is by one of the sight-seeing boats that cruise up and down the Seine. Don't, however, take one of the overpriced dinner or lunch cruises — they cost between 85€ and 125€ per person. Instead, opt for an evening cruise. With its dramatically lit monuments and romantic bridges, Paris is truly breathtaking at night.

Three companies offer the tours, which are all similar and cost about the same price. Perhaps the most well known are the **Bateaux-Mouches** that sail from the pont de l'Alma on the Right Bank and have huge floodlit boats. They offer recorded commentary in up to six languages. You can't miss the huge neon sign at night.

Bateaux-Parisiens sail from the port de la Bourdonnais on the Left Bank, while **Vedettes Pont Neuf** sail from the riverside where the Pont Neuf crosses the Ile de la Cité. Vedettes boats are smaller, more intimate, and not all of them are covered. Commentary is live.

For a boat ride without commentary, take one of the **Bat-o-bus** shuttles that stop at Trocadéro, Musée d'Orsay, Louvre, Notre-Dame, and Hôtel de Ville. A ticket costs 3.50€ plus 2.00€ for each stop, and you can jump off and on when you want.

Bateaux-Mouches, pont de l'Alma, Right Bank, 8e. ☎ 01-42-25-96-10 or 01-42-76-99-99 for reservations. Métro: Alma Marceau. Departures: March to mid-November every 30 min. 10:00 a.m.–8:00 p.m., every 20 min. 8:00–11:00 p.m.; Nov–Mar 11:00 a.m., 2:30 p.m., 4:00 p.m., 6:00 p.m., and 9:00 p.m. Rates: 7€ for adults, 4€ for children 4–12 and adults older than 65; children younger than 4 ride free.

Bateaux-Parisiens, port de la Bourdonnais, Left Bank, 7e. ☎ 01-44-11-33-44. Métro: Bir-Hakeim. Departures: From Easter through Halloween every half-hour from 10 a.m.–11 p.m.; November 1 to Easter every hour from 10 a.m.–1 p.m., and 5–8 p.m., every half-hour 1–5 p.m. and 8–10 p.m. Rates: 8.50€ before 8 p.m., 9.00€ after 8 p.m. adults; 4.10€ children 12 and younger.

Vedettes Pont Neuf, square du Vert-Galant, 1er. ☎ 01-46-33-98-38. Métro: Pont-Neuf, sail from the riverside where the Pont Neuf crosses the Ile de la Cité. Departures: Mar–Oct every half-hour 10:30 a.m.–10:30 p.m.; Nov–Feb every 45 min. 10:30 a.m. to noon and 2:00–10:00 p.m., Sat and Sun every half-hour from 10:00 a.m.–10:30 p.m. Rates: 9.00€ adults, 4.50€ children 12 and younger.

Some advice: Six million people visit the Eiffel Tower each year. To avoid loonnnggg lines, go early in the morning or in the off-season. If this isn't possible, allow at least three hours for your visit: one hour to line up for tickets and another two just to access the elevators on levels one and two.

Food is available at the Altitude 95 restaurant on the first floor, which is simply gorgeous, but overpriced for the quality of its meals. A first-floor snack bar and second-floor cafeteria are open, but again they're not the best values. The best food at the Eiffel Tower is also its most expensive, without a doubt: The Michelin-starred Jules Verne, one of Paris's most celebrated restaurants, is on the Eiffel Tower's second level.

Since 1999, double sweeping beacons have preceded the Eiffel Tower's illumination each night. If you have the patience to wait until sunset, the Eiffel Tower at night is recommended! Its lights frame the lacy steelwork in a way that daylight doesn't; beneath you, the city twinkles, and the Seine reflects it all.

Parc du Champ de Mars, 7e. ☎ *01-44-11-23-23. Internet:* www.tour-eiffel.fr. *Métro: Trocadéro, Bir-Hakeim, or École-Militaire. RER: Champs-de-Mars. Bus: 42, 69, 82, 87. Admission: 9.80€, adults, 5.30€ ages 4–12 to highest level (1,060 ft.); 6.90€ adults, 3.90€ ages 4–12 to 2nd level (380 ft.); 3.70€ adults, 2.10€ ages 4–12 for elevator to 1st level (188 ft.); 3€ for stairs to 1st and 2nd levels. Children younger than 3 are free. Open: Sept 1–June 13 daily 9:30 a.m.–11:00 p.m.; June 14–Aug 31 daily 9 a.m. to midnight. Fall and winter, stairs close at 6:30 p.m. Closed major holidays.*

Hôtel des Invalides (Napoléon's Tomb)
Eiffel Tour/Les Invalides

Louis XIV, who liked war and waged many, built Invalides as a hospital and home for all veteran officers and soldiers. It still has offices for departments of the French armed forces, and part of it is still a hospital. The best way to get the sense of the awe that the Hôtel des Invalides inspires is to walk to it by crossing the Alexander III bridge. The dome of the **Église du Dôme** (gilded with 12 kilograms of real gold), is one of the high points of classical art, rising 107 meters from the ground. Sixteen green copper cannons point outward in a powerful display.

Enemy flags captured during the military campaigns of the 19th and 20th centuries hang from the rafters in two impressive rows at the **Église de St-Louis,** known as the Church of the Soldiers, but most visitors come to see the **Tomb of Napoléon,** where the emperor is buried in six coffins, one inside the other under the great dome. The first coffin is iron, the second mahogany, the third and fourth lead, the fifth ebony, and the outermost oak. The emperor's remains were transferred here 20 years after his death in 1820 on the island of St. Helena, where he was exiled following his defeat at Waterloo.

A must-see is the **Musée de l'Armée,** one of the world's greatest military museums; admission is included when you buy your ticket for Napoléon's tomb. It features thousands of weapons from prehistory to World War II such as spearheads, arrowheads, maces, cannons, and guns, in addition to battle flags, booty, suits of armor and uniforms from around the world. The DeGaulle wing opened in 2000 with the goal of telling the story of World War II on touch screens, with videos, a decoding machine, and other artifacts. Set aside two hours for a complete visit or a half-hour to see the tomb.

Place des Invalides, 7e. ☎ *01-44-42-37-65. Métro: Latour-Maubourg, Invalides, or Varenne. Bus: 63, 83, 93. Admission 6€ adults; 4.50€ children 12–17; free for children younger than 12. Open: Oct–Mar daily 10:00 a.m.–4:45 p.m.; Apr–Sept 30 daily 10:00 a.m.–5:45 p.m. Tomb of Napoléon open until 6:45 p.m. June–Sept. Closed major holidays.*

Jardin des Tuileries
Louvre

The Tuileries are a great place to rest your feet and catch some rays on conveniently placed wrought-iron chairs surrounding the garden's fountains. In keeping with the French style of parks, trees are planted according to an orderly design and the sandy paths are arrow straight. Spread out across 63 acres, the city's most formal gardens originally ran between the Louvre and the Tuileries Palace, which was burned down during the 1871 Paris Commune. You can get a light snack at one of the outdoor cafés. During the summer, a carnival features an enormous Ferris wheel (with great views of the city), a log flume, fun house, arcade-style games, snacks and machine-made soft ice cream (but I find the best is the home-made ice cream sold from a stand right beyond the Arc de Triomphe du Carrousel at the entrance to the Tuileries). Come for a stroll before or after visiting the Louvre.

Quai des Tuileries, 1er. Entrances on rue de Rivoli and place de la Concorde, 1er. Métro: Concorde or Tuileries. Bus: 42, 69, 72, 73, 94. Admission: Free. Free guided visits of the gardens (in French) Sun, Wed, Fri 3 p.m. Open: Daily 7:30 a.m. to dusk.

Jardin du Palais-Royal
Louvre

Cardinal Richelieu ordered the Royal Palace built in 1630 as his personal residence, complete with grounds landscaped by the royal gardener. Today the palace is no longer open to the public, but its statue-filled gardens, including the controversial prison-striped columns built in 1986 (which make a great photo-op), remain one of the most restful places in the city. The square is also ringed by restaurants, art galleries, and specialty boutiques, and it's home to the Comédie Française.

Entrances on rue de Rivoli and place de la Concorde, 1er. Métro: Concorde or Tuileries. Bus: 42, 69, 72,73,94. Admission: Free. Open: Daily 7:30 a.m. to dusk.

Jardin et Palais du Luxembourg
St-Germain-des-Prés

Not far from the Sorbonne and just south of the Latin Quarter is the 6e arrondissement's **Jardin du Luxembourg,** one of Paris's most beloved parks. Children love it for its playground, toy boat pond, pony rides, and puppet theater. Besides pools, fountains, and statues of queens and poets, there are tennis and *boules* courts (*boule* means ball; in this game, players compete to see who can roll their small steel ball closest to a larger steel ball that lies farther down the court).

The park was commissioned by King Henri IV's queen, Marie de Medici, who also had the **Palais du Luxembourg** built at the northern edge of the park. The Palais resembles the Palazzo Pitti in Florence, where Marie had spent her childhood and for which she was homesick. When the queen was banished in 1630, the palace was abandoned until the Revolution, when it was used as a prison. Now the seat of the French Senate, it is not open to the public.

Orchards in the park's southwest corner contain 360 varieties of apples, 270 kinds of pears, and various grapevines. Members of the French Senate get to eat the fruit, but leftovers go to a soup kitchen. Walk north, and you come across a bevy of beehives behind a low fence. A beekeeping (apiculture) course is taught here on weekends. See whether you can find the Statue of Liberty tucked away nearby.

St-Germain-des-Prés, 6e. Main entrance at the corner of bd. St-Michel and rue des Médicis. ☎ 01-43-29-12-78. Métro: Odéon. RER: Luxembourg, Port-Royal. Bus: 38, 82, 84, 85, 89. Open: Daily dawn to dusk. Admission: Free.

Montmartre
On the Right Bank

This neighborhood is for anyone who loved the film *Amélie*. The film's heroine lived here and worked in an actual Montmartre bar, Les Deux Moulins, located at 15 rue Lépic. The bar was recently sold, but the new owners have promised not to change a thing. You can get to Montmartre by taking the Métro to the Anvers or Abbesses stop, the entrance of which is graced by a fabulous Art Nouveau MÉTRO sign. You can either walk to the top of the *butte* (hill) or take the funicular (railway) up. (Walk from the Anvers Métro station the short distance from rue Steinkerque and turn left onto rue Tardieu, where the *funiculaire* whisks you from the base of the Montmartre butte right up to the outside of Sacré-Coeur.) After visiting Sacré-Coeur and the touristy but fun place du Tertre, a square with overpriced restaurants and artists clamoring to sketch your portrait, wander down the hill where you eventually stumble across Paris from another era — surprisingly unspoiled lanes, quiet squares, ivy-clad shuttered houses with gardens, and even Paris's only vineyard. Together, it all creates a sense of the rustic village it once was. See Chapter 20 for an in-depth walking tour of Montmartre.

Musée d'Orsay
Eiffel Tower/Les Invalides

To get a sense of the train station that this museum was during its previous incarnation, take a moment at the top of the central staircase to envision where trains once pulled into the station under the curved roof.

Then enjoy the Musée d'Orsay's real claim to fame — its unsurpassed collection of Impressionist masterpieces. There are three floors of exhibits. On the ground floor are Ingres's *La Source,* Millet's *L'Angelus,* the Barbizon school, Manet's *Olympia,* and other works of early impressionism. Impressionism continues on the top level, with Renoir's *Le Moulin de la Galette,* Manet's *Déjeuner sur l'Herbe,* Degas's *Racing at Longchamps,* Monet's cathedrals, van Gogh's *Self-Portrait,* and Whistler's *Portrait of the Artist's Mother.* Works by Gauguin and the Pont-Aven school, Toulouse-Lautrec, Pissarro, Cézanne, and Seurat also are exhibited. Symbolism, naturalism, and Art Nouveau are represented on the middle level; the international Art Nouveau exhibit includes wonderful furniture and objets d'art as well as Koloman Moser's *Paradise,* a beautiful design for stained glass. Give yourself three hours, including a lunch break in the museum's gorgeous, turn-of-the-20th-century Musée d'Orsay restaurant on the middle level. For less expensive and quicker light bites, the Café des Hauteurs is on the fifth floor (it has a great view of the Seine through its clock window) and a snack bar on the mezzanine.

62 rue de Lille/1 rue Bellechasse, 7e. ☎ *01-40-49-48-14, or 01-40-49-48-48 for information desk. Internet:* www.musee-orsay.fr. *Métro: Solférino. RER: Musée-d'Orsay. Bus: 24, 63, 68, 69, 73, 83, 94, 94. Admission (may cost more to include major temporary exhibits): 7€ adults; 5€ ages 18–24 and seniors and on Sun; free for children younger than 18. Free the first Sun of every month. Open: Tues–Wed and Fri–Sat 10 a.m.–6 p.m.; Thurs 10:00 a.m.–9:45 p.m.; Sun 9 a.m.–6 p.m. From mid-June through the end of Sept, the museum opens at 9 a.m.*

Musée du Louvre

Louvre

The huge Louvre palace (see "The Louvre" map nearby) evolved during several centuries, first opening as a museum in 1793, which is why it would take you a month of visits to see the more than 30,000 treasures it houses. But, don't fear, a visit to the Louvre doesn't have to be overwhelming. In fact, the three steps to an enjoyable Louvre experience are: 1) Decide what you want to see before you go, and see it first. Trust me on this one. 2) Grab a free map of the Louvre at the Information Desk under the Pyramid or get a guide. The Louvre bookstore in the Carrousel de Louvre sells many comprehensive guides and maps in English; you can also grab brochures for "Visitors in a Hurry," or a guidebook, "The Louvre, First Visit." 3) Take a guided tour. You can try a 90-minute tour by a museum guide (☎ 01-40-20-52-63) that covers the most popular works and gives you a quick orientation to the museum's layout. If you prefer to set your own pace, a four-hour "audiotour" (5€) can be rented at the entrance to any of the wings.

I.M. Pei's glass pyramid is the main entrance to the museum; pregnant women, visitors with children in strollers and the disabled have priority. Avoid this entrance and its long lines by using **the 99 rue de Rivoli/Carrousel du Louvre** entrance, or take the stairs at the **Porte des Lions** near the Arc du Triomphe du Carrousel. Those who already have

The Louvre

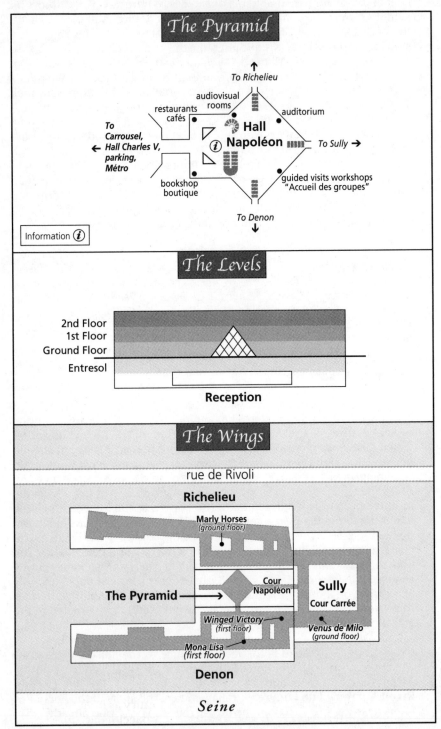

tickets or have the Carte Musées et Monuments can use the special entrance to the Louvre at the **passage Richelieu** between rue de Rivoli and the courtyard.

The Louvre is organized in three wings — Sully, Denon, and Richelieu over four floors exhibiting art and antiquities from Oriental, Islamic, Egyptian, Greek, Etruscan, Roman, Oceanic, European, and North and South American civilizations, and sculpture, objets d'art, paintings, prints, drawings, and the moats and dungeon of the medieval Louvre fortress.

When you're in a hurry, but want to do the Louvre on your own, do a quick, "best of the Louvre" tour. Start with Leonardo da Vinci's *Mona Lisa* (Denon wing, first floor); on the same floor nearby are two of the Louvre's most famous French paintings, Géricault's *The Raft of Medusa* and Delacroix's *Liberty Guiding the People*. Next, visit the *Winged Victory* and Michelangelo's *Slaves* (both Denon wing, ground floor) before seeing the *Venus de Milo* (Sully wing, ground floor). After that, let your own interests guide you. Consider that only Florence's Uffizi Gallery rivals the Denon wing for its Italian Renaissance collection, which includes Raphael's *Portrait of Balthazar Castiglione* and Titian's *Man with a Glove*. And the revamped Egyptian antiquities department is the largest exhibition of Egyptian antiquities outside Cairo. In 2000, a new exhibit featuring 120 arts and antiquities from the earliest civilizations in Africa, Asia, Oceania, and the Americas opened on the ground floor near the Denon wing. The exhibit is housed in the Louvre until 2004, when Musée de Quai Branly, to which it belongs, opens.

Order tickets by phone from FNAC ☎ **08-92-68-46-94** (0.34€/min.), and pick them up at any FNAC store (except FNAC photo shops). A 1.10€ commission is charged by FNAC. A nearby branch is at Forum des Halles, 1 rue Pierre Lescure. You can also buy Louvre tickets at Le Printemps, Galeries Lafayette, Le Bon Marché, and BHV; ask at the information desks in these stores.

Rue de Rivoli, 1er. ☎ *01-40-20-50-50 for recorded message, 01-40-20-53-17 for information desk. Internet:* www.louvre.fr. *Métro: Palais-Royal–Musée du Louvre. Admission: 7.50€ adults; 5€ after 3 p.m. and on Sun; free first Sun of month, Bastille Day (July 14) and for children younger than 18. Tours in English (call 01-40-20-52-63 for hours) 5.95€ adults, 3.05€ seniors, 3.51€ younger than age 18. Open: Mon (certain rooms only) and Wed 9:00 a.m.–9:45 p.m.; Thurs–Sun 9 a.m.–6 p.m. Closed Tues.*

Musée Jacquemart André
Champs-Elysées

The combination of an outstanding art collection and a gorgeous 19th-century mansion makes this museum one of the jewels of Paris and a paradise for Renaissance art fans. It's worth visiting as much for a glimpse of how filthy rich Parisians lived in the 19th century as for its Italian and Flemish masterpieces by Bellini, Botticelli, Carpaccio, Uccello, Rubens,

Rembrandt, and van Eyck. Edouard André, the heir of a prominent banking family, and his wife, Nélie Jacquemart, a well-known portraitist, commissioned architect Henri Parent to build their "house," then set about filling it with French, Flemish, and Italian paintings, furniture, and tapestries. Highlights of the collection include Rembrandt's *Docteur Tholinx,* Van Dyck's *Time Cutting the Wings of Love,* a fresco by Jean Baptiste Tiepolo, Fragonard's naturalistic *Portrait d'un Vieillard,* and a portrait of *Catherine Skavronskaia* by Elisabeth Vigée-Lebrun, one of Marie Antoinette's favorite artists. As you wander the ornate gilt-ridden rooms, pause in the "winter garden," a tour de force of marble and mirrors flanking an unusual double staircase. Take advantage of the free audio that guides you through the mansion with fascinating narrative. Allow an hour to visit the museum, then take a break in what was Madame Jacquemart's lofty ceilinged dining room, now a pretty tearoom serving light lunches and snacks.

158 bd. Haussmann, 8e. ☎ *01-45-62-11-59. Métro: Miromesnil. Bus: 22, 28, 43, 52, 54, 80, 83, 84, 93. Admission: 8€ adults; 6€ students and children younger than 18. Open: Daily (including Dec 25) 10 a.m.–6 p.m.*

Musée Nationale d'Auguste Rodin
Eiffel Tower/Les Invalides

Auguste Rodin, often regarded as the greatest sculptor of all time, lived and worked here from 1908 until his death in 1917. His legendary sensuality, which outraged 19th-century critics, is expressed here in this collection that includes all of his greatest works. *The Kiss* immortalizes in white marble the passion of doomed 13th-century lovers Paolo Malatesta and Francesca da Rimini. In the courtyard, *Burghers of Calais* is a harrowing commemoration of the siege of Calais in 1347, after which the triumphant Edward III of England kept the town's six richest burghers as servants. Also in the courtyard is *The Thinker.* The *Gates of Hell* is a portrayal of Dante's *Inferno.* Intended for the Musée des Arts Decoratifs, the massive bronze doors were not completed until seven years after Rodin's death. The museum is in the 18th-century Hôtel Biron, which was a convent before it became a residence for artists and writers. Matisse, Jean Cocteau, and the poet Rainer Maria Rilke lived and worked in the mansion before Rodin moved there at the height of his popularity. Count on spending at least an hour and a half in the museum.

If you don't have much time or money, pay the 1€ admission to visit just the gardens, where Rodin's works stand among 2,000 rosebushes. Allow at least an hour to visit the garden, longer if you want to break for coffee in the garden café.

Hôtel Biron, 77 rue de Varenne, 7e. ☎ *01-44-18-61-10. Métro: Varenne. Bus: 69, 82, 87, 92. Admission: 5€ adults; 3€ ages 18–24 and seniors and on Sun; 1€ for garden only; free for children younger than 18. Open: Apr–Sept Tues–Sun 9:30 a.m.–5:45 p.m.; Oct–Mar Tues–Sun 9:30 a.m.–4:45 p.m. Garden closes at 6:45 p.m. in summer, 5:00 p.m. in winter, last admittance one hour before closing.*

Musée Picasso
Le Marais

You can pay a visit to the Musée Picasso on each trip to Paris and see something different each time because the works are rotated. The museum was created in 1973 by Picasso's heirs, who donated his personal art collection to the state in lieu of paying outrageous inheritance taxes after his death. The spectacular collection includes more than 200 paintings, nearly 160 sculptures, 88 ceramics, and more than 3,000 prints and drawings. Every phase of Picasso's prolific 75-year career is represented. Works can be viewed chronologically; budget at least a few hours here, if not more. The museum also displays works by other artists collected by Picasso, including Corot, Cézanne, Braque, Rousseau, Matisse, and Renoir. The 17th-century Hôtel Salé housing it all has a gorgeous carved stairway and is worth a visit in its own right (the name "Salé" means salty; the former owner was a salt tax collector).

Hôtel Salé, 5 rue de Thorigny, 3e. ☎ 01-42-71-25-21. Métro: Chemin-Vert, St-Paul, or Filles du Calvaire. Bus: 29, 69, 75, 96. Admission: 5.50€ adults; 4€ ages 18–25 and on Sundays; free for children younger than 18. Free the first Sun of each month. Open: Apr–Sept Wed–Mon 9:30 a.m.–6:00 p.m.; Oct–Mar Wed–Mon 9:30 a.m.–5:30 p.m., Thurs until 8 p.m.

Panthéon
Latin Quarter

The Panthéon is to France what Westminster Abbey is to England: a final resting place for many of the nation's greatest citizens. Inside the domed church's barrel-vaulted crypt are the tombs of Voltaire, Rousseau, Hugo, Braille, and Zola. André Malraux was the last to be entombed there in 1996. Louis XV originally built the Panthéon as a church in thanksgiving to St-Geneviève after his recovery from gout. Construction started in 1755, but after the French Revolution, the church was renamed the Panthéon, in remembrance of ancient Rome's Pantheon, and rededicated as a burying ground for France's heroes. All Christian elements were removed and windows were blocked. From 1806 to 1884, officials turned the Pantheon back into a church two more times before finally declaring it what it currently is today. You can't miss the Panthéon at night, it's lit from the inside with eerie blue lights that give it the appearance of a UFO — or a trendy disco.

Place du Panthéon, 5e. ☎ 01-44-32-18-00. Métro: Cardinal-Lemoine or Maubert-Mutualité. Bus: 21, 27, 83, 84, 85, 89. Admission: 7€ adults; 4.50€ ages 18–25; free for children younger than 18. Open: Apr–Sept daily 10:00 a.m.–6:30 p.m. (Oct–Mar till 6 p.m.).

Père-Lachaise Cemetery
Montmartre and Beyond

Cresting above a high hill overlooking Paris, the world's most visited cemetery is more outdoor museum than place of mourning. No wonder

Père-Lachaise Cemetery

N

0   100 yds
0   100 m

Père-Lachaise
Cemetery
Seine
P A R I S

rue Ramus

avenue du Père-Lachaise

rue des Rondeaux

avenue Aguado

avenue Carette

77

1

89

avenue Transversale No. 3

avenue des Combattants-Étrangers

88

83   78   84

Colombarium

3   **2**

90

85   **4**

87 **6**   **7**

avenue Transversale No. 2

8

82

44

91

79

avenue Circulaire

81

86

5

9

80   46

45

avenue Transversale No. 1

47   48

49

15

49

50

23 **12**

13

11 **10**

24

16

52

avenue des Feuillants

avenue St-Morys

51

22

14

72

71

54

53

55

21

69   70

56   **19**

20

12   11

avenue de la Chapelle

17

68

57

Monument
aux
Morts

avenue Latérale du Sud

10

65

67

4

18

66

58

21

22

9

2

avenue Circulaire

23

avenue du Puits

Conservati

63

3

62   61   60   59

1   2

boulevard de Ménilmontant

Entrance

Abélard & Héloïse **37**

Guillaume Apollinaire **5**

Pierre-Auguste
   Beaumarchais **30**

Hans Bellmer **24**

Sarah Bernhardt **9**

Georges Bizet **17**

Maria Callas **3**

Frédéric Chopin **36**

Colette **23**

Auguste Comte **34**

Jean Baptiste Camille
   Corot **11**

Honoré Daumier **10**

Jaques-Louis David **19**

Honoré de Balzac **16**

Eugène Delacroix **15**

Gustave Doré **14**

Isadora Duncan **6**

Paul Eluard **26**

Max Ernst **2**

Théodore Géricault **20**

Jean-Auguste-Dominique
   Ingres **13**

Jean La Fontaine **33**

René Lalique **12**

Lefebvre Masséna **29**

Amedeo Modigliani **28**

Molière **32**

Jim Morrison **35**

Alfred de Musset **21**

Edith Piaf **27**

Camille Pissarro **38**

Marcel Proust **4**

Gioacchio Antonio
   Rossini **22**

Rothschild family plot **39**

Henri de Saint-Simon **31**

Georges Seurat **18**

Simone Signoret &
   Yves Montand **8**

Gertrude Stein &
   Alice B. Toklas **25**

Oscar Wilde **1**

Richard Wright **7**

Parisians have always come here to stroll and reflect; with its winding, cobbled streets, park benches, and street signs, the 110-acre Père-Lachaise is a minicity unto itself. Many visitors leave flowers or notes scrawled on Métro tickets for their favorite celebrity residents, who include Isadora Duncan, Edith Piaf, Oscar Wilde, Chopin, Jim Morrison, Modigliani, Molière, Pissarro, Proust, Sarah Bernhardt, and Gertrude Stein.

If you're interested in nothing else, go for the striking and often poignant statuary: the boy who seems to sit up in bed as if he'd heard a noise or the young woman who's frozen, mid-dance, as if turned to stone without warning. You can obtain a free map from the gatekeeper at the main entrance, but the better map is one sold outside the entrance for 2€. Or you can just use the "Père-Lachaise Cemetery" map I provide in this chapter. Allow at the very least two hours to visit.

16 rue du Repos, 20e. Main entrance on bd. du Ménilmontant. Métro: Père-Lachaise. Bus: 61, 69, 102. Admission: Free. Open: Mar 16–Nov 5 Mon–Fri 8 a.m.– 6 p.m., Sat 8:30 a.m.–6:00 p.m., Sun 9 a.m.–6 p.m.; Nov 6–Mar 15 Mon–Fri 8:00 a.m.–5:30 p.m., Sat 8:30 a.m.–5:30 p.m., Sun 9:00 a.m.–5:30 p.m.

Place des Vosges
Le Marais

The most beautiful square in Paris sits right in the middle of Le Marais — a symmetrical block of 36 rose-colored town houses, nine on each side, with handsome slate roofs and dormer windows. At ground level is a lovely arcaded walkway that's now home to galleries, cafés, antiques dealers, and smart boutiques. In the early 17th century, Henri IV transformed this area into the most prestigious neighborhood in France, putting his royal palace here, and the square quickly became the center of courtly parades and festivities. After the Revolution, it became place de l'Indivisibilité and later place des Vosges, in honor of the first *département* in France that completely paid its taxes. Victor Hugo lived at No. 6 for 16 years.

Allow 30 minutes to walk all the way around the square under the arcades and a brief stroll in the park.

3e. Métro: St-Paul. Bus: 69, 76, 96.

Sacré-Coeur
Montmartre

The white Byzantine-Romanesque church dominating Paris's highest hill — the one that you can see from all around the city — is Basilique du Sacré-Coeur. Built from 1876 (after France's defeat in the Franco-Prussian War) to 1919, the church's interior is not as striking as its exterior and is, in fact, vaguely depressing. The best reason to come here is for the city-spanning views from its dome — visibility is 30-miles across the rooftops of Paris on a clear day. The climb from church floor to dome, however, is on a flight of nail-bitingly steep corkscrew steps. A better idea, and one that kids enjoy, is to conserve your pre-Dome climbing energy by taking the elevator up from the Anvers Métro station, walking the short distance from rue Steinkerque and turning left onto rue Tardieu, where a *funiculaire* whisks you from the base of the Montmartre butte right up to the outside of the church.

On the other side of Sacré-Coeur is the **place du Tertre,** where Vincent van Gogh once lived; he used it as a scene for one of his paintings. The place is usually swamped by tourists and quick-sketch artists in the spring and summer. Following any street downhill from the place du Tertre leads you to the quiet side of Montmartre. The steps in front of the church come alive around dusk, when street musicians entertain the crowd that gathers to watch the city's lights come on. Be alert: Pickpockets are all around Montmartre.

25 rue du Chevalier-de-la-Barre, 18e. ☎ *01-53-41-89-00. Métro: Abbesses. Take elevator to surface and follow signs to funiculaire, which runs to the church (fare: 1 Métro ticket). Bus: The only bus that goes to the top of the hill is the local Montmartrobus. Admission: Basilica free; dome and crypt 4.50€ adults, 2.50€ all others. Open: Basilica daily 6:45 a.m.–10:30 p.m.; dome and crypt daily 10:00 a.m.–5:45 p.m.*

Sainte-Chapelle
Ile de la Cité

If you save Sainte-Chapelle for a sunny day, its 15 perfect stained-glass windows soaring 50 feet high to a star-studded vaulted ceiling take your breath away. You may think you've stepped into a kaleidoscope by mistake. Louis IX, the only French king to become a saint, had Sainte-Chapelle, the "Holy Chapel," built as a shrine to house relics of the crucifixion, including the Crown of Thorns that Louis bought from the Emperor of Constantinople. Building Sainte-Chapelle certainly cost less than the outrageously expensive Crown of Thorns, which was said to have been acquired at the crucifixion and now resides in the vault at Notre-Dame.

Built between 1246 and 1248, Sainte-Chapelle consists of two chapels, one on top of the other. Palace servants used the *chapelle basse* (lower chapel), ornamented with fleur-de-lis designs. The *chapelle haute* (upper chapel, accessed by 30 winding steps) is one of the highest achievements of Gothic art. If you spend the time (which can take hours or even a day!), you can see that the 1,134 scenes in the stained glass of the 15 windows trace the Biblical story from the Garden of Eden to the Apocalypse. The first window to the right represents the story of the Crown of Thorns; St. Louis is shown several times. Some evenings, when the upper chapel becomes a venue for classical-music concerts, the effect of its chandelier lights dancing off the windows is magical.

4 bd. du Palais, Palais de Justice, Ile de la Cité, 4e. ☎ 01-53-73-78-50. Métro: Cité or St-Michel. RER: St-Michel. Bus: 21, 27, 38, 85, 96. Admission: 5.50€ adults; 3.50€ 12–25; free for children younger than 12. Open: Apr–Sept daily 9:30 a.m.–6:00 p.m. Closed major holidays.

Index of Top Attractions by Neighborhood

The Right Bank

Louvre (1er)
Jardin des Tuileries
Jardin du Palais-Royal
Musée du Louvre

Le Marais, Ile de la Cité (3e, 4e)
Cathédral de Notre-Dame
Centre Georges Pompidou
Musée Picasso
Place des Vosges
Sainte-Chapelle

Champs-Elysées (8e, 16e)
Arc de Triomphe
Champs-Elysées
Musée Jacquemart-André

Montmartre (18e) and Beyond
Montmartre
Père-Lachaise Cemetery (20e)
Sacré-Coeur

The Left Bank

Latin Quarter (5e)
Panthéon

St-Germain-des-Prés (6e)
Jardin et Palais du Luxembourg

Eiffel Tower/Les Invalides (7e)
Eiffel Tower (La Tour Eiffel)
Hôtel des Invalides (Napoléon's Tomb)
Musée d'Orsay
Musée Nationale d'Auguste Rodin

Index of Top Attractions by Type

Cemeteries
Père-Lachaise Cemetery (20e)

Churches
Cathédral de Notre-Dame (4e)
Sacré-Cœur (18e)
Sainte-Chapelle (4e)

Museums
Centre Georges Pompidou (4e)
Musée d'Orsay (7e)
Musée du Louvre (1er)
Musée Jacquemart-André (8e)
Musée Nationale d'Auguste Rodin (7e)
Musée Picasso (3e)

Monuments and Architecture

Arc de Triomphe (8e)
Champs-Elysées (8e)
Eiffel Tower (La Tour Eiffel; 7e)
Hôtel des Invalides (Napoléon's
    Tomb; 7e)
Panthéon (5e)

Neighborhoods

Montmartre (18e)

Parks

Jardin des Tuileries (1er)
Jardin du Palais-Royal (1er)
Jardin et Palais du Luxembourg (6e)
Place des Vosges (3e)

Chapter 17

More Cool Things to See and Do

A fter you hit all of the city's top attractions, you may want to search out some of its lesser known but still captivating sights. This chapter introduces you to some of those spots; organized with specific interests in mind, it gives you ideas about how to make Paris truly your own. Because, after all, visiting Paris is more than seeing the Eiffel Tower or *Mona Lisa* (but if that's what you're after, see Chapter 16). The "More Fun Things to Do in Paris" map can help you locate the fun zones.

Especially for Kids

Both you and your kids can have a great time in Paris climbing to the top of the Eiffel Tower, Notre-Dame, or the Arc de Triomphe (all covered in Chapter 16). Or you can attend puppet shows (*les guignols*), which are a great Paris tradition. Even though the shows are in French, your kids will probably be able to figure out what's going on. You can find the shows in the Jardin du Luxembourg, the Champ de Mars, and the Jardin des Tuileries. All Parisian parks, in fact, are wonderful for children, even without the puppet shows; one of the best is the **Bois de Vincennes,** which is located at the most eastern edge of the city. It has a lake where you can rent a boat for a leisurely row, ride miles of bike paths (bike rental is also available), and explore a cave. You can also find a wonderful maze at the **Jardin des Enfants aux Halles,** 105 rue Rambuteau (☎ 01-45-08-07-18; Métro: Chatelet).

Children may also enjoy taking a boat cruise on the Seine (see Chapters 16 and 18) and seeing art and history made real before their eyes in museums.

More Fun Things to Do in Paris

place du Mal. Juin
rue de Prony
avenue de Villiers
av. du Roule
place du Gal Koenig
av. de Gouvion St-Cyr
avenue Niel
rue de Courcelles
bd. des Batignolles
rue de Constantinople
av. Charles de Gaulle
Palais des Congrès
bd. Pereire des Ternes
de Courcelles
PARC MONCEAU
bd. Malesherbes
rue de Rome
Conservatoire de Musique
BOIS DE BOULOGNE
bd. de l'Amiral Bruix
av. de la Gr. Armée
St-Ferdinand
place des Ternes
Salle Wagram
avenue de Wagram
rue du Faubourg St-Honoré
Salle Pleyel
bd. Haussmann
St-Augustin
place St-Augustin
Gare St-Lazare
place Charles de Gaulle
Arc de Triomphe
av. de Friedland
bd. Haussmann
bd. Malesherbes
av. de la Malakoff
Foch
avenue
Centre de Conférences Internationales
av. des
place de la Madeleine
La Madele
pl. Victor Hugo
avenue Victor Hugo
avenue Kléber
avenue Marceau
Rond Point des Champs-Elysées
Théâtre Marigny
Palais de l'Elysée
av. Bugeaud
rue Lauriston
rue Bissière
av. F. D. Roosevelt
Champs-Elysées
place de la Concorde
avenue Victor Hugo
Belles Feuilles
Raymond Poincaré
rue de Longchamp
av. W. Churchill
JARDIN D
place du Trocadéro et du 11 Novembre
avenue du Président Wilson
place de l'Alma
Seine
pont de la Concorde
rue de Passy
av. Paul Doumer
New York
Débilly
passerelle Debilly
quai d'Orsay
Egouts
pont des Invalides
pont Alex. III
Aerogare des Invalides
quai Anatole France
JARDINS DU TROCADÉRO
pont d'Iéna
quai Branly
avenue de la Bourdonnais
rue de l'Université
rue St-Dominique
Musée d'Orsa
Ste-Clotilde
Tour Eiffel
av. de Gustave Eiffel
CHAMP
av. Joseph Bouvard
DE
rue de Grenelle
Hôtel des Invalides
rue de Varenne
pont de Grenelle
Bir Hakeim
av. du Président Kennedy
allée des Cygnes
quai de Grenelle
avenue de Suffren
av. Charles Risler
MARS
place Joffre
av. de La Motte Picquet
av. de Tourville
rue de Babylone
rue du Bac
place de Brazzaville
St-Léon
Ecole Militaire
av. de Lowendal
av. de Ségur
St-François Xavier
rue de Vaneau
rue Linois
U.N.E.S.C.O.
bd. Garibaldi
place de Breteuil
rue du Cherche-Midi
avenue Emile Zola
rue Fremicourt
bd. du Montparnasse
rue de Vaugirard
Imprimerie Nationale
rue de la Croix Nivert
rue du Commerce
place Henry Queuille
MONTPARNASSE
place du 18 Ju 1940
rue de la Convention
rue St-Charles
rue de Vaugirard
rue Lecourbe
Institut Pasteur
Tour Montparnasse
Gare Montparnasse
bd. Edga
rue Balard
avenue Félix Faure
St-Lambert
rue P. Barruel
rue Dutot
Cimet
rue de la Convention
rue Lecourbe
bd. Victor
place d'Alleray

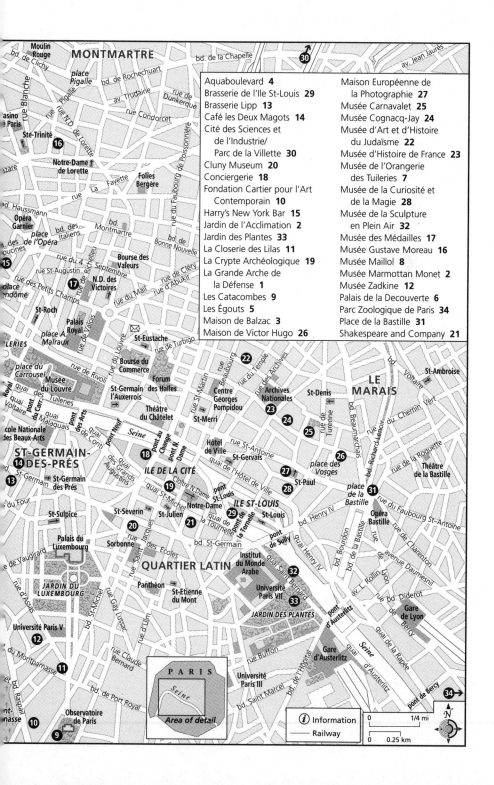

Aquaboulevard **4**
Brasserie de l'Ile St-Louis **29**
Brasserie Lipp **13**
Café les Deux Magots **14**
Cité des Sciences et
  de l'Industrie/
  Parc de la Villette **30**
Cluny Museum **20**
Conciergerie **18**
Fondation Cartier pour l'Art
  Contemporain **10**
Harry's New York Bar **15**
Jardin de l'Acclimation **2**
Jardin des Plantes **33**
La Closerie des Lilas **11**
La Crypte Archéologique **19**
La Grande Arche de
  la Défense **1**
Les Catacombes **9**
Les Égouts **5**
Maison de Balzac **3**
Maison de Victor Hugo **26**

Maison Européenne de
  la Photographie **27**
Musée Carnavalet **25**
Musée Cognacq-Jay **24**
Musée d'Art et d'Histoire
  du Judaïsme **22**
Musée d'Histoire de France **23**
Musée de l'Orangerie
  des Tuileries **7**
Musée de la Curiosité et
  de la Magie **28**
Musée de la Sculpture
  en Plein Air **32**
Musée des Médailles **17**
Musée Gustave Moreau **16**
Musée Maillol **8**
Musée Marmottan Monet **2**
Musée Zadkine **12**
Palais de la Decouverte **6**
Parc Zoologique de Paris **34**
Place de la Bastille **31**
Shakespeare and Company **21**

Cité des Sciences et de l'Industrie

If your kids are 3 or older, head to this enormous, modern science complex with interactive exhibits on everything from outer space to genetically manipulated plants. You'll find a planetarium, movie cinemas, and an aquarium, as well as an adventure playground designed specifically for 3- to 12-year-olds. On the complex's east side is Explora, which features exhibits, models, robots, and interactive games, demonstrates scientific techniques, and presents subjects that include the universe, the earth, the environment, space, computer science, and health (in one experiment, you can test your sense of smell). The Children's City is divided into exhibits for 5- to 12-year-olds, including: Machines and Mechanisms, the Living Species, and Techniques of Communications (in one demonstration, kids can be part of a weather broadcast). A separate exhibit on electricity will stand your kids' hair on end. A small section of the Children's City is reserved for 3- to 5-year-olds. Organized around a stream, children learn about themselves in relation to the world around them (in one activity, they get to wear a tortoise shell). The gigantic Géode sphere, on the complex's south side, is a wonder, with a huge hemispheric IMAX screen on which six or so films are shown daily. Another theater, the Cinaxe, is a "simulator" that projects movies on a screen while accelerating and moving the audience in different directions (children younger than 3, pregnant women, and the disabled are not allowed). Kids can climb aboard an actual submarine in the l'Argonaute exhibit (on the complex's south side next to Géode) and participate in technology demonstrations at the Technocité. A free aquarium is located in the basement. After the visit, let your kids run wild in the expansive, green Parc de la Villette. You'll find a restaurant in the complex and food stands in the park. This could easily be an all-day visit. Music lovers take note: The Musée de la Musique is located on the other side of the canal and is accessible by a bridge. Its exhibits and concerts are worth a stop.

30 av. Corentin-Cariou, 19e. ☎ *01-40-05-81-00. Internet:* www.cite-sciences.fr. *Métro: Porte-de-la-Villette. Admission: Exhibitions (including l'Argonaute submarine) 3€, free for children younger than 7; to the Géode, 8.75€ adults, 6.75€ ages 25 and younger and per person in large families or groups; to Cinaxe theater, 5.20€, combined with another ticket (Explora or Géode) 4.50€; to Explora 7.50€ adults, 5.50€ ages 7–25, free for children younger than 7. Admission to Cité des Enfants 5€ (children must be accompanied by an adult). Open: Tues–Sat 10 a.m.–6 p.m.; Sun 10 a.m.–7 p.m.*

Jardin de l'Acclimatation Bois de Boulogne

This 25-acre amusement park on the north side of the former royal hunting ground is a must for young children. The park's layout is simple: Just follow its circular road in either direction, and it will eventually get you back to where you started. Attractions include a house of mirrors, an archery range, a miniature golf course, a petting zoo and farm, an American–style bowling alley, a playground, pony rides, paddle boats, and a "City of Merry-Go-Rounds," where young "citizens" can drive cars, fire trucks, and planes, try their hand at carnival games, and ride the carousel. The park also has an "enchanted river," a lake bordered by a bright blue-topped Korean pavilion, a restaurant, and snack and ice cream stands. After a half-day here, your little ones will sleep well!

16e. ☎ 01-40-67-90-82. Take Métro Line 1 to Les Sablons, exit on rue d'Orléans, entrance is about 50 feet away. Or take bus nos. 43, 73, 82, or 174. Or take the open-air "Petit Train" from the Bois de Boulogne's Porte Maillot entrance; 4.60€ round-trip adults, 3.45€ round-trip children and students. Admission to the Jardin d'Acclimatation: 2.30€ adults and children ages 3 and older. Free for children younger than 3. Open: Daily 10 a.m.–6 p.m.

Jardin des Plantes

The rows of trees, beds of herbs and flowers, 17th-century maze, green-houses, and specialized gardens are only some of the sights to marvel at within these immense former royal medicine gardens. Children will stare in awe at the bugs, bones, minerals, meteorites, dinosaurs, fossils, and endangered species in the galleries of the Jardin's Musée National d'Histoire Naturelle. Here, the Grand Gallery of Evolution traces life and humankind's relationship to nature. Don't miss the endangered and extinct species room, which displays (stuffed versions of) Gabonese monkeys, Sumatran tigers, lemurs of Madagascar, and a mock-up of the dodo bird. English explanations of some exhibits are available. Also part of the natural history museum are the Mineralogical Gallery (1,800 minerals, meteorites, and precious stones), the Entomological Gallery (1,500 insect specimens for bug-loving kids), and the Paleobotanical Gallery (plant evolution and specimens of fossil plants). Save for last the medium-sized menagerie, one of the oldest zoos in the world, containing live bears, buffalo, big cats, apes, antelope, reptiles (including an alligator found in a room at the Hôtel de Paris), tortoises, and birds. Don't overlook the Vivarium — the spiders and insects are remarkable, especially the bugs that look like living tree branches! — or the Microzoo, where kids use microscopes to get a look at the life of the tiniest animals. A small restaurant on the zoo's premises offers pick-me-ups for the tired and cranky and their parents.

Take the Métro to Gare d'Austerlitz and exit from the rue Buffon side; you're right next to the Gallery of Anatomy and Paleontology. You can also take the Métro to Jussieu and walk up rue Geoffroy St-Hilaire to the Grand Gallery of Evolution. Admission: Grande Galerie 7€ adults, 5€ students, seniors, and children; other galleries 4.57€ adults, 3.04€ students, seniors, and children; ménagerie (zoo) 7.63€ adults, 4.57€ students, seniors, and children. Open: Park summer 7:30 a.m.–8:00 p.m., winter until 5:30 p.m.; galleries Apr–Oct Wed–Mon 10 a.m.–6 p.m., Oct–Apr till 5 p.m.; zoo daily summer 9:00 a.m.–6:30 p.m., winter 9:00 a.m.–5:30 p.m.

La Grande Arche de la Défense

Kids will love the cool outdoor elevator to the top of modernity's answer to the Arc de Triomphe. The Grand Arche de la Défense is the center-piece of a very futuristic Paris suburb rife with glass and chrome sky-scrapers lending their height to surreal sculptures. Built in 1989 to commemorate France's bicentennial, this 35-story cube completes a continuous line of perspective running from the Arc de Triomphe du Carrousel in the courtyard of the Louvre, down the Champs-Elysées, and through the Arc de Triomphe to the suburb of La Défense. The netting you see here is for catching any pieces of the façade that may fall down; several chunks have already come down. Allow about two hours for the round-trip journey from central Paris, including the climb to the top.

1 parvis de la Défense, 92040 Paris-La Défense. ☎ *01-49-07-27-57. Métro, RER: Grande Arche de la Défense. Admission: 7€ adults, 5.50€ ages 6–17 and students, free for children younger than 6. Open: Wed and Sat–Sun 2–7 p.m.; Apr 1–Sept 30 10 a.m.–8 p.m. and Nov 1–Mar 31 10 a.m.–7 p.m.*

Musée de la Curiosité et de la Magie

Bona fide magicians escort you through a collection of trick mirrors, animated paintings, talking genies, and the history of illusion in general. You and your kids can play with the many interactive displays — who is brave enough to stick his hand in the open mouth of a lion and see if it really is an illusion? Live magic shows performed throughout the afternoon are also highly entertaining. The museum shop sells all the tools your kids need to cast spells back home.

11 rue St-Paul, 4e. ☎ *01-42-72-13-26. Métro: St-Paul. Admission: 7€ adults, 5€ children younger than 13. Open: Wed, Sat, and Sun 2–7 p.m.*

Palais de la Découverte

You can find a full funhouse of things for kids to do inside the Art Nouveau glass and metal Grand Palais. Your kids' hair will stand on end in the electrostatics room; they can light up displays, test their muscle reactions on special machines, and watch live experiments. And there's a brand new dinosaur exhibit!

Grand Palais Av. Franklin-D-Roosevelt, 8e. ☎ *01-56-43-20-21. Métro: Franklin-D-Roosevelt. (The museum is just up the street on the left.) Admission: 5.60€ adults, 3.65€ students and children 5–17. Planetarium supplement 3.05€. A family of two adults and two children older than age 5 is 12.20€, each additional child older than 5 years is 2.25€. Open: Tues–Sat 9:30 a.m.–6:00 p.m.; Sun 10 a.m.–7 p.m.*

Parc Zoologique de Paris

The zoo is big enough (1,200 animals) to keep your kids occupied for an afternoon, with lions, tigers, bears, and a cool climbing tower (*Le Grand Rocher*) that offers a great view of the animals. Most animals live in settings that closely resemble their natural habitats; you can even watch while some are fed lunch (bears at 11:30 a.m., pelicans 2:15 p.m., seals and sea lions 4:00 p.m.). The zoo has picnic areas on site as well as a snack bar.

53 av. de St-Maurice, Bois de Vincennes, 12e. ☎ *01-44-75-20-10. Fax: 01-43-43-54-73. Métro: Porte Dorée. (Take av. Daumesnil past the Square des Combattants*

Indochine to av. de St-Maurice and turn right; it's a 5- to 10-minute walk.) Admission: 8€ adult, 5€ ages 4–25, free for children younger than 4. Open: Summer daily 9:00 a.m.–6:00 p.m. (Sun till 6:30 p.m.); winter 9:00 a.m.–5:00 or 5:30 p.m.

Especially for Teens

The kid-friendly sights previously mentioned are appropriate for teenagers, as well. But here are a few more suggestions for kids who are a bit older.

Aquaboulevard

If your teens are griping about the heat, send them here. It may not be the beach, but its seven water slides, indoor and outdoor pools, and wave machines make it a fun substitute, and it's safer than swimming in the Seine. A McDonald's, an Oh! Poivrier!, a pizza place, and a first-run movie theater are located on the premises, as well.

4 rue Louis-Armand, 15e. ☎ *01-40-60-10-00. Take the Métro to Balard, head down avenue de la Porte de Sèvres; just after you walk under the overpass, you will see Aquaboulevard straight ahead. Admission: 16.05€ people ages 12 and older, 10.55€ children 3–11. Children 3–11 must be accompanied by an adult. Open: Mon–Thurs 9 a.m.–11 p.m., Fri and Sat 8 a.m. to midnight, Sun 8 a.m.–11 p.m.*

Champs-Elysées

On this famous street, teens can shop to their hearts' content at clothing stores such as O'Neill, Quiksilver, Zara, Naf Naf, and Kookaï, and music stores such as Virgin and FNAC. They can catch movies in French or English (look for "v.o." for *version originale* on the marquee or in newspaper listings for U.S. releases that have not been dubbed into French) in one of the many movie theaters and eat familiar fast food at McDonald's or KFC. Many of the stores on this street are open Sunday, and plenty of teens — both residents and tourists — hang out here.

Métro: Concorde, Champs-Elysées, Clémenceau, Franklin-D-Roosevelt, George V, Charles de Gaulle-Etoile. Many bus lines cross the Champs, but only the 73 travels its entire length.

Les Catacombes

The Catacombes is perfect for hardy kids older than 10, because its tunnels are dark, damp, and spooky. Les Catacombes, a former quarry, began housing bones in 1785 from the Cimetière des Innocents and an assortment of other overstocked Parisian cemeteries. Now about 6 million skulls and skeletons are stacked in thousands of yards of tunnels (a visit is bound to provoke at least a little bit of fear, even among the bravest adults).

Those prone to claustrophobia should think twice about entering! The deep, dark tunnels close in rapidly and tightly. Equip yourself with flashlights to navigate the poorly lit corridors and read the inscriptions, and wear proper shoes (such as hiking boots) to avoid a misstep on the rocky, often slippery passageways. Wear a hood to protect yourself from the water dripping overhead. Les Catacombes earned the nickname *place d'Enfer* ("Hell Square"), which later became *place Denfert-Rochereau*, and you can take Métro line 4 or 6, or RER B to the stop of the same name.

1 place Denfert-Rochereau, 14e. ☎ 01-43-22-47-63. Admission: 4.12€ adults; 2.90€ ages 8–26; free for children younger than 8. Open: Tues–Fri 2–4 p.m.; weekends 9–11 a.m. and 2–4 p.m.

Les Égouts

Believe it or not, this tour of the city's sewers is so popular that you sometimes have to wait as long as a half-hour in line. The tour starts with a short film about the history of sewers, followed by a visit to a small museum, and finally a short trip through the maze. Paris's sewers are laid out like an underground city, with streets clearly labeled and each branch pipe bearing the name of the building to which it's connected. Don't worry; you won't trudge through anything *dégoutant* (disgusting), but the visit may leave your clothes smelling a bit ripe. Make this the last of the day's attractions, and wear something you don't plan to wear again until after the next wash day.

7e. ☎ 01-47-05-10-29. Fax: 01-47-05-34-78. Get off Métro line 9 at Alma-Marceau, then walk across the bridge to the Left Bank. Or take RER C to Pont de l'Alma. The entrance is a stairway on the Seine side of the Quai d'Orsay, facing no. 93. Admission: 3.81€ adults; 3.05€ students and adults older than 60; 2.29€ children 5–12; free for children younger than 5. Open: May–Sept Sat–Wed 11 a.m.–5 p.m.; Oct–Apr 11 a.m.–4 p.m. Closed three weeks in Jan.

Especially for History Buffs

Paris resounds with history. Blue plaques on buildings tell you the names of famous people and the dates that that they lived there. Brown-and-orange signs in French give you an overview of an area's particular story. The city is filled with wonderful museums to satisfy even the pickiest buff's thirst for knowledge. In this section, you find a few of the particularly good ones.

Cluny Museum

If the idea of a medieval museum (officially the Musée National du Moyen Age/Thermes de Cluny) sounds too boring to visit, please reconsider. This museum is one of Paris's treasures, and you won't see only religious art and artifacts, but ancient Roman hot and cold baths, the original statues that furious revolutionaries tore from Notre-Dame in 1790 (thinking they represented royalty), and one of the most beautiful tapestry series in the world. You'll also find remnants of clothing that royalty wore in the Middle Ages, coins, leatherwork, and gothic furniture, as well as *church art* — jewelled crosses, statues, sculptures, clothing, tapestries, and paintings of saints.

In the 19th century, the Hôtel de Cluny belonged to a collector of medieval art; upon his death in the 1840s, the government acquired the house and its contents. You enter through a medieval cobblestone courtyard, the *Cour d'Honneur* (Courtyard of Honor) — be sure to take in the turreted building and its gargoyles; this is one of the only medieval residences left in Paris. After paying for admission in the tiny lobby, turn left past the gift shop (save it until last) and try to take it all in. The fascinating Roman baths and the Notre-Dame statues are one floor down; one floor up is the famous 15th-century tapestry series of *The Lady and the Unicorn*. The tapestries hang in a dimly lit room by themselves. You can sit in one of the cushioned seats and try to figure out the meaning of the sixth tapestry. (The first five are an allegory representing the five senses; the meaning of the sixth tapestry remains a mystery.) The gift shop here is a wonderful place for souvenirs, and the renovated gardens are an oasis of calm off one of the Latin Quarter's busiest streets. Every plant (except two) in *The Lady and the Unicorn* tapestries was extensively researched and tracked down to be planted here.

6 place Paul-Painlevé, 5e (between rue du Sommerard and rue des Écoles). ☎ *01-53-73-78-00. Métro: Cluny-Sorbonne. Admission: 5.50€ adults; 4€ ages 18–26, seniors older than 60 and on Sun; free for children younger than 18. Free for all the first Sun of every month. Open: Wed–Mon 9:15 a.m.–5:45 p.m.*

Conciergerie

The Conciergerie is probably most famous for its days as a prison during "The Terror" years of the French Revolution, when those deemed "enemies of the people" passed through here. Built in the 14th century as part of the administrative offices of the crown, the Conciergerie was turned into a prison in the 15th century. Visitors pass through the Tour d'Argent, where the crown jewels were once stored, and the Tour César to the Salle des Gardes (Guard Room) entrance. Probably the most famous exhibit is the 11-square-foot cell of Marie Antoinette, who was kept here in squalor to await her fate. More than 4,000 of those imprisoned here headed for the guillotine on the place de la Révolution (now the place de la Concorde), including revolutionary ringleaders Danton and Robespierre, assassin Charlotte Corday, and the poet André Chenier. The far western tower, the Tour Bonbec, came to be known facetiously as the Tower of Babel because of the frequent screams from the many prisoners tortured there. Marie Antoinette's cell is now a chapel, and the other cells have been transformed with exhibits and mementos designed to convey a sense of prison life in a brutal era.

Palais de Justice, Ile de la Cité, 1er. ☎ *01-53-73-78-50. Métro: Cité, Châtelet–Les Halles, or St-Michel. (Exit the Métro at Cité, which is between rue de la Cité and bd.*

du Palais; the Palais is directly across bd. du Palais.) RER: St-Michel. Admission: 5.50€ adults; 3.50€ ages 18–25; free for children younger than 18. Combined Sainte-Chapelle and Conciergerie ticket 7.62€. Open: Apr–Sept daily 9:30 a.m.–6:30 p.m.; Oct–Mar daily 10 a.m.–5 p.m.

La Crypte Archéologique

In 1965, excavations for a new parking lot under the parvis (a portico in front of the church) of Notre-Dame revealed Gallo-Roman ramparts, third-century Gallo-Roman rooms heated by an underground furnace system called a hypocaust, and cellars of medieval houses. The parking lot project was abandoned, and the excavations were turned into this neat archaeological museum. When you go down to the crypt, you are at the Ile de la Cité's original level. Over the centuries, builders erected new structures over the ruins of previous settlements, raising the island about 23 feet. To help you visualize the buildings that once stood here, scale models show how Paris grew from a small settlement to a Roman city, and photographs show the pre-Haussmann parvis. Allow about 45 minutes, longer if you're a history buff.

Place du Parvis Notre-Dame, 4e (about 200 feet directly in front of Notre-Dame, accessed by downward-leading stairs). ☎ *01-43-29-83-51. Métro: Cité, RER: St-Michel-Notre-Dame. Admission: 3.30€ adults; 2.20€ 25 and younger. Open: Tues–Sun 10 a.m.–6 p.m.*

Musée Carnavalet

If you prefer to see history rather than read about it, this is the museum for you. Housed inside two beautiful Renaissance mansions, Paris history comes alive through an incredible selection of paintings, reassembled rooms in all their period glory, and other items from daily life long ago. The blue and yellow rooms of Louis XV and Louis XVI are here in all their ornately furnished glory. The chess pieces that Louis XVI played with while awaiting his beheading are here, as are Napoléon's cradle and a replica of Marcel Proust's cork-lined bedroom. Many salons depict events related to the revolution, and the paintings of what Paris used to look like are fascinating. In 2000, the museum opened a $1.6 million dollar wing devoted to the archaeology of Paris's earliest settlements (some artifacts, such as the fishing boats used by settlers, date back to between 2200 and 4400 B.C.). Visitors can even touch some of the exhibits here. You may want to buy an English-language guidebook in the museum's gift shop, because audio guides are in French.

23 rue de Sévigné, 3e. ☎ *01-44-59-58-58. Métro: St-Paul. (Turn left on rue de Sévigné.) Admission: Free for permanent collections; temporary exhibits 6€ adults, 4.50€ students. Open: Tues–Sun 10 a.m.–6 p.m.*

Musée d'Art et d'Histoire du Judaïsme

This enormous collection displayed in the beautiful 17th-century mansion Hôtel de St-Aignan traces the development of Jewish culture in

France and Europe, from life in the Middle Ages to the 20th century. In addition to beautifully crafted religious objects, including torahs, shofars, menorahs, ark curtains, and spectacular velvet cloaks reflecting both the Sephardic and Ashkenazi traditions throughout Europe and North Africa, the museum has medieval gravestones and 20th-century paintings and sculptures. The museum also presents newly available documents relating to the Dreyfus affair, the notorious scandal that falsely accused a Jewish army captain of providing secret military information to the German government in 1894. The free audio tour is very informative. The exhibits end with a collection of works by Jewish artists, including paintings by Modigliani, Soutine, Zadkine, and Chagall. Allow at least two hours. Security is tight here.

71 rue du Temple, 3e (between rue Rambuteau and rue de Braque). ☎ *01-53-01-86-60. Métro: Rambuteau. Bus: 29, 38, 47, 75. Admission: 6.10€ adults; 3.80€ ages 18–26 and seniors; free for children younger than 18. Open: Mon–Fri 11 a.m.–6 p.m.; Sun 10 a.m.–6 p.m.*

Musée des Médailles

This is the site of France's original national library, still referred to as the Bibliothèque Nationale de France Richelieu, and home to the Musée des Médailles. Ten million books were removed in 1998 to the new Bibliothèque Francois Mitterand in the 13e, but the impressive display of archaeological objects, cameos, bronzes, medals, and money originally amassed by French kings remains. Among the more exceptional objects are the Treasure of Berthouville, a collection of Gallo-Roman money; the Cameo of Sainte-Chapelle, a huge multicolored cameo dating from the first century; and the Treasure of Childéric, one of the oldest remnants of the French monarchy. Take a peek into the Salle Labrouste, a lovely reading room built in 1868, which now echoes sadly without its book collection. The garden, a virtual mini-Versailles, also merits a stop. Security is tight here.

Bibliothèque Nationale de France, 58 rue de Richelieu, 2e (between rue des Filles St-Thomas and rue Colbert). ☎ *01-53-79-83-30. Métro: Palais-Royal–Musée du Louvre or Bourse. Bus: 20,29, 39, 48, 67, 74, 85, 95. Admission: Free. Open: Mon–Fri 1:00–5:45 p.m.; Sat 1:00–4:45 p.m.; Sun noon to 6 p.m.*

Musée d'Histoire de France/Archives Nationales

This incredible palace was purchased in 1700 by François de Rohan, prince de Soubise. The prince received many gifts from Louis XIV — not only due to his position as heir to one of the most powerful families in France, but for the many "favors" imparted by his wife, Anne Chabot de Rohan, onto the King. In 1808, Napoléon ordered the acquisition of the Rohan-Soubise estate to house Empire archives; the palace also contains the National Archives. The interior includes works by François Boucher, whose delicate rococo paintings of landscapes and shepherdesses won him the favor of Madame de Pompadour, Louis XV's influential mistress. It also houses works by Charles Joseph Natoire, a contemporary painter of Boucher's and director of Rome's French Academy, and Louis-Michel van Loo, first painter to Louis XV. The first floor is devoted to the *Musée de l'Histoire de France* (the Museum of the History of France), which contains some of the most important documents that pertain to the country's history, as well as personal papers of some famous French citizens. Exhibits include Henry IV's Edict of Nantes (a document which guaranteed religious liberty), Louis XIV's will, Louis XVI's diary and will, the Declaration of Human Rights, Marie Antoinette's last letter, Napoléon's will, and the French constitution. Rooms are devoted to the Middle Ages, the French Revolution, and other themes.

Hôtel de Soubise, 60 rue des Francs-Bourgeois, 3e. ☎ 01-40-27-60-96. Métro: Rambuteau. Bus: 29, 75, 96. Admission: Museum 3.05€ adults; 2.29€ ages 18–25; free for children younger than 18. Open: Mon, Wed–Fri 10:00 a.m.–5:45 p.m., Sat–Sun 1:45–5:45 p.m.

Place de la Bastille

Ignore the traffic and try to imagine the place de la Bastille just more than 200 years ago, when it contained eight towers rising 100 feet. It was here, on July 14, 1789 (now commemorated in France as Bastille Day), that a mob attacked the old prison, launching the French Revolution. Although the Bastille had long since fallen into disuse, it symbolized the arbitrary power of a king who could imprison anyone for any reason. Prisoners of means could buy a spacious cell and even host dinner parties, but the poor disappeared within the prison's recesses and sometimes drowned when the Seine overflowed its banks. The attack on the prison was therefore a direct assault on royal power. The Bastille was razed in 1792. In its place stands the Colonne de Juillet, a 171-foot bronze column built between 1830 and 1849 to commemorate Parisians killed in civil uprisings in 1830 and 1848.

11e. Métro: Bastille. (The Colonne de Juillet is across from the Métro.)

Especially for Art Lovers

Art in Paris is not merely French art. Many French movements began or developed here, but generations of artists from all parts of the world have thrived in Paris, and the city's museums and galleries hold enough art for several lifetimes of daily viewing. From galleries in the Marais, Bastille, St-Germain-des-Prés, and near the Champs-Elysées, to the Egyptian, Assyrian, and Greco-Roman art at the Louvre, through realism, impressionism, and Art Nouveau at the Musée d'Orsay, to the modern international masters at the Centre Pompidou, Paris offers a vast wealth of art.

Each October, Paris also presents the *Foire Internationale d'Art Contemporain,* one of the largest contemporary art fairs in the world. This art fair has stands from more than 150 galleries, half of them foreign (see Chapter 2). You may find the following museums often less crowded than their larger and more famous counterparts, but each is still capable of wowing you.

Fondation Cartier pour l'Art Contemporain

This building, designed by architect Jean Nouvel, is too striking to miss — it has a glass and metal screen that stands between the street and the glass and metal building, creating an optical illusion that makes the court-yard greenery appear as if it is growing indoors. The offices for the Cartier jewelry empire are upstairs, and most of the first-rate contemporary art exhibits that the foundation hosts are in the basement. The collection is built around large groups of work by living artists and includes paintings by artists such as Vija Celmins, Sam Francis, and Simon Hantai, as well as photography, sculpture, huge installations, and video works. Reservations are necessary for the *très cool* performance art and music of *Les Soirees Nomades* (Nomadic Evenings) every Thursday night at 8:30. Recent programs included a Japanese anime screening, a Franco-American poetry/performance art evening, and performances set to techno music.

261 bd. Raspail, 14e (200 meters from the Métro stop, past Passage d'Enfer and rue Boissonade). ☎ *01-42-18-56-50, 01-42-18-56-72 for Nomadic Evenings reservations. Internet:* www.fondation.cartier.fr. *Métro: Raspail. Admission: 5€ adults; 3.50€ students younger than 25; free for children younger than 10. Open: Tues–Sun noon to 8 p.m.*

Maison Européenne de la Photographie

This museum's goal is to make the three fundamental mediums of pho-tography — exhibition prints, the printed page, and film — accessible to all, and it succeeds on all fronts. In addition to the ever-changing displays of photographs from the 1950s and up, the museum has a projection room, permanent collections of Polaroid art, and an excellent video library that allows you to look up thousands of photographs. The museum was created from two restored mansions. Exhibits in 2002 included works by Irving Penn and William Klein.

5–7 rue de Fourcy, 4e. ☎ *01-44-78-75-00. Internet:* www.mep-fr.org. *Métro: St-Paul or Pont-Marie. Bus: 67, 69, 96, 76. Admission: 5€ adults; 2.50€ ages 8–26 and older than 60; free for children younger than 8. Free admission for all visitors on Wed 5–8 p.m. Guided tours 7.55€ adults, 5€ reduced; reservations necessary. Open: Wed–Sun 11 a.m.–8 p.m.*

Musée Cognacq-Jay

Though not in the same class as the grand museums in this neighborhood, the collection at this museum in the 16th-century Hôtel Donon is still worth a look, if only as a window into the aristocratic lifestyle that pre-ceded the French Revolution. The 18th-century rococo art and the col-lection of everyday objects, like dance cards, and snuff and candy boxes, were amassed by La Samaritaine department store founder Ernest

Cognacq and his wife. The museum features works by François Boucher, Jean-Honoré Fragonard, Peter Paul Rubens, Louis-Michel van Loo, Jean-Antoine Watteau, Elisabeth Vigée-LeBrun, and Giambattista Tiepolo in elegant Louis XV and Louis XVI paneled rooms. Shelves of porcelain and porcelain figures, rich cabinets, and furniture are also on display. You can walk through a little manicured garden, open May to September, and enjoy sunny days. Temporary exhibits are presented two to three times a year.

8 rue Elzévir, 3e (between rue des Francs Bourgeois and rue Barbette). ☎ *01-40-27-07-21. Métro: St-Paul. Admission: Permanent collections free; temporary exhibits 6.10€ adults; 3.05€ students 14–26 and seniors; free for children younger than 14. Open: Tues–Sun 10:00 a.m.–5:40 p.m.*

Musée de la Sculpture en Plein Air

Displayed here are the sculptures of 29 artists, including César, Ossip Zadkine, and Stagio Stahly. Located on the banks of the Seine, you may have passed it on one of your strolls without realizing that this graceful waterside park is really a museum.

Quai St-Bernard, 5e (on the quai of the Seine between the Institut du Monde Arabe and the Jardin des Plantes). Métro: Sully-Morland or Gare d'Austerlitz. Admission: Free. If you go on a summer Thurs evening around 8 p.m., you can see outdoor dancing nearby.

Musée de l'Orangerie des Tuileries

Will this museum in the Tuileries ever reopen? It's been closed for renovations since the late 1990s, and its reopening dates are regularly estimated and then pushed back. At press time, the museum was slated to open in early 2004. If you're lucky enough to be in Paris when the Orangerie again admits the public, pay it a visit. The highlight is its two oval rooms wrapped nearly 360 degrees with Monet's *Nymphéas,* the water lily series he painted especially for the Orangerie. (It's partly to improve their presentation that the museum is undergoing the overhaul.) Since 1984, the museum has also housed the remarkable John Walter and Paul Guillaume art collection, comprising works by Cézanne, Renoir, Rousseau, Matisse, Dérain, Picasso, and Soutine. You can check with the Paris Tourist Office for an official update on the museum.

Jardin des Tuileries, 1er. Métro: Concorde.

Musée Gustave Moreau

This house and studio displays more than 6,000 works of the teacher of Henri Matisse, Gustave Moreau (1826–1898). A symbolist painter, Moreau embraced the bizarre and painted mythological subjects and scenes in a sensuous, romantic style. Among the works displayed are *Orpheus by the Tomb of Eurydice* and *Jupiter and Semele.* Moreau taught at the École des Beaux-Arts; his museum's first curator, Georges Rouault, was once his student. Moreau's modest apartment is also here.

For fans of Princess Diana

The Center for Nature Discovery, Garden in Memory of Diana, Princess of Wales recently opened at 21 rue des Blancs-Manteaux in the Marais (Métro: Rambuteau). In the small park, which is open during daylight hours, children discover how to grow flowers, vegetables, and decorative plants and learn about nature. The city of Paris is trying to get Diana fans to bring their messages and bouquets here instead of to the flame at place de l'Alma (Métro: Alma-Marceau), near the entrance to the tunnel where the princess, her friend Dodi Fayed, and driver Henri Paul were killed in an automobile accident on August 31, 1997. The bronze flame is a replica of the flame in the Statue of Liberty. It was a 1989 gift by the *International Herald Tribune* to honor Franco-American friendship.

14 rue de la Rochefoucault, 9e (between rue la Bruyère and rue St-Lazare). ☎ *01-48-74-38-50. Métro: Trinité d'Estienne d'Orves. Bus: 68 or 74. Admission: 3.40€ adults; 2.30€ students, ages 18–25, seniors older than 60, and on Sun; free for children younger than 18. Open: Wed 11:00 a.m.–5:15 p.m.; Tues, Thurs–Sun 10:00 a.m.–12:45 p.m. and 2:00–5:15 p.m.*

Musée Maillol

This restored town house is known for the sculpted fountain of the four seasons by Edme Bouchardon. But it is the important modern art collection inside that rightly draws the most notice. Curvaceous and graceful bronze statues of Aristide Maillol's (1861–1944) favorite model, Diana Vierny, as well as the works of impressionist and postimpressionist artists, are on display. The elegant upper floors of the museum display crayon and pastel sketches of Vierny. Maillol's personal collection includes the work of his friends, Matisse and Bonnard, as well as two sculptures by Rodin, works by Gauguin, Dégas, Rousseau, Odilon Redon, Maurice Denis, Kandinsky, and Renoir. Vierny, who collected art most of her life, has an important collection of modern primitives that include Douanier Rousseau and Camille Bombois, as well as drawings by Suzanne Valadon, Degas, Picasso, and Foujita. The museum features splendid temporary exhibits; a recent exhibit was devoted to the last ten years of Robert Rauschenberg.

59–61 rue de Grenelle, 7e. ☎ *01-42-22-59-58. Internet:* www.museemaillol.com. *Métro: Rue du Bac. Admission: 7€ adults; 5.50€ students 18–26; free for children younger than 18. Open: Wed–Mon 11 a.m.–6 p.m. (last ticket sold at 5:15 p.m.).*

Musée Marmottan Monet

The Musée Marmottan Monet celebrates the painter Claude Monet and contains an outstanding collection of his water lily paintings, as well as his more abstract representations of the Japanese Bridge at Giverny. The painting *Impression: Sunrise,* is located here; it was from this painting that the term "impressionism" was coined to describe the painting style and subsequent artistic movement. Also on hand is Monet's personal collection that includes works by his contemporaries Pissarro, Manet, Morisot, and Renoir.

The museum, located between the Ranelagh garden and the Bois de Boulogne, is in a 19th-century mansion that belonged to the art historian Paul Marmottan. Marmottan donated the mansion and his collection of Empire furniture and Napoleonic art to the Académie des Beaux-Arts upon his death in 1932.

When Claude Monet's son and heir bequeathed his father's collection to the Marmottan, the museum paid permanent homage to Monet's unique vision. Subsequent donations have expanded the collection to include more impressionist paintings and the stunning Wildenstein collection of late medieval illuminated manuscripts.

2 rue Louis-Boilly, 16e. ☎ *01-42-24-07-02. Internet:* www.marmottan.com. *Métro: La-Muette. Admission: 6.50€ adults; 4€ ages 8–25; free for children younger than 8. Open: Tues–Sun 10 a.m.–6 p.m.*

Musée Zadkine

The beautiful garden of Ukrainian sculptor Ossip Zadkine (1890–1967) is free, and the museum doesn't cost much more. It's worth a visit if you like contemporary sculpture or are familiar with the artist's work. Zadkine lived and worked in this house and studio until his death. His art, books, tools, and furniture are all on display, as well as many of his works in brass, wood, and stone.

100 bis rue d'Assas, 6e. ☎ *01-43-26-91-90. Métro: Notre-Dame-des-Champs or Vavin. Bus: 38, 82, 83, 91. Admission: 4€ adults; 3€ children and students ages 7–26 and adults older than 60; free for children younger than 7. Open: Tues–Sun 10:00 a.m.–5:30 p.m.*

Especially for the Literary

Paris's literary landmarks aren't all connected to Ernest Hemingway or F. Scott Fitzgerald.

Brasserie de l'Île St-Louis

If you're a fan of *From Here to Eternity* or *The Thin Red Line*, pay a visit to this brasserie (see also Chapter 14 for a review of the food), where novelist and regular customer James Jones kept his own *chope* (mug) at the bar. Not only is the location excellent — the building is situated directly off the foot bridge from Ile de la Cité to Ile St-Louis with an unparalleled view of the eastern tip of Ile de la Cité (including the back of Notre-Dame) — but this eatery is also the last remaining independent brasserie in Paris. Jones lived with his family around the corner on Ile de la Cité, and the film about their lives, *A Soldier's Daughter Never Cries,* was filmed in the neighborhood.

Ile St-Louis, 55 quai de Bourbon, 1er. ☎ 01-43-54-02-59. Métro: Pont Marie.

Brasserie Lipp and Café les Deux Magots

You can't talk about literary Paris without mentioning Ernest Hemingway, and two of his favorite hangouts are just across the street from each other on boulevard St-Germain-des-Prés. Brasserie Lipp is where Hemingway lovingly recalls eating potato salad in *A Moveable Feast,* and the Café les Deux Magots is where Jake Barnes meets Lady Brett in *The Sun Also Rises.* Tourism has driven up prices, so just go for a glass of wine or a coffee (and remember that it's cheaper standing up at the bar than sitting down at a table).

Brasserie Lipp: 151 bd. St-Germain, 6e. ☎ 01-45-48-53-91. Open: Daily 9–1 a.m. Café les Deux Magots: 170 bd. St-Germain, 6e. ☎ 01-45-48-55-25. Open: Daily 7:30–1:30 a.m. Both are less than 50 yards from the St-Germain-des-Prés Métro stop.

Harry's New York Bar

They say that the Bloody Mary was invented at Harry's New York Bar, a place that's still going strong all these years after — guess who? — Ernest Hemingway and F. Scott Fitzgerald went on a few famous benders. Unfortunately, Harry's is now a high-priced tourist trap, so peek in for the ambience and maybe one drink. They do make great martinis.

5 rue Danou, 2e. ☎ 01-42-61-71-14. Take the Métro to Opéra, then head down the rue de la Paix and take the first left. Open: Daily 10:30–4:00 a.m.

La Closerie de Lilas

Author John Dos Passos and painter Pablo Picasso hung out here, and Soviet revolutionary Leon Trotsky played chess here. But the true claim to fame is that Hemingway completed *The Sun Also Rises* on the terrace here in just six weeks. Much of the novel also takes place at Closerie des Lilas, which means "the courtyard of lilacs." Lilac bushes still bloom here, and the place is just as crowded as it was in the 1930s, although its high, high prices are geared toward an American tourist crowd.

171 bd. du Montparnasse, 6e. ☎ 01-40-51-34-50. Take RER Line B to the Port-Royal stop. Exit onto bd. du Port-Royal and walk west. Cross av. de l'Observatoire. Bd. du Port-Royal turns into bd. du Montparnasse. The restaurant will be on the north corner of av. de l'Observatoire and bd. du Montparnasse. Open: Daily noon to 1 a.m.

Maison de Balzac

The very modest Honoré de Balzac lived in this rustic cabin in the very posh residential Passy neighborhood from 1840 to 1847 under a false name to avoid creditors, only allowing entrance to those who knew the password. He wrote some of his most famous novels here, including those that make up his *La Comédie Humaine* (*The Human Comedy*). His study is preserved, and portraits, books, letters, and manuscripts are on display. You can also see his jewel-encrusted cane and the Limoges coffee pot that bears his initials in mulberry pink — leaving you to wonder just how bad his money problems *really* were.

47 rue Raynouard, 16e. ☎ *01-55-74-41-80. Take Métro line 6 to Passy, walk 1 block away from the river and turn left into rue Raynouard. Bus: 32, 50, 70, 72. Admission: Permanent collections free; temporary exhibits 3.30€ adults, 2.20€ adults older than 60, 1.60€ ages 14–26, free for children 13 and younger. Open: Tues–Sun 10 a.m.– 6 p.m. Closed holidays.*

Maison de Victor Hugo

If you or your kids have read *The Hunchback of Notre-Dame* and *Les Miserables,* you may want to visit this house. The novelist and poet lived on the second floor of this town house (built in 1610) from 1832 to 1848. You can see some of Hugo's furniture, samples of his handwriting, his inkwell, first editions of his works, and a painting of his funeral procession at the Arc de Triomphe in 1885. Portraits of his family adorn the walls, and the Chinese salon from Hugo's house on Guernsey (where he was exiled) has been reassembled here. The highlight is more than 450 of Hugo's drawings, illustrating scenes from his own works.

6 place des Vosges, 4e (between rue des Tournelles and rue de Turenne, nearer to rue de Turenne). ☎ *01-42-72-10-16. Métro: St-Paul. Bus: 20,29, 65, 69, 96. Admission: Free. Open Tues–Sun 10 a.m.–6 p.m. (ticket window closes at 5:15 p.m.).*

Shakespeare and Company

This is *not* the original Shakespeare and Company, even though it looks old and dusty enough to be. That original was opened in 1919 at 6 rue Dupuytren (take the Métro to Odéon, walk through the square there, and turn left) by Sylvia Beach. Two years later, Beach moved the shop to 12 rue de l'Odéon (the building is no longer there) and stayed until the United States entered into World War II (in Germany-occupied Paris, Beach was considered an enemy alien and was forced to abandon shop). The newest of the Shakespeares was opened by George Whitman in the mid-1960s and named in honor of Beach. It serves as a haven for Americans and English speakers, playing the dual role of gathering place and bookstore. Poetry readings take place on Sunday nights.

37 rue de la Bûcherie, 5e. ☎ *01-43-26-96-50. Métro or RER: St-Michel.*

Especially for Nature Lovers

Most parks are open until sunset, unless otherwise noted, and all parks are wonderful places to visit with children.

Parc de Belleville

Topped by the Maison de l'Air, a museum with displays devoted to the air that we breathe, the Parc de Belleville is a superb place to visit with children. You can enjoy fountains, a children's play area, and an open-air theater with many concerts during the summer, and rock formations and grottoes that evoke the days when the hill was a strategic point for fighting enemies like Attila the Hun. The park is also a wonderful place to watch the sun set over western Paris. Access the park by taking the rue Piat off rue de Belleville and enter through an iron gate spelling out the words Villa Ottoz. A curved path leads you to tree-lined promenades (more than 500 trees are here), with the first of the magnificent Left Bank views peeping through the spaces between pretty houses. Beds of roses and other seasonal flowers line walks, and views of the city's Left Bank become more pronounced the higher up the terraced pathways you go.

20e. Take the Métro to Pyrénées, then walk down rue de Belleville and turn left onto rue Piat where you see arched iron gates leading into the park. You can also take the Métro to Courrones, cross bd. de Belleville and turn left onto rue Julien Lacroix where you find another entrance.

Parc de la Bagatelle

The rose gardens here are gorgeous, and the thematic gardens reveal the art of gardening through the centuries. A water lily pond pays homage to a certain famous painter (think *Monet*). The château here, which you can view from the outside only, was built by the Comte d'Artois in 1775, after he made a bet with his sister-in-law, Marie Antoinette, that he could do it in less than 90 days. It took 66 days. Under Napoléon, it was used as a hunting lodge.

16e. Take the Métro to Porte Maillot and exit the station at av. Neuilly. Or take bus No. 244 to the Bagatelle-Pré-Catalan stop.

Parc de la Villette

In the summer, you can catch an outdoor movie or listen to a concert, and your kids can play on a giant dragon slide. You can also visit the children's museum, the Cité des Sciences et de l'Industrie, and the Musée de la Musique, which are all located on the grounds separated by the Canal de l'Orq. This modern park has a series of theme gardens, including an exotic bamboo garden and a garden featuring steam and water jets. Scattered throughout the park are playgrounds and other attractions. (See Chapter 20.)

You can get to the Parc de la Villette by Métro, but a fun, alternative route worth trying is the guided canal trip to the park from Pont l'Arsenal or Musée d'Orsay with **Paris Canal** (☎ **01-42-40-96-97;** Métro: Bastille). The three-hour cruises leave the Musée d'Orsay at 9:30 a.m. and end at the Parc de la Villette. The same voyage in reverse leaves the park at 2:30 p.m. Reservations are essential. The trip costs 16€ for adults, 12€ for students and seniors, and 9€ for children 4 to 11. **Canauxrama** (☎ 01-42-39-15-00; Métro: Jaurés) offers similar tours at 9:45 a.m. and 2:30 p.m., leaving from Port l'Arsenal in the 12e and ending at the Parc de la Villette. This trip costs 13€ for adults, 10€ for students and seniors, and 8€ for children 6 to 12. Children younger than 6 are free. Reservations are required.

19e. Métro: Porte de la Villette.

Parc des Buttes-Chaumont

Featuring cliffs, waterfalls, a lake, and a cave topped by a temple, this former gypsum quarry and centuries-old dump is one of four man-made parks Napoléon III commissioned to resemble the English gardens he grew to love during his exile in England.

19e. Métro: Buttes-Chaumont. (The station is located within the park.)

Parc Floral de Paris

The Bois de Vincennes houses the spectacular Parc Floral de Paris, with a butterfly garden, library, and miniature golf, as well as the Parc Zoologique de Paris. You can rent bikes here and ride around the extensive grounds, or row a rented canoe around a winding pond. (See also Chapter 20.) You can even rent *quadricycles* — bicycles built for four (10€).

12e. ☎ 01-55-94-20-20. Métro: Château de Vincennes. Exit at cours des Maréchaux and walk south; the chateau will be on your right. Cross av. des Minimes into the park.

Parc Monceau

Kids love this park for its oddities, including a Dutch windmill, a Roman temple, a covered bridge, a waterfall, a farm, medieval ruins, and a pagoda, all designed by Carmontelle. It was a favorite place for Marcel Proust to stroll, and it contains Paris's largest tree, an Oriental plane tree with a circumference of almost 23 feet. Have a picnic on a bench here with supplies from the rue de Levis (open Tues–Sun; Métro: Villiers).

Boulevard de Coucelles, 8e. Métro: Monceau. (The Métro station is at the edge of the park.)

Parc Montsouris

Parc Montsouris is another of Napoléon III's English parks, and it resembles an English garden, with waterfalls, copses, and winding paths. Swans and ducks gather on the pond, and the bandstand is still in use for concerts.

14e. RER:Cité Universitaire. (The RER station is at the edge of the park.)

Promenade Plantée

This old railroad bridge has been converted into a neat 5-kilometer-long garden that begins behind the Opéra Bastille, runs along the length of avenue Daumesnil, the Reuilly Garden, and the Porte Dorée to the Bois de Vincennes (it makes a great jogging path). Beneath the promenade, artisans have built boutiques and studios into the bridge, collectively known as the Viaduc des Arts. Check them out for eclectic, unusual gifts.

12e. Métro: Bel Air or Dugommier. (Walk from the Métro to avenue Daumesnil. The elevated railroad bridge above av. Daumesnil is the Promenade Plantée.)

Chapter 18

Seeing Paris by Guided Tour

· ·

In This Chapter

▶ Touring by bus

▶ Seeing Paris on foot

▶ Cruising down the river and canals

▶ Pedaling through Paris by bike

· ·

*I*f you're a newcomer to the wonders of Paris, an orientation tour can help you understand the city's geography. But even if you've been coming to Paris for ten years or more, one of the various tours can introduce you to sides of the city you never knew existed. As you see from this chapter, you have many good reasons for taking a guided tour. Being lucky enough to be shown around by guides whose enthusiasm makes the city come to life can be the high point of your entire trip.

Getting Orientated with Bus Tours

Paris is the perfect city to explore on your own, but if time is a priority, or your energy is at low ebb, consider taking an introductory bus tour. The biggest company is **Cityrama** (4 place des Pyramides, 1er. ☎ **01-44-55-61-00**; Métro: Palais-Royal–Musée du Louvre). The two-hour orientation tour is a bit pricey at 24€, but kids younger than 12 ride free. Also available are half-day tours for 53€ adults, 26€ children and full-day tours for 89€ adults, 44.50€ children. Tours to Versailles (from 32€ adults, 16€ children) and to Chartres (44€ adults, 22€ children) are a better bargain because they take the hassle out of visiting these monuments. Nighttime illumination tours include a Seine boat cruise and start at 30€ for adults, 15€ for children.

Paris L'OpenTour (☎ **01-42-66-56-56**; Internet: www.paris-opentour.com), from Paris's public transportation system (the RATP), has quickly come to rival Cityrama. Its bright yellow and green convertible double-decker buses take you to three different areas, and you listen to recorded commentary in English through a set of headphones given to you when you board. The Paris Grand Tour covers Paris's most central sights, minus the Islands: the Madeleine, Opéra, the Louvre, Notre-Dame, Jardin du Luxembourg, St-Germain-des-Prés, Musee d'Orsay, place de la

Concorde, Champs-Elysées, Arc de Triomphe, Trocadéro, Eiffel Tower, and Invalides. The Montmartre tour goes to the Montmartre funiculaire (but not up the Montmartre hill), the Gare du Nord, Gare de l'Est, and the Grands Boulevards. The Bastille-Bercy tour goes east to Notre-Dame, Ile de la Cité, Bastille, Gare de Lyon, and Parc Bercy. L'OpenTour makes its stops at regular city bus stops marked with the L'OpenTour logo. You can board at any of these stops and buy a pass right on the bus. The pass is also on sale at the Paris Tourist Office, L'OpenTour kiosks near the Malesherbes (8e) and Anvers (9e) bus stops, the RATP office at place de la Madeleine (8e), the Montmartre tourist office (21 place du Tertre), some hotels, and the main Batobus docks on the Seine.

A two-day pass costs 26€ for adults, 12€ for children 4 to 11, and 20€ for holders of the Paris Visite pass. You can get on or off the bus as many times as you want, which, in my opinion, makes this the more worthwhile tour. The buses run daily every 25 minutes throughout the year from about 9:30 a.m. to 6:30 p.m.

The **RATP** (☎ 08-36-68-41-14) also runs the **Balabus,** a fleet of orange-and-white buses that only runs on Sundays and holidays, noon to 8 p.m. from April to September. Routes run between the Gare de Lyon and the Grand Arche de La Défense, in both directions, and cost just one Métro ticket. A "Bb" symbol can be found across the side of the bus and on signs posted along the route.

Touring by Boat: Anchors Aweigh

One of the most romantic and beautiful ways to see Paris is by taking a sightseeing boat cruise up and down Paris's waterways. In addition to the Seine River cruises (see Chapter 16), try a longer and more unusual tour with **Paris Canal** (☎ 01-42-40-96-97; Métro: Bastille). Its three-hour cruises leave the Musée d'Orsay at 9:30 a.m. and end at Parc de la Villette. The boat passes under the Bastille and enters the Canal St-Martin for a lazy journey along the tree-lined quai Jemmapes. You cruise under bridges and through many locks. The boat leaves the Parc de la Villette at 2:30 p.m. for the same voyage in reverse. Reservations are essential. The trip costs 16€ for adults, 12€ for ages 12 to 25 and older than 60, and 9€ for children 4 to 11.

If you have restless young children, the wait for each lock to let the boat pass may prove too long. You may want to consider one of the shorter Seine boat trips mentioned in Chapter 16.

Canauxrama (☎ 01-42-39-15-00; Métro: Jaurès) offers tours similar to Paris Canal's at 9:45 a.m. and 2:30 p.m., leaving from Port l'Arsenal in the 12e and ending at the Parc de la Villette in the 19e. The cost is 13€ for adults, 10€ for ages 12 to 25, 8€ for children 6 to 11, and free for children younger than 6. Reservations are required. (See the nearby sidebar "Paris by canal: The bridge and tunnel crowd.")

Paris by canal: The bridge and tunnel crowd

If you've toured the Seine but still long for a boat ride, pick up the *Canauxrama* tour at pont l'Arsenal and enjoy a pleasant cruise along the Canal St. Martin, which winds for 4.5 watery kilometers (about 2½ miles) through Paris's northeast *quartiers* (quarters). In contrast to the Seine's elegant scenery, the canal passes through neighborhoods, where entire families sit along the banks, fishing. These neighborhoods are shabby but vibrant, and they're filled with street life and children. This is the Paris of the working class.

The canal, built by Napoleon in the early 19th century, gives access to barges when high waters prevent them from passing under the bridges of the Seine. You sail into a 2-kilometer-long underground vault, which was once lit by 37 lanterns to guide bargemen. Today, however, the vault is pitch dark, lit only occasionally in daylight by circular grates cut into the tunnel's roof; you feel like you've stepped into Greek mythology and are taking a ferry along the River Styx to the Underworld. The tunnel passes beneath the famous *Colonne de Juillet* in the center of place de la Bastille (a landmark erected in honor of citizens killed in the less famous revolutions of 1830 and 1848) — most visitors never realize that you can see it from below!

People wave as your boat passes under the many pedestrian bridges and through the canal's locks (*écluses*). The double *écluse de Temple* in the tenth arrondissement played a role in the 1938 film *Hotel du Nord.* The cruise turns around at the Parc de la Villette, at the tip of the *bassin* (basin) *de la Villette* where the Canal St. Martin splits into two other canals — the Saint Denis and the l'Ourcq. Nineteenth-century Parisians made their Sunday outings here, and the *bassin* still provides Paris with water for its fountains. The area is surrounded by wonderful old factories and warehouses, some of which are restored and used as artists' studios.

You can remain onboard for the return trip or disembark to play in the sprawling park that serves as a backyard for the surrounding population, many of whom are African immigrants. This is a great place to spend an afternoon with two huge museum complexes, the Cité des Sciences et de l'Industrie and the Musée de la Musique. In the summer, free movie festivals and concerts abound. Whatever you choose, you can enjoy a nice afternoon seeing a part of Paris you may have otherwise missed.

— *Alice Alexiou*

Walking Your Way across Paris

WICE (20 bd. du Montparnasse, 15e. ☎ **01-45-66-75-50,** outside France, 01-45-66-75-50, inside France; Fax: 01-40-65-96-53; Internet: www.wice-paris.org; Métro: Duroc or Falguière), a nonprofit cultural association for Paris's English-speaking community, gives comprehensive walking tours of Paris. The walking tours are in-depth tours for travelers who want to do more than skim the surface. Recent tours included: The Senate, The Paris Commune of 1871, and The Medieval Splendor of Paris. The commentary is always excellent, and the guides are experts in their respective fields.

Tours vary in length and cost, but most start at 16€ for a two- to three-hour tour. Paris residents and returning visitors love these tours, so book a few weeks ahead to reserve a spot. Unfortunately, the Web site isn't yet equipped to handle online payments, so you'll have to send in payment or pay in person at the WICE office in Paris.

Paris Walks (☎ 01-48-09-21-40; Internet: www.paris-walks.com) was founded by Peter and Oriel Caine and has become a popular English-language outfit whose guided walks cost 10€ for adults, 7€ for students younger than 25, and 5€ for children. Specific tours concentrate on a single neighborhood (The Village of Montmartre, The Historic Marais), a particular theme (Hemingway's Paris), or perhaps a single sight (Les Invalides, the Paris Sewers). Call for the designated meeting place.

Moveable Feast (☎ 06-66-92-34-12; Internet: www.moveablefeast tours.com) offers offbeat two-hour guided walks such as Paris is a Woman, which takes visitors to the haunts and former residences of some of Paris's most famous women (Colette, Josephine Baker, Sarah Bernhardt, Janet Flanner, Gertrude Stein, Coco Chanel). The Belly of Paris takes aspiring gourmands to Les Halles (called the Belly of Paris by writer Émile Zola), where they explore restaurants, markets, and the culinary history of Paris. You may also choose the Medieval Paris itinerary. Tours cost 12€ for adults, 10€ for students and seniors. Call to reserve a place and find a starting point.

Paris à Pied (☎ 800-594-9535 in the U.S., 01-46-27-11-56 or 06-64-77-11-56 in Paris; Internet: www.parisapied.com) has three three-hour tours geared to first-time visitors to Paris. Tours cost $45 (they prefer to be paid in dollars) and are made up of no more than six people. Recent tours included The Heart of Old Paris, The Latin Quarter, Montmartre, and The Marais.

Seeing Paris by Bike

For cyclists, **Paris à Vélo C'est Sympa** (☎ 01-48-87-60-01; Internet: www.parisvelosympa.com; Métro: Bastille; meeting place 37 bd. Bourdon) has three-hour Heart of Paris tours of Paris at 10 a.m. Friday through Monday from April to November, and Saturday and Sunday at 10 a.m. from November to March. Reservations are required, and most tours are in French (call or stop in for times of English-speaking tours). The company also has night (*nocturne*) bike tours Saturday at 8:30 p.m.

May to September. Other tours include Paris Contrasts, Unusual Paris, and Paris at Dawn. Prices for all tours are 30€ for adults, 26€ for ages 12 to 26, and 16€ for ages 10 and 11. Children younger than 10 are not permitted. Daylong tours for groups can also be arranged; call for information. Bike rental is available at 12.50€ a day, 9.50€ for a half-day, and 24€ for the weekend. Tandem bike rentals are 25€ a day, 19€ for a half-day, and 32€ for 24 hours. A 200€ credit-card deposit is required for bike rentals.

You can also try **Mike's Bike Tours** (24 rue Edgar Faure, 15e ☎ **01-56-58-10-54;** Internet: www.mikesbiketoursparis.com). Look for the Mike's Bikes flags in front of the *Pilier Sud* (South Pillar) of the Eiffel Tower (*Pilier Sud* is spelled out above the ticket booth). Friendly guides will take you on day or night bike tours of the city (22€ day, 26€ night, 44€ both tours). The tours last three to four hours. Day tours are at 11 a.m. and 3:30 p.m. May 1 through August 15, and 11 a.m. only March 1 through April 30 and August 26 through October 31. Night tours, which are beautiful (especially the ride past the Grand Pyramid through the courtyard at the Louvre), take place at 7 p.m. Monday through Friday May 1 through Aug 15. Call or e-mail for times March 1 through April 30 and August 16 through October 31. Reservations are optional for day tours but required for night tours. Bike rental is available at 2€ per hour, 15€ for 24 hours, 25€ for a weekend, and 50€ per week.

Formerly known as Bullfrog Bikes, Mike's Bike Tours now boasts a brand-new "tourist office," where owner Dave Mebane claims English-speakers from all over Paris like to congregate. The office has bathrooms, free daily storage for bags and luggage, snacks, drinks and Starbucks coffee, computers, CD burner, and low-cost Internet access, as well as Air France bus tickets and telephone cards for sale. If you're homesick for the United States, or English-speakers in general, this is the place to be!

Chapter 19

A Shopper's Guide to Paris

*E*very first-time visitor to Paris should set aside a little time for shopping. Paris simply has some of the best shopping in the world! Even the window-shopping is good; you notice that even the tiniest *pâtissier* (pastry shop) has exquisite, enticing goods arranged just so in windows, beckoning you to come inside. Window-shopping in French is aptly translated to *faire du leche-vitrines,* or window licking. Paris is truly a shopper's heaven, from the toniest haute couture shop, to the hidden *dêpot-vente* (resale shop) selling last year's Yves St-Laurent at fabulously reduced prices. Even nonshoppers find something: the eye-popping hardware store in the basement of BHV, the inexpensive furnishings at Conforama, and the mouth-watering *epicerie* (grocer) at Bon Marché. This chapter gives you an overview of the Parisian shopping scene, providing hints about where to find the bargains, how to get it all home, and even how to get some of your money back.

Surveying the Shopping Scene

The cost of shopping in Paris doesn't mean you have to scrape your chin on the pavement in awe of the expense. If you plan only to buy haute couture clothing, then yes, you'll pay top prices. However, Paris has many stores that sell clothing and goods at prices comparable to what you'd pay in the United States. And some items in Paris are cheaper even than they are in your hometown, including some French and European brands of perfume and cosmetics, shoes, clothing from French-based companies like Petit Bateau and Lacoste, and French-made porcelain, cookware, and glassware. You'll obviously pay more for any name brand imported from the United States, such as Donna Karan and Calvin Klein, and for any souvenirs in areas heavily frequented by tourists.

Keep in mind that a 20.6% value-added tax (VAT) is tacked on to the price of most products, which means that most things cost less at home. (For details on getting a VAT refund, see the section "Getting the VAT back" later in this chapter.) Appliances, paper products, housewares, computer supplies, electronics, and CDs, are notoriously expensive in France, but the cost of computers is beginning to come down. Checking out prices of French products before your trip can help you recognize a bargain.

Probably the best time to find a bargain in Paris is during the government-mandated twice-annual sales (*soldes*) in January and July when merchandise gets marked down 30% to 50% or more. Parisians line up outside their favorite stores the first days of the sales. If you can brave the crowds, you just may find the perfect designer outfit at a fraction of its retail price.

Generally, store hours are Monday through Saturday from 9:00 or 9:30 a.m. (sometimes 10 a.m.) to 7 p.m., and later on Thursday evenings, without a break for lunch. Some smaller stores are closed Monday or Monday mornings, and break for lunch for one to three hours, beginning at around 1 p.m., but this schedule is becoming increasingly rare. Small stores also may be closed for all or part of August and on some days around Christmas and Easter. Sunday shopping is gradually making inroads in Paris but is limited mostly to tourist areas; try the Carrousel du Louvre at the Louvre, rue de Rivoli across from the Louvre, rue des Francs-Bourgeois in the Marais, and the Champs-Elysées.

Politeness is imperative when you shop in Paris. Always greet the salespeople with *"Bonjour, madame"* or *"Bonjour, monsieur"* when you arrive (the Glossary in Appendix B will help with pronunciation). And regardless of whether you buy anything, say, *"Merci, au revoir"* (Thank you, goodbye) when you're leaving.

Clothing sizes are different around the world. To determine what size you need to start looking for, check out Table 19-1, which lists conversions for U.S. and Continental sizes.

Table 19-1	The Right Fit: Size Conversions		
U.S.	**Continental**	**U.S.**	**Continental**
Women's Clothes		**Women's Shoes**	
6	36	5	36
8	38	6	37
10	40	7	38
12	42	8	39

U.S.	Continental	U.S.	Continental
Women's Clothes		Women's Shoes	
14	44	9	40
16	46	10	41
Men's Shirts		Men's Shoes	
14½	37	7	39½
15	38	8	41
15½	39	9	42
16	41	10	43
16½	42	11	44½
17	43	12	46

Getting the VAT back

Whenever you spend more than 175€ in a single store, you're entitled to a partial refund on the value-added tax (VAT), also referred to in France as TVA. The refund, however, isn't automatic. Food, wine, and tobacco don't count, and the refund is granted only on purchases that you take out of the country — not on merchandise that you ship home.

When applying for a refund, you must show the store clerk your passport to prove your eligibility. You're then given an export sales document (in triplicate — two pink sheets and a green one), which you must sign, and usually an envelope addressed to the store. Or, when you're shopping in a store that participates in the Europe Tax-free shopping program (indicated by the TAX-FREE sticker in the store's windows), you're given a Tax-free Shopping Cheque that shows the amount of refund owed to you when you leave the country. Department stores that cater to foreign visitors, like Au Printemps and Galeries Lafayette, have special *détaxe* areas where clerks will prepare your invoices for you. Otherwise, when you leave the country, bring all documents to the airport's *détaxe* booth where a Customs official stamps them. To receive an immediate cash refund, you pay a fee of 4.60€. Otherwise, enclose the appropriate document (the pink one) in the store envelope the clerk provided when you bought your merchandise and mail it from the airport. The wait for a refund is anywhere from one to three months. Travelers leaving from Charles-de-Gaulle Airport can visit the *détaxe* refund point in Terminal 1 on the departure level between Gate 14 and 16; in Terminal 2, Hall B between Doors 6 and 7 near the baggage claim area or in Hall A between Doors 5 and 6; and in Terminal T9, near the departure gates. At Orly the *détaxe* booth is in Orly West between Halls 3 and 4 on the departure level.

Whenever you're claiming a tax refund, try to arrive at the airport as early as possible because you must show everything you're declaring to a Customs official, and you may have to wait in line. Plus, after you've finished with *détaxe,* you must to stand in line again to check your luggage.

If you're traveling by train, go to the *détaxe* area in the station before boarding, because you can't have your refund documents processed on the train. Give the three sheets to the Customs official, who stamps them and returns a pink and a green copy to you. Keep the green copy and mail the pink copy to the store.

Your reimbursement is either mailed as a check (in euros) or credited to your credit-card account. If you don't receive your tax refund within four months, write to the store, giving the date of purchase, and the location where the forms were given to Customs officials. Include a photocopy of your green refund sheet.

Getting your goodies through Customs

Returning **U.S. citizens,** who've been away for 48 hours or more, are allowed to bring back, once every 30 days, $800 worth of merchandise duty-free (a duty is a tax). You'll be charged a flat duty of 10% on the next $1,000 worth of purchases; on gifts, the duty-free limit is $100 (any item that costs more than $100 is subject to the full tax). You can't bring fresh food into the United States; canned foods, however, are allowed.

Citizens of the United Kingdom and **Ireland** who are returning from a European Union country have no limit on what they can bring back from an EU country, as long as the items are for personal use (including gifts), and the necessary duty and taxes have been paid. Limits are set at: 800 cigarettes, 200 cigars, 1kg smoking tobacco, 10 liters of spirits, 90 liters of wine, and 110 liters of beer.

Canada allows its citizens a once-a-year C$750 exemption after spending seven days out of the country, and you're allowed to bring back duty-free: 200 cigarettes, 1.5 liters of wine or 1.14 liters of liquor, and 50 cigars. In addition, you can mail gifts to Canada from abroad at the value of C$60 a day, provided they're unsolicited and don't contain alcohol, or tobacco, or advertising matter. Write on the package UNSO-LICITED GIFT, UNDER $60 VALUE. All valuables need to be declared on the Y-38 form before your departure from Canada, including serial numbers of valuables you already own, such as expensive foreign cameras.

The duty-free allowance in **Australia** is A$400 or A$200 for those younger than 18. Upon returning to Australia, citizens can bring in 250 cigarettes or 250 grams of loose tobacco, and 1.125 liters of alcohol. If you're returning with valuable goods that you already own, such as foreign-made cameras, you need to file form B263.

The duty-free allowance for **New Zealand** is NZ$700. Citizens older than 17 can bring in 200 cigarettes or 50 cigars or 250 grams of tobacco (or a mixture of all three as long as the combined weight doesn't exceed 250 grams), plus 4.5 liters of wine or beer or 1.125 liters of liquor.

Checking Out the Big-Name Stores

Two of Paris's major department stores, Au Printemps and Galeries Lafayette, offer visitors a 10% discount coupon, good in most departments. If your hotel or travel agent doesn't give you one of these coupons (they're sometimes attached to a city map), you can ask for it at the stores' welcome desks; the clerks speak English. And check out the "Paris Shopping" map for the locations of the stores I indulge in here.

Au Printemps

Au Printemps is one of Paris's largest department stores, and a recent renovation costing millions of euros has made it one of Paris's best. Merchandise is sold in three different buildings: Printemps de l'Homme (menswear), Printemps de la Maison (furniture and accessories), and Printemps de la Mode (women and children's fashion). Designers include Dolce & Gabbana and Burberry. Fashion shows take place under the 1920s glass dome at 10:15 a.m. every Tuesday year-round, and every Friday from March to October. Be sure to obtain one of the store's 10% discount coupons from the reception desk inside the store (if you don't already have one).

64 bd. Haussmann, 9e. ☎ *01-42-82-50-00. Métro: Havre-Caumartin.*

BHV

Near the Marais, BHV (*Bazar de l'Hôtel de Ville*) sells the usual clothing, cosmetics, luggage, and leatherware at decent prices, but it's really worth a visit because of its giant basement-level hardware store with everything you need to fix up your home plus a café (decorated like a tool shed) serving light bites.

52 rue de Rivoli, 1er. ☎ *01-42-74-90-00. Métro: Hôtel de Ville.*

Galeries Lafayette

This store gets downright crowded, and if you visit during the sales, you'll be thoroughly fatigued. Fortunately, choices for refreshment abound from Ladurée tea salon to burgers to the self-serve Lafayette Café on the sixth floor, which, by the way, has great views of Paris. Merchandise here is good quality with excellent deals during the sales: Look for women's clothing from Comptoir des Cotoniers and Agnès B and check out the gourmet grocery store, Lafayette Gourmet, in the Men's

Paris Shopping

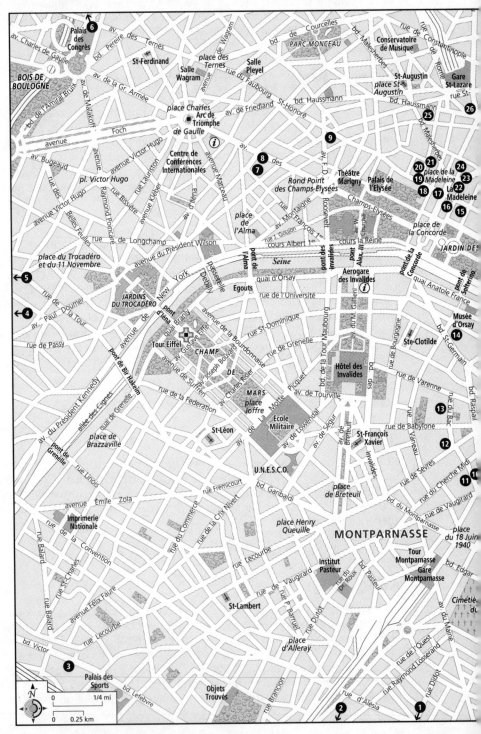

ⓘ Information

------ Railway

PARIS

Seine

Area of detail

store. If you don't already have one, ask at the front desk for the 10% discount coupon, good in most departments.

40 bd. Haussmann, 9e. ☎ *01-42-82-34-56. Métro: Opéra or Chaussée-d'Antin.*

La Samaritaine

Right now, probably the best thing about La Samaritaine, besides the fact that its prices are slightly lower than Galeries Lafayette and Au Printemps, is its views. Look for signs in its main building to the *panorama,* a free observation point with a wonderful view of Paris that actually takes in the Eiffel Tower. (Catch the elevator to the 9th floor, then climb two flights of stairs to the 11th floor "panorama." On the 10th floor is a terrace, also with good views, where meals are served.) Located between the Louvre and the Pont Neuf, La Samaritaine is housed in four buildings with Art Nouveau touches, and has an Art Deco facade on quai du Louvre. The fifth floor of store No. 2 has a nice, inexpensive restaurant. LVMH (Louis Vuitton Moet Hennessy) is the new owner, so count on an expensive renovation in the near future.

19 rue de la Monnaie, 1er. ☎ *01-40-41-20-20. Métro: Pont-Neuf or Châtelet–Les Halles.*

Le Bon Marché

If you're lucky enough to be here during the sales, you can find tons of deals at Paris's only Left Bank department store. Elegant, but small enough to be manageable, much of the store's merchandise is exquisite and includes designers such as Vivienne Westwood, Burberry, and Yohji Yamamoto. The third floor is particularly renowned for its large shoe selection and grand lingerie department (where dressing rooms have phones to summon your salesperson!). But it isn't cheap. Make sure to visit the huge supermarket (in a separate building next door), where you can find nearly any kind of food. A small antiques market, café, and cafeteria are on the second floor.

24 rue de Sèvres, 7e. ☎ *01-44-39-80-00. Métro: Sèvres-Babylone.*

Monoprix

Clothing is low-priced and stylish at Monoprix, stores that also are great for accessories, low-priced cosmetics, lingerie, and housewares. Many locations also have large grocery stores.

Various locations. ☎ *01-40-75-11-02.*

Tati

For the most part, Tati (originally opened to cater to budget-conscious shoppers) is frankly tacky. But you never know what you may find here if you dig; the occasional gem rewards those who are persistent.

4 bd. Rochechouart, 18e. ☎ *01-55-29-50-00. Métro: Barbés-Rochechouart. Other branches are located at 172 rue du Temple, 4e (*☎ *01-42-76-04-93 or 01-48-04-56-49), 13 place de la République, 3e (*☎ *01-48-87-72-81), 11 bis rue Scribe (01-47-42-20-28). A branch, Tati Or, specializes in gold (see "Gifts and jewelry," later in this chapter).*

Taking It to the Street (Markets)

If you have the time on a Saturday, Sunday, or Monday, try visiting the huge **Marché aux Puces de la Porte de St-Ouen,** 18e, which purportedly is the largest flea market in the world. It features several thousand stalls, carts, shops, and vendors selling everything from vintage clothing to antique chandeliers, paintings, furniture, and toys. It's a real shopping adventure, and you need to arrive early to snag the deals — if you can find any. The best times for bargains are right at opening time and just before closing time. To reach the market, take the Métro to the Porte de Clignancourt stop; exit onto av. de la Porte de Clignancourt. (You can also exit onto bd. Omano, which turns into av. de la Porte de Clignancourt.) Head north a block and cross beneath an underpass; the markets will begin on your left. Open Saturday through Monday 9 a.m. to 8 p.m.

Don't pay the ticketed price or the price the vendor first quotes you; always haggle. You can usually get at least 10% off.

You'll see stalls where cheap junk is sold starting at the underpass just past the Clignancourt Métro stop, but watch out for pickpockets, and don't stop here! Turn left onto rue des Rosiers, the market's main street.

Visitors to Paris usually choose the Clignancourt market over the convivial market at **Porte de Vanves,** 14e, a gem waiting to be discovered. Probably the smallest of the fleas, and a bit more upscale (so are its prices), it's nevertheless a good place to browse among friendly dealers. To reach the market, take the Métro to the Porte de Vanves stop; exit at bd. Brune; follow it east to av. Georges Lafenestre, and turn right. Open Saturday and Sunday 8:30 a.m. to 1:00 p.m.

Scoring Bargains in Paris

How do Parisian women afford to look as put-together as they do and still have enough money to eat? Four words: *soldes* (sales), *dégriffés* (designerwear with the labels cut out), *stock* (overstock), and *dépot-vente* (resale). The savvy Parisienne waits for sales, knows the addresses of discounters, and knows that some of the best fashion deals are found in resale shops that deal directly with designer showrooms and people in the fashion industry. Designer clothing that has been worn on a runway or for a fashion shoot is on sale for half price, along with other gently used clothing and accessories. Most *depôts-vente* are on the Right

Bank in the 8e, 16e, and 17e arrondissements. If you're itching for a bargain after shopping for full-price items, visit one of the streets where discount stores abound:

- ✔ **Rue d'Alésia,** 14e (Métro: Alésia), is filled with French designer discount outlets selling last year's overstock at up to 70% below retail. These stock boutiques are more downscale than their sister shops; be prepared to rifle through the racks to find the gems. Outlets include **Chevignon** at No. 12, **Sonia Rykiel** at No. 54, **Cacharel** at No. 114, **Sergent Major** at No. 82, **Toute Compte Fait** at No. 101, and **Jacadi** at No. 116.

- ✔ **Rue Paradis,** 10e (Métro: Poissonnière), is filled with wholesale china and porcelain stores such as **Paradis Porcelaine** at No. 56 and **La Tisanière Porcelaine** at No. 21.

- ✔ **Rue St-Placide,** 6e (Métro: Sèvres-Babylone), is also a street of dreams with many discount stores, including **Le Mouton à Cinq Pattes** (8, 10, 14–18, and 48 rue St-Placide, 6e) and **Kookaï** (15Ter). Discounted no-name shoes and housewares are also sold here.

You can also try the discount stores spread throughout the city.

Anna Lowe

It's hard to believe that this discount shop is within such close range of the deluxe Hotel Bristol! It's a find for those who want the very best designers such as Yves Saint-Laurent, Chanel, and Giorgio Armani at a steep discount — at least 50%. The clothes may be overstock or last year's models with samples from the runway. Most of the staff speaks English.

Keep in mind that a steep discount off an incredibly expensive couture price can still mean an expensive item.

104 rue du Faubourg-St-Honoré, 8e. ☎ *01-42-66-11-32 or 01-40-06-02-42. Métro: Miromesnil or St-Phillippe-de-Roule.*

Bonpoint

Bonpoint clothes make children look like royalty (hand-smocked dresses, lace collars, velvet), and the prices usually reflect this level of craftsmanship. However, this Bonpoint branch sells end-of-season clothes at reduced prices; it's particularly good during the yearly sales in January and July.

42 rue de l'Université, 7e. ☎ *01-40-20-10-55. Métro: Rue-du-Bac.*

Guerrisold

This resale shop can be compared to Goodwill or the Salvation Army — there are loads of clothes and accessories for men and women that will look just great after they're cleaned up.

17 bd. de Rochechouart, 9e. ☎ 01-45-26-38-92. Métro: Anvers. Other locations in the city including 19, 29, 33 av. de Clichy, 17e. ☎ 01-53-42-31-31. Métro: La Fourche.

La Clef des Marques

This large boutique, with other branches at 86 rue Faubourg St-Antoine, 12e (☎ 01-40-01-95-15) and 20 place Marché St-Honoré, 1er (☎ 01-47-03-90-40), sells shoes, baby clothes, lingerie, and end-of-series couture items. Check here first before buying Doc Martens, because the selection usually is good.

124 bd. Raspail, 6e. ☎ 01-45-49-31-00. Métro: Notre-Dame des Champs.

La Marelle

Located in the wonderful Galerie Vivienne, this store resells clothing from some of the top designers in very good condition.

21 Galerie Vivienne, 2e. ☎ 01-42-60-08-19. Métro: Palais Royal.

Le Depôt-Vente de Buci, Le Depôt-Vente de Bourbon

These great shops (which are right next to each other) carry vintage and not-so-old clothing and resale and not-quite-antique furniture.

4, 6 rue Bourbon Le Chateau, 6e. ☎ 01-42-96-99-04. Métro: St-Germain-des Prés or Mabillon.

Le Mouton à Cinq Pattes

The packed racks here often carry extremely well-known designer names on women's, men's, and children's clothing, shoes, and accessories, so visit when you're feeling energetic! The stock changes constantly, and if you see something you like, grab it; it won't be there the next time. Other branches are located at 19 rue Gregoire de Tours, 6e (☎ 01-43-29-73-56), and 15 rue Vieille du Temple, 4e (☎ 01-42-71-86-30), and 138 bd. St-Germain (☎ 01-43-26-30). The name means "the sheep with five legs." Hmmm.

8, 10, 14–18, and 48 rue St-Placide, 6e. ☎ 01-45-48-86-26 for all stores. Métro: Sèvres-Babylone.

Mi-prix

Karl Lagerfeld, Alaia, Missoni, and Gianfranco Ferre are just some of the labels that are steeply discounted in this men's discount store.

27 bd. Victor, 15e. ☎ 01-48-28-42-48. Métro: Balard or Porte de Versailles.

Nip Shop

Yves Saint-Laurent, Sonia Rykiel, and Guy Laroche are big labels here, but lesser-known designers are also represented. It's in the same neighborhood as Réciproque (see the next listing), but much more intimate.

6 rue Edmond-About, 16e. ☎ *01-45-04-66-19. Métro: Rue de la Pompe.*

Réciproque

This *depôt-vente* (resale shop) is the largest in Paris for men, women, and children. Exhaust yourself among the jewelry, furs, belts, antiques, and designer purses (Hermès, Gucci, and Vuitton are just a few of the names I've seen). This store is for shoppers willing to spend upwards of $1,000 on a "gently-worn" Chanel suit, less for other designers. Mid-range labels are also well represented.

89–123 rue de la Pompe, 16e. ☎ *01-47-04-30-28. Métro: Rue de la Pompe.*

Hitting the Great Shopping Neighborhoods

The shopping in Paris is terrific, and you don't need *beaucoup* bucks to afford it. Great finds for every taste and dollar amount can be found. Read this section to get a significant head start in the hunt.

The land of luxe: The 8e

When people around the world need a luxury-shopping fix, they go to Paris, and all you have to do is head for the 8e to see why. Nearly every French designer is based on two streets — **avenue Montaigne** (Métro: Alma-Marceau, Franklin-D-Roosevelt) and **rue du Faubourg St-Honoré** (Métro: Concorde) — where prices more than 1,000€ are normal, and snooty sales clerks are par for the course. You can still have a good time window-shopping here, even when you don't have a platinum card.

Although these streets boast some of the same big designer names, they are completely different in temperament. Avenue Montaigne is wide, graceful, lined with chestnut trees, and undeniably hip, attracting the likes of **Dolce & Gabbana** at Nos. 2 and 22 (☎ 01-47-20-42-43; 01-42-25-68-78, respectively) and **Prada** at No. 10 (☎ 01-53-23-99-40). Other designers on this street include **Céline,** 36 av. Montaigne (☎ 01-56-89-07-92); **Chanel,** 42 av. Montaigne (☎ 01-47-23-74-12); **Christian Dior,** 30 av. Montaigne (☎ 01-40-73-54-44); **Escada,** 53 av. Montaigne (☎ 01-42-89-83-45); **Ferragamo,** 45 av. Montaigne (☎ 01-47-23-36-37); **Christian Lacroix,** 26 av. Montaigne and 73 rue du Faubourg St-Honoré

(☎ 01-47-20-68-95; 0142-68-79-04, respectively); **Thierry Mugler,** 49 av. Montaigne (☎ 01-47-23-37-62); **Ungaro,** 2 av. Montaigne (☎ 01-53-57-00-00); and **Valentino,** 17 av. Montaigne (☎ 01-47-23-64-61).

Rue du Faubourg St-Honoré is jammed with shoppers walking along the small, narrow sidewalks. **Gucci** is located at No. 23 and is opening a store at 60 av. Montaigne (☎ 01-42-96-83-27). **Hermès** (pronounced "air-mess") occupies No. 24 (☎ 01-40-17-47-17), and **Yves St-Laurent** is at No. 38 (☎ 01-42-65-23-16). Begin at the rue Royale intersection and head west. Other designer stores you'll run across here include **Ferragamo,** 50 rue du Faubourg St-Honoré (☎ 01-43-12-96-96); **Gianni Versace,** 62 rue du Faubourg St-Honoré (☎ 01-47-42-88-02); **La Perla,** 20 rue du Faubourg St-Honoré (☎ 01-43-12-33-60); **Chloé,** 54 rue du Faubourg St-Honoré (☎ 01-44-94-33-00); **Sonia Rykiel,** 70 rue du Faubourg St-Honoré (☎ 01-42-65-20-81); and **Missoni,** 1 rue du Faubourg-St-Honoré (☎ 01-44-51-96-96).

Arty and individual: The 3e and 4e

The Marais (3e, 4e) is a beautiful neighborhood crammed with magnificent Renaissance mansions, artists' studios, secret courtyards, and some of the most original shops in the city. Fifteen museums are in the Marais alone, so divide your time between culture and commercialism, and when you're hungry, Jo Goldenberg, another Marais institution, should fill you up nicely.

Rue des Francs-Bourgeois (Métro: St-Paul or Rambuteau), the highlight of the area, is full of small shops selling everything from fashion to jewels. And don't miss **Rue des Rosiers** (Métro: St-Paul), a fashion destination in its own right, with white-hot designers standing shoulder-to-shoulder with Jewish delis. Everything is really close in the Marais, so don't be afraid to ramble down the tiniest lane whenever whim dictates. Part of the fun of this neighborhood is that it's such a mixed (shopping) bag.

Marais highlights include **Paule Ka,** 20 rue Mahler (☎ 01-40-29-96-03), for the sort of 1960s clothing made famous by Grace Kelly, Jackie Onassis, and Audrey Hepburn; **Autour du Monde Home,** 8 rue des Francs-Bourgeois (☎ 01-42-77-06-08), a clothing/housewares store with everything from relaxed and sporty cotton dresses to delicate linen sheets and inventive tableware; and **Issey Miyake,** 3 pl des Vosges (☎ 01-48-87-01-86), for loose, structured clothing that screams "artist." Fans of hot brand **Camper,** 9 rue des Francs-Bourgeois (☎ 01-48-87-09-09), can buy their comfortable men's and women's shoes made in Spain; **Plein Sud,** 21 rue des Francs-Bourgeois (☎ 01-42-72-10-60), sells sexy curve-hugging women's fashion; and check out **Zadig et Voltaire,** 1 rue Guillemites (☎ 01-42-72-15-20), for casual clothes with a flair from new and established European designers.

"BCBG" bourgeois chic: The 6e

Be part of the BCBG (*Bon Chic Bon Genre* — or what the French call stylish young professionals with old family money) who call this area home, and shop amid art and antiques galleries, high-end designer clothing shops, decently priced shoe and accessories stores, and sophisticated and trendy boutiques. This is one the prettiest neighborhoods in Paris. You won't go thirsty with famed literary hangouts such as Café de Flore, Les Deux Magots, and Brasserie Lipp nearby, and you may not even go broke — all price ranges are represented here.

Louis Vuitton recently opened a huge store behind Les Deux Magots on 6 place St-Germain (☎ 01-45-49-62-32), and **Christian Dior** is nearby at 16 rue de l'Abbaye (☎ 01-56-24-90-53). Plenty of stores here are a better value than **Emporio Armani,** 149 bd. St-Germain (☎ 01-53-63-33-50); **Céline,** 58 rue de Rennes, (☎ 01-45-48-58-55); **Christian Lacroix,** 2 place St-Sulpice (☎ 01-46-33-48-95); or **Prada,** 5 rue de Grenelle (☎ 01-45-48-53-14). Check out **Stefanel,** 54 rue de Rennes (☎ 01-45-44-06-07), **Comptoir des Cotonniers,** 59T rue de Bonaparte (☎ 01-43-26-07-56), **APC Surplus,** 45 rue Madame Bonaparte (☎ 01-45-48-43-71), and **Tara Jarmon,** 18 rue de Four, Bonaparte (☎ 01-46-33-26-60).

It was bound to happen — Gap and other international chain stores have taken up residence in the Marché St-Germain, a modern shopping mall that's a bit out of place in a neighborhood known for bookstores and upscale boutiques. Visit if you need to experience air conditioning, otherwise don't waste your time; prices are higher, and the styles are the same at home.

Young and branché: The 2e

Branché is a high compliment among Paris's younger set, meaning "plugged in," or hip, and the 2e is where you head if you are. The area sells a mix of high fashion and discount, with Jean-Paul Gaultier in the pretty Galerie Vivienne on one end and Kookaï le Stock on the other. The cheapest shopping is in the Sentier area, around the Sentier Métro stop, which is Paris's garment district, overlapping parts of the 3e and 1er. The best — but not the cheapest — shops are found within a square formed on the south by rue Rambuteau, on the west by rue du Louvre, on the north by rue Réamur, and on the east by rue St-Martin. This area is where you can find hip secondhand clothes, funky clubwear, and *stock* boutiques selling last season's designs at a discount.

Prostitutes frequent the area later in the day and evening.

For last year's unsold stock of women's and teen's clothing visit **Et Vous Stock,** 15 rue de Turbigo, 2e (☎ 01-40-13-04-12), and **Kookaï Le Stock,** 82 rue Réamur, 2e (☎ 01-45-08-93-69). **Kiliwatch,** 64 rue Tiquetonne, 2e (☎ 01-42-21-17-37), sells the cool looks of up-and-coming designers mixed in with vintage clothing, while **Kokon To Zai,** 48 rue Tiquetonne, 2e

The arcades

Picture shopping at the turn of the 19th century: People, horses, and carriages crowd unpaved, dirty, badly lit streets. When it rains, the scene gets even worse — everything turns to mud. Now, imagine you're a 19th-century shopkeeper looking for innovative ways to draw crowds to your store. Someone proposes displaying wares in pretty covered passageways with other merchants. You jump at the chance to set up business in what will become some of the western world's first shopping malls. These days, the charming iron and glass arcades are still shopping havens, and the 2e has Paris's greatest concentration, each with its own character.

✔ **Passage Choiseul,** 44 rue des Petits-Champs (Métro: Quatre-Septembre), dates from 1827 and is the longest and most colorful arcade selling discount shoes and clothing and used books. French writer Céline grew up here and included it in his books *Journey to the End of Night* and *Death on the Installment Plan.*

✔ **Passage des Panoramas,** 11 bd. Montmartre and 10 rue St-Marc (Métro: Grands Boulevards), opened in 1800 and was enlarged with the addition of galleries Variétés, St-Marc, Montmartre, and Feydeau in 1834. Its stores sell stamps, clothes, and gifts, and it's the passage with the largest choice of dining options: Korean food, a cafeteria, tea salons, and bistros.

✔ **Passage Jouffroy,** across the street at 10 bd. Montmartre (Métro: Grands Boulevards), was built between 1845 and 1846. It became an instant hit as Paris's first heated gallery. After an extensive restoration of its tile floors, the gallery now houses a variety of arty boutiques, including a dollhouse store.

✔ **Passage Verdeau,** 31 bis rue du Faubourg-Montmartre (Métro: Le Peletier), was built at the same time as its neighbor, Passage Jouffroy. You can find old prints, books, and postcards here.

✔ **Galerie Vivienne,** 4 place des Petits-Champs, 5 rue de la Banque, or 6 rue Vivienne (Métro: Bourse), is hands down, the most gorgeous of all the arcades. Its classical friezes, mosaic floors, and graceful arches have been beautifully restored. Built in 1823, this neoclassical arcade is now a national monument that has attracted upscale art galleries, hair salons, and boutiques, including Jean-Paul Gaultier.

✔ **Galerie Colbert** is linked to the adjoining **Galerie Vivienne.** It was built with a large rotunda and decorated in Pompeian style in 1826 to capitalize on the success of Galerie Vivienne.

✔ The pretty **Passage du Grand Cerf,** 10 rue Dussoubs (Métro: Etienne-Marcel), has more of a modern bent, with jewelry designers, trendy clothing stores, and an ad agency.

For a complete change of pace, head over to the following arcades, but keep in mind that the neighborhoods aren't the nicest. The **Passage Brady,** 46 rue du Faubourg St-Denis (Métro: Strasbourg St-Denis), has become an exotic bazaar where Indian restaurants and spice shops scent the air. The passage opened in 1828. The **Passage du Caire,** 2 place du Caire (Métro: Sentier), is one of the oldest arcades built in 1798 to commemorate Napoléon's triumphant entry into Cairo. It reflects the "Egyptomania" of the time with fake columns and "death masks" of pharaohs on its exterior. In the heart of Paris's Sentier garment district, it's home to clothing wholesalers and manufacturers.

(☎ **01-42-36-92-41**), sells funky designerwear in a small store that dazzles with mirrors and neon. **Le Shop,** 3 rue d'Argout, 2e (☎ **01-40-28-95-94**), sells two floors of clubwear, skateboards, and CDs — all to tunes spun by a DJ. Those with a more sophisticated palate can go to **Barbara Bui,** 23 rue Etienne-Marcel, 1er (☎ **01-40-26-43-65**), for elegant, contemporary fashion. (She also has a trendy café two doors down.) For sophistication with an edge, head to **Jean-Paul Gaultier,** 6 rue Vivienne (☎ **01-42-86-05-05**). **Agnès b.,** 3–6 rue du Jour (☎ **01-45-08-56-56**), is timelessly chic with plenty of black clothes for men and women. Other stores include **Mon Amie Pierlot,** 3 rue Montmartre, 1er (☎ **01-40-28-45-55**), for casual wear that includes the striped sailor sweater, a French wardrobe basic.

Shopping in Paris from A to Z

From antiques to wine (okay, so maybe not quite to Z), here are some great stores representing both economy and first-class shopping in the City of Light.

Antiques

Le Louvre des Antiquaires

This is an enormous mall filled with all kinds of shops selling everything from Jean Cocteau sketches to silver cutlery. Items are pricey, but rumors have it that some good deals exist here. A café and toilets are located on the second floor.

2 place du Palais-Royal, 1er. ☎ *01-42-97-29-86. Métro: Palais-Royal-Musée du Louvre.*

Le Village St-Paul

This secluded 17th-century village has been turned into an indoor-outdoor arts and antiques fair with shops that display paintings, antiques and other items, both inside and in the courtyard. It's easy to walk past the entrances, so look for the signs just inside the narrow passageways between the houses on rue St-Paul, rue Jardins St-Paul, and rue Charlemagne. Keep in mind that this is a very popular destination on the weekend. Closed Tuesday and Wednesday.

23–27 rue St-Paul, 4e (no phone). Métro: St-Paul.

Bookstores

Bouquinistes

These booksellers hawking posters, postcards, and used books from green wooden boxes on some of the Seine's quais are worth a browse.

Many of these merchants come from a long line of booksellers dating back to the time of Henri IV in the 17th century.

Quai de Montebello, Quai St-Michel, and various others.

Gibert Joseph

Gibert Joseph is *the* Parisian students' bookstore, selling new and secondhand books, records, videos, and stationery on several floors and in several branches on bd. St-Michel.

26, 30 bd. St-Michel, 6e. ☎ 01-44-41-88-88. Métro: Odéon or Cluny-Sorbonne.

Librarie La Hune

Sandwiched between cafés Les Deux Magots and de Flore, this bookstore has been a center for Left Bank intellectuals since 1945 when Sartre was among its clients. Most books are in French. It's open until midnight every night except Sunday.

170 bd. St-Germain, 6e. ☎ 01-45-48-35-85. Métro: St-Germain.

Shakespeare and Company

No, this *isn't* the original, but English-speaking residents of Paris still gather in this wonderfully dark and cluttered store, named after Sylvia Beach's legendary literary lair. There is a selection of new books, but most books are used. *Note:* It's a great place to find used travel guides! Poetry readings are held on Sundays.

37 rue de la Bûcherie, 5e. ☎ 01-43-26-96-50. Métro or RER: St-Michel.

Village Voice

Quality fiction in English is the highlight of this small two-level store in St-Germain-des-Prés, along with an excellent selection of poetry, plays, nonfiction, and literary magazines. Owner Odile Hellier has been hosting free poetry and prose readings with celebrated authors and poets since 1982.

6 rue Princesse, 6e. ☎ 01-46-33-36-47. Métro: Mabillon or St-Germain.

Ceramics, china, and glass

Baccarat

Baccarat's crystal has been world-renowned since the 18th century. This store is also a museum, so even if its prices are too high for your wallet, you feel comfortable browsing the collections that include perfume bottles, 19th- and 20th-century glassware, and coats of arms.

30 rue de Paradis, 10e. ☎ *01-47-70-64-30 or 01-40-22-11-00. Métro: Château-d'Eau, Poissonnière, or Gare-de-l'Est.*

La Maison Ivre

The Left Bank between St-Germain-des-Prés and the Seine is the unofficial antiques and art gallery district. This store sits right in the district's heart and carries an excellent selection of handmade pottery from across France, with emphases on Provençal and southern French ceramics. Wonderful pieces of ovenware, bowls, platters, plates, pitchers, mugs, and vases are here.

38 rue Jacob, 6e. ☎ *01-42-60-01-85. Métro: St-Germain-des-Prés.*

Lumicristal

For discounted crystal by Daum, Limoges, and Baccarat, Lumicristal is the place to shop.

22 bis rue de Paradis, 10e. ☎ *01-47-7027-97. Metro: Château-d'Eau, Poissonnière, or Gare-de-l'Est*

Clothing for children

Du Pareil au Même

Du Pareil au Même is *the* store to buy clothes for every child on your list — clothes are practical, *très mignons* (very cute), and very reasonably priced.

168 bd. St-Germain, 6e. ☎ *01-46-33-87-85. Other branches include 1 rue St-Denis, 1er (☎ 01-42-36-07-57) and 14 rue St-Placide, 6e (☎ 01-45-44-04-40).*

Jacadi

When BCBG women (see the "'BCBG' bourgeois chic: The 6e" section earlier in this chapter) have children, Jacadi is where they buy their very proper children's clothes.

256 bd. St-Germain, 7e. ☎ *01-42-84-30-40. Many branches are located across the city, including 17 bd. Poissonière, 2e (☎ 01-42-36-69-91).*

Natalys

Part of a French chain with a dozen stores in Paris, Natalys sells children's wear, maternity wear, and related products.

92 av. des Champs-Elysées, 8e. ☎ *01-43-59-17-65. Métro: Franklin-D-Roosevelt. Other branches include 69 rue de Clichy, 9e (☎ 01-48-74-07-44), and 47 rue de Sèvres, 6e (☎ 01-45-48-77-12).*

Tartine et Chocolat

This store features typically French, precious, and pricey clothes.

105 rue du Faubourg-St-Honoré, 8e. ☎ *01-45-62-44-04. Métro: Concorde. Another branch is located at 266 bd. St-Germain, 7e (☎ 01-45-56-10-45).*

Clothing for men

Façonnable

For quality shirts in nearly every color and casual pants, in addition to jackets, suits, and other men's furnishings (all a bit on the conservative side), Façonnable is the place. In the United States, Nordstrom carries Façonnable, but this store has the entire line.

9 rue du Faubourg-St-Honoré, 8e. ☎ *01-47-42-72-60. Métro: Sèvres-Babylone. Another branch is located at 174 bd. St-Germain, 6e (☎ 01-40-49-02-47).*

Loft Design

Although the store sells women's clothing, this shop is worth a visit for the menswear, which is reasonably priced and fashion-forward, especially the thick cotton sweaters and casual trousers.

56 rue de Rennes, 6e. ☎ *01-45-44-88-99.*

Madelios

This huge store offers one-stop shopping for men, selling everything from overcoats to lighters. If companions get bored waiting, the store is part of a small mall that has some nice stores for browsing.

23 bd. de la Madeleine, 1er. ☎ *01-53-45-00-00.*

Clothing for teens and the young at heart

Antoine et Lili

This bright store is a nice place to stop if you're strolling the quays of the Canal St-Martin; it sells fun bohemian-style clothes and accessories, and decorations that look great in dorm rooms. A garden and small canteen also are located here.

95 quai Valmy, 10e. ☎ *01-40-37-41-55. Métro: Gare de l'Est. Another branch is at 7 rue d'Albioni, 16e (☎ 01-45-27-95-00).*

Cop-Copine

Cutting-edge and flattering, Cop-Copine makes great youthful clothes for which even my 60-something mother has flipped!

80 rue Rambuteau, 1er. ☎ 01-40-28-03-72. Métro: Les Halles, RER: Châtelet-Les Halles.

H&M

Hennes & Mauritz, the Swedish "IKEA of fashion," has a large selection of up-to-the-minute men and women's fashion at very low prices.

120 rue de Rivoli, 1er. ☎ 01-55-34-96-86. Métro: Hôtel-de-Ville, Louvre-Rivoli.

Mango

With locations throughout the city, this store is popular with young Parisian women for its inexpensive, fashion-conscious, body-hugging clothes.

82 rue de Rivoli, 1er. ☎ 01-44-59-80-37. Métro: Hôtel-de-Ville, Louvre-Rivoli.

Morgan

Form-fitting suits, dresses, and casual wear in synthetics and blends can be found at low prices for young women at Morgan.

44Bis bd. St-Michel, 6e. ☎ 01-53-10-98-00. RER: Luxembourg.

Zara

Zara offers well-made copies of today's hottest styles for women, men, and children at extremely low prices.

128 rue de Rivoli, 1er. ☎ 01-44-82-64-00. Métro: Hôtel-de-Ville, Louvre-Rivoli. Locations all over the place, including 2 rue Halévy, 9e (☎ 01-44-71-90-90 and 01-44-71-90-93), near the Opéra, 44 av. Champs-Elysées (☎ 01-45-61-52-81 and 01-45-61-52-81), and 45 rue de Rennes, 6e (☎ 01-44-39-03-50).

Clothing for women

Cacharel

Beautiful and reasonably priced women's, children's, and men's clothes are featured at Cacharel, some in pretty Liberty-flower printed fabrics.

64 rue Bonaparte, 6e. ☎ 01-40-46-00-45.

Colette

Some of the city's most cutting-edge fashion is for sale here, in *très* artistic displays. You can also find artsy chotchkes, art magazines, and art exhibits. Even if you don't buy (the prices are steep), just looking or having a bite to eat, or drinking one of the extensive selection of waters at the basement café and water bar is fun.

213 rue St-Honoré, 1er. ☎ *01-55-35-33-90. Métro: Tuileries.*

Corinne Sarrut

Sarrut designed the charming outfits with nipped-in waists and swingy skirts worn by Audrey Tautou in the film *Amèlie.* An overstock boutique is located at 24 rue du Champ de Mars, 7e (☎ **01-45-56-00-65**).

4 rue de Prè aux Clercs, 6e. ☎ *01-42 61-71-60. Métro: École Militaire.*

Etam

Merchandise at Etam is made mostly from synthetic or synthetic blend fabrics, but the fashions are recent, and the stores are *everywhere.* The Etam lingerie store at 47 rue de Sèvres, 6e (☎ **01-45-48-21-33**), has some pretty and affordable nightclothes and underwear.

9 bd. St Michel, 5e. ☎ *01-43-54-79-20. Métro: St-Michel.*

La City

You can find some nice young and modern styles at La City, and although everything is synthetic, the prices are reasonable.

37 rue Chaussée d'Antin, 9e. ☎ *01-48-74-41-00. Métro: Chaussée d'Antin. Other branches are located at 18 rue St-Antoine, 4e (*☎ *01-42-78-95-55), and 5Bis rue St-Placide, 6e (*☎ *01-42-84-32-84).*

1-2-3

Stylish women's suits, blouses, sweaters, most in synthetics, and accessories are sold at moderate prices at 1-2-3.

146 rue de Rivoli, 1er. ☎ *01-40-20-97-01. Métro: Louvre-Rivoli. Other branches include 30 av. Italie, 13e (*☎ *01-45-80-02- 88).*

Rodier

Prices are high, but the quality of the stylish knits here is good, and you can often find bargains during sales.

72 av. Ternes, 17e. ☎ *01-45-74-17-17. Métro: Ternes. Other branches include 47 rue de Rennes, 6e (*☎ *01-45-44-30-27).*

Shoe Bizz

This store carries the latest fashions for your feet at budget-friendly prices.

42 rue Dragon, 6e. ☎ 01-45-44-91-70. Métro: Ternes. Another branch is at 48 rue de Beaubourg, 3e (☎ 01-48-87-12-73).

Crafts

Viaduc des Arts

When the elevated railroad cutting across the 12e was transformed into the Promenade Plantée, the space beneath was redesigned to accommodate a long stretch of artisan shops, galleries, furniture stores, and craft boutiques. If you plan to visit the Bois de Vincennes via the Promenade Plantée, duck in for a look on any day, except Sunday, when it's closed. The Viaduc Café here (43 av. Daumensil) is a pleasant place for a light bite or glass of wine.

9-147 av. Daumensil, 12e. ☎ 01-44-75-80-66. Métro: Bastille, Lédru-Rollin, Reuilly-Diderot, or Gare-de Lyon.

Food

Fauchon

This large gourmet store stocked with pink-labeled cans of coffee, caviar, foie gras, biscuits, wines, oils, candy, pastries, and on, and on isn't so much a good value as worth a visit for the store's long history. Its tea salon is next door.

26 place Madeleine, 8e. ☎ 01-47-42-60-11. Métro: Madeleine.

Hédiard

Right across the street from its rival, Fauchon, is Hédiard, a gourmet food shop that sells most of the same products packaged in red and black stripes. Hédiard is slightly cheaper than Fauchon and has good prepared hot and cold food. Branches are located across the city.

21 place Madeleine, 8e. ☎ 01-43-31-88-94. Métro: Madeleine.

Jacques Papin

This butcher shop has some of the most exquisite foods you can ever see, including trout in aspic, fine patés and salads, lobsters, and smoked salmon.

Prestige et Tradition, 8 rue de Buci, 6e. ☎ 01-43-26-86-09. Métro: Odéon.

Lafayette Gourmet

This large, well-stocked supermarket in the men's building at Galeries Lafayette is a terrific spot to browse for gifts or for yourself. It has a good selection of wines, and the house-brand merchandise, often cheaper than other labels, is of very good quality. Eat at the prepared-food counters or sit at the small bar for a glass of wine.

97 rue Provence, 9e (or enter through the men's dept. of Galeries Lafayette, 52 bd. Haussmann, 9e). ☎ *01-48-74-46-06. Métro: Chaussée-d'Antin.*

La Grande Epicerie de Paris (at Le Bon Marché)

Although it isn't cheap, this is one of the best luxury supermarkets in Paris and a great place to look for gourmet gifts, such as olive oils, home-made chocolates, or wine. It makes for wonderful one-stop picnic shopping, too, offering a wide array of prepared foods and cheeses.

38 rue de Sèvres, 7e. ☎ *01-44-39-81-00. Métro: Sèvres-Babylone.*

La Maison du Chocolat

Each candy here is made from a blend of as many as six kinds of South American and African chocolate, flavored with just about everything imaginable. All the merchandise is made on the premises. If the smell doesn't lure you in, the windows will.

225 rue du Faubourg-St-Honoré, 8e. ☎ *01-42-27-39-44. Métro: Ternes.*

La Maison du Miel

This little shop has varieties of honey you never dreamed possible (pine tree, for example), identified according to the flower to which the bees were exposed.

24 rue Vignon, 9e. ☎ *01-47-42-26-70. Métro: Madeleine or Havre-Caumartin.*

Gifts and jewelry

Biche de Bère

Chunky and unusual jewelry in sterling silver and gold plate can be found here.

16 rue des Innocents, 1er. ☎ *01-40-41-02-13. Métro: Châtelet.*

Bijoux Burma

Visit Bijoux Burma for some of the best costume jewelry in the city — the secret weapon of many a Parisian woman.

50 rue François 1er, 8e. ☎ *01-47-23-70-93. Métro: Franklin-D-Roosevelt. With branches at 8 bd. Des Capucines (☎ 01-42-66-27-09) and 23 bd. Madeleine, 1er (☎ 01-42-96-05-00).*

Eric et Lydie

This shop in the arty Passage du Grand Cerf, contains unusual, beautiful, and reasonably-priced costume jewelry, hair ornaments, and other accessories.

7 passage du Grand Cerf, 2e. ☎ *01-40-26-52-59. Métro: Etienne-Marcel.*

Monic

At this store in the Marais — open Sunday afternoons — you find a wide range of affordable costume jewelry and designer creations at a discount.

5 rue des Francs-Bourgeois, 4e. ☎ *01-42-72-39-15. Métro: St-Paul.*

Pylones

This boutique sells Simpsons collectibles, children's umbrellas that stand on their own, bicycle bells shaped like ladybugs, and a variety of other unusual gift items. It's a fun place to browse.

57 rue de St-Louis-en-l'Ile, 4e. ☎ *01-46-34-05-02. Métro: Cité. Branches at 7 rue Tardieu, 18e (☎ 01-46-06-37-00), and 54 Galerie Vivienne, 2e (☎ 01-56-83-81-11).*

Tati Or

Eighteen-carat gold jewelry for up to 40% less than traditional jewelers, and more than 3,000 bracelets, earrings, necklaces, rings, and pins are offered, with about 500 items selling for less than 75€.

19 rue de la Paix, 2e. ☎ *01-40-07-06-76. Métro: Opéra.*

Why?

This is for those who are teenagers at heart. Inflatable chairs, dirty cards and jokes, Tantin figurines, notebooks, and T-shirts are highlighted.

41 rue des Francs-Bourgeois, 4e. ☎ *01-44-61-72-75. Métro: St. Paul.*

Home and housewares

Alessi

Bright and affordable kitchen implements, such as magnetized salt and pepper shakers, and wine openers that look a tad, well, *human*. Some cutlery, dishes, and linens, too.

14 rue du Faubourg St-Honoré, 8e. ☎ *01-42-66-14-61. Métro: Madéleine or Concorde.*

Cedre Rouge

Cedre Rouge sells that urban rustic look made with natural materials for apartment, country home, and garden. It isn't cheap, but you can find some unusual gifts (like cute, but tiny, snail candleholders for 20€). Finds include Tuscan pottery, Irish linen tablecloths and napkins, murano glass, teak and wicker furniture, and beeswax candles.

116 rue du Bac, 6e. ☎ *01-42-84-84-00. Métro: Sèvres-Babylone or Rue du Bac.*

Conforama

This huge store sells everything for your home at reasonable prices: furniture, appliances, garden tools and accessories, and everyday china and glass.

2 rue de Pont-Neuf, 1er. ☎ *01-42-33-78-58. Métro: Pont Neuf.*

Déhillerin

Cooks love this store, because it's filled with high-quality copper cookware, glasses, dishes, china, gadgets, utensils, pots, and kitchen appliances, but they especially love it because the prices are discounted.

18–20 rue Coquillière, 1er. ☎ *01-42-36-53-13. Internet:* www.e-dehillerin.fr. *Métro: Les Halles.*

Verrerie des Halles

China and glassware made for restaurants are available here at discount prices.

15 rue du Louvre, 1er. ☎ *01-42-36-80-60. Métro: Louvre-Rivoli.*

Toys

Au Nain Bleu

For more than 150 years, Au Nain Bleu has been selling toy soldiers, stuffed animals, games, and puppets. More modern toys are also on hand, including airplanes and model cars.

408 rue St-Honoré, 8e. ☎ *01-42-60-39-01. Métro: Concorde.*

FNAC Junior

In addition to the books, videos, and music for children, FNAC Junior has story hours and other activities for its young guests.

19 rue Vavin, 6e. ☎ 01-56-24-03-46. Métro: Vavin.

Galeries Lafayette

Floor 4 of the Galeries Lafayette main store is devoted to toys and children's clothing, and there's a play area kids love.

40 bd. Haussman, 9e. ☎ 01-56-24-03-46. Métro: Havre-Caumartin, Chaussée-d'Antin-La Fayette, Opéra, or Trinité.

Le Bon Marché

The basement of Le Bon Marché is a children's wonderland filled with adorable clothing and loads of toys, both educational and purely fun.

24 rue de Sèvres rue Vavin, 6e. ☎ 01-56-24-03-46. Métro: Vavin.

Wine

Legrand Filles et Fils

In addition to fine wines, this store stocks brandies, chocolates, coffees, and oenophile (which means "wine lover," in case you're not one) paraphernalia. It also conducts wine tastings one night a week.

1 rue de la Banque, 2e. ☎ 01-42-60-07-12. Métro: Bourse.

Le Jardin des Vignes

Bottles of rare wines, champagne, and cognac are sold here at reasonable prices. The friendly owners are really excited about wine, and they offer tastings.

91 rue de Turenne, 3e. ☎ 01-42-77-05-00. Métro: St-Sébastien-Froissart.

Les Caves Augé

This is the oldest wine shop in Paris with a sommelier (wine steward) on site.

116 bd. Hausmann, 8e. ☎ 01-45-22-16-97. Métro: St-Augustin.

Nicolas

Nicolas is the flagship store of the wine chain that has more than 110 branches in and around Paris, and it offers good prices for bottles you may not be able to find in the United States.

31 place de la Madeleine, 8e. ☎ 01-42-68-00-16. Métro: Madeleine.

Chapter 20

Three Great Paris Itineraries and a Stroll

*P*aris offers so much to see and do that first- and even second-time visitors to the city can feel overwhelmed just trying to figure out where to begin. When you're short on time, or have young children with you, you want to maximize your opportunities to see the best Paris has to offer in the most efficient way possible. I've designed the itineraries in this chapter to help you figure out where to start and what to do. But please feel free to branch out and explore those interesting alleyways and pretty green spaces you encounter all around you. That's what's so much fun about Paris; it reveals itself in all kinds of ways, making the trips of each individual visitor different, and special.

Making the Most of Paris in Three Days

Watch out: This itinerary is jam-packed!

On **Day One,** start early by having coffee and croissants at a café. Then begin at the true center of Paris: **Notre-Dame,** on the **Ile de la Cité.** The cathedral is a great starting point for any tour, and it's Paris's starting point, as well; you're at Kilometre Zéro, from which all distances in France are measured. From there, take a short walk to the island's other Gothic masterpiece — **St-Chapelle** in the **Palais de Justice.** Afterward, cross the Seine to the **Louvre.** Select just a few rooms in a particular collection for your first visit — this is one of the world's largest and finest museums, and it would take months to see everything. Take a well-deserved lunch break in the museum's comfortable **Café Marly** (see Chapter 15 for a description).

From the museum, stroll through the beautiful **Jardin des Tuileries** to the **place de la Concorde,** with its Egyptian obelisk and fountains. Walk up the **Champs-Elysées** to the **Arc de Triomphe** and browse the stores (**FNAC** and **Virgin Megastore** are good places to buy music, and each has a café on the premises for a break; **Zara** is good for the latest fashion at low prices). Walk south on avenue Marceau or take bus 92 to Alma Marceau and board the **Bateaux-Mouches** for a **Seine boat ride** (see Chapter 16). After you disembark, have dinner at the friendly and reasonably priced **L'Assiette Lyonnaise,** 21 rue Marbeuf, 8e (from Pont L'Alma walk down av. George V to rue Marbeuf and make a right; L'Assiette Lyonnaise is on your right).

Explore the **Left Bank** on **Day Two.** Take the Métro to LaMotte-Picquet-Grenelle and stop into **Monoprix** just across the street for cheap picnic food. Walk down av. de Suffren until you reach the **École Militaire.** Facing it is the **Champs-de-Mars** where you can spread out to have a picnic before visiting the **Eiffel Tower.** After you climb the tower, visit the **Église du Dôme** (which contains the **Tomb of Napoléon**) on the other side of the Ecole Militaire. Admission also includes entrance to the **Musée de l'Armée.** Across bd. des Invalides is the **Musée Rodin,** where you can enjoy a slow walk around the beautiful gardens before gazing at the artwork inside. Then walk down bd. des Invalides to the Seine, and head east for quai Anatole France (this is a long walk) and the **Musée d'Orsay** to spend a few hours with the impressionist masters. (Instead of tackling this leg of your journey on foot, you can hop on the Métro at Varenne, at the corner of bd. des Invalides and Varenne, change to RER Line C, and arrive at Musée d'Orsay.) Afterward, walk over to the Métro's **Assemblée Nationale** station at the intersection of bd. St-Germain and rue de Lille. Take the Métro two stops to rue du Bac and exit onto bd. St-Germain, making sure to walk in the direction traffic is heading, all the while browsing in upscale shops and art galleries. At pl. St-Germain-des-Près, look for one of the famous cafés, **Café de Flore, Les Deux Magots** (see Chapter 15), or **Brasserie Lipp** and have a drink. When you've finished, take rue Bonaparte (which intersects St-Germain-des-Près) to Parisians' favorite park, the **Jardin du Luxembourg.** Stroll through the park and exit at the bd. St-Michel gates. Walk down bd. St-Michel toward the river. You'll be in the **Latin Quarter.** The **Panthéon** is at the top of the hill on rue Soufflot. Many inexpensive restaurants where you can enjoy a nice meal are located behind the Panthéon on rue Mouffetard.

On **Day Three,** get up early and hop on the Métro to St-Paul, in the heart of the **Marais.** Walk over to Paris's oldest square, the aristocratic **place des Vosges,** bordered by 17th-century town houses. Then head over to rue Thorigny for the **Musée Picasso.** Try to arrive when it opens at 9:30, and allow two hours for your visit. Afterward follow rue du Vieille Temple to rue des Rosiers and pick up lunch from **Florence Finkelsztajn** or **Jo Goldenberg** (see Chapter 14). Browse the stores here and on rue des Francs Bourgeois, which turns into rue Rambuteau. Follow rue Rambuteau to rue Beaubourg, where you'll face the back of the wonderful **Centre Georges Pompidou.** Spend two hours exploring it. Afterward, jump on the Métro and head for Père-Lachaise. Spend the afternoon searching out **Cimitière Père-Lachaise**'s famous residents with the 2€ map (it's the best one) sold outside the gates on bd. de Ménilmontant. Afterward, take the Métro's Line 2 to the Anvers station. Walk down rue Tardieu to the base of **Sacré Coeur.** Take the funicular (one Métro ticket) to the top and then spend 15 to 20 minutes inside Sacré Coeur before climbing to its dome. After climbing down, head behind the church to the **place du Tertre,** which still looks like an old-fashioned Parisian square, despite artists begging to paint your picture (some can be quite persuasive, but they're too expensive, and it's better to just politely tell them *"non, merci"*). Even though the cafés are picturesque — and more expensive — save your appetite for **Au Poulbot Gourmet,** 39 rue Lamarck (follow rue Lamarck down the hill to No. 39). See the "Strolling through Montmartre" section later in this chapter.

Planning a Five-Day Visit

Spend the first three days as outlined in the "Making the Most of Paris in Three Days" itinerary. Add the **Conciergerie** to your tour of Ile de la Cité on Day One; the entrance is on the Seine side of the Palais de Justice.

On **Day Four,** visit **Versailles.** On **Day Five,** take the Métro to Opéra to visit the stunning and newly renovated **Opéra Garnier** with its mural by Marc Chagall. Cash the last of your traveler's checks at nearby **American Express** and then head over to bd. Haussmann where you can shop the rest of the afternoon away at department stores **Au Printemps** and **Galeries Lafayette.** The sixth-floor cafeteria at Galeries Lafayette offers plenty of lunch or dinner choices — from a salad bar to grilled steaks and dessert.

Playing in Paris with the Family

These itineraries take into account short attention spans, so the restaurants listed tend to be on the fast-food side. I haven't broken these outlines down into day-by-day schedules because your kids probably have varying (and, if more than one, probably competing) interests. So feel free to mix-and-match.

Taking a magical history tour: Version 1

Climb the **Eiffel Tower;** then cross over the Champs-de-Mars to visit **Napoleon's Tomb** and the **Musée de l'Armée** at **Invalides.** Afterward cross the Pont Alexandre III and pay a visit to the kid-friendly science museum, **Palais de la Découverte.** You'll be more than ready to eat, and you have your pick of places on the Champs-Elysées. **Lina's Sandwiches,** 8 rue Marbeuf, is a nearby inexpensive (and delicious) choice. After lunch, continue walking up the Champs-Elysées until you face the **Arc de Triomphe.**

Never cross the traffic circle to get to the Arc; make sure you use the pedestrian tunnel.

Climb to the top of the Arc and watch 12 lanes of traffic converge around the circle below. Afterward take bus No. 83 from the Friedland-Haussmann stop across the traffic circle to the **Jardin du Luxembourg,** Parisians' favorite park. Exit the park on bd. St-Germain or bd. St-Michel for some quick shopping before having dinner at one of the many restaurants in the area. You get an authentic French meal in upscale surroundings at **Chez Maître Paul,** 12 rue Monsieur-le-Prince. For something a little less fancy, but just as good, the Corsican restaurant, **Vivario,** is nearby at 6 rue Cochin. (Check out other eateries in Chapter 14.)

Sampling science, slides, and stalagmites: Version 2

Take half of a **Canauxrama** boat trip (if they're restless or very young, your kids won't stand for more) to **Parc de la Villette** and cross over the pedestrian bridge to visit the **Cité des Sciences et de l'Industrie.** Try to catch one of the six short films shown on the giant **Géode** IMAX screen on the grounds. Afterward, grab lunch in the complex's cafeteria, at restaurant chain **Quick,** or from one of the vendors in the park grounds and watch your kids tackle the giant-dragon sliding board and explore the submarine. Then, cross the pedestrian bridge to the other side where your small kids can enjoy kiddie rides, and your bigger ones can enjoy the **Musée de la Musique.** Afterward, take the Métro to the **Buttes-Chaumont** stop; you'll be at the edge of the park Buttes-Chaumont. Admire the waterfalls, cliffs, and the cave with stalactites and stalagmites (all man-made). Then, if it's between 8 and 11 p.m., jump back on the Métro's Line 7, change to Line 11 at Place des Fêtes, and exit at the Belleville stop. Walk up bd. de la Villette, turn left onto rue de Sambre et Meuse, and make another quick left onto pl. St-Marthe. Walk about 200 feet and on your left will be **Le Galopin** brasserie, which serves traditional French food in a casual atmosphere and is just terrific. If it's a

Friday night, you're treated to live traditional music. Their ice cream is homemade and comes in some unusual flavors (lavender, cinnamon).

Picnicking through the parks: Version 3

Bring a picnic lunch with you, then take the Métro to Porte Dorée and follow the signs for the **Bois de Vincennes.** Rent a bike in the park to explore the park's extensive grounds, or rent a canoe and lazily take in the lush surroundings. Have lunch near the cave crowned by a pseudo-Greek temple. Afterward walk over to the **Parc Zoologique** on av. St-Maurice and spend a few hours observing the animals in very natural settings. Your kids may want to climb the neat futuristic observation tower from which they get a great view of the animals, park, and surrounding city. Afterward, hop on the Métro for the Château de Vincennes stop. After a tour of the *chateau,* head over to the **Parc Floral,** which has a great playground, a butterfly garden, and a large amphitheatre where jazz musicians play on summer Saturdays. Then get on the Métro and shoot over to Hôtel de Ville. Walk over the Pont d'Arcole onto Ile de la Cité and stroll over the Pont St-Louis, which connects the two islands. Ile St-Louis's best ice cream shop, **Berthillon,** is right down the street at 31 rue St-Louis en l'Ile. If you have any energy left, try taking one of the nearby **Seine boat tours** from Vedettes Pont Neuf, moored next to Pont Neuf, or take a **Batobus** from the Notre-Dame stop.

Strolling through Montmartre

The winding roads in Montmartre still follow today the same paths medieval villagers used when the hilltop was the city's vineyard. The lamps, steep stairs, and the tiny, whitewashed houses seem a world away from the city beneath them. This walk takes you along the rustic lanes that inspired artists as diverse as Renoir, Toulouse-Lautrec, Utrillo, and Picasso. This is the Montmartre of windmills and vineyards, of neighborhood parks and compact cottages half buried in vines and foliage. You also take in a panoramic view of Paris from the Sacré-Coeur church, and explore some of the lesser-known attractions on the hill. You can do this stroll in a morning.

Begin your walk at the **Place des Abbesses,** the centerpiece of this unpretentious and slightly offbeat neighborhood. Notice the entrance to the Métro station; the glass-and-iron shell is one of the few surviving examples of the many stations designed by Art Nouveau master Hector Guimard. Also here is the **Je T'Aime** wall, a 152-square-foot wall made of enameled lava and tiles with 311 versions of the phrase, "I love you," in 250 languages against the background of a broken heart. The artist, Frédéric Baron, asked 311 people to write "I love you" in their own language. He transferred their handwriting to the wall, which he claims represents humanity torn apart by war and which the words try to gather together. Continue up rue des Abbesses, a lively street of shops, boutiques, cafés, and restaurants. Notice the view of the **windmill Moulin de la Galette** as you pass rue Tholozé on the right (more about that follows). A few steps farther, rue des Abbesses branches off to the right into **rue Lepic,** which climbs to the top of the Butte. **Les Deux Moulins,** where the character Amélie Poulain worked in the 2001 film, *Amélie,* is located at No. 15, which is down the hill. **No. 54,** on the right, is the building in which Vincent van Gogh and his brother, Théo, lived from 1886 to 1888 on the third floor.

Continue along rue Lepic to **Moulin de la Galette** and **Moulin Radet.** Early in the 16th century, the first windmills appeared in Montmartre to press grapes from the nearby vineyards and grind grain from surrounding villages. At one time 13 windmills were situated here; now only two remain. **No. 75** is the **Moulin de la Galette,** built in 1622. It was a popular outdoor dance hall in the 19th century, and the subject of a painting by Renoir. A few steps away at the intersection of rue Lepic and rue Girardon is the second windmill, **Moulin Radet,** now part of a restaurant.

Turn left on rue Girardon and head to its intersection with avenue Junot, where you'll find **Place Marcel-Aymé,** named for writer Marcel Aymé, who lived in the building here until his death in 1967. The curious sculpture of a man emerging from a wall, executed by actor and Montmartre resident Jean Marais in 1989, was inspired by Aymé's novel *Le Passe-Muraille* (*The Man Who Passed Through Walls*).

Across the street is the **Square Suzanne-Buisson,** a tranquil park where you often find a *boules* game (French lawn bowling) in progress. The statue in the center is of St-Denis, who allegedly washed his decapitated head in the fountain that used to be here. Continue along avenue Junot to **No. 25 Villa Léandre,** a cul-de-sac of houses surrounded by creeping vines and tiny gardens in proper English style. Return to avenue Junot, go down the hill a few steps and turn right at rue Simon-Dereure. Ahead of you is the **Château des Brouillards,** an impressive 18th-century mansion that has been inhabited by the Casadesus family of musicians since 1928.

Take the stairs on the left that lead up to the **allée des Brouillards.** One of the houses behind the foliage on the left was the studio and family residence of painter Pierre-Auguste Renoir from 1890 to 1897. His son, Jean, was born here in 1894 and went on to direct the classic French films *Rules of the Game* and *The Grand Illusion.* At the end of the allée des Brouillards you'll arrive at **Place Dalida,** a tiny square dominated by a bust of the beloved French singer Dalida, who lived nearby on rue d'Orchampt.

Take the road opposite the allée des Brouillards, and follow rue de l'Abreuvoir to **No. 2.** This is the "little pink house" painted by Utrillo; it was his earliest success.

Take a break at **La Maison Rose,** 2 rue de l'Abreuvoir (☎ 01-42-57-66-75). Utrillo's subject is now an inexpensive cafe and restaurant set amid vine-draped cottages that recall a typical village lane. At the end of rue de l'Abreuvoir, cross rue des Saules and take a few steps to the right onto rue Cortot. At **No. 12** is the **Musée du Vieux Montmartre,** where exhibits focus on the artists who lived and worked in Montmartre.

At the end of rue Cortot, turn left on rue du Mont-Cenis, and go down the stairs to rue St-Vincent. Turn left. A little way down the road is the **Vineyard of Montmartre.** This tiny vineyard is a tribute to the days when Montmartre was covered with vines and supplied Paris with most of its wine. The vineyard produces approximately 500 bottles of Clos Montmartre red annually. Every year on the first Saturday of October there's a celebration, the Vendanges, in honor of the harvest. If you're lucky enough to be in Paris at harvest time, you'll find it's quite a party — there's even a parade. The wine is more notable for its nostalgic value than its taste, however. On your right is the cabaret **Au Lapin Agile.** Dating to 1860, when it was called *Au Rendez-vous des Voleurs* (The Meeting Place of Thieves), the cabaret is named for the painting of a rabbit (*lapin*) by the artist A. Gill, a copy of which hangs outside this often-photographed spot.

Walk up rue des Saules. Utrillo frequently painted the crossroads of rue des Saules, rue St-Rustique, and rue Norvins — although without the shops selling trinkets, postcards, and T-shirts. On your left you'll see rue Poulbot. Follow the curve to **No. 11,** the **Espace Montmartre Salvador-Dalí,** housing a permanent display of 330 works by the Spanish artist. When you leave the museum, turn left and walk up a few steps to place du Calvaire, and enjoy the view over south Paris.

Turn left and you'll come to **Place du Tertre,** the old town square of Montmartre, now overflowing with pleading quick-sketch artists and overpriced cafés. Despite the nonstop fleece-the-tourists fest, you can just about make out a typical village square surrounded by low-rise 18th-century dwellings. Continue across the square to rue Norvins, where you turn right and arrive at the historic church of **St-Pierre de Montmartre,** one of the oldest churches in Paris and the last remnant of the powerful Montmartre Abbey that once dominated the hill.

When you leave the church, head left along place du Tertre, go downhill, and take the first left, rue Azais, to the **Basilique du Sacré-Coeur.** The gleaming white stone was chosen for its ability to secrete calcium when it rains, making this a self-whitening (and possibly a self-dissolving) church. The dome rises 262 feet and contains one of the world's heaviest bells, weighing in at 19 tons. Admire the spectacular view over Paris (and keep firm hold of your wallet; pickpockets love the area).

When you exit the church, go down the stairs that lead to the funicular and follow the road right. Immediately after the funicular, go down the stairs on the left, called rue Chappe, and you arrive at rue Gabrielle.

Turn right. At **No. 49** is **Pablo Picasso's first Paris studio.** He obtained the space from another Spanish painter in 1900 and supported himself by supplying a Spanish art dealer with a certain number of paintings in exchange for 150 francs a month.

Follow rue Gabrielle as it turns into rue Ravignan, which leads you to the cobblestone **Place Emile-Goudeau.** At **No. 13** on your right is the **Bateau-Lavoir,** a small building that many artists, including Picasso, Modigliani, and Juan Gris, have called home. Here Picasso painted his famous portrait of Gertrude Stein, *The Third Rose,* and *Les Demoiselles d'Avignon.* The original building burned in 1970 and was rebuilt in 1978; the studios now house 25 artists and sculptors.

The stairs at the end of the square take you to rue Ravignan. Follow the street down to rue des Abbesses, turn left, and you'll be back at the Abbesses Métro station.

Chapter 21

Exploring Beyond Paris: Five Great Day-Trips

In This Chapter

▶ Enjoying the excesses of Versailles

▶ Reliving French history at Fontainebleau

▶ Basking in the stained-glass light at Chartres's cool cathedral

▶ Hanging out with the giant rats at Disneyland Paris

▶ Lingering in Giverny's gardens

*J*ust as you're getting used to Paris, it's time to leave. Don't worry; it's just for the day, and you should be back in time to have a nightcap in a café. The "Day-Trips from Paris" map can help you plan your excursions.

The Château de Versailles

When you first set eyes on the royal château of Versailles (☎ 01-30-84-74-00; Internet: www.chateauversailles.fr), you won't know where to look first. "Incredible" doesn't do it justice, especially when you realize that it attests to the power royalty once had and to one king — Louis XIV — who truly believed he deserved it. Louis hired the best to build Versailles: Louis Le Vau and Jules Hardouin-Mansart, France's premier architects; André Le Nôtre, designer of the Tuileries gardens; and Charles Le Brun, head of the Royal Academy of Painting and Sculpture, for the interior. Construction got underway in 1661.

In 1682, Louis XIV transferred the court to Versailles to live with him and thus prevent plots against him. (Because his citizens' taxes paid for Versailles, he was a little paranoid.) Historians estimate that anywhere from 3,000 to 10,000 people, including servants, lived at Versailles, and court etiquette grew to be absurd. (Sometimes power struggles occurred between attendants about who ranked high enough to dress Marie Antoinette while the young queen waited, shivering.)

Day-Trips from Paris

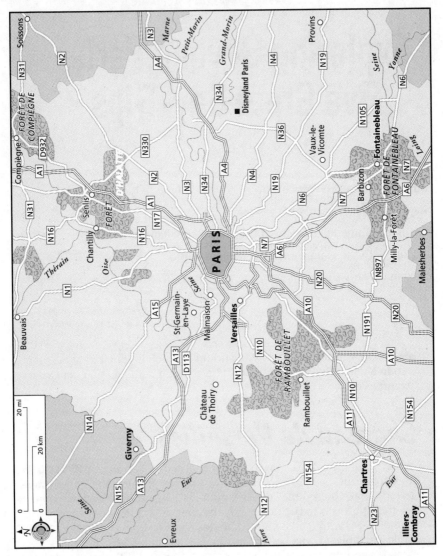

When you see all this over-the-top magnificence and try to estimate the cost, you may have a better understanding of the anger of the revolutionaries a century later.

Louis enjoyed an incredibly long reign of 72 years. When he died in 1715, he was succeeded by his great-grandson, Louis XV, who continued the outrageous pomp and ceremony and made interior renovations and redecorations until lack of funds forced him to stop. His son and daughter-in-law, Louis XVI and Marie Antoinette, had simpler tastes and made no major changes at Versailles. But by then, it was too late. On October 6, 1789, a mob marched on the palace and forced the royal couple to return to Paris, and Versailles ceased to be a royal residence.

Louis-Philippe, who reigned from 1830 to 1848 and succeeded Louis XVIII, prevented the château's destruction by donating his own money to convert it into a museum dedicated to the glory of France. John D. Rockefeller also contributed to the restoration of Versailles, and the work from that contribution continues to this day. The nearby "Versailles" map shows the current configuration.

Getting there

To reach Versailles by car, drive west on the A13 highway from Porte d'Auteuil toward Rouen. Take the Versailles-Château exit, about 14 miles from Paris. Park in the visitors' parking lot at place d'Armes for 4.50€ Monday through Friday, 5.50€ on weekends. The drive takes about a half-hour, but in traffic, it can take more than an hour.

You can also take a tour bus to Versailles. **Cityrama,** 4 place des Pyramides, 1er (☎ **01-44-55-61-00;** Internet: www.cityrama.fr), has different trips to Versailles ranging from 34€ to 67€ for adults, 17€ to 33.50€ for children. **Paris Vision,** 214 rue de Rivoli, 1er (☎ **01-42-60-30-01;** Internet: www.parisvision.com), offers bus excursions starting from 34€ to 58€; it's half price for ages 4 to 11.

Exploring Versailles

Two words of advice — arrive early! More than 3 million tourists visit Versailles each year, and you'll want to have as much of a head start as possible.

Kings used the six Louis XIV–style **Grands Appartements** for ceremonial events, and lived with their families in **the Petits Appartements.** Louis XV stashed his mistresses, Madame du Barry and Madame de Pompadour, in his second-floor apartment, which can be visited only with a guide. Attempts have been made to restore the original decor of the Queen's bedchamber, which Marie Antoinette renovated with a huge four-poster bed and silks in patterns of lilacs and peacock feathers.

The **Salons of War and Peace** flank its most famous room, the 236-foot-long **Hall of Mirrors.** Hardoin-Mansart began work on it in 1678, and Le Brun added 17 large windows and corresponding mirrors. The ceiling paintings represent the accomplishments of Louis XIV's government. Jacques-Ange Gabriel designed the **library** with its delicately carved panels. The **Clock Room** contains Passement's astronomical clock, which took 20 years to make; it's encased in gilded bronze.

Versailles

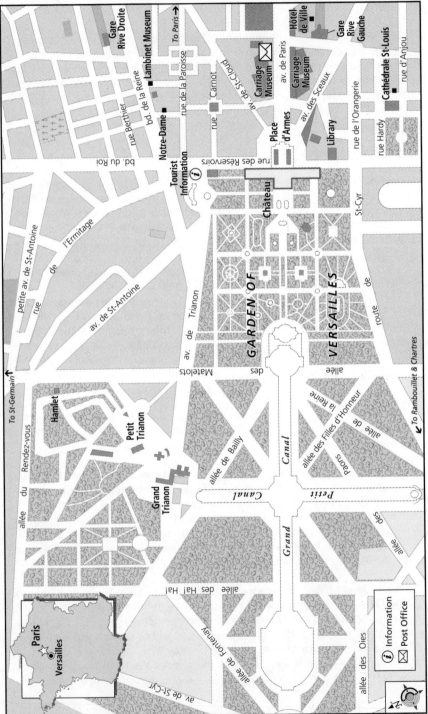

Gare Rive Droite

Lambinet Museum

To Paris →

rue de la Paroisse

Hôtel de Ville

Carriage Museum

av. de Paris

Gare Rive Gauche

Cathédrale St-Louis

rue d'Anjou

bd. de la Reine

rue Berthier

rue Carnot

av. de St-Cloud

Carriage Museum

av. des Sceaux

rue de l'Orangerie

rue Hardy

Notre-Dame

bd. du Roi

Tourist Information

rue des Réservoirs

Place d'Armes

Library

Château

St-Cyr

l'Ermitage

petite av. de St-Antoine

rue de

av. de St-Antoine

av. de Trianon

GARDEN OF

VERSAILLES

de

route

de

To St-Germain

Rendez-vous

Hamlet

Petit Trianon

Matelots

des

allée

allée de

la Reine

allée des Filles d'Honneur

paris

To Rambouillet & Chartres

allée du

allée de Bailly

Grand Trianon

Petit Canal

Canal

Grand Canal

des

allée

allée des Hal Hal

allée de Fontenay

av. de St-Cyr

allée des Oies

Paris

Versailles

ⓘ Information

☒ Post Office

Gabriel also designed the **Royal Opéra** for Louis XV. Try to imagine it the way it used to be — floor coverings of bearskin, lit by 3,000 powerful candles. Hardoin-Mansart built the gold-and-white **Royal Chapel** between 1699 and 1710. After his father's death, Louis XVI and Marie Antoinette prayed for guidance here, thinking they were too young to run the country.

After you've seen the château, plan to spend at least an hour strolling through the **Formal Gardens.** Spread across 250 acres, Le Nôtre created a Garden of Eden, using ornamental lakes and canals, geometrically designed flowerbeds, and avenues bordered with statuary. Louis XV, imagining he was in Venice, used to take gondola rides with his "favorite" of the moment on the mile-long Grand Canal.

Because of the crowds and long lines, most guests are content with visiting only the château and gardens, but you can see much more at Versailles if you have the stamina. The most important of the remaining sights are the **Grand Trianon** and the **Petit Trianon,** both opulent love nests constructed for the mistresses of kings. A long walk across the park takes you to the pink-and-white-marble Grand Trianon, designed in 1687 by Hardouin-Mansart for Louis XIV. It has traditionally served as a residence for the country's important guests, although former President Charles de Gaulle wanted to turn it into a weekend retreat for himself. Napoléon I spent the night here, and U.S. President Richard Nixon slept in the room where Madame de Pompadour (Louis XV's mistress) died. Gabriel, the designer of the place de la Concorde, built the Petit Trianon in 1768 for Louis XV; Louis used it for his trysts with Madame du Barry, his mistress after La Pompadour. Marie Antoinette adopted it as her favorite residence, where she could escape the constraints of palace life.

Behind the Petit Trianon is the **Hamlet,** a collection of small thatched farmhouses and a water mill, a setting where Marie Antoinette pretended she was back at her family's country retreat in Austria. Near the Hamlet is the Temple of Love, built in 1775 by Richard Mique, Marie Antoinette's favorite architect. In the center of its Corinthian colonnade is a reproduction of Bouchardon's Cupid shaping a bow from the club of Hercules.

Near the stables is the entrance to the **Carriage Museum,** which houses coaches from the 18th and 19th centuries, among them are one used at the coronation of Charles X and another used at the wedding of Napoléon I and Marie-Louise. One sleigh rests on tortoiseshell runners. A ticket to the Petit Trianon also admits you to this museum.

Admission to the palace is 7.50€ for adults, 5.30€ for ages 18 to 24 and older than 60, and free for those younger than 18 and for all on Sunday. Combined admission to the Grand and Petit Trianons is 5€ for adults, 3€ for ages 18 to 24 and seniors, and free for those younger than 18.

Admission to the gardens is 3.50€ for adults, 3€ for ages 10 to 17. Admission to the coach museum is 1.90€, free for children younger than 18. Admission to Jeu de Paume is free.

One-hour audio tours of the respective King's Chambers are admission price plus 4€ for ages 18 and older, admission plus 2.70€ for ages 10 to 17. Lecturer-led one-hour tours of the palace are admission price plus 4€ for adults, 2.70€ for ages 10 to 18; 1½-hour tours are admission plus 6€ for adults, 4.20€ for ages 10 to 18; two-hour tours are admission plus 8€ for adults, 5.50€ for ages 10 to 18. Tours are free for children younger than 10.

From May 2 to September 30, the palace is open Tuesday through Sunday from 9:00 a.m. to 6:30 p.m.; from April to October, the Grand Trianon and Petit Trianon are open daily from noon to 6:30 p.m. The rest of the year, the palace is open Tuesday through Sunday from 9:00 a.m. to 5:30 p.m.; the Grand Trianon and Petit Trianon are open daily from noon to 5:30 p.m. The park and the gardens are open every day except in bad weather from 7:00 a.m. in summer, 8:00 a.m. in winter, until sunset (between 5.30 p.m. and 9.30 p.m. depending on the season).

Dining options

The town of Versailles has no shortage of places where you can break for lunch, but after you're on palace grounds, you may find it infinitely more convenient just to stay put — otherwise you have to hike back into town and back out to the palace again. In the château, you can eat at a cafeteria just off the Cour de la Chapelle. In the Formal Gardens is an informal restaurant, **La Flotille,** on Petite Venise. (To get there from the château, walk directly back through the gardens to where the canal starts. Petite Venise and the restaurant are to your right.) Finally, several **snack bars** are located in the gardens near the Quinconce du Midi and the Grand Trianon.

The Palais de Fontainebleau

Fontainebleau (☎ 01-60-71-50-70; check out the nearby "Fontainebleau" map) contains more than 700 years of royal history from the enthronement of Louis VII in 1137, to the fall of the Second Empire in 1873. What this place is probably most famous for, however, is Napoléon's farewell to his Imperial Guard, which he delivered on the grand curved stairway before leaving for exile. If you get tired of the palace's splendor, you can walk around the beautiful gardens and then rent bikes to ride in the 42,000 acres of the kings' old hunting grounds, the Forêt de Fontainebleau.

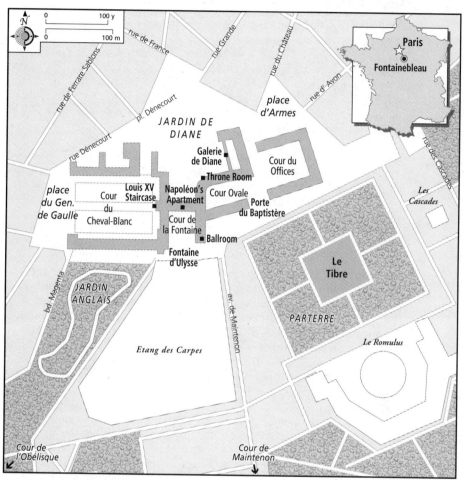

Fontainebleau

Getting there

To reach Fontainebleau by train, take the Montargie line to Fontainebleau Avon station; it departs hourly from the Gare de Lyon in Paris. The trip takes 35 to 60 minutes and costs 7.30€. Fontainebleau Avon station is just outside the town in Avon, a suburb of Paris. From the station, the town bus (direction Château) makes the 2-mile trip to the château every 10 to 15 minutes on weekdays, every 30 minutes on Saturdays and Sundays.

You can also reach Fontainebleau on a tour bus. **Cityrama,** 4 place des Pyramides, 1er (**☎ 01-44-55-61-00;** Internet: www.cityrama.fr), combines both Fontainebleau and the village of Barbizon for 53€ adult, 26.50€ child.

Exploring Fontainebleau

François I transformed a run-down royal palace into Fontainebleau in 1528 for his mistress, and his successor, Henri II, left a beautiful memorial to the woman he loved — a **ballroom** decorated with the intertwined initials of his mistress, Diane de Poitiers and himself. The Mona Lisa once hung here; François I bought the painting from da Vinci himself. Stucco-framed paintings now hanging in the **Gallery of François I** include *The Rape of Europa* and depict mythological and allegorical scenes related to the king's life.

Make sure to see the racy ceiling paintings above the **Louis XV Staircase.** Originally painted for the bedroom of a duchess, the stairway's architect simply ripped out the bedroom floor, using its ceiling to cover the stairway. One fresco depicts the Queen of the Amazons climbing into Alexander the Great's bed.

When Louis XIV ascended the throne, Fontainebleau was largely neglected because of his preoccupation with Versailles, but it found renewed glory under Napoléon I. You can walk around much of the palace on your own, but most of the Napoleonic Rooms are accessible only on guided tours, which are in French. Napoleon had two bedchambers; mirrors adorn either side of his bed in the grander chamber (look for his symbol, a bee), while a small bed is housed in the aptly named **Small Bedchamber.** A red-and-gold throne with the initial "N" is displayed in the **Throne Room.** You can also see Napoléon's **offices** where the emperor signed his abdication; however, the document on exhibit is only a copy.

After a visit to the palace, wander through the gardens, paying special attention to the lovely, bucolic carp pond with its fearless swans. If you'd like to promenade in the forest, a detailed map of its paths is available from the **Office de Tourisme,** 4 rue Royale, near the palace (☎ 01-60-74-99-99). You can also rent bikes nearby from **A la Petite Reine,** 32 rue des Sablons (☎ 01-60-74-57-57), for about 12€ a day, 20€ on weekends, with a credit-card deposit. The **Tour Denencourt,** about 3 miles north of the palace, makes a nice ride and has a pretty view.

The Palais de Fontainebleau is open Wednesday through Monday from 9:30 a.m. to 6:00 p.m. in July and August; from 9:30 a.m. to 5:00 p.m. in May, June, September, and October; from 9:30 a.m. to 12:30 p.m. and from 2:00 to 5:00 p.m. November through April. Admission to the Grands Appartements is 5.34€ for adults, 3.51€ for ages 18 to 26 and older than 60, and for all on Sunday. Children younger than 18 are admitted free.

Dining options

If you're arriving by train and plan only to visit Fontainebleau, consider bringing a picnic from Paris. In fine weather, the château's gardens and nearby forest beckon. But, if you have a car, save your appetite for Barbizon.

On the western edge of France's finest forest, lies the village of Barbizon, home to a number of noted landscape artists — Corot, Millet, Rousseau, and Daumier. The colorful town has a lively mix of good restaurants, boutiques, and antiques shops — the perfect place to while away an afternoon. For lunch, try the **Relais de Barbizon,** 2 av. Charles-de-Gaulle (☎ **01-60-66-40-28**). The 24€ prix fixe features such hearty homestyle dishes as duckling in wild cherry sauce or braised lamb with thyme. The restaurant is open Thursday through Monday noon to 2:30 p.m. and 8:00 to 10:00 p.m. (Only lunch is served on Tuesdays.)

If you stay in Fontainebleau for lunch, try **Le Table des Maréchaux,** 9 rue Grande (☎ **01-60-39-50-50**); its 26€ prix-fixe lunch (served Monday through Friday) may include starters of smoked salmon in a creamy mustard sauce or gazpacho with grilled almonds and pine nuts and main courses of grilled duck breast with regional spices or tuna sautéed in herbs. In warm weather, diners can eat on the outdoor terrace.

The Cathédral at Chartres

The Cathédrale de Notre-Dame de Chartres (☎ **02-37-21-56-33**; see the nearby "Notre-Dame de Chartres" map), one of the world's greatest Gothic cathedrals and one of the finest creations of the Middle Ages, comes second in importance to a majority of its visitors. Instead, a small scrap of material — said to be worn by the Virgin Mary when she gave birth to Jesus — draws the masses here.

Getting there

Pick up one of the hourly SNCF trains from Paris's Gare Montparnasse to the town of Chartres. A round-trip ticket costs about 23€; the trip takes an hour.

If you'd like to drive to Chartres, take the A10/A11 highway from Porte d'Orléans and follow the signs to Le Mans and Chartres. The drive takes about 75 minutes.

Traveling to Chartres by tour bus is another option. **Cityrama,** 4 place des Pyramides, 1er (☎ **01-44-55-61-00**; Internet: www.cityrama.fr), offers five-hour excursions leaving from Paris every Tuesday, Thursday, and Saturday for 47€ adult, 23.50€ child. **Paris Vision,** 214 rue de Rivoli, 1er (☎ **01-42-60-30-01**; Internet: www.parisvision.com), also has a tour that departs the same days for the same amount.

Notre-Dame de Chartres

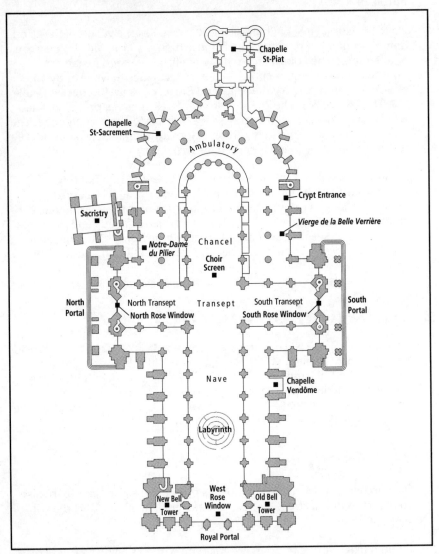

Exploring the cathedral

Take one of Malcolm Miller's excellent guided tours of Chartres Cathedral (☎ **02-37-28-15-58**). He gives fascinating tours Monday through Saturday at noon and 2:45 p.m. from Easter to November; he's sometimes available in winter, too.

A good time to visit is on Sunday afternoons when free organ concerts (4:45 to 5:45 p.m.) and the filtered light coming in from the western windows make the church come wonderfully alive.

The cathedral that you see today dates principally from the 13th century, when it was built with the combined efforts and contributions of kings, princes, church officials, and pilgrims from across Europe. This Notre-Dame was among the first to use flying buttresses.

Begin at the beginning — with the **entryway.** People say that Rodin sat for hours on the edge of the sidewalk, contemplating the portal, spellbound by its sculptured bodies draped in long, flowing robes with amazingly lifelike faces. Before entering, walk around to both the north and south portals, which date from the 13th century. The bays depict such biblical scenes as the expulsion of Adam and Eve from the Garden of Eden, and episodes from the life of the Virgin.

Next, just inside, are the **Clocher Vieux** (Old Tower) with its 350-foot steeple dating from the 12th century, and the **Clocher Neuf** (New Tower). Originally built in 1134, the new tower's elaborate ornamental tower was added between 1507 and 1513 following one of the many fires that swept through the cathedral.

You can climb to the top of the Clocher Neuf, but make sure your shoes aren't slippery — parts of the tower are without a railing and are quite steep and narrow.

The cathedral is also known for its celebrated **choir screen.** Don't let the term fool you; this is a carved wood structure that took nearly 200 years to complete. The niches, 40 in all, contain statues illustrating scenes from the life of Mary. The screen is in the middle of the cathedral toward the back.

Few of the rushed visitors ever notice the screen; they're transfixed by the **stained-glass windows.** Bring a pair of binoculars to better focus on the panes covering more than 3,000 square yards. The glass is unequaled anywhere in the world and is truly mystical. It was spared in both world wars, because in both wars, the glass was removed piece by piece.

Most of the stained glass dates from the 12th and 13th centuries. Many visitors find it difficult to single out one panel or window of particular merit; however, the oldest is the 12th-century **Notre Dame de la belle verrière** (Our Lady of the Beautiful Window, sometimes called the Blue Virgin) on the south side. The colors from the glass are such a vibrant, startling blue that many find it hard to believe that the window is 1,000 years old.

Look down in the **nave** — the widest in France — at the 13th-century labyrinth. It was designed for pilgrims to navigate on their hands and knees as a form of penance, all 1,000 feet of it. These days, much of it is covered with fold-up chairs for mass. The **Sancta Camisia,** the holy relic that some people believe Mary wore during the birth of Jesus, is behind the choir screen in a chapel to the left of the church's treasury.

The cathedral is open daily April through September from 8:00 a.m. to 8:00 p.m., October through March from 7:30 a.m. to 7:00 p.m. Ask at the Chartres tourist office (☎ 02-37-21-50-00) outside the cathedral for information about tours in English and a schedule of masses that are open to the public. From April to September, the North Tower is open Monday through Saturday from 9:30 to 11:30 a.m. and daily from 2:00 to 5:30 p.m.; October through March, Monday through Saturday from 10:00 to 11:30 a.m. and daily from 2:00 to 4:00 p.m. Admission to the tower is about 3.70€ for adults, 2.20€ for seniors and students; children younger than 12 are admitted free.

Dining options

You can find plenty of restaurants, cafés, and snack bars around town, but just a stone's throw from the cathedral is **Le Buisson Ardent,** 10 rue au Lait (☎ 02-37-34-04-66). The restaurant serves well-prepared fare made with farm-fresh ingredients in a quaint, wood-beamed dining room. A variety of fresh fish dishes are available, and the roast pigeon with lemon juice, served with potato pancakes and fresh vegetables, is also recommended. *Calvados* (a cider brandy) is a specialty of the Normandy region, and for dessert, try the crispy hot apples with sorbet and Calvados-flavored butter sauce. Priced between 20€ and 35€ for three courses. The restaurant is open daily for lunch, and Monday through Saturday for dinner. MasterCard and Visa are accepted.

If you have extra time, spend it by exploring the medieval cobbled streets of the **Old Town.** At the foot of the cathedral are lanes with gabled and turreted houses and humped bridges spanning the Eure River. One house, on rue Chantault, dates back nine centuries.

Stop in to the **Musée de Beaux-Arts de Chartres,** 29 Cloître Notre-Dame (☎ 02-37-36-41-39), to see paintings by old masters such as Watteau, Brosamer, and Zurbarán. The museum is open Monday and Wednesday through Friday from 9:30 a.m. to noon, and from 2:00 to 5:00 p.m. Admission is 2€.

Disneyland Paris

Disneyland Paris (☎ 01-64-74-30-00) opened in 1992 to much resistance and controversy. Ten years later, it's France's number 1 attraction, with more than 50 million visitors a year; 40% of them are French, and half of those Parisian. Set on a 5,000-acre site (about one-fifth the size of Paris) in the suburb of Marne-la-Vallée, the park incorporates the elements of its Disney predecessors but gives them a European flair. Allow a full day to see Disneyland Paris.

Admission (subject to change) to either the theme park or the new Walt Disney Studios Park for one day is 38€ for visitors older than 11 years of age, 29€ for children ages 3 to 11 years, and free for children younger than 3. Admission for a three-day "Hopper" pass good for unlimited access to both the theme park and the Studios Park costs 99€ for adults, 80€ for children. Entrance to Le Festival Disney (the consortium of shops, dance clubs, and restaurants) is free; a cover charge is usually in order for the dance clubs.

Disneyland Paris is open from the middle of June to the middle of September daily from 9 a.m. to 11 p.m.; off-season hours vary but are generally Monday through Friday from 10 a.m. to 6 p.m., and Saturday and Sunday from 9 a.m. to 8 p.m. Hours vary with the weather and season, so call ☎ **01-60-30-60-00** before setting out.

A guide for visitors in wheelchairs gives important information about access to rides and other attractions all around the park. You can pick up a copy at City Hall in the Disneyland Park or call to have a copy sent to you (☎ **01-60-30-60-30**).

Getting there

To get to Disneyland Paris by train, take the RER Line A from the center of Paris (Invalides, Nation, or Châtelet–Les Halles) to Marne-la-Vallée/ Chessy, a 35-minute ride. Trains run every 10 to 20 minutes, depending on the time of day. The station is at the entrance to the park.

Avoid lines at the resort by buying Disneyland passes at all RER A stations, except Marne-la-Vallée, and Métro stations including Charles de Gaulle-Étoile, Franklin-D-Roosevelt, Gare de Lyon, Porte Maillot, Esplanade de la Défense, Anvers, Père-Lachaise, Place de Clichy, Gallieni, Havre-Caumartin, Villiers, Alésia, Barbès-Rochechouart, Châtelet, Denfert-Rochereau, and Gare de l'Est. The pass is good for either Disneyland Park or Walt Disney Studios but not both.

Another option is to take a bus to Disneyland Paris. Shuttle buses connect the resort's hotels (except the Davy Crockett Ranch) with Orly Airport (every 45 minutes daily between 9 a.m. and 7 p.m.) and Roissy–Charles-de-Gaulle (every 45 minutes daily between 8 a.m. and 8 p.m.). One-way transport to the park from either airport costs 14€ for adults, 11.50€ for ages 3 to 11. Within the park, a free shuttle bus connects the various hotels with the theme park, stopping every 6 to 15 minutes, depending on the time of year. Service begins an hour before the park opens and stops an hour after closing.

If you prefer to drive to Disneyland Paris, take the A4 highway east and exit at "Park Euro Disney." Guest parking at any of the thousands of spaces costs 8€. A series of moving sidewalks speeds up pedestrian transit from the parking areas to the theme park entrance.

Exploring the park

The Disneyland Paris resort now consists of two theme parks: the **Disneyland Park** and the new **Walt Disney Studios Park.** Disneyland is conceived as a total vacation destination, clustering together five "lands" of entertainment (Main Street, U.S.A; Frontierland; Adventureland; Fantasyland; and Discoveryland), six massive and well-designed hotels, a campground, a nightlife center (Le Festival Disney), swimming pools, tennis courts, a 27-hole golf course, and dozens of restaurants, shows, and shops.

Walt Disney Studios Park is a movie studio come to life where children participate in the process. The entrance is called the Front Lot and resembles the Hollywood Disney studios, water tower, gates, and all. En Coulisse restaurant is located here, serving the kind of food kids like and Americans are known for — hamburgers, pizza, salads, and ice cream. In a film studio resembling a street, kids can become a part of the filming of impromptu comedy sketches as they walk around the park; later in the day, they get to see themselves on screen. In the Animation Courtyard, cartoon characters come to life via black light and mirrors, and children can play at being animators at interactive displays. The French Disney Channel has its studios here, in the Production Courtyard; kids get to see how a TV studio really works and may be asked to serve as extras. An international buffet, Rendez-Vous des Stars, is located here. The Back Lot features the Backlot Express Restaurant serving sandwiches and other quick fare, and the Rock-n-Roller Coaster, a very fast and very loud ride (120 speakers playing Aerosmith) that whips you through an Aerosmith rock video. Calm down afterward by watching the stunt show spectacular, which is highlighted by a high-speed car chase. Food kiosks sell popcorn, ice cream, hot dogs, and so on throughout the park.

If your kids are younger than 7, they'd be best suited for Main Street, U.S.A., Fantasyland, Sleeping Beauty's Castle, and the afternoon parade. Children ages 7 through 12 enjoy Frontierland, the Phantom Manor ghost house, the Big Thunder Mountain roller coaster, Adventureland, Indiana Jones and the Temple of Doom roller coaster, and the Pirates of the Caribbean ride. Teens like Discoveryland, the Space Mountain roller coaster, and the Star Tours simulated spacecraft ride.

Avoid waiting in long lines with the free Fast Pass. After presenting the pass at the ride you want, you're given a time frame for when to come back and board the ride first upon your return. Ask for it at the ticket booth or City Hall.

Staying at Disneyland

If you want to stay at Disneyland overnight or for a few days, you need to book well in advance. Plenty of hotels are available at different price levels, and you can explore the options and book accommodations on the park's Web site at www.disneylandparis.com.

Monet's Gardens at Giverny

Monet moved to Giverny (☎ 02-32-51-28-21 for Fondation Claude Monet, which runs the museum) in 1883, and the water lilies beneath the Japanese bridge in the garden and the flower garden became his regular subjects until his death in 1926. In 1966, the Monet family donated Giverny to the Académie des Beaux-Arts in Paris, perhaps the most prestigious fine arts school in France, which subsequently opened the site to the public. Giverny has since become one of the most popular attractions in France, but even the crowds can't completely overwhelm the magic.

Getting there

Catch an SCNF train at the Gare St-Lazare in Paris approximately every hour for the 45-minute trip to Vernon, the town nearest the Monet gardens. The round-trip fare is about 21€. From the station, buses make the 3-mile trip to the museum for 2€ or you can go on foot — the route along the Seine makes for a nice walk.

If you're driving to Giverny, take the A13 highway from the Porte d'Auteuil to Bonnières, then D201 to Giverny. The whole trip takes about an hour.

Traveling to Giverny by tour bus is another option. **Cityrama,** 4 place des Pyramides, 1er (☎ 01-44-55-61-00; Internet: www.cityrama.com), has two trips to Giverny: a five-hour trip on Tuesday through Saturday for 58€ adult, 29€ child; and an all-day Giverny–Auvers-sur-Oise trip on Sunday or Wednesday for 96€ for adults, 86.40€ for children, which includes lunch at the American Museum. Call for specific dates. **Paris Vision,** 214 rue de Rivoli, 1er (☎ 01-42-60-30-01; Internet: www.parisvision.com), offers two trips: a Versailles-Giverny all-day trip on Tuesday and Friday that includes lunch at the **Moulin de Fourges** for 98€ for adults, 49€ for children; and a trip without lunch on Tuesday through Sunday for 58€ for adults and 29.50€ for children.

Exploring the gardens

Even before you arrive at Giverny, you probably have some idea of what you're going to see. The gardens are usually at their best in May, June, September, and October. Should you yearn to have them almost to yourself, plan to be at the gates when they open. Plan to spend at least a half-day at Giverny, longer if you plan to eat lunch and visit the American Museum.

Giverny: It's not just for Monet any more

At one point, more than 50 American artists lived in Giverny with their families, and you can see much of their work at the **Musée d'Art Américain Giverny** (☎ 02-32-51-94-65), just 100 yards from Monet's house and gardens.

Some say Monet's influence was responsible for the influx of American artists into the village of Giverny in the late 1880s. Others say that Monet had little contact with the Americans, and it was Giverny's beauty that captured the hearts of painters like John Singer Sargent and William Metcalf, who began spending their summers there.

The museum is open April through November, Tuesday through Sunday from 10 a.m. to 6 p.m., as well as Easter Monday and Whit Monday (the 51st day after Easter). Admission is 5€ for adults, 4€ for students and seniors, 3€ for ages 12 to 18, and free for children younger than 12. Admission is free for all on the first Sunday of every month.

The gardens are open from April to November Tuesday through Sunday from 9:30 a.m. to 6:00 p.m., as well as Easter Monday and Whit Monday (51 days after Easter). Admission to the house and gardens is 5.50€ for adults, 4€ for students, and 3€ for ages 7 to 12; admission to only the gardens is 4€, and admission to only the house is 1.50€. No advanced tickets are sold.

Dining options

Your entry ticket is no longer valid once you leave Monet's home, so think ahead about whether you want to eat lunch before or after your visit. Most people arrive in early afternoon, so crowds are slightly lighter in the mornings.

The square directly across from Monet's house and the adjacent street has many little cafés and crêperies. But if you're in the mood for more substantial fare, walk back to town and treat yourself to **Le Relais Normand,** an old Norman manor house with fireplace and terrace. It serves delicious dishes like Neufchâtel cheese in pastry, stewed beef à la Provençal, and young rabbit in green peppercorn sauce. The four-course, prix-fixe menu at around 26€ is the best deal in the house. The restaurant is open for lunch Tuesday through Sunday from noon to 3 p.m. Visa and MasterCard are accepted.

Part VI
Living It Up after the Sun Goes Down: Paris Nightlife

The 5th Wave   By Rich Tennant

"It serves you right for requesting a lap dance from someone doing the can-can."

In this part . . .

*P*aris may not be a city that never sleeps, but it's just as fabulous after the sun sets as it is during the day. There is so much to do! Take your pick of French-language, English-language, and avant-garde theater productions or ballet, opera, and symphony. But beware! Events can sell out quickly. The Ménilmontant neighborhood is still a haven for bar hoppers (although residents complain that it's getting trendy), and clubs have opened up in barges on the Seine. You can always check out the overpriced can-can cabaret spectacles at venues like the Moulin Rouge, the Lido, and the Crazy Horse — even though Parisians wouldn't be caught dead at 'em, there's still plenty of healthy business from visitors. Chapter 22 gives you the lowdown on Paris's vibrant theater scene, while Chapter 23 previews the symphony, opera, ballet, and cabaret. Chapter 24 hits the bars and clubs (hope you like house music; it's de rigueur), jumping jazz spots, live music venues, classy cocktail joints, and *boites des nuits* (nightspots).

Chapter 22

The Play's the Thing: Paris's Theater Scene

. . . .

In This Chapter

▶ Saving money on tickets

▶ Attending the national theaters

▶ Tracking down English-language theater

. . . .

*P*aris gave the world playwrights like Molière, Victor Hugo, Corneille, and Racine and actors Sarah Bernhardt and Antonin Artaud. It also nourished expatriate playwrights like Samuel Beckett and Eugene Ionesco. The city's theater scene has nearly always been dynamic, with plenty of experimentation, and today is no different. Recently, Paris audiences have been seeing something rare for them: musicals, like *Le Dix Commandments* (*The Ten Commandments*), based on the Bible, and *Le Petit Prince,* from the book by Antoine St-Exupéry. A staged version of Tolstoy's *War and Peace* and a play about the Biblical character, *Job,* are other recent works of note.

If your French is rusty, you may want to consider alternatives to French-language productions — like ballet (see Chapter 23) or one of the many avant-garde productions in which language is secondary, or not spoken at all (remember, Paris also gave the world mime Marcel Marceau). Paris is home to a thriving English-language theater scene, so you should be able to find something that suits your tastes. In this chapter, find out where to go to save money on tickets, where to catch a classic performance, and the best spots for English-language theater.

Saving Money on Tickets

For half-price theater tickets for national theaters and other venues, go to the **Kiosque-Théâtre** at the northwest corner of the Madeleine church (Métro: Madeleine) to buy tickets for same-day performances. The panels all around the kiosk indicate sold out shows with a little red man, and a little green man tells you that tickets are still available. The Kiosque-Théâtre is open Tuesday through Saturday from 12:30 to 8:00 p.m., Sunday from 12:30 to 4:00 p.m. A second branch of the discount-ticket counter is in front of the Gare Montparnasse. Try to arrive no later than noon, because lines are usually long.

Students may be able to pick up last-minute tickets by applying at the box office an hour before curtain time. Have your International Student Identity Card (ISIC) with you — you can order one from **Council Travel** (☎ 800-2COUNCIL in the U.S.; Internet: www.counciltravel.com). Students can also buy seats for 10.62€ in 46 theaters; call the ticket hotline at ☎ 08-00-80-07-50.

National Theater in Paris

The theaters listed here are national theaters supported by the government, but many private ones also exist. For full listings, consult *Pariscope: Une Semaine de Paris* (.40€), a weekly guide with thorough listings of movies, plays, ballet, art exhibits, and clubs sold at all newsstands.

A good mix of modern and classic tragedies and comedies comes alive in wonderful performances in the **Salle Richelieu** of the **Comédie Française,** 2 rue de Richelieu, 1er (☎ 01-44-58-15-15; Internet: www.comedie-francaise.fr; Métro: Palais-Royal–Musée du Louvre). Performances are in French, however, and can be difficult to understand. Tickets cost 11€ to 30€, or 7.50€ to 13€ for people 27 and younger. Last-minute seats for people 27 and younger are on sale 30 minutes before the start of the performance and cost 10€. Reduced visibility seats are 4.50€. To make a reservation up to 14 days in advance, phone daily from 11 a.m. to 6 p.m. To order tickets 15 days to two months in advance, fax information to 01-44-39-87-19 or purchase online (no phone reservations are accepted).

In 1996, the Comédie Française took over the **Théâtre du Vieux Colombier,** 21 rue Vieux Colombier, 6e (☎ 01-44-39-87-00/01; Métro: St-Sulpice), an intimate 300-seat venue where mostly modern works are performed. Tickets cost 26€ for adults (8€ on Saturdays), 13€ for people 27 and younger (6€ on Saturdays), and 19€ for seniors (6€ on Saturdays). To make a reservation up to 14 days in advance, call Tuesday through Saturday from 11 a.m. to 6 p.m., or Sunday and Monday from 1 to 6 p.m. To order tickets 15 days to two months in advance, fax information to 01-44-39-87-19 or purchase online (no phone reservations are accepted).

The Comédie Française also has a workshop in the Carrousel du Louvre **Studio-Théâtre,** where actors perform one-hour plays and readings. Video projections of plays and films are also shown here. Tickets are sold at the ticket window one hour before the performance and cost 13€ for adults, 11€ for seniors, and 7.50€ for people 27 and younger.

For popular, contemporary plays, the **Théâtre National de Chaillot,** place du Trocadéro, 16e (☎ **01-53-65-30-00;** Internet: www.theatre-chaillot.fr; Métro: Trocadéro), is your place. Part of the Art Deco Palais de Chaillot, the theater is located directly across the Seine from the Eiffel Tower. Tickets are 18€ to 30€ for adults, 15€ to 25€ for seniors, and 9.50€ to 17.50€ for people 26 and younger.

The **Théâtre National de la Colline,** 15 rue Malte-Brun, 20e (☎ **01-44-62-52-52;** Internet: www.colline.fr; Metro: Gambetta), has modern drama from around the world, and the **Petit Théâtre,** located upstairs, has short plays and offerings from international theater's less famous and up-and-coming playwrights. Arrive early to have a glass of wine and admire the view from the Café de la Colline in the lobby. Tickets cost 24.50€ for adults, 20€ for seniors, and 12€ for people younger than 30. On Tuesdays, adults and seniors pay 17€.

The show must go on! Because of renovations of its building at 6 pl. de l'Odéon, the troupe of the Odéon, Théâtre de l'Europe has temporarily relocated until 2004 to 32 bd Berthier, 17e, once home to the Opéra Comique. Known for now as the **Théâtre de l'Europe aux Ateliers Berthier** (☎ 01-44-41-36-36; Internet: www.theatre-odeon.fr; Métro: Porte de Clichy), performances are still varied and eclectic. (Lou Reed once read his poems at the Odéon.) Tickets are 26€ for adults, 20€ for seniors, and 12€ for people younger than 30.

English-Language Theater

On any given day, close to 100 theatrical productions may be going on in Paris and the surrounding area. However, without a firm grip on the French language — or at least the plays written by Molière — a night at the Comédie Française is likely to confuse more than entertain. What's a traveling theater fan to do? Fear not — English speakers of all types flock to Paris. Because Paris is just a hop, skip, and Eurostar Channel Tunnel train away from London, some of that city's finest actors have found their way across the Channel and into the city's English-language theater community, where they've joined up with American, Australian, and even some bilingual French *confrères* (colleagues). Productions may not be plentiful, but quality is high, and a wide range of styles is offered.

Summer is a good time to catch English-language theater in Paris. The **Théâtre de Nesle,** 8 rue de Nesle, 6e (☎ **01-46-34-61-04;** Métro: St-Michel), or the **Théâtre des Déchargeurs,** 3 rue des Déchargeurs, 1er (☎ **01-42-36-00-02;** Métro: Châtelet), sometimes stages English-language plays. Or, for comedy in English, try **Laughing Matters,** in the historic Hôtel du Nord, 102 quai de Jemmapes, 10e (☎ **01-53-19-98-98;** Métro: Jacques Bonsergent). This company is thriving; the line-ups are always terrific, featuring award-winning comics from the United States, the United Kingdom, Ireland, and Australia. Shows start at 8:30 p.m.; admission is 15.30€ and 18.30€ (depending on seat location) at the door.

Your easiest (and cheapest) ticket is the weekly play reading at the **Café de Flore,** 172 bd. St-Germain, 6e (☎ **01-45-48-55-26;** Métro: St-Germain-des-Prés). Every Monday night at 8:15, **Brava Productions** rounds up a group of talented actors to present works by authors such as Tom Stoppard, David Mamet, and George Bernard Shaw. The evening is free, although you may end up paying 4€ for a cup of coffee. The company also does full-blown productions in English at various theaters around town. Plays presented include *Love Letters, Waiting for Godot,* and *A Girl's Guide to Chaos.*

Other English-language theaters include **Dear Conjunction** (☎ **01-42-62-35-00**), known for its interpretations of Harold Pinter, and **Paris Festival Theatre Company** (☎ **01-53-01-45-22**), which perform musicals. You can find listings for English-language productions in the *Paris Voice* or the *TimeOut Paris* section of *Pariscope* — just be sure to call the theater ahead of time to double-check the curtain time.

And don't forget: Some theater isn't meant to be understood. In fact, sometimes not understanding the language can actually be a bonus. Several well-known avant-garde theater companies are located in Paris, including **Les Bouffes du Nord** (☎ **01-46-07-34-50**), run by the legendary Peter Brook, and **Le Théâtre du Soleil** (☎ **01-43-74-24-08**), known for its stunning adaptations of both classics and original works. Even though these performances are usually in French, the scope of these productions is so large, and the visuals are so profound, you may not even notice that you haven't understood a single word.

Chapter 23

The Performing Arts

In This Chapter

▶ Getting the latest performance info

▶ Seeing the best opera and ballet

▶ Experiencing Paris's world-famous cabarets

Composers Bizet and Offenbach staged operas in Paris, and the city welcomed Diaghilev, who formed the *Ballet Russes*. It's no wonder — Paris is a cultured city with citizens who enjoy enlightening themselves, repeatedly selling out performances in advance. The Opéra Bastille has revived with great success such classics as *The Marriage of Figaro, The Tales of Hoffman* (*Les Contes d'Hoffman*), and *Swan Lake*. This chapter helps you find out what's going on and then gets you there.

Finding Out What's On and Getting Tickets

Several local publications provide up-to-the-minute listings of performances and other evening entertainment. *Pariscope: Une Semaine de Paris* (0.40€) is a weekly guide with thorough listings of movies, plays, ballet, art exhibits, clubs, and more, and contains an English-language insert with selected listings. It can be found at any newsstand. *L'Officiel des Spectacles* (0.35€) is another weekly guide in French. *Paris Nuit* (3.05€) is a French monthly that contains good articles and listings. You can pick up the free music monthlies, *La Terrasse* and *Cadences,* outside concert venues. The *Paris Free Voice* is a free monthly publication that spotlights events of interest to English speakers, including poetry readings, plays, and literary evenings at English-language bookstores and libraries. You can find it at cybercafés and English-language bookstores.

You can also get information on the Web from the **French Government Tourist Office** (www.francetourism.com), the **Office de Tourisme et de Congrès de Paris** (www.paris-touristoffice.com), and the **Maison de la France** (www.franceguide.com). Likewise, try **Culture Kiosque** (www.culturekiosque.com) for excellent magazine-style sites about opera and dance, including schedules, reviews, and phone numbers for ordering tickets. The *Paris Free Voice* also has a Web site (http://parisvoice.com), featuring an events calendar and reviews of current opera, dance, and theater.

Ticket prices in this chapter are approximate; costs vary, depending on who is performing what on which day of the week. Call the theaters for information, or consult *Pariscope* and other entertainment listings. Many concert, theater, and dance tickets are sold through **FNAC** department stores and at the box office. You can find a dozen or so FNAC outlets throughout Paris; the most prominent is 74 av. des Champs-Elysées (Métro: George V). You can also reserve by phone (☎ **08-92-68-36-22;** 0.34€/min.) Monday through Friday from 9 a.m. to 8 p.m., Saturday from 10 a.m. to 5 p.m. **TicketNet** (Internet: www.ticketnet.fr), in French and English, also sells tickets to cultural events (☎ **08-92-69-70-73;** 0.34€/min.).

Listening to Classical Music and the Symphony

Classical music concerts occur throughout the year, and many of them are quite affordable. Look for flyers at churches announcing schedule times, prices, and locations.

More than a dozen Parisian churches regularly schedule inexpensive or free organ recitals and concerts. Among them are **Notre-Dame** (☎ **01-42-32-16-70;** Métro: Cité); **St-Eustache,** 1 rue Montmartre, 1er (☎ **01-42-33-77-87;** Métro: Châtelet); **St-Sulpice,** place St-Sulpice (☎ **01-46-33-21-78;** Métro: St-Sulpice), which has an amazing eight-columned pipe organ; **St-Germain-des-Prés,** place St-Germain-des-Prés (☎ **01-55-42-81-33;** Métro: St-Germain-des-Prés); the **Madeleine,** place de la Madeleine (☎ **01-42-65-52-17;** Métro: Madeleine); and **St-Louis en l'Ile,** 19 rue St-Louis-en-l'Ile (☎ **01-44-62-00-55;** Métro: Pont-Marie). In a less magnificent setting, the Sunday concerts at 6 p.m. at the **American Church,** 65 quai d'Orsay (☎ **01-45-56-09-50;** Métro: Invalides), are friendly and inviting.

Free concerts are staged occasionally in the parks and gardens. (See Chapter 2 for a calendar.) **Maison de la Radio,** 116 av. du President Kennedy, 16e (☎ **01-56-40-15-16;** Métro: Kennedy-Radio France), offers free tickets to recordings of some concerts. Tickets are available on the spot an hour before the recording starts. The **Conservatoire National Superieur de Musique** at the Cité de la Musique, 209 av. Jean Jaurés, 19e (☎ **01-40-40-45-45;** Métro: Porte de Pantin), also stages free concerts and ballets performed by students at the conservatory.

Orchestras from across Europe play at the Paris's main concert hall, **Salle Pleyel,** 252 rue du Faubourg-St-Honoré, 8e (☎ **01-45-61-53-00;**

Métro: Ternes). The 2002–2003 season featured the Royal Philharmonic Orchestra of Stockholm performing Mahler and Prokofiev, among others, and the Philharmonic Orchestra of Berlin performing Mahler and Haydn. Tickets range from 30€ to 170€.

The **Théâtre Mogador,** 25 rue de Mogador, 9e (☎ **01-56-35-12-00;** Métro: Trinité, Chausée d'Antin, St-Lazare), is the new home of the Orchestre de Paris, which used to be based in the Salle Pleyel. The orchestra, directed by Christoph Eschenbach, performed "Brahms: A New Messiah of Art," and Berlioz's "Te Deum" during the 2002–2003 season. Tickets range from 10€ to 65€; chamber music concerts cost 10€.

Enjoying Opera and Ballet

Jessye Norman, performing one act of *La Voix Humaine* and *Erwartung,* was one of the draws of the 2002–2003 season at **Châtelet, Théâtre Musical de Paris,** 1 place du Châtelet, 1e (☎ **01-40-28-28-40;** Internet: www.chatelet-theatre.com; Métro: Châtelet). Tickets for opera and ballet range from 8€ to 130€; tickets for concerts and recitals are 12€ to 76€. The box office is open daily from 10 a.m. to 7 p.m. Phone and Internet reservations can be made for a 2€ charge.

You can see the national opera and ballet troupes perform at both the radiant **Palais Garnier,** place de l'Opéra, 9e (☎ **08-92-89-90-90** at 0.34€/min. for reservations; Fax: 01-40-01-25-60; Internet: www.opera-de-paris.fr; Métro: Opéra; RER: Auber) and the ultramodern **Opéra National de Bastille** (see the next paragraph). The Palais Garnier conducts more ballet performances, and the Opéra Bastille puts on more opera. The Palais had an eclectic 2002–2003 program schedule with such operas as the surrealist *Juliette ou la Cle des Songes* and Rossini's Cinderella tale, *Cenerentola. Casanova* was one of the highlights of the Garnier's ballet season, and so were dances by Jerome Robbins and Roland Petit. Tickets are priced from 7€ for seats that have little or no visibility to 109€. Reserve by phone up to four weeks in advance and buy at the ticket windows for performances up to 14 days in advance (including same-day tickets). Making reservations online or by phone adds a 3€ surcharge. The box office is open Monday through Saturday from 11:00 a.m. to 6:30 p.m.

The **Opéra National de la Bastille** (☎ **08-92-89-90-90** at 0.34€/min. for reservations; Fax: 01-40-01-25-60; Internet: www.opera-de-paris.fr; Métro: Bastille) offers first-class comfort, and magnificent acoustics at each level of the auditorium, although Parisians still think the building is a badly designed eyesore. The opera house is located at the place de la Bastille; at night, young adults crowd the steps, showing off their skateboarding moves, talking on cellphones, and flirting. *Les Contes d'Hoffman* and *Boris Gudonov* were just two of the performances scheduled here for the 2002–2003 season, and so were ballet favorites like *La*

Lac des Cygnes (*Swan Lake*). Tickets cost 7€ for limited or no visibility seats to 109€. Reserve by phone up to four weeks in advance and buy at the ticket windows for performances up to 14 days in advance (including same-day tickets). Making reservations online or by phone requires a 3€ surcharge. The box office is open Monday through Saturday from 11:00 a.m. to 6:30 p.m.

The **Opéra-Comique/Salle Favart,** 5 rue Favart, 2e (☎ **08-25-00-00-58** for reservations; Fax: 01-49-26-05-93; Internet: www.opera-comique.com; Métro: Richelieu Drouot), offers wonderful musical theater in the Salle Favart, a more intimate venue (the auditorium is so small you can hear people whispering onstage) than its opera hall counterparts. Jerome Savary is musical director. Highly entertaining shows that ran during the 2002–2003 season included *La Vie Parisienne,* a musical about Offenbach's life in Paris, and *La Toujours Belle et La Toute Petite Bete,* based lightly on *Beauty and the Beast.* Tickets are priced from 7€ to 90€ depending on the performance. The box office is open Monday through Saturday from 9 a.m. to 9 p.m., and Sunday from 11 a.m. to 7 p.m.

Spending an Evening at a French Cabaret

Although the club names Lido, Crazy Horse Saloon, and Moulin Rouge may conjure up images of performances by Edith Piaf or Maurice Chevalier, today it's the topless cancan dancers who draw in the crowds. The dancers are often overshadowed by light shows, special effects, and recorded music, but if you're expecting to see lots of flesh in today's Parisian revues, you won't be disappointed. The shows are highly overrated and very expensive but continue to be a huge attraction for tourists.

When seeing a Parisian cabaret show, have dinner somewhere else and save yourself some cash. For the money you'd spend at the cabaret, you can have an absolutely fabulous meal at one of the pricier suggestions in Chapter 14. Be aware that none of the cabaret shows is suitable for children and that every other member of the audience may be from another country — these are some of the least "Parisian" experiences you can have while still being in Paris.

The sexiest acts are at **Crazy Horse, Paris,** 12 av. George V, 8e (☎ **01-47-23-32-32;** Internet: www.lecrazyhorseparis.com; Métro: George V). Dancers, who have names like Chica Boum, Pussy Duty-Free, and Zany Zizanie, appear on swing seats or slithering and writhing in cages — you get the picture. Cover and two drinks cost from 49€ to 90€, with additional drinks from 20€. Two shows nightly at 8:30 and 11:00 p.m., with an additional show April 1 through June 30 on Saturday at 10:15 p.m.

At the **Lido,** 116 av. des Champs-Elysées, 8e (☎ **01-40-76-56-10;** Internet: www.lido.fr; Métro: George V), award-winning chef Paul Bocuse designed the above-average menu, but it still isn't worth the money to dine here. Its revue, *C'est Magique,* offers "flying" dancers, and an ascending stage that periodically delivers feathered women, fountains, and an ice rink, as well as high-tech laser lighting and video projections. Other acts include a magician who performs rabbit tricks. The show with a half-bottle of champagne is 90€ on Friday and Saturday, and 80€ from Sunday to Thursday. Dinner with a half-bottle of champagne costs 160€. Two shows nightly at 10 p.m. and midnight.

Probably the most famous of the cabarets is the **Moulin Rouge,** place Blanche, Montmartre, 18e (☎ **01-53-09-82-82;** Internet: www.moulin rouge.fr; Métro: place-Blanche). The place has been packing in crowds since 1889, and singers such as Edith Piaf, Yves Montand, and Charles Aznavour made their reputations here. Even Frank Sinatra performed here. The show, *Féerie,* features comedy, animal, and magic acts with the requisite scantily clad women bumping and grinding around the stage. A bar seat and two drinks cost 89€ for the 9 p.m. show, 79€ for the 11 p.m. show. Dinner is available at the 9 p.m. show and costs 125€ to 155€; you must arrive for dinner by 7 p.m.

Gustav Eiffel designed the building of the **Paradis Latin,** 28 rue Cardinal-Lemoine, 5e (☎ **01-43-25-28-28;** Internet: www.paradislatin.fr; Métro: Cardinal-Lemoine), the club that's probably the most French of the cabarets. A genial master encourages audience participation during a show that's less gimmick-filled than the others. To save money, forego dinner for the lower-priced Champagne Revue, which includes a half-bottle of bubbly and costs 75€; dinner plus show packages range from 109€ to 200€. Performances are Wednesday through Monday, with a 9:30 p.m. showtime.

Chapter 24

Hitting the Clubs and Bars

• •

In This Chapter

▶ Getting the lowdown on the latest hot spots

▶ Searching out your kind of music and dancing

▶ Unwinding over cocktails

• •

*P*aris may not be another "city that never sleeps" — the Métro closes at a "mere" 1 a.m. — but you can still paint the town a lovely shade of *rouge*. Whether you want to spend the evening chatting over cocktails, chatting up the beautiful people, or dancing till you drop, Paris has a bar or club for you. Bars usually close around 2 a.m., but most clubs don't open until 11 p.m., and the music doesn't stop pumping until dawn. Check the listings in *Night Life, Nova* magazine, or the English *TimeOut Paris* section of the weekly *Pariscope* magazine for special theme nights at clubs.

Heading to the Hot Spots for Cool Jazz

The city's longstanding love affair with American jazz music dates back to 1918, when James Reese Europe and his band were a hit on a tour of Paris. Paris's warm welcome to black musicians led legions of them to flee segregation at home and come to Paris to perform — and often to stay. Montmartre became home to a number of thriving jazz clubs, among them Bricktop's, run by the black American singer of the same name. Cole Porter's songs debuted at Bricktop's, which eventually became a regular stop for jazz musicians on tour. A number of American musicians were more famous in Paris than they ever were in the United States; Sidney Bechet, a clarinetist, is remembered in Paris with awe. Today, the Paris jazz scene is still vibrant as new generations develop a taste for the sound. Look through the current *Pariscope* for the artists you admire. If you don't care who's playing, and you're just out for a night of good music, you can stop by the following clubs.

A noisy crowd of foreigners and locals appreciates **Caveau de la Hûchette,** 5 rue de la Hûchette, 5e (☎ 01-43-26-65-05; Métro or RER: St-Michel), for a rollicking good time. Cover is 9€ Monday through Thursday and before 9 p.m. Friday through Sunday; it's 13€ Friday through Sunday between 9 p.m. and 1 a.m. Music starts at 9:30 p.m. **Baiser Sale,** 56 rue des Lombards, 1er (☎ 01-42-33-37-71; Métro: Châtelet), is a small space that gets crowded with fans of fusion jazz, funk, and Caribbean music. The cover on Tuesday and Thursday through Sunday varies from 10€ to 13€. On Monday and Wednesday nights admission is free. The club is open daily from 7 p.m. to 6 a.m.

The crowd is casual and down to earth, and the jazz is some of France's most interesting at **Duc des Lombards,** 42 rue des Lombards, 1er (☎ 01-42-33-22-88; Métro: Châtelet–Les Halles). Cover is 15.24€. You can dine and drink at **Le Petit Journal Saint-Michel,** 71 bd. St-Michel, 5e (☎ 01-43-26-28-59; Métro: Cluny-La-Sorbonne, RER: Luxembourg), with its warm and relaxed French atmosphere. Recent jazz acts included Les Dixieland Seniors, the Paris Swing Orchestra, and the Claude Luter Orchestra. Cover is 15.25€, or you can do dinner plus a show for 30€ to 63€.

New Morning, 7–9 rue des Petites-Ecuries, 10e (☎ 01-45-23-56-39; Métro: Château-d'Eau), is one of Paris's best jazz clubs, and the best from around the world perform here. Recent acts included jazz band Blind Boys of Alabama, folk act Faiz al Faiz, and rock group Mighty Mo Rodgers. Cover starts from 16€, depending on the act. With its medieval look and vaulted ceilings, **Slow Club,** 130 rue de Rivoli, 1er (☎ 01-42-33-84-30; Métro: Châtelet–Les Halles), is a dungeon filled with dancers and fans of big American and European artists who perform swing, Dixieland, and classic jazz. Cover is 10.50€. Anything goes at **Le 7 Lézards**, 10 rue des Rosiers 4e (☎ 01-48-87-08-97; Métro: St-Paul) — the more experimental, the better. Depending on the performer, entry is free to 14€. This is the place where jazz musicians go to wind down. Check out the program on the Web at www.7lezards.com.

Listening to Live Music

A bar known for great live gigs (usually free) is **The Chesterfield Café,** 124 rue La Boétie, 8e (☎ 01-42-25-18-06; Métro: Franklin-D-Roosevelt). It's the place to find up-and-coming or just-arrived rock and blues bands, and the occasional oldie. Webb Wilder, Alanis Morissette, and Eagle Eye Cherry have played here. Concerts start at 11:30 p.m. You can also check out Sunday gospel at 2 p.m. Open daily from 10 a.m. to 5 a.m.

Ménilmontant has become known in recent years for its nightlife, and **Cithéa,** 114 rue Oberkampf, 11e (☎ 01-40-21-70-95; Métro: Parmentier or Ménilmontant), is one reason to visit this district not far from the Bastille. Reasonable prices and an eclectic mix of world, jazz, and funk bands play Wednesday through Saturday, and a DJ spins whenever the bands aren't playing. Cover is 6.10€ Wednesday and Thursday and 7.62€ Friday and Saturday (cover includes one drink). Open daily from 9:30 p.m. to 5:00 a.m.

World music acts reign at **La Divan du Monde,** 75 rue des Martyrs, 18e (☎ 01-44-92-77-66; Métro: Pigalle), with everything from Brazilian samba to British pop to Bretagnon folk. Concerts start at 7:30 p.m. Monday through Saturday and at 4:00 p.m. Sunday. On weekends a DJ spins music after the concerts. Cover is 10€ to 20€ depending on the act. Call for closing hours.

La Flèche d'Or, 102 bis rue de Bagnolet, 20e (☎ 01-43-72-04-23; Métro: Alexandre-Dumas), is only two Métro stops from Pére-Lachaise Cemetery (take the 2 to Alexandre-Dumas; see Chapter 16), and worth a visit on the weekend. In another life, it was the Charonne train station, but now it's a restaurant turned music venue on Friday and Saturday nights. You may hear reggae, alternative rock, Celtic rock, or blues rock. Sundays at 5 p.m., a live dance band usually plays salsa or swing, and on other nights there could be, well, anything. This cavernous space pulls in a funky, artsy, racially mixed crowd. Open Tuesday through Sunday from 10 a.m. to 2 a.m. and Monday from 6 p.m. to 2 a.m. Cover ranges from free to 5€ depending on the act.

Getting Down at the Best Dance Clubs

Paris clubs change their programming from night to night. The current fad is the international DJ spinning his or her own mix of house music. If you don't like house, try one of the *bal musettes* (dances), where local bands usually perform. The barges along the Seine in the 13e attract a good mix and play everything from house to blues, and you can have a good, though often crowded, time right on the river. Check the *TimeOut* section in *Pariscope* magazine (in English) for barge concert schedules. Salsa, the hottest trend a few years back, is still going strong. Whether you like dancing to techno, house, salsa, world, classic rock, or swing, you'll find it somewhere in Paris (and legions of Parisians eager to dance with you!).

To club on a budget, go out during the week when cover charges may be (officially or unofficially) waived. Yes, it's sexist, but women often get in free, especially if they're dressed in something slinky, low-cut, or short (or all three). Black clothes are de rigueur for men and women, and the later you go — or earlier in the morning as the case may be — the more fashionable.

Many nightclubs accept reservations, so if you're worried about getting past the bouncers, give your club of choice a call.

The Irish light ship (a boat that lights the path for other ships) **Batofar,** 11 quai François Mauriac, 13e (☎ **01-56-29-10-00;** Métro: Bibliothèque François Mitterand or Quai de la Gare), has concerts Tuesday through Sunday, starting around 8 p.m., and the party can go on all night. Drinks are reasonable (3€ to 6€), the clientele are in their 20s, and it can get crowded, but it's still a bunch of sweaty fun. Music can be anything from drum-and-bass to British pop. Open Tuesday to Sunday; hours vary (check listings in *Pariscope*). Cover ranges from 5€ to 12€ depending on the band or DJ for the night. A small snack bar is onboard.

You can catch a monthly *bal* (dance) and have a ball at **Elysée Montmartre,** 72 bd. De Rochechouart, 18e (☎ **01-42-23-46-50;** Métro: Anvers), a club that serves the dual function of disco and major concert hall. Moby was a recent headliner, adding his name to a long list of illustrious acts that include Björk, U2, and the Red Hot Chili Peppers. Dance music is usually house; the monthly *bals* usually have live local bands. Check *Pariscope* for events and prices. Dances are open 11 p.m. to 5 a.m. Cover charges vary from 12€ to 18€ for dancing and more for concerts.

One of the best things about **Le Wax,** 15 rue Daval, 11e (☎ **01-40-21-16-16;** Métro: Bastille), is the price — free. You have to really like house music; the club is the premiere place for DJs who spin it all night long. The decor is very *A Clockwork Orange,* with plastic bubbles on the walls, yellow plastic couches, and lots of crimson and orange. Open Monday through Saturday from 10 p.m. to 4 a.m.

La Coupole, 102 bd. du Montparnasse, 14e (☎ **01-43-27-56-00;** Métro: Montparnasse-Bienvenüe), has a basement dance hall — a retro venue with plush banquettes and old-fashioned sounds that's a big draw for out-of-towners. Come on Friday for house; Tuesdays are salsa nights, with dance classes starting at 8:30 p.m. for 22€ (including a drink). Regular cover is 16€ on Saturday from 10 p.m. to 5 a.m., on Tuesday from 9:30 p.m. to 3:00 a.m., and Friday 10 p.m. to 5 a.m.

At **La Java,** 105 rue du Faubourg-du-Temple, 10e (☎ **01-42-02-20-52;** Métro: Belleville), a diverse crowd comes to dance without restraint to mostly Cuban and Brazilian music, played by a live band on Friday and Saturday nights. If you have a taste for something fun, funky, and very authentic, and you like Latin music, this charming old dance hall may be your great night out. Salsa classes are in session Thursday nights. Cover on Thursday is 0.76€; on Friday and Saturday the cover is 15.24€. Open 9:30 p.m. to dawn.

The huge tri-level **La Locomotive,** 90 bd. de Clichy, 18e (☎ **08-36-69-69-28;** Métro: place-Clichy), is popular with American students, and is especially busy on Sundays. People dance to rock and techno, although occasionally metal bands pay a visit. This place is very big; and in the *sous-sol* (basement, which I think is the coolest of the three levels), you can even see the remnants of an old railway line (hence the name). The

Bar Americain looks more Roman with fake statuary and columns crowned by lions. Beers and Evian start at a high 9€ during the week, 10€ on weekends. Cover Monday through Thursday and Sunday is 12€ with one drink, 16€ with two drinks, and 19€ with three drinks; cover on Friday and Saturday night is 20€ with one drink. Women get in free on Sunday until 1 a.m. Open 11 p.m. to 5 a.m.

Formerly one of the most famous rock dance clubs in Paris, **Le Gibus,** 18 rue du Faubourg-du-Temple, 11e (☎ **01-47-00-78-88;** Métro: République), changed its style to DJ-spun 1990s music, although Crystal Waters was a recent live music act. Wednesday nights are Club Trance, where entry is free and atmosphere is psychedelic. Cover is 11€. Soft drinks are 3€, alcoholic beverages start at 6€. Open Tuesday through Sunday from 10:30 p.m. to noon.

Queen, 102 av. des Champs-Elysées, 8e (☎ **01-53-89-08-89;** Métro: George V), is one of the hottest clubs in town, with nightly crowds so thick you can find it difficult to get a drink. The clientele is about two-thirds gay. Having a beautiful face and body, or at least the ability to disguise your faults with great clothes helps you get past the strict drag queens at the door. Women usually get in only with male friends. Cover (including one drink, with or without alcohol) is 10€ Sunday through Thursday; Friday and Saturday cover (including one drink, with or without alcohol) is 18€. Open daily midnight to 7 a.m., 8 a.m. on weekends.

Kicking Back for Classy Cocktails

If you're looking for a quiet, romantic place to unwind with a drink — or if you're on the prowl for where the hip, hot folks hang out — these places should fit the bill. Most bars and lounges in Paris open daily at 9 p.m., but no one arrives until after midnight. They generally close around 4 a.m.

At **Alcazar,** 62 rue Mazarine, 6e (☎ **01-53-10-19-99;** Métro: Odéon), elements of traditional brasserie style, such as banquettes and mirrors, are slicked up and mixed with innovations such as a glassed-in kitchen theatrically installed along the left wall. The comfortable upstairs bar is great for a view over the downstairs restaurant, once one of Paris's hottest eateries.

The atmosphere at the **China Club,** 50 rue de Charenton, 12e (☎ **01-43-43-82-02;** Métro: Bastille), is one of hushed elegance. The Colonial-decorated restaurant just a few steps from the Bastille is a popular nighttime attraction. If you hate cigars, avoid the trendy upstairs *fumoir* (smoking room). All cocktails are well made (7.50€), but the Chinese food is overpriced.

It's not hip, it's not even new, but **Harry's New York Bar,** 5 rue Daunou, 2e, (☎ **01-53-05-90-00;** Métro: Opéra or Pyramides), definitely serves a classy cocktail. In fact, it's one of Europe's most famous bars, and as popular today as it was in the time of that notorious Lost Generation of writers who really knew how to ring up a bar tab. The Bloody Mary was said to have been invented here, and the selection of whiskeys is amazing. Make sure you step downstairs if only to look at the 1930s Piano Bar resembling the inside of a cozy yacht. It isn't cheap, of course — the lowest priced alcohol (beer) is 6.80€ a glass.

Beautiful people dressed in black come to **La Fabrique,** 53 rue du Faubourg St-Antoine, 11e (☎ **01-43-07-67-07;** Métro: Bastille), a sleek dark bar and restaurant, to drink at the minimalist bar and eat the delicious Alsatian specialty, *Flammekueche* — large, square, thin-crusted pizzas topped with cream, herbs, and toppings of your choice, including salmon, ham, and goat cheese. Although the bar is open until around 5 a.m., depending on the crowds, food is served only until midnight. Be ready to stand in line on the weekends, and look out for private parties when the restaurant is closed to the public.

At **La Veranda,** 40 av. George V, 8e (☎ **01-53-57-49-49;** Métro: George V), the elegant clientele is outfitted from nearby shops on the chic rue du Faubourg–St. Honoré. Glossy wood floors and paneled walls provide an unobtrusive setting for the glamorous clientele to sip expensive drinks. Drink prices start at 10€.

At **The Lizard Lounge,** 18 rue du Bourg-Tibourg, 4e (☎ **01-42-72-81-34;** Métro: Hôtel-de-Ville), the music is loud, but the heavy-gauge steel balcony overlooking the main bar offers a chance for quieter conversation. This stylish but easygoing bar is a pleasant place to hang out with an arty, international crowd. You can also come early in the evening for a reasonably priced light meal prepared in the open kitchen. A DJ spins dance music in the refurbished basement Wednesday through Saturday.

The huge downstairs restaurant at **Man Ray,** 34 rue Marbeuf, 8e (☎ **01-56-88-36-36;** Métro: Franklin-D-Roosevelt), is dominated by statues of two winged Asian goddesses who appear concerned — possibly about the food. But don't visit for dinner, have a drink at the upstairs bar while listening to jazz. Take note that as the restaurant winds down around 11 p.m., the music takes on a harder edge, and a sleek international crowd stands shoulder-to-shoulder along the curving bar. American artist and photographer Man Ray's photos adorn several walls. Celebrity owners include Sean Penn, Johnny Depp, and John Malkovich. Drinks start at 5€.

Part VII
The Part of Tens

In this part . . .

*O*kay, these little extras won't make or break your trip, but they may just make it a little more fun. In Chapter 25, you can find out where to make like Manet and have *dejeuner sur l'herbe* — in other words, ten places to go for a fabulous picnic. And in Chapter 26, I narrow the field to ten wonderful books that have Paris at their heart — books that will move you, thrill you, and inspire you to create your very own Paris adventure.

Chapter 25

Ten Great Places for a Picnic

In This Chapter

▶ Living the "a loaf of bread, a jug of wine, and thou" dream

▶ Finding that special place to enjoy a meal in *plein air*

*P*aris abounds with parks and green spaces to picnic in. (The city is home to so many of these expanses that I couldn't limit this list to ten.) You can get delicious meats, sweets, and wine (see Chapter 15 for recommendations) from plenty of open-air markets, *traiteurs* (gourmet food shops), and grocery stores. You won't need to worry about tipping, dressing to dine, or speaking the language, and best of all, you can lay down for a snooze right after you eat.

A word of advice, however: Some parks, such as the Luxembourg Gardens or the Tuileries, jealously guard their lawns; you may have to walk a bit before you find a spot where you can spread out on the grass. But chairs are everywhere — some even have reclining backs! — and you can pull a few chairs right up to a fountain and eat amidst the spray from the water. If this seems too public, your best bet is to try the vast Bois de Vincennes or Bois de Boulogne where you can picnic nearly anywhere. Don't forget to clean up afterward.

Banks of the Seine near the Musée de Sculpture en Plein Air

Wander amid the sculptures before you spread out your meal in this waterside park that's really a museum (the name ***Musée de Sculpture en Plein Air*** translates to *Open-Air Sculpture Museum*). Twenty-nine artists created abstract works that compliment the meditative mood that the banks of the Seine inspire (kids still climb all over them). Sculptures include César, and Zadkine. (Métro: Sully-Morland or Gare d'Austerlitz.)

Bois de Boulogne

A former royal forest and hunting ground, the Bois de Boulogne is a vast reserve of more than 2,200 acres with jogging paths, horseback riding paths, cycling (rentals are available), and boating on two lakes. The **Longchamp** and **Auteuil racecourses** are located here, as is the **Jardin Shakespeare** in the Pré Catelan, a garden containing many of the plants and herbs mentioned in Shakespeare's plays. (Métro: Porte Maillot, Porte Dauphine, or Porte Auteuil.)

Bois de Vincennes

Rent canoes or bikes or visit the *Parc Zoologique* (zoo) and petting zoo after your picnic on the extensive grounds at the Bois de Vincennes, which also has a Buddhist center, complete with temple, and the Chateau de Vincennes, where early monarchs like Charles V and Henri III sought refuge from wars. The **Parc Floral de Paris** (☎ 01-43-43-92-95) is here with its spectacular amphitheatre (and jazz concerts on summer Saturdays), a butterfly garden, library, and miniature golf. (Métro: Porte Dorée or Chateau de Vincennes.)

Jardin des Tuileries

The Tuileries is a restful space in the center of Paris that houses the Orangerie and the Jeu de Paume at its western edge and plays home to 40 beautiful Maillol bronzes scattered among the trees to its east. This spot is the city's most formal garden, with pathways and fountains that invite you to sit on the metal chairs provided and munch on picnic treats while cooling off in the breezes off the waters.

The name means *tuiles* (tiles) — the clay here was once used to make roof tiles. The gardens were originally laid out in the 1560s for Catherine de Medici in front of the Tuileries Palace, which burned down in 1871. In the 17th century, landscape artist André Le Nôtre, creator of the gardens at Versailles, redesigned a large section. (Métro: Tuileries or Concorde.)

Jardin du Luxembourg

The 6e arrondissement's **Jardin du Luxembourg** is one of the most beloved parks in Paris. You can sit on metal chairs near the boat pond or spread out on grass open to picnickers directly across from the Palais de Luxembourg, on the park's south edge. Not far from the

Sorbonne and just south of the Latin Quarter, the large park is popular with students and children who love it for its playground, toy-boat pond, pony rides, and puppet theater. Besides pools, fountains, and statues of queens and poets, tennis and *boules* (lawn bowling) courts are available. See whether you can find the miniature Statue of Liberty. (Métro: Odéon; RER: Luxembourg.)

Parc de Belleville

The Parc de Belleville is a wonderful place to visit with children, watch the sun set across western Paris, or nosh on a baguette with *saucisson sec* (cured sliced sausage, a bit like French salami). The park has fountains, a children's play area, an open-air theater with concerts during the summer, rock formations, and grottoes that evoke the long-ago days when the hill was a strategic point to fight enemies like Attila the Hun. Beds of roses and other seasonal flowers line the walks, and views of the city's Left Bank become more pronounced the higher up the terraced pathways you go.

Access the park by taking the rue Piat off rue Belleville and enter through an iron gate spelling out the words Villa Ottoz. A curved path leads you to tree-lined promenades (more than 500 trees are here) with the first of the magnificent Left Bank views peeping through the spaces between pretty houses. Take the Métro to Pyrénées; then walk down rue de Belleville and turn left onto rue Piat, where you see arched iron gates leading into the park. You can also take the Métro to Courrones, cross bd. de Belleville, and turn left onto rue Julien Lacroix where another entrance is located.

Parc de la Villette

Picnic at Parc de la Villette in the summer while watching an outdoor movie or listening to a concert. Afterward, you and your kids can visit the children's museum, the **Cité des Sciences et de l'Industrie** (Museum of Science and Industry), and the **Musée de la Musique** (Music Museum), located on the grounds. This modern park has a series of theme gardens and includes an exotic bamboo garden and a garden featuring steam and water jets. Scattered throughout the park are playgrounds and other attractions (see Chapter 20). The most fun way to get here is to take a canal trip from Pont l'Arsenal or the Musée d'Orsay (see Chapter 18). You can also take the Métro to Porte de la Villette.

Parc des Buttes-Chaumont

Parc des Buttes-Chaumont is one of the four man-made parks that Napoléon III commissioned to resemble the English gardens he grew to love during his exile in England. Built on the site of a former gypsum (a mineral used to make plaster) quarry and a centuries-old dump, it features cliffs, waterfalls, a lake, and a cave topped by a temple. You have plenty of places to lay out your picnic spread here. (Métro: Buttes-Chaumont.)

Parc du Champ de Mars

Once a parade ground for French troops, Parc du Champ de Mars is a vast green esplanade beneath the Eiffel Tower, extending to the École Militaire (Military Academy), at its southeast end, where Napoléon was once a student. You have plenty of places to relax and contemplate the tower. After your picnic, take a boat tour of the Seine from the nearby Bateaux Mouches. (Métro: Bir-Hakeim.)

Parc Monceau

The painter Carmontelle designed several structures for Parc Monceau, including a Dutch windmill, a Roman temple, a covered bridge, a waterfall, a farm, medieval ruins, and a pagoda. Garnerin, the world's first parachutist, landed here. In the mid-19th century, the park was redesigned in the English style. A favorite place for author Marcel Proust to stroll, the park contains Paris's largest tree, an Oriental plane tree with a circumference of almost 23 feet. (Métro: Ternes.)

Square du Vert Galant

Descend the stairs near the middle of Pont Neuf (near the Pont Neuf tour boats) to this beautiful spot commemorating Paris's favorite king, Henri IV. You're at the very tip of Ile de la Cité, in the middle of the Seine. You can spread out on a bench under the trees and enjoy the stunning views of both banks and the river stretching out ahead. The square is 23 feet lower than the rest of the island; this was the original level of Paris during the Gallo-Roman period. At sunset, this is a popular spot for romantics.

Chapter 26

Ten Great Books about Paris

In This Chapter

▶ Reading to prepare for your trip

▶ Savoring some great fiction (and nonfiction)

*I*n keeping with the name of this part of the book, this list is made up of only ten books, but it could easily contain three times as many. Scores of authors have lived (and still live) in Paris, and all have been enchanted by the city's charms (or in the case of George Orwell, its seedier side). As a result, you have countless terrific books to enjoy. This is a subjective list. I'm not saying these are the ten best books ever written about Paris, they're just an excellent place to start. I have listed them alphabetically by author.

"The Piano Shop on the Left Bank" by Thad Carhart

Thad Carhart, an American writer living in Paris, began noticing the funny little shop, Desforges Pianos, while walking his children to school. Was it a piano repair shop? Or did the proprietor sell pianos? When Carhart visits the first time, the gruff owner refuses to let him in. It seems that the only way Carhart can gain entry is if someone introduces him, and he finally manages it. Once entry is secured, Carhart meets a most unusual society of piano lovers, and discovers his own love of music. He recounts this story of the shop, music, and the only city where such a magical place could exist in this wonderful read.

"A Moveable Feast" by Ernest Hemingway

A chronicle of the author's years with his first wife, Hadley, in 1920s Paris, these stories encompass a whole cast of famed literary expatriates: F. Scott and Zelda Fitzgerald, James Joyce, Ezra Pound,

T.S. Eliot, Gertrude Stein, and more. Hemingway describes everything so vividly — from his chilly writing studio on rue Cardinal Lemoine, to his marathon writing sessions at Closerie des Lilas — that you may want to take the book with you to see whether his destinations still exist (many of them do). In the end, however, this book is a tribute to his love for Hadley.

Written at the end of Hemingway's life and published with the permission of his fourth wife, Mary, after he committed suicide, the book exudes a palpable nostalgia for happy, magical memories.

"The American" by Henry James

A *nouveau riche* American visiting Europe falls in love with a beautiful but impoverished Frenchwoman of nobility, shocking her family when he proposes. This novel of manners is wry and sometimes humorous, and a well-observed social portrait. The story takes place in late 19th-century Paris, giving the reader a feel for Paris of a bygone era. Readers will be happy that many sights James described in this novel still exist as they did then.

"Le Divorce" by Diane Johnson

An American woman visits her distraught pregnant sister, who has just learned her husband wants to leave her for another woman. With treachery, a scandalous affair, and a murder, this comedy of manners is a fun way to learn how bourgeois Parisians live.

"The Pleasing Hour" by Lily King

A young American woman travels to Paris to be an *au pair* to a family with three children. But is she really fleeing something else? An evocative story about a young woman's search for a family and ultimately herself. Set mostly in Paris, the author realistically describes Paris and the life of some of its late 20th-century upper class.

"Honeymoon" by Patrick Modiano

Set in the 1940s during World War II, this novel is about a documentary filmmaker who becomes fed up with his life and pretends to leave Paris on assignment. He remains in his neighborhood and reflects back to Paris of 20 years before when he met the love of his life.

"Down and Out in Paris and London" by George Orwell

Many know George Orwell for his savvy political critiques *Animal Farm* and *1984*, but this, his first book, has a more autobiographical bent. An unemployed writer becomes one of the desperately poor of Paris and London in the 1920s, working as a dishwasher in a series of hotels and restaurants. A shockingly sad, funny, and scary look at society and poverty — a piece of Paris's less palatable past.

"Paris Noir: African Americans in the City of Light" by Tyler Stovall

This is a terrific history of black Americans in Paris, from World War I when black soldiers first discovered a social equality they had never before experienced, through the jazz age, which made stars out of performers and club owners. Stovall looks at some of America's most famous African-American expatriates — including Josephine Baker, Richard Wright, and James Baldwin — who found new and better lives in the City of Light.

"The Way I Found Her" by Rose Tremain

Lewis, a young British teenager, travels to Paris's 8e arrondissement during the 1980s with his mother, who is hired to translate a romance novel for a Russian expatriate writer. The boy falls in love with Valentina, the writer. His mother, Alice, falls in love with a roofer. And when Valentina is kidnapped, Lewis takes it upon himself to solve the crime in this poignant mystery/coming-of-age tale.

"The Flâneur" by Edmund White

A *flâneur* is someone who strolls, who ambles through a city without apparent purpose but is secretly attuned to the history of the place and in covert search for adventure. White lived in Paris for 16 years, and he shares lesser-known tales of the city: the history of Jews in France, of black Americans in Paris, even of his own gay cruising. It's a short but terrific read.

Part VIII

Appendixes

"I know it's a wedding present from your niece, I just don't know why you had to wear it to the Louvre."

In this part . . .

1 tucked some really useful information into these appendixes. Appendix A — the Quick Concierge — gives you straight-to-the-point, bare-bones info on how to contact your embassy, find a pharmacy, cash a check, and generally take care of business. Appendix B is a glossary of some of the French terms you may need. It features pronunciation guides so you can at least attempt to sound like a native.

Quick Concierge

* * *

*H*ow do you use the telephones? Where can you find your embassy or consulate? The Quick Concierge offers answers to a variety of "Where do I . . . ?" and "How do I . . . ?" questions.

Fast Facts: Paris

American Express

The big Paris office, 11 rue Scribe, 9e (☎ 01-47-14-50-00; Métro: Opéra Chaussée-d'Antin or Havre-Caumartin; RER: Auber), is open weekdays from 9 a.m. to 6 p.m. The bank is open from 9 a.m. to 5 p.m. Saturday, but the mail pickup window is closed.

ATM Locators

ATMs are widely available. If you'd like a list of ATMs that accept MasterCard or Visa cards before you leave home, ask your bank, or print out lists from the following sites: www.visaeu.com or www.mastercard.com.

Baby Sitters

Check out **Ababa,** 8 av. du Maine, 15e (☎ 01-45-49-46-46), or **Kid Services,** 17 rue Molière, 9e (☎ 01-42-61-90-00). Specify when calling whether you'd like a sitter who speaks English. Also, try the American Church's basement bulletin board where English-speaking (often American) students post notices offering baby-sitting services. The church is located at 65 quai d'Orsay, 7e (☎ 01-45-56-09-50; Métro: Invalides).

Business Hours

The *grands magasins* (department stores) are generally open Monday through Saturday from 9:30 a.m. to 7:00 p.m.; **smaller shops** close for lunch and reopen around 2:00 p.m., but this practice is rarer than it used to be. Many stores stay open until 7:00 p.m. in summer; others are closed Monday, especially in the morning. **Large offices** remain open all day, but some close for lunch. **Banks** are normally open weekdays from 9:00 a.m. to noon and from 1:00 or 1:30 to 4:30 p.m. Some banks also open on Saturday morning. Some currency-exchange booths are open very long hours; see "Currency Exchange," later in this list.

Climate

From May to September you can expect clear sunny days and temperatures in the 70s and 80s (Fahrenheit). But be prepared for rainy or searingly hot summers, too. From late October to April the weather is often gray and misty with a dampness that gets into your bones. Always bring an umbrella. Temperatures average about 45 degrees Fahrenheit in winter, and the low 60s in spring and autumn. *Note:* Ignore the song "April in Paris," and pack layers for your early spring trip to the City of Light. It is often quite chilly.

Collect Calls

For an AT&T operator: ☎ 0800-99-00-11; MCI: ☎ 0800-99-00-19; Sprint: ☎ 0800-99-00-87. See also "Telephone," later in this Appendix.

Credit Cards

Visa, MasterCard, American Express, and the Diner's Club cards are all accepted in Paris, but not at all establishments.

Currency Exchange

Banks and *bureaux de change* (exchange offices) almost always offer better exchange rates than hotels, restaurants, and shops, which should be used only in emergencies. For good rates, without fees or commissions, and quick service, try the **Comptoir de Change Opéra**, 9 rue Scribe, 9e (☎ 01-47-42-20-96; Métro: Opéra; RER: Auber). It is open weekdays from 9:00 a.m. to 6:00 p.m., Saturday from 9:30 a.m. to 4:00 p.m. The bureaux de change at all train stations (except gare de Montparnasse) are open daily; those at 63 av. des Champs-Elysées, 8e (Métro: Franklin-D-Roosevelt), and 140 av. des Champs-Elysées, 8e (Métro: Charles-de-Gaulle–Étoile), keep long hours.

Despite disadvantageous exchange rates and long lines, many people prefer to exchange their money at **American Express** (see the "American Express" listing earlier in this Appendix).

Customs

Non-EU nationals can bring into France duty-free 200 cigarettes or 100 cigarillos or 50 cigars or 250 grams of smoking tobacco; 2 liters of wine and 1 liter of alcohol over 38.80 proof; 50 grams of perfume, one-quarter liter of toilet water; 500 grams of coffee, and 100 grams of tea. Travelers 15 years old and older can also bring in 183€ in other goods; for those 14 and younger, the limit is 91€. **EU citizens** may bring any amount of goods into France as long as it is for their personal use and not for resale.

Returning U.S. citizens who have been away for 48 hours or more are allowed to bring back, once every 30 days, $800 worth of merchandise duty-free. You'll be charged a flat rate of 10% duty on the next $1,000 worth of purchases; on gifts, the duty-free limit is $100. You can't bring fresh food into the United States; canned foods, however, are allowed.

Returning U.K. citizens have no limit on what can be brought back from an EU country as long as the items are for personal use (including gifts), and the necessary duty and tax have been paid. Guidance levels are set at: 800 cigarettes, 200 cigars, 1kg smoking tobacco, 10 liters of spirits, 90 liters of wine, and 110 liters of beer.

Canada allows its citizens a once-a-year C$750 exemption after seven days, and you're allowed to bring back duty-free 200 cigarettes, 1.5 liters of wine or 1.14 liters of liquor, and 50 cigars. In addition, you may mail gifts to Canada from abroad at the rate of C$60 a day, provided they're unsolicited and don't contain alcohol, tobacco, or advertising matter. Write on the package *Unsolicited gift, under $60 value.* All valuables need to be declared on the Y-38 form before departure from Canada, including serial numbers of valuables you already own, such as expensive foreign cameras.

The duty-free allowance in **Australia** is A$400 or, for those younger than 18, A$200. Upon returning to Australia, citizens can bring in 250 cigarettes or 250 grams of loose tobacco, and 1.125 liters of alcohol. If you're returning with valuable goods you already own, such as foreign-made cameras, you need to file form B263.

The duty-free allowance for **New Zealand** is NZ$700. Citizens older than 17 can bring in 200 cigarettes or 50 cigars or 250 grams of tobacco (or a mixture of all three if their combined weight doesn't exceed 250 grams), plus 4.5 liters of wine or beer or 1.125 liters of liquor.

Dentists

You can call your consulate and ask the duty officer to recommend a dentist. For dental emergencies, call **SOS Urgences Stomatologique Dentaire** (☎ 01-43-36-36-00) daily from 9 a.m. to midnight.

Doctors

Call your consulate (see "Embassies and Consulates" later in this list for numbers) and ask the duty officer to recommend a doctor, or call **SOS Médecins** (☎ 01-43-37-77-77), a 24-hour service. Most doctors and dentists speak some English. You can also call for an appointment at the **Centre Médicale Europe,** 44 rue d'Amsterdam (☎ 01-42-81-93-33). Consultations cost about 20€, and specialists are available.

Drugstores

Pharmacies are marked with a green cross and are often upscale, selling toiletries and cosmetics in addition to prescription drugs and over-the-counter remedies. If you're shopping for products other than drugs, buying them elsewhere, such as a *supermarché* (supermarket), is almost always cheaper.

Electricity

The French electrical system runs on 220 volts. Adapters are needed to convert the voltage and fit sockets, and are cheaper at home than they are in Paris. Many hotels have two-pin (in some cases, three-pin) sockets for electric razors. Asking your hotel whether you need an adapter is a good idea before plugging in any electrical appliance.

Embassies and Consulates

If you have a passport, immigration, legal, or other problem, contact your consulate. Call before you go: They often keep strange hours and observe both French and home-country holidays. Here's where to find them: **Australia,** 4 rue Jean-Rey, 15e (☎ 01-40-59-33-00; Métro: Bir-Hakeim); **Canada,** 35 av. Montaigne, 8e (☎ 01-44-43-29-00; Métro:

Franklin-D-Roosevelt or Alma Marceau); **New Zealand,** 7 ter rue Léonard-de-Vinci, 16e (☎ 01-45-01-43-43; Métro: Victor-Hugo); **Consulate of Great Britain,** 18 bis rue d'Anjou, 8e (☎ 01-44-51-31-02; Métro: Madeleine); **Embassy of Ireland,** 4 rue Rude, 16e (☎ 01-44-17-67-00); **United States,** 2 rue St-Florentin, 1er (☎ 01-43-12-22-22); Métro: Concorde).

Emergencies

Call ☎ 17 for the **police.** To report a **fire,** dial ☎ 18. For an **ambulance,** call ☎ 15. For English-language assistance, call **SOS Help** at ☎ 01-47-23-80-80 between 3 and 11 p.m. The main police station, 7 bd. du Palais, 4e (☎ 01-53-71-53-71; Métro: Cité), is open 24 hours a day.

Holidays

See Chapter 2.

Hospitals

Two hospitals with English-speaking staff are the **American Hospital of Paris,** 63 bd. Victor-Hugo, Neuilly-sur-Seine (☎ 01-46-41-25-25), just west of Paris proper (Métro: Les Sablons or Levallois-Perret), and the **Hôpital Franco-Brittanique,** 3 rue Barbes Levallois-Perret (☎ 01-46-39-22-22), just north of Neuilly, across the city line north-west of Paris (Métro: Anatole-France). Note that the American Hospital charges about $600 a day for a room, not including doctor's fees. The emergency department charges more than $60 for a visit, not including tests and x-rays.

Information

Before you go, contact the **French Government Tourist Office,** 444 Madison Ave., 16th floor, New York, NY 10022-6903 (Internet: www.francetourism.com). This office doesn't provide information over the phone. When you arrive, contact **Office de Tourisme de Paris,** 127 av. des Champs-Elysées, 8e (☎ 08-92-68-31-12; 0.34€/min.).

Internet Access

To surf the Web or check your e-mail, open an account at a free-mail provider, such as Hotmail (www.hotmail.com) or Yahoo! Mail (http://mail.yahoo.com), and all you need to check e-mail while you travel is a Web connection, available at Internet cafés around the world. After logging on, just point the browser to your e-mail provider, enter your username and password, and you'll have access to your mail.

The following Paris Web bars, listed by arrondissement, charge modest fees (4–7€ per hr.) to their customers:

Cybercafé de Paris, 11 and 15 rue des Halles, 1er. ☎ 01- 42-21-11-11. Métro: Châtelet.

Web Bar, 32 rue de Picardie, 3e. ☎ 01-42-72-66-55. Métro: République or Temple.

Café Orbital, 13 rue de Medicis, 6e. ☎ 01-43-25-76-77. Métro: Odéon, RER: Luxembourg.

Laundry and Dry Cleaning

The more expensive your hotel, the more it costs to have your laundry or dry cleaning done there. Instead, find a laundry near you by consulting the Yellow Pages under *Laveries pour particuliers.* Take as many coins as you can. Washing and drying 6 kilos (13¼ lbs.) usually costs 4.00 to 5.50€. Dry cleaning is *nettoyage à sec;* look for shop signs with the word PRESSING, and don't expect to have your clothes back within an hour; you may be able to get them back the next day if you ask nicely. The dry cleaning chain **5 à Sec** has stores across Paris.

Liquor Laws

Supermarkets, grocery stores, and cafés sell alcoholic beverages. The legal drinking age is 16. Persons younger than 16 can be served an alcoholic drink in a bar or restaurant when accompanied by a parent or legal guardian. Wine and liquor are sold every day of the year. *Be warned:* The authorities are very strict about drunk-driving laws. If convicted, you face a stiff fine and a possible prison term of two months to two years.

Lost Property

Paris's Prefecture of Police runs the central Lost and Found, **Objets Trouvés,** 36 rue des Morillons, 15e (☎ 01-55-76-20-20; Métro: Convention), at the corner of rue de Dantzig. The office is open Monday, Wednesday, and Friday from 8:30 a.m. to 5:00 p.m. and Tuesday and Thursday from 8:30 a.m. to 8:00 p.m. (except in July and August). For Lost and Found on the **Métro,** call ☎ 01-40-06-75-27. If you lose your **Visa** card, call ☎ 08-00-90-11-79; for **MasterCard,** call ☎ 08-00-90-13-87. To report lost **American Express** cards, call ☎ 06-39-31-11-11.

Luggage Storage/Lockers

Most hotels will store luggage for you free, and that's your best bet, especially when you plan to return to Paris after a tour of the provinces. Otherwise, try the *consignes* (lockers) at railway stations.

Mail

Large **post offices** are normally open weekdays from 8 a.m. to 7 p.m., Saturday from 8 a.m. to noon; small post offices may have shorter hours. Many post offices (PTT) are scattered around the city; ask anybody for the nearest one. Airmail letters and postcards to the United States cost 0.67€; within Europe 0.58€; and to Australia or New Zealand, 0.79€.

The city's **main post office** is at 52 rue du Louvre, 75001 Paris (☎ 01-40-28-76-00; Métro: Louvre-Rivoli). It's open 24 hours a day for urgent mail, telegrams, and telephone calls. It handles Poste Restante mail: sent to you in care of the post office and stored until you pick it up; be prepared to show your passport and pay 0.75€ for each letter you receive. If you don't want to use Poste Restante, you can receive mail in care of **American Express.** Holders of American Express cards or traveler's checks get this service free; others pay a fee.

Maps

Maps printed by the department stores are usually available free at hotels, and they're good for those visiting Paris for only a few days and hitting only the major attractions. But if you plan to really explore all the nooks and crannies of the city, the best maps are those of the *Plan de Paris par Arrondissement,* pocket-sized books with maps and a street index, available at most bookstores. They're extremely practical, and prices start at around 9€. You can find them in Paris bookstores, Monoprix, and some of the bigger newsstands. Most Parisians carry a copy because they, too, get lost at times.

Newspapers and Magazines

Most newsstands carry the latest editions of the *International Herald Tribune,* published Monday through Saturday, and the major London papers. *Time* and *Newsweek* are readily available in Paris and so is the International edition of *USA Today.* The weekly entertainment guide *Pariscope,* which comes out on Wednesdays, has an English-language insert that gives you up-to-the-minute information on the latest cultural events. You can also get the *New York Times* in some of the bigger English-language bookstores.

Police

Dial ☎ **17** in emergencies; otherwise, call ☎ 01-53-71-53-71.

Post Office

See the "Mail" listing.

Restrooms

Public restrooms are plentiful, but you usually have to pay for them. Every café has a restroom, but it's supposed to be for customers only. The best plan is to ask to use the telephone; it's usually next to the *toilette.* For a 2€ coin, you can use the street-side toilets, which are automatically flushed out and cleaned after every use. Some Métro stations have serviced restrooms; you're expected to tip the attendant 0.50€.

Safety

Paris is a relatively safe city; your biggest risks are **pickpockets** and **purse snatchers,** so be particularly attentive in museum lines, popular shopping areas, around tourist attractions, on the Métro, and on crowded buses (especially in the confusion of getting on and off). Popular pickpocket tactics include someone asking you for directions or bumping into you while an accomplice takes your wallet and bands of children surrounding and distracting you and then making off with purchases and/or your wallet.

Women need to be on guard in crowded tourist areas and on the Métro against **overly friendly men** who seem to have made a specialty out of bothering unsuspecting female tourists. Tricks include asking your name and nationality and then taking advantage of your politeness by sticking like a burr to you for the rest of the day. They're usually more harassing than harmful, but if you're too nice, you may be stuck spending time with someone with whom you prefer not to. A simple *laissez-moi tranquille* (lay-say mwa tran-*keel;* leave me alone) usually works.

Smoking

Although restaurants are required to provide nonsmoking sections, you may find yourself next to the kitchen or the restrooms. Even there, your neighbor may light up and defy you to say something about it. Large brasseries, expensive restaurants, and places accustomed to dealing with foreigners are more likely to be accommodating.

Taxes

Watch out: You can get burned. As a member of the European Community, France routinely imposes a standard 20.6% value-added tax (VAT) on many goods and services. The tax on merchandise applies to clothing, appliances, liquor, leather goods, shoes, furs, jewelry, perfume, cameras, and even caviar. You can get a rebate — usually 13% — on certain goods and merchandise, but not on services. The minimum purchase is 175€ in the same store for nationals or residents of countries outside the European Union.

Taxis

Taxis Bleus (☎ 08-25-16-10-10), **Alpha Taxis** (☎ 01-45-85-85- 85), or **G7** (☎ 01-47-39-47-39). Be aware that the meter starts running as soon as you call a cab, so they're more expensive than hailed taxis. You can hail taxis in the street (look for a taxi with a white light on; an orange light means it's occupied), but most drivers won't pick you up if you're within 200 meters (218 yards) of a taxi stand (look for the blue TAXI sign).

Telephone/Telex/Fax

Most **public phone booths** take only telephone debit cards called *télécartes,* which you can buy at post offices and at *tabacs* (cafes and kiosks that sell tobacco products). You insert the card into the phone and make your call; the cost is automatically deducted from the "value" of the card recorded on its magnetized strip. The télécarte comes in 50- and 120-unit denominations, respectively costing about 7.40€ and 14.80€, and can be used only in a phone booth.

Cashiers almost always try to sell you a card from France Télécom, the French phone company, but cards exist that give you more talk time for the same amount of money. Instead of inserting the card into a public phone, you dial a free number and tap in a code. The cards come with directions, some in English, and can be used from public and private phones, unlike France Télécom's card, which you can use only on public phones. Look for *tabacs* that have advertisements for Delta Multimedia or Kertel, or ask for a *télécarte international avec un code.*

For placing **international calls from France,** dial 00 and then the country code (for the United States and Canada, 1; for Britain, 44; for Ireland, 353; for Australia, 61; for New Zealand, 64), then the area or city code, and then the local number (for example, to call New York, you'd dial 00 + 1 + 212 + 000-0000). **To place a collect call to North America,** dial ☎ 00-33-11, and an English-speaking operator will assist you. Dial ☎ 00-00-11 for an American AT&T operator; MCI ☎ 0800-99-00-19; Sprint ☎ 0800-99-00-87.

For **calling from Paris to anywhere else in France** (called *province*), the country is divided into five zones with prefixes beginning 01, 02, 03, 04, and 05; check a phone directory for the code of the city you're calling.

If you're **calling France from the United States,** dial the international prefix, 011; then the country code for France, 33; followed by city code and the local number, but leave off the initial zero (for example, 011 + 33 + 1-00-00-00-00).

Avoid making phone calls from your hotel room; many hotels charge at least 0.75€ for local calls, and the markup on international calls can be staggering.

You can send **telex** and **fax** messages at the main post office in each arrondissement of Paris, but asking at your hotel or going to a neighborhood printer or copy shop is often cheaper.

Time

Paris is six hours ahead of Eastern Standard Time; noon in New York is 6 p.m. in Paris.

Tipping

Service is supposedly included at your hotel, but the custom is to tip the **bellhop** about 1€ coin per bag, more in expensive (splurge) hotels. If you have a lot of luggage, tip a bit more. Don't tip housekeepers unless you do something that requires extra work. Tip a few euros if a reception staff member performs extra services.

Although your *addition* (restaurant bill) or *fiche* (café check) bears the words *service compris* (service charge included), always leave a small tip. Generally, 5% is considered acceptable. Remember, service has supposedly already been paid for.

Taxi drivers appreciate a tip of 0.50€ to 1.0€ or whatever it costs to round up the fare to the next euro. On longer journeys, when the fare exceeds 20€, a 5% to 10% tip is appropriate. At the theater and cinema, tip 0.50€ if an usher shows you to your seat. In **public toilets,** a fee for using the facilities often is posted. If not, the maintenance person will expect a tip of 1.0 or 2.0€. Put it in the basket or on the plate at the entrance. **Porters** and **cloakroom attendants** are usually governed by set prices, which are displayed. If not, give a porter 1.0€ per suitcase, and a cloakroom attendant 0.50€ per coat.

Trains

The telephone number for reservations on France's national railroads (SNCF) is ☎ 08-92-35-35-35 (0.46€/min.; open daily from 7 a.m. to 10 p.m.). *Remember:* You must validate your train ticket in the orange ticket *composteur* on the platform or pay a fine.

Water

Tap water in Paris is perfectly safe, but if you're prone to stomach problems, you may prefer to drink mineral water.

Weather updates

Call ☎ 08-92-69-02-75 (0.46€/min.) for France and abroad. Or try this Web site: http://europe.cnn.com/WEATHER.

Toll-Free Numbers and Web Sites

Major airlines

Air Canada
☎ 888-247-2262
www.aircanada.ca

Air France
☎ 800-237-2747
www.airfrance.com

American Airlines
☎ 800-433-7300
www.aa.com

British Airways
☎ 800-247-9297
www.british-airways.com

Continental Airlines
☎ 800-525-0280
www.continental.com

Delta Air Lines
☎ 800-221-1212
www.delta.com

Iceland Air
☎ 800-223-5500
www.icelandair.com

Northwest/KLM
☎ 800-225-2525
www.nwa.com

United Airlines
☎ 800-241-6522
www.ual.com

US Airways
☎ 800-428-4322
www.usairways.com

Major car rental agencies in Paris

Avis
gare d'Austerlitz, 13e
☎ 01-45-84-22-10
www.avis.com

National
gare de Lyon, 12e
☎ 01-40-04-90-04
www.nationalcar.com

Hertz France
gare de l'Est, 10e
☎ 01-42-05-50-43
www.hertz.com

Where to Get More Information

The information sources listed here are the best of the bunch; dig in before you go, and you'll be well prepared for your trip.

Tourist offices

For general information about France, contact an office of the **French Government Tourist Office** at one of the following addresses:

✔ **In the United States: The French Government Tourist Office,** 444 Madison Ave., 16th floor, New York, NY 10022-6903 (☎ 212-838-7800; Internet: www.francetourism.com); 676 N. Michigan Ave., Chicago, IL 60611-2819 (☎ 312-751-7800).

✔ **In Canada: Maison de la France/French Government Tourist Office,** 1981 av. McGill College, Suite 490, Montréal PQ H3A 2W9 (☎ 514-876-9881).

✔ **In the United Kingdom: Maison de la France/French Government Tourist Office,** 178 Piccadilly, London W1V 0AL (☎ 0891-244-123).

✔ **In Australia: French Tourist Bureau,** 25 Bligh St. Level 20, Sydney, NSW 2000 Australia (☎ 02-231-5244; Fax: 02-231-8682).

✔ **In New Zealand:** You won't find a representative in New Zealand; contact the Australian representative.

✔ **In Paris: The Office de Tourisme et des Congrès de Paris,** 127 av. des Champs-Elysées, 75008 Paris (☎ 08-92-68-31-12 [0.34€/min.]; Métro: Charles-de-Gaulle–Étoile or George V).

Surfing the Web

You can find plenty of excellent information about Paris on the Internet — the latest news, restaurant reviews, concert schedules, subway maps, and more.

✔ **Aeroports de Paris** (www.paris-airports.com). Click the American flag on this site's home page for an English version that provides transfer information into Paris and lists terminals, maps, airlines, boutiques, hotels, restaurants, and accessibility information for travelers with disabilities.

✔ **Bonjour Paris** (www.bparis.com). This site should be one of the first you browse before your trip; it's just full of useful information about Paris. You can find everything from cultural differences to shopping to restaurant reviews, all written from an American expatriate point of view.

✔ **Café de la Soul** (www.cafedelasoul.com). A sleekly designed Web site for African-American travelers in Paris. The site features articles, travelogues, and links to resources in the City of Light.

✔ **French Government Tourist Office** (www.francetourism.com). Here you can find information on planning your trip to France and practical tips, family activities, events, and accommodations.

✔ **ISMAP** (www.ismap.com). Type in a Paris address on this site, and ISMAP will map it, including nearby sights of interest and the closest Métro stops.

✔ **Paris Digest** (www.parisdigest.com). Paris Digest selects "the best sights in Paris" and provides photos and links to them and to restaurants with views and good décor, and information about shopping, hotels, and things to do.

✔ **Paris France Guide** (www.parisfranceguide.com). This site has plenty of useful information about Paris, with current nightlife, restaurant, music, theater, and events listings. This guide is brought to you by the publishers of the *Living in France, Study in France,* and *What's on in France* guides.

✔ **Paris Free Voice** (www.parisvoice.com or www.thinkparis.com). This is the online version of the free Paris monthly, *The Paris Voice.* It's hip and opinionated with lots of listings for the performing arts, music, and theater.

✔ **Paris Pages** (www.paris.org). So much information is on this site that you won't know where to begin. Lodging reviews are organized by area and the monuments standing nearby, and you can find photo tours, shop listings, and a map of attractions with details. Some of the information may be out of date.

✔ **Paris Tourist Office** (www.paris-touristoffice.com). The official site of the Paris Tourist Office provides information on the year's events, museums, accommodations, nightlife, and restaurants.

✔ **RATP (Paris Urban Transit)** (www.ratp.fr). Find subway and bus line maps, timetables and information, and routes and times for Noctambus, Paris's night buses that run after the Métro closes. Click on the word *English* for the English-language version.

✔ **Smartweb: Paris** (www.smartweb.fr/paris). The big attractions, such as the Louvre and the Eiffel Tower, are featured along with shop and gallery listings organized by arrondissement. Airport terminal information and click-on subway maps are also posted here.

✔ **SNCF (French Rail)** (www.sncf.fr). The official Web site of the French railway system, this site sells seats online for trips through France. You can also find timetables and prices here. Click on the Union Jack on the upper-left corner of the screen for English.

✔ **Subway Navigator** (www.subwaynavigator.com). This site provides detailed subway maps for Paris and other cities around the world. You can select a city and enter your arrival and departure points, and then Subway Navigator maps out your route and estimates how long your trip will take.

Hitting the books

Most bookstores have several shelves devoted entirely to Paris-related titles, given that the city is one of the most-visited on the planet. Here are a few other books that may be useful for your trip. All Frommer's guides are published by Wiley, Inc.

✔ *Frommer's Paris,* updated every year, is an authoritative guide that covers the city and its surroundings.

✔ *Frommer's Paris from $80 a Day* is the guide for travelers who want to visit Paris comfortably but don't want to spend a fortune doing it.

✔ *Frommer's Portable Paris* is the pocket-sized version of *Frommer's Paris.*

✔ *Frommer's Memorable Walks in Paris* is for folks who want to explore the city in depth and on foot with easy directions and descriptions of important sights.

✔ *Frommer's Irreverent Guide to Paris* is a fun guide for sophisticated travelers who want the basics without much excess.

Appendix B

A Glossary of French Words and Phrases

● ●

*W*hy **La** *Tour Eiffel* but **Le** *Tour de France?* Why **un** *cabinet* but **une** *cabine?* Simply put, in French and other Romance languages, nouns are assigned a gender. The articles preceding the noun, such as *le* and *la* (which mean *the*) and *un* and *une* (which mean *a* or *one*) correspond to that gender. *La* and *une* are feminine; *le* and *un* are masculine. Plural nouns are preceded by *les.* An extra letter is also added to the noun itself to signify feminine gender. So Dan Rather is *un journalist,* but Diane Sawyer is *une journaliste.* French schoolchildren spend years memorizing the gender of nouns; fortunately no one expects you to do the same!

Basic Vocabulary

English	*French*	*Pronunciation*
Yes/no	**Oui/non**	wee/nohn
Okay	**D'accord**	dah-*core*
Please	**S'il vous plaît**	seel-voo-*play*
Thank you	**Merci**	mair-*see*
You're welcome	**De rien**	duh ree-*ehn*
Hello (during daylight hours)	**Bonjour**	bohn-*jhoor*
Good evening	**Bonsoir**	bohn-*swahr*
Goodbye	**Au revoir**	o ruh-*vwahr*
What's your name?	**Comment vous appelez-vous?**	ko-mahn-voo-za-pel-ay-*voo?*
My name is . . .	**Je m'appelle . . .**	jhuh ma-*pell*
Happy to meet you	**Enchanté(e)**	ohn-shahn-*tay*
Miss	**Mademoiselle**	mad mwa-*zel*

(continued)

Basic Vocabulary *(continued)*

English	French	Pronunciation
Mr.	**Monsieur**	muh-*syuh*
Mrs.	**Madame**	ma-*dam*
How are you?	**Comment allez-vous?**	kuh-mahn-tahl-ay-*voo?*
Fine, thank you, and you?	**Très bien, merci, et vous?**	tray bee-ehn, mare-see, ay *voo?*
Very well, thank you	**Très bien, merci**	tray bee-ehn, mair-*see*
So-so	**Comme ci, comme ça**	kum-*see,* kum-*sah*
I'm sorry/excuse me	**Pardon**	pahr-*dohn*
I'm so very sorry	**Désolé(e)**	day-zoh-*lay*
Do you speak English?	**Parlez-vous anglais?**	par-lay-voo-ahn-*glay?*
I don't speak French	**Je ne parle pas français**	jhuh ne parl pah frahn-*say*
I don't understand	**Je ne comprends pas**	jhuh ne kohm-*prahn* pah
Could you speak more slowly?	**Pouvez-vous parler un peu plus lentement?**	poo-*vay* voo par-*lay* uh puh ploo lan-te-*ment?*
Could you repeat that?	**Répetez, s'il vous plaît**	ray-pay-*tay,* seel voo *play?*
What is it?	**Qu'est-ce que c'est?**	kess-kuh-*say?*
What time is it?	**Qu'elle heure est-il?**	kel uhr eh-*teel?*
What?	**Quoi?**	kwah?
Pardon?	**Pardons?**	par-*doh?*
Help!	**Aidez-moi!**	*Ay*-day moi!
How? *or* What did you say?	**Comment?**	ko-*mahn?*
When?	**Quand?**	cohn?
Where is . . . ?	**Où est . . . ?**	ooh-eh?
Where are the toilets?	**Où sont les toilettes?**	ooh-sohn lay twah-*lets?*
Who?	**Qui?**	kee?
Why?	**Pourquoi?**	poor-*kwah?*

English	French	Pronunciation
Here/there	**Ici/là**	ee-*see*/lah
Left/right	**à gauche/à droite**	ah goash/ah drwaht
Straight ahead	**Tout droit**	too-drwah
I'm American/Canadian/ British	**Je suis américain(e)/ canadien(e)/ anglais(e)**	jhe swee a-may-ree-*kehn*/canah-dee-*en*/ ahn-*glay (glaise)*
I'm going to . . .	**Je vais à . . .**	jhe vay ah
I want to get off at . . .	**Je voudrais descendre à**	jhe voo-*dray* day-son-drah-ah

Health Terms

English	French	Pronunciation
I'm sick	**Je suis malade**	jhuh swee mal-*ahd*
I have a headache	**J'ai une mal de tête**	jhay oon mal de tet
I have a stomachache	**J'ai une mal de ventre**	jhay oon mal de *vahn*-trah
I would like to buy some aspirin	**Je voudrais acheter des aspirines**	jhe *voo*-dray *ash*-tay days as-peh-*reen*
hospital	**l'hôpital**	low-pee-*tahl*
insurance	**les assurances**	lez ah-sur-*ahns*

Travel Terms

English	French	Pronunciation
airport	**l'aéroport**	lair-o-*por*
bank	**la banque**	lah bahnk
bridge	**pont**	pohn
bus station	**la gare routière**	lah gar roo-tee-*air*
bus stop	**l'arrêt de bus**	lah-*ray* duh boohss
by means of a bicycle	**en vélo/par bicyclette**	ahn *vay*-low/par bee-see-*clet*

(continued)

Travel Terms *(continued)*

English	*French*	*Pronunciation*
by means of a car	**en voiture**	ahn vwa-*toor*
cashier	**la caisse**	lah *kess*
driver's license	**permis de conduire**	per-*mee* duh con-*dweer*
elevator	**l'ascenseur**	lah sahn *seuhr*
entrance (to a building or a city)	**porte**	port
exit (from a building or a freeway)	**une sortie**	ewn sor-*tee*
ground floor	**rez-de-chausée**	ray-duh-show-*say*
highway to . . .	**la route pour . . .**	lah root por
luggage storage	**consigne**	kohn-*seen*-yuh
museum	**le musée**	luh mew-*zay*
no entry	**sens interdit**	sehns ahn-ter-*dee*
no smoking	**défense de fumer**	day-*fahns* duh fu-may
on foot	**à pied**	ah pee-*ay*
one-day pass	**ticket journalier**	tee-kay jhoor-nall-ee-*ay*
one-way ticket	**aller simple**	ah-*lay sam*-pluh
police	**la police**	lah po-*lees*
round-trip ticket	**aller-retour**	ah-*lay* re-*toor*
second floor	**premier étage**	prem-ee-*ehr* ay-*taj*
slow down	**ralentissez**	rah-lahn-tis-*ay*
store	**le magasin**	luh ma-ga-*zehn*
street	**la rue**	roo
suburb	**la banlieue**	lah bahn-*liew*
subway	**le Métro**	luh may-tro
telephone	**le téléphone**	luh tay-lay-*phun*
ticket	**un billet**	uh *bee*-yay

English	French	Pronunciation
ticket office	**vente de billets**	vahnt duh bee-*yay*
toilets	**les toilettes**	lay twa-*lets*
I'd like . . .	**Je voudrais . . .**	jhe voo-*dray*
a room	**une chambre**	ewn *shahm*-bruh
the key	**la clé (la clef)**	lah clay

Shopping Terms

English	French	Pronunciation
How much does it cost?	**C'est combien?/** **Ça coûte combien?**	say comb-bee-*ehn?/* sah coot comb-bee-*ehn?*
That's expensive	**C'est cher/chère**	say share
That's inexpensive	**C'est raisonnable/** **C'est bon marché**	say ray-son-*ahb*-bluh/ say bohn mar-*shay*
Do you take credit cards?	**Est-ce que vous acceptez les cartes de credit?**	es-kuh voo zaksep-*tay* lay kart duh creh-*dee?*
I'd like to buy . . .	**Je voudrais acheter . . .**	jhe voo-dray ahsh-*tay*
aspirin	**des aspirines**	deyz ahs-peer-*eens*
cigarettes	**des cigarettes**	day see-ga-*ret*
condoms	**des préservatifs**	day pray-ser-va-*teefs*
contraceptive suppositories	**des ovules contraceptives**	days oh-*vyules* kahn-trah-cep-*teef*
a dictionary	**un dictionnaire**	uh deek-see-oh-*nare*
a gift (for someone)	**un cadeau**	uh kah-*doe*
a handbag	**un sac à main**	uh sahk ah man
a magazine	**une revue**	ewn reh-*vu*
a map of the city	**un plan de ville**	uh plahn de *veel*
matches	**des allumettes**	dayz a-loo-*met*
lighter	**un briquet**	uh *bree*-kay
a newspaper	**un journal**	uh zhoor-*nahl*

(continued)

Shopping Terms *(continued)*

English	*French*	*Pronunciation*
a phone card	**une carte téléphonique**	ewn cart tay-lay-fone-*eek*
a postcard	**une carte postale**	ewn carte pos-*tahl*
a road map	**une carte routière**	ewn cart roo-tee-*air*
shoes	**des chaussures**	day show-*suhr*
soap	**du savon**	dew sah-*vohn*
socks	**des chaussettes**	day show-*set*
a stamp	**un timbre**	uh *tam*-bruh
writing paper	**du papier à lettres**	dew pap-pee-*ay* a *let*-ruh

Elements of Time

English	*French*	*Pronunciation*
Sunday	**dimanche**	dee-*mahnsh*
Monday	**lundi**	luhn-*dee*
Tuesday	**mardi**	mahr-*dee*
Wednesday	**mercredi**	mair-kruh-*dee*
Thursday	**jeudi**	jheu-*dee*
Friday	**vendredi**	vawn-druh-*dee*
Saturday	**samedi**	sahm-*dee*
Yesterday	**hier**	ee-*air*
Today	**aujourd'hui**	o-jhord-*dwee*
This morning	**ce matin**	suh ma-*tan*
This afternoon	**cet après-midi**	set ah-preh mee-*dee*
Tonight	**ce soir**	suh *swahr*
Tomorrow	**demain**	de-*man*
Now	**maintenant**	mant-*naw*

Making Dollars and Sense of It

Expense	Daily cost	x	Number of days	=	Total
Airfare					
Local transportation					
Car rental					
Lodging (with tax)					
Parking					
Breakfast					
Lunch					
Dinner					
Snacks					
Entertainment					
Babysitting					
Attractions					
Gifts & souvenirs					
Tips					
Other					
Grand Total					

Fare Game: Choosing an Airline

When looking for the best airfare, you should cover all your bases — 1) consult a trusted travel agent; 2) contact the airline directly, via the airline's toll-free number and/or Web site; 3) check out one of the travel-planning Web sites, such as www.frommers.com.

Travel Agency_____ Phone_____
   Agent's Name_____ Quoted fare_____

Airline 1_____ Quoted fare_____
   Toll-free number/Internet_____

Airline 2_____ Quoted fare_____
   Toll-free number/Internet_____

Web site 1_____ Quoted fare_____

Web site 2_____ Quoted fare_____

Departure Schedule & Flight Information

Airline_____ Flight #_____ Confirmation #_____

Departs_____ Date_____ Time_____ a.m./p.m.

Arrives_____ Date_____ Time_____ a.m./p.m.

Connecting Flight (if any)

Amount of time between flights_____ hours/mins

Airline_____ Flight #_____ Confirmation #_____

Departs_____ Date_____ Time_____ a.m./p.m.

Arrives_____ Date_____ Time_____ a.m./p.m.

Return Trip Schedule & Flight Information

Airline_____ Flight #_____ Confirmation #_____

Departs_____ Date_____ Time_____ a.m./p.m.

Arrives_____ Date_____ Time_____ a.m./p.m.

Connecting Flight (if any)

Amount of time between flights_____ hours/mins

Airline_____ Flight #_____ Confirmation #_____

Departs_____ Date_____ Time_____ a.m./p.m.

Arrives_____ Date_____ Time_____ a.m./p.m.

Sweet Dreams: Choosing Your Hotel

Make a list of all the hotels where you'd like to stay and then check online and call the local and toll-free numbers to get the best price. You should also check with a travel agent, who may be able to get you a better rate.

Hotel & page	Location	Internet	Tel. (local)	Tel. (Toll-free)	Quoted rate

Hotel Checklist

Here's a checklist of things to inquire about when booking your room, depending on your needs and preferences.

- ❏ Smoking/smoke-free room
- ❏ Noise (if you prefer a quiet room, ask about proximity to elevator, bar/restaurant, pool, meeting facilities, renovations, and street)
- ❏ View
- ❏ Facilities for children (crib, roll-away cot, babysitting services)
- ❏ Facilities for travelers with disabilities
- ❏ Number and size of bed(s) (king, queen, double/full-size)
- ❏ Is breakfast included? (buffet, continental, or sit-down?)
- ❏ In-room amenities (hair dryer, iron/board, minibar, etc.)
- ❏ Other_____

Places to Go, People to See, Things to Do

Enter the attractions you would most like to see and decide how they'll fit into your schedule.

Attraction/activity	Page	Amount of time you expect to spend there	Best day and time to go

Index

See also separate Accommodations and Restaurant indexes following General index.

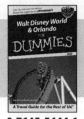
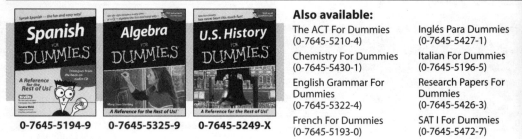

FOR DUMMIES®

A world of resources to help you grow

HOME & BUSINESS COMPUTER BASICS

0-7645-0838-5   **0-7645-1663-9**   **0-7645-1548-9**

Also available:

Excel 2002 All-in-One Desk Reference For Dummies (0-7645-1794-5)

Office XP 9-in-1 Desk Reference For Dummies (0-7645-0819-9)

PCs All-in-One Desk Reference For Dummies (0-7645-0791-5)

Troubleshooting Your PC For Dummies (0-7645-1669-8)

Upgrading & Fixing PCs For Dummies (0-7645-1665-5)

Windows XP For Dummies (0-7645-0893-8)

Windows XP For Dummies Quick Reference (0-7645-0897-0)

Word 2002 For Dummies (0-7645-0839-3)

INTERNET & DIGITAL MEDIA

0-7645-0894-6   **0-7645-1642-6**   **0-7645-1664-7**

Also available:

CD and DVD Recording For Dummies (0-7645-1627-2)

Digital Photography All-in-One Desk Reference For Dummies (0-7645-1800-3)

eBay For Dummies (0-7645-1642-6)

Genealogy Online For Dummies (0-7645-0807-5)

Internet All-in-One Desk Reference For Dummies (0-7645-1659-0)

Internet For Dummies Quick Reference (0-7645-1645-0)

Internet Privacy For Dummies (0-7645-0846-6)

Paint Shop Pro For Dummies (0-7645-2440-2)

Photo Retouching & Restoration For Dummies (0-7645-1662-0)

Photoshop Elements For Dummies (0-7645-1675-2)

Scanners For Dummies (0-7645-0783-4)

Get smart! Visit www.dummies.com

- **Find listings of even more Dummies titles**

- **Browse online articles, excerpts, and how-to's**

- **Sign up for daily or weekly e-mail tips**

- **Check out Dummies fitness videos and other products**

- **Order from our online bookstore**

Available wherever books are sold. Go to www.dummies.com or call 1-877-762-2974 to order direct

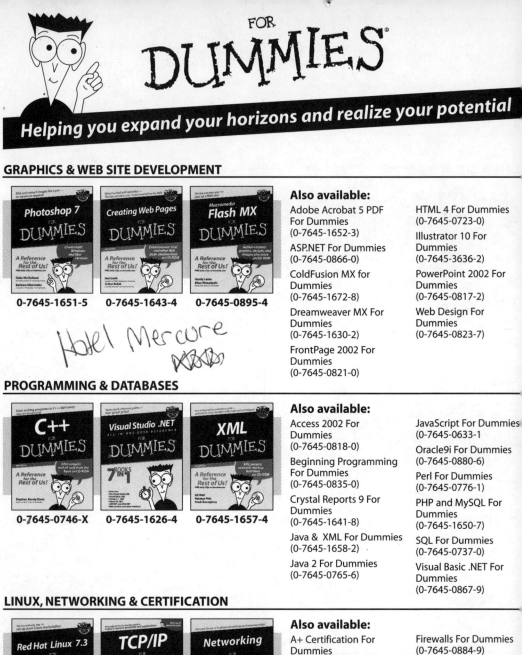